Oxford Archaeological Guides
General Editor: Barry Cunliffe

Spain

Roger Collins is a Fellow of the Institute for Advanced Study in
the Humanities, University of Edinburgh. He is the author of
*Early Medieval Spain, 400–1000, The Basques, The Arab Conquest
of Spain, 710–797*, and *Early Medieval Europe, 300–1000*.

Barry Cunliffe is Professor of European Archaeology at the
University of Oxford. The author of over forty books, including
The Oxford Illustrated Prehistory of Europe and *The Ancient
Celts*, he has served as President of the Council for British
Archaeology and the Society of Antiquaries, and is currently a
member of the Ancient Monuments Board of English Heritage.

'For the traveller who wishes to be generally well informed and who
wishes to examine sites and buildings of Spain in detail, and, above
all, within their proper cultural context, Roger Collins's guide is the
best available in any language. ... No serious traveller in Spain can
be without this volume. For those who visit the land for the first
time it offers an essential guide to the many-layered culture of the
peninsula. And for those who know Spain well, it will still contain
many surprises.'
MALCOLM TODD
University of Durham

Oxford Archaeological Guides

Spain

An Oxford Archaeological Guide

Roger Collins

Oxford · New York
OXFORD UNIVERSITY PRESS
1998

Oxford University Press, Great Clarendon Street, Oxford OX2 6DP

Oxford New York

Athens Auckland Bangkok Bombay
Calcutta Cape Town Dar es Salaam Delhi
Florence Hong Kong Istanbul Karachi
Kuala Lumpur Madras Madrid Melbourne
Mexico City Nairobi Paris Singapore
Taipei Tokyo Toronto Warsaw

and associated companies in
Berlin Ibadan

Oxford is a trade mark of Oxford University Press

First published as an Oxford University Press
paperback 1998

British Library Cataloguing in Publication Data
Data available

Library of Congress Cataloging in Publication Data
Collins, Roger, 1949–
Spain: an Oxford archaeological guide/Roger Collins.
p.   cm. — (Oxford archaeological guides)
Includes bibliographical references and index.
1. Spain — Antiquities — Guidebooks.   2. Excavations (Archaeology) —
Spain — Guidebooks.   I. Title.   II. Series.
DP44.C675   1998   936.6 — dc21   97–30251
ISBN 0–19–285300–7

1 3 5 7 9 10 8 6 4 2

Designed by First Edition, London
Typeset by Best-set Typesetter Ltd., Hong Kong
Printed by
Book Print, F. L.
Barcelona, Spain

Series Editor's Foreword

Travelling for pleasure, whether for curiosity, nostalgia, religious conviction, or simply to satisfy an inherent need to learn, has been an essential part of the human condition for centuries. Chaucer's 'Wife of Bath' ranged wide, visiting Jerusalem three times as well as Santiago de Compostela, Rome, Cologne, and Boulogne. Her motivation, like that of so many medieval travellers, was primarily to visit holy places. Later, as the Grand Tour took a hold in the eighteenth century, piety was replaced by the need felt by the élite to educate its young, to compensate for the disgracefully inadequate training offered at that time by Oxford and Cambridge. The levelling effect of the Napoleonic Wars changed all that and in the age of the steamship and the railway mass tourism was born when Mr Thomas Cook first offered 'A Great Circular Tour of the Continent'.

There have been guidebooks as long as there have been travellers. Though not intended as such, the *Histories* of Herodotus would have been an indispensable companion to a wandering Greek. Centuries later Pausanias' guide to the monuments of Greece was widely used by travelling Romans intent on discovering the roots of their civilization. In the eighteenth century travel books took on a more practical form offering a torrent of useful advice, from dealing with recalcitrant foreign innkeepers to taking a plentiful supply of oil of lavender to ward off bedbugs. But it was the incomparable 'Baedekers' that gave enlightenment and reassurance to the increasing tide of enquiring tourists who flooded the Continent in the latter part of the nineteenth century. The battered but much-treasured red volumes may still sometimes be seen in use today, pored over on sites by those nostalgic for the gentle art of travel.

The needs and expectations of the enquiring traveller change rapidly and it would be impossible to meet them all within the compass of single volumes. With this in mind, the Oxford Archaeological Guides have been created to satisfy a particular and growing interest. Each volume provides lively and informed descriptions of a wide selection of archaeological sites chosen to display the cultural heritage of the country in question. Plans, designed to match the text, make it easy to grasp the full extent of the site while focusing on its essential aspects. The emphasis is, necessarily, on seeing, understanding, and above all enjoying the particular place. But archaeological sites are the creation of history and can only be fully appreciated against the *longue durée* of human achievement. To provide this, each book begins with a wide-ranging historical overview introducing the changing cultures of the country and the landscapes which formed them. Thus, while the Guides are primarily intended for the traveller they can be read with equal value at home.

Barry Cunliffe

Contents

How to use this Guide

Maps

Directions have been given using the Michelin 1/400,000 series (map numbers 440 to 446, covering the whole peninsula). A national programme of road numbering has been introduced recently for the minor as well as the major roads, some of which has been included on recent printings of these maps. Where possible this has been included here.

Travel

While most visitors may wish to use their own or hired cars, it is worth pointing out that Spanish taxis are still amongst the cheapest in western Europe, operating on fixed prices per kilometre. For getting to remote and difficult sites, and for making contact with sometimes elusive key-holders, the services of a taxi driver are invaluable. An approximate price or even an agreed total fare can be obtained in advance, and a quarter century of experience has never produced a rogue 'taxista'.

Sites

A small number of the sites described here are on private land, and permission should be obtained from the owners before entering. An enquiry at the nearest Tourist Office (*Oficina del Turismo*) or, failing this, the Town Hall (*Ayuntamiento*) should suffice to locate the proprietor. Some sites, e.g. EL BOVALAR and BOBASTRO, are enclosed and in theory viewable only through the perimeter fence. In practice, gates may be wide open or removed. In all such cases care should be taken to look out for possible hazards, such as an unprotected well, and to prevent any damage to the site. Some unrestored castles may be particularly dangerous, with unsecured loose masonry and hazardous battlement walks. If close to centres of population, these can be infested by opportunistic muggers and/or local youths capable of making a nuisance of themselves. One or two such sites, such as the upper fortress at MÁLAGA, which are distant from normal police patrols, have particularly unsavoury reputations. Visit at sensible hours, and, if in doubt, enquire at the Tourist Office for advice.

Timings

Museum and site opening times are not given here, as this might imply a greater degree of assurance than is warranted. Most major museums and sites will be open roughly between 10 a.m. and 1 p.m. and again in the afternoon between about 4 and 6, but there are variations, and some establishments can be quite erratic. Spanish museums also close for restoration (*obras*) rather more frequently than might seem necessary, and if not the whole institution then it is invariably the section that the visitor particularly wants to see that is closed (*cerrado*). Local Tourist Offices have been known to be unaware of such closures! In almost all cases Monday is the weekly closing day, while admission, though for more restricted hours, can be gained on Sundays. There is a government publication: *Museos y colecciones de España* (Madrid: Ministerio de Cultura, 1990) listing all museums and private collections to which access can be gained, giving their official opening times.

Weather and dress

There are considerable climatic variations in Spain, both between regions and between seasons, and standard guides may provide some account of these. Most archaeological sites present no special difficulties in these respects, but it is worth remembering that summer temperatures in the south and centre of the peninsula can be well over 40 °C and the power of the sun is considerable throughout the day. So be careful about overexposure in large open country locations, such as SEGÓBRIGA or CALATRAVA LA VIEJA, where there is no shade and quite a time will have to be spent if the whole site is to be seen. It is worth taking a supply of water on such trips. Large bottles of mineral water are easily and cheaply obtained at all grocers. While poisonous snakes are not a major problem in Spain (I have only ever seen two), they do like to take refuge under rocks or in holes in the heat of the day, and so can be found in such locations in rural archaeological sites. Sensible precautions as to dress should be taken when visiting slightly out of the way mountainous sites, such as MONTE MARINET, and it may be well to let someone know where you expect to be and by what time you should return.

Starred sites

Twenty-six exceptionally important and interesting sites have been awarded star points. Those sites which have two stars are unmissable, and those with one star are highly reccommended.

Key to map

★★ Outstanding sites (see
   p. x)
★ Highly recommended

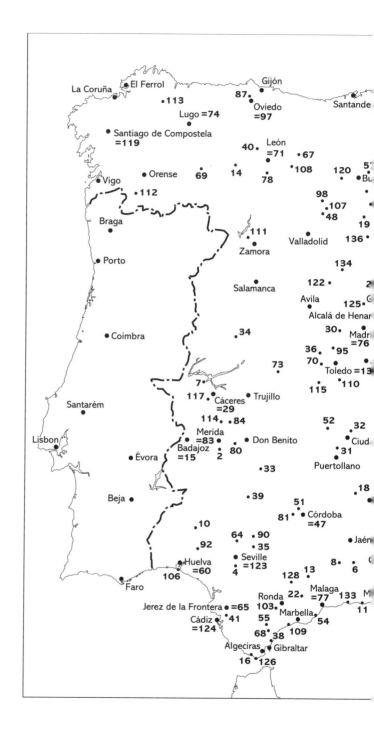

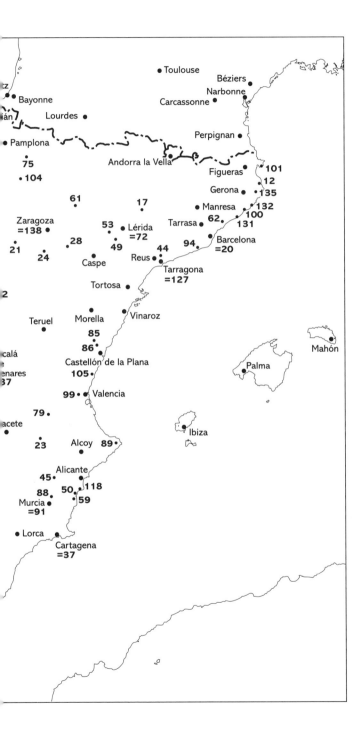

Toulouse

Béziers

Bayonne

Narbonne

Carcassonne

Lourdes

Perpignan

Pamplona

Andorra la Vella

Figueras

•101

•104

•12

Gerona

•135

•61

•17

Manresa

•132

•100

Zaragoza

•53

Lérida

Tarrasa

•62

•131

=138

•28

=72

94

Barcelona

•21

•24

49

44

=20

Caspe

Reus

Tarragona

=127

Tortosa

2

Teruel

Morella

Vinaroz

•85

•86

cala

Castellón de la Plana

enares

•105

37

•99

Valencia

•79

acete

Mahón

•23

Alcoy

•89

Palma

Alicante

Ibiza

•45

•88

•50

•118

Murcia

•59

=91

Lorca

Cartagena

=37

Sites listed by archaeological period

1. Prehistoric

Alava Dolmens ★
Antequera★
Bonete
Cabezo de Alcalá
Cancho Roano
Castillo de Doña
    Blanca
Castro de la
    Coronilla
El Oral
Fraga★
Gran Dolina
Huelva
Ilduro
La Hoya
Meca
Montgó
Orce
Puig Castellet
Santa Pola
South coast
    Phoenician
    settlements
Trayamar
Ullastret

2. Roman

Alange
Alcalá de Henares
Alcántara
Almedinilla
Almuñecar
Ampurias ★★
Astorga
Baelo ★
Baños de
    Valdearados
Barcelona ★
Bilbilis
Botorrita
Bruñel
Cáceres★
Cancho Roano
Caparra
Carmona
Carranque
Cartagena
Carteia
Casas de Reina
Castulo
Centcelles
Clunia ★
Córdoba ★★
Dueñas
Fraga ★
Huelva
Irún
Itálica ★★
La Pedrosa de la
    Vega
Lacipo
Las Médulas
Las Vegas de Puebla
    Nueva
León ★★
Lérida
Lugo
Lumbier
Medellín
Medinacelli
Mérida ★
Muñigua
Niebla
Numantia
Ronda la Vieja
Sádaba
Sagunto
San Pedro de
    Alcántara
Sasamón
Segóbriga ★
Segovia
Tarragona ★★
Tiermes
Toledo ★★
Torre Llauder
Tossa de Mar
Uxama
Valeria
Zaragoza ★

3. Visigothic

Barcelona ★
El Bovalar
Las Vegas de Puebla
    Nueva
Marialba
Mérida
Niebla
Palencia
Pla de Nadal
Puig de les
    Muralles/Puig
    Rom
Reccopolis ★
San Juan de Baños ★
San Pedro de la
    Mata
San Pedro de la
    Nave ★
Sta Comba de
    Bande
Sta Lucía del
    Trampal
Sta María de
    Melque ★
Sta María de
    Quintanilla de
    las Viñas
Sta Olalla de
    Cáceres
Segóbriga★
Toledo ★★

4. Medieval: Christian and Islamic

Aistra
Alcalá de
    Guadaira
Alcalá de Henares
Alcalá la Real
Almería
Almonaster la
    Real
Antequera ★
Bádajoz
Balaguer
Baños de la Encina
Barcelona ★
Bobastro
Bonete
Buitrago de
    Lozoya
Bujarrabal
Cáceres ★
Calatalifa
Calatrava la
    Nueva ★
Calatrava la Vieja ★

Castillo de Alba
Cieza
Córdoba ★★
El Vacar
Fontanarejo
Fraga ★
Fuengirola
Gaucín
Gormaz ★★
Granada ★★
Guardamar
Huesca
Jerez de la
    Frontera
Las Vegas de
    Puebla Nueva
León ★★
Lérida
Los Vascos ★
Madrid ★★
Málaga
Medina Azahara
Medinacelli
Montánchez
Monte Marinet
Monte Mollet
Monte Naranco

Monteagudo
Murcia
Niebla
Olérdola
Olmos
Oviedo ★
Ronda
Sagunto
Saltés
San Miguel de
    Escalada
Sta Eulalia de
    Bóveda
Santiago de
    Compostela
Segovia
Seville
Talamanca del
    Jarama
Tarifa
Teba
Toledo ★★
Turégano
Zaragoza ★
Zorita

Introduction

PREHISTORIC SOCIETIES IN SPAIN

A note on terminology. While the chronological division of prehistory into a series of ages named after their principal technologies—stone tool-making, the use of bronze, and the working of iron—has been standard scholarly practice for a long time and will be found in most museum displays, it can blur periods of transition and give deceptive impressions of the societies under consideration. Thus, for example, stone tools and weapons were still being made and used in the Early Bronze Age, just as bronze would continue to be employed for many high status items, including swords, in the opening phases of the Iron Age. These metal-working technologies spread only gradually, and some parts of Europe could have developed them well in advance of others. Thus, Spain was still in the Bronze Age at a time when the Near East was firmly into the Iron Age. Even within the Iberian peninsula the subsequent spread of the use of iron would be at differential rates. Some regions would be importing and then making items in the new metal long before others. While the existence of such periods of overlap and gradual dissemination of new technology matter less in the chronologically much longer spans of the various parts of the Stone Age, the relative brevity of the ensuing Copper, Bronze, and Iron Ages calls into question the value of such a relative system of classification. It can also seem to over-emphasize one feature of a period, its tool and weapon-making technology, and ignore others of equal or greater significance. For example, it is likely that the development of agriculture opened the way to far more significant social changes than did the transition from the use of copper to bronze or from bronze to iron. While the traditional divisions will be retained here for convenience of reference to other publications and in museums, they will be put into rather wider contexts.

Hunters and Gatherers

The Palaeolithic or Old Stone Age

Recently, Spain has managed not only to become the first place in Europe where fossilized dinosaur eggs (about 300,000 of them!), from the Upper Cretaceous Period, have been discovered, but where the earliest traces of hominid life in the continent have been found.[1] Two sites, at ORCE and GRAN DOLINA, have revealed traces of occupation and tool-making at dates around 1.8 million and 780,000 BC respectively. The Orce site, which has also produced bone fragments dated to *c.*1.6–1.4 million BC, is a particularly exciting site, as hitherto the only comparable hominid discoveries dating to such a period from outside Africa were made at Dmanisi in Georgia and in Java. Even the Gran Dolina discovery, at half the age, is important as it undermines the previous view that climatic conditions made Europe uninhabitable for early man before about 500,000 BC. The hominid form represented in the Orce site may be related to *Homo heidelbergensis* (named after a fragment of jaw found near Heidelberg), while that at Gran Dolina would have been *Homo erectus*. It must be admitted that these conclusions are not yet secure, and their interpretations remain somewhat controversial. This is largely due to the wider significance of these findings, which may contradict what had become the accepted version of the processes of human occupation of Europe, in the form of a movement of early hominids out of Africa, and into western Europe via the Near East. The Spanish findings, if accepted, would not only cast doubt on this particular route for hominid expansion, but might cast further doubt on the previously dominant view that the earliest stages of human evolution took place exclusively in Africa.[2] A conference was held in Valladolid in 1992 to debate these issues, and it must be said that so far the conclusions given above remain *sub judice*, but they, and the sites that produced them, remain exciting, if provisional, and revolutionary.[3]

Whatever the outcome of these controversies, there remains a considerable gap in the evidence between the period to which these sites may relate and the next indications of human activity in the Iberian peninsula. It is possible that, should the conclusions drawn about the age of these sites be accepted, anthropologists will be more inclined to look for further evidence to try to fill a gap whose existence had not previously been recognized. The more orthodox expectations relate to the appearance of man in the Iberian peninsula in the Lower Palaeolithic period, around 300,000–250,000 BC. What seems to be a camp, marked by the presence of stone hand axes and scrapers, as well as elephant bones and the presence of fires, has been located near the village of Torralba (province of Soria), and has been dated to this period.[4]

Another hominid form, Neanderthal man, whose relationship to the later *Homo sapiens* remains a perennial topic of debate, flourished in the succeeding Middle Palaeolithic period (*c*.100,000–40,000 BC). A substantial number of cave sites from the Pyrenees southwards, containing finds of large, simply cut, flint tools and animal bones have been associated with the Neanderthals. One recent discovery at Capellades, 56 km. north-east of Barcelona, may serve to revise older views of Neanderthal man's limited skills. Work continues on this site, which in part dates back to *c*.80,000 BC. But particularly important are a group of fifteen furnaces that have been found here, dating to *c*.50,000 BC, which seem to have served for both cooking and tool-making. The excavation has uncovered a wide range of stone and bone tools, and also the largest known collection of wooden utensils from any Neanderthal site. It has often been wondered if there was any significant interbreeding between Neanderthal men and other hominid groups more closely related to modern man, as there is evidence to show that chronologically they coexisted. However, no trace has been found of such a genetic contribution in a recent study of the DNA of the current European populations.[5]

The third stage of the Old Stone Age, the Upper Palaeolithic (*c*.40,000–10,000 BC), is linked with the presence of *Homo sapiens*, the immediate ancestor of the present form of man (emerging *c*.35,000 BC, and categorized as *Homo sapiens sapiens*), who is also associated with a very widely distributed group of cave sites. More substantial quantities of fossil bones and of worked flints have been found from this period. The most distinctive feature of this phase is the first appearance, around 15000 BC, of cave paintings, primarily large and vivid representations of animals, perhaps associated with rituals for ensuring success in hunting. In the absence of any other form of evidence, the exact purpose of these paintings remains a matter for speculation.[6] The paintings of Palaeolithic date are principally concentrated in the north of Spain, where the most famous and still perhaps the finest collection of them was found in the cave of Altamira.[7]

The Mesolithic or Middle Stone Age (c.10,000 – c.5000 BC)

This period is marked primarily by developments in flint technology, in particular by the use of more complex microliths for cutting and scraping instruments. These are small, more carefully cut and shaped, pieces of flint, which could be set into wood or other forms of holder to produce sharper and finer cutters. These tools and weapons would also be capable of reuse by replacing lost or damaged microliths. In tandem with this went the creation of smaller, sharper, and more carefully shaped arrowheads. A distinction is also made between the Palaeolithic and the Mesolithic in terms of the introduction of food gathering to supplement hunting in the latter period. Traces of seeds from berries and other forms of fruit in Mesolithic sites would seem to confirm this distinction, but this may reflect the vagaries of the evidence rather than an absolute difference between the two periods. In addition, it was probably in this period that fishing was first developed, using light, finely cut flints for fish spears. The earliest known boats were made at this time, using techniques that are still employed in some cultures. These involved the controlled use of fire to hollow out tree trunks, thus producing simple but perfectly seaworthy canoes. From about 8000 BC dates a major new phase in cave art, particularly well represented in the south-east coastal region of Spain, which extended into the succeeding Neolithic period. This involved painting smaller but more animated scenes, often involving human figures as well as the animals that they hunted. Some of these paintings also contain clear indications of dress and weapons, notably bows and arrows, and also of apparent communal activities such as dancing and hunting.

Early Farmers and the Beginnings of Metallurgy

The Neolithic or New Stone Age (c.5000 – c.2500 BC)

This period saw more rapid changes in economic and social organization, possibly largely thanks to cultural influences transmitted from the eastern Mediterranean. In particular, in what has been called the 'Neolithic Revolution', the basic techniques of farming, and also of the domestication of certain species of animals, were discovered. Grains of cultivated barley found in a cave site near Alicante have been dated by Carbon-14 to the very beginning of this period, establishing the presence of farming in the peninsula by at least 4500 BC. The sedentary nature of agriculture in turn fostered the need for greater co-operation between communities that grew to form villages consisting of huts made from branches, and animal pens. Stone, primarily flint, continued to be used for both weapons and simple farming implements, such as hoes and sickles. The growth of agriculture did not displace the importance of hunting in this society, and particularly fine stone arrowheads and axes were made at this time. The Late Neolithic period also saw the appearance of the first pottery, hand-made by coiling and without use of the wheel. This earliest pottery is striking for its fine shapes and the intricate decoration cut into the clay before firing.

The Chalcolithic or Copper Age (c.2500 – c.1700 BC)

This used to be classified as the final stage of the Neolithic or as the 'Eneolithic' (a word that may be encountered in some Spanish museums). The very significant social and technological developments that took place at this time, however, including the emergence of organized agriculture which led to more complex political organization, and the discovery of metallurgical arts, particularly of copper smelting, have led prehistorians in recent years to give this period a chronological label of its own. Two areas of the Iberian peninsula in particular have provided evidence relating to this period: the south-east and the south-west (the latter being primarily represented by sites within the modern boundaries of Portugal). The south-east is marked in particular by the important site of Las Millares (see ALMERÍA), for which evidence has been found for continuous occupation between c.2500 and c.1800 BC. As well as the construction of the first complex forms of fortification, this society is noted for its *tholoi* or beehive-shaped stone tombs, and its metallurgical skills. Other Chalcolithic sites in the south-east include Los Castillejos[8] and Almizaraque, where a flint-napping workshop has been found, emphasizing the continuing importance of stone for certain tools, notably axes and chisels.[9] A distinctive item of pottery of this period, which is found widely distributed over western Europe in funerary contexts, is the so-called Bell Beaker, named after its shape. Arguments that this style originated in

Spain and spread thence across the Pyrenees are now less well regarded than once they were.

The most characteristic physical features of the Chalcolithic, however, are the megalithic (i.e. large stone) dolmens or stone burial mounds that begin to appear in the third millennium BC, and continue to be erected during the succeeding Copper Age. These are very well represented in Spain, not least by the three great monuments of this kind at ANTEQUERA. They have been classified and given a chronology on the basis of variations in their style and the sophistication of their techniques of construction. Such monuments usually consisted of a central chamber, roofed with large flagstones, which was approached via a stone walled and roofed passage, the whole being covered in earth to form a large mound. Some of the mounds contain more complex arrangements with more than one chamber, or with subsidiary areas opening off from the central space. In some cases erosion over the millennia has entirely removed the earth covering, leaving the stones exposed, as is true of many examples in the province of Alava (see DOLMENS OF ALAVA). In numerous such instances the stones themselves were broken up and removed at later periods. Constructed at ground level, these dolmens were clearly intended to be conspicuous, and in many cases were re-used for burials of various kinds in later periods. Although traces of burials have been found in central locations in the main chamber, it is not necessarily the case that burial was the primary intention of the builders in all cases. It has been suggested, for example, that some of the Pyrenean dolmens were erected to serve as shelters for pastoralists, the equivalents of the high-pasture huts of much later centuries.[10]

The Growth of Social Complexity

The Early Bronze Age (c.1700–c.1200 BC)

With all of the divisions into the chronological and cultural periods employed by prehistorians, it is important not to imagine either necessarily rapid or uniform rates of change. There is less of a tendency now to explain the major developments in technology in these periods as being the result of large-scale immigrations or conquests, resulting in the speedy imposition of change. Instead, the spread can better be seen as the result of gradual diffusion, affecting local societies at different periods and with variable rates of rapidity. Moreover, within the human population of a geographically defined area, such as the Iberian peninsula, elements of cultural unity (such as the common employment of bronze technology) can be contrasted with social and cultural differences (e.g. in burial practices), that may have had far greater weight at the time in differentiating ethnic groups. In the case of the Early Bronze Age, which in Spain may be dated to between 1700 and 1200 BC, variable rates in the spread and employment of the new metal technology can be detected, as can the social consequences that are usually thought to result from it, such as the development of social hierarchies. As with the Chalcolithic, certain parts of the Iberian peninsula are still very poorly represented in the archaeological record for this period, and much more remains to be learnt. It is also worth noting that the spread of metallurgy still did not entirely displace the continuing use of flint, particularly in items such as sickles.

The archetypal Early Bronze Age site has long been taken to be the settlement at El Argar in the province of Almería, where over nine hundred tombs have been found.[11] These are of two types: cists and urns. A variety of funerary goods have been found in them. Two separate phases have been identified in the burials, although there seems to have been absolute continuity in occupation of the site between about 1700 and 1400 BC. There are a number of other settlements in this south-east area, such as the much-studied Fuente Alamo (near Antas, ALMERÍA), whose material culture, in terms of buildings, including tombs, and ceramic and metal personal items, indicates that they belonged to the same society as the inhabitants of El Argar. The role of metallurgy in this society has been a subject of debate. Did its possession lead to the social stratification that is demonstrated by the differing degrees of wealth displayed in the tombs? Similarly, the evidence for mining and for metal-working is unevenly distributed amongst these sites. Was there, therefore, co-operation between mining and metal-working communities, with a regular pattern of trade to distribute the finished products? If so, were these politically independent settlements or did they form part of a larger whole? This would argue for the existence of more complex forms of social and political organization by this time.[12] A lack of homogeneity in some of the evidence for social customs, for example, the relative importance of cist as opposed to urn burials, might argue in favour of political and cultural diversity rather than unity. In general, in these pre-literate periods (writing only developed in the Iberian peninsula in the first millennium BC), prehistorians can only speculate on the basis of broad patterns and divergences in the material record.

In the same period other comparable societies, but with distinct features in their buildings, burial practices, and material culture, flourished in the Levant, the Algarve (in Portugal) and La Mancha. The last of these is particularly noteworthy for the *motillas*, fortified settlements with a central tower and several rings of concentric walls, which in their decay have left distinctive mounds in the landscape shaped like small volcanoes. In the province of Albacete, where a sub-branch of this particular culture flourished, such mounds are called *moras*. In most cases all such fortified settlements are located in naturally defensible hill-top sites. Whether this concern for defence reflects the dangers of attacks from outside this society or the prevalence of internal conflict between the various settlements cannot be gauged.

The Later Bronze Age (c.1200–c.700 BC)

Two cultures in particular have attracted scholarly interest in this period. The first is known from a key-find site in the province of Avila as the Las Cogotas culture. (Las Cogotas itself is a hill fort, built by subsequent Iron Age inhabitants on a site previously occupied by elements of this Late Bronze Age population.) It is distinguished by its rather crudely shaped but highly decorated pottery, which seems to divide into two periods. What is called Las Cogotas I dates from c.1100 to c.900 BC, and Las Cogotas II is assigned to c.800 to c.700 BC. The main concentration of finds of these wares has been in the valleys of the Duero and its tributaries, but their overall distribution is surprisingly wide. Thus, there have been finds of Las Cogotas pottery as far south as CARMONA in the Guadalquivir valley. The people associated with the production of these pots, located on the Meseta, appear to have lived in caves or simple wooden huts, and to have practised individual burials (inhumations). Little is known of other features of their material culture, but it does seem generally of poor quality and limited in its extent, despite the widespread distribution of their pottery. It seems that they were pastoralists, and some features of their art and society have been thought to link them with a section of the preceding 'Bell Beaker people' in this north-west region.

Very different are the so-called Urn Folk, who form a distinctive presence in the north-east, especially around the lower Ebro and the valleys of the Segre and Jalón in modern Catalonia, in this same period (i.e. c.1100–c.700). They are representatives of a culture that was to be found at this time throughout western and central Europe. Like the Las Cogotas people, they used cave sites in the earlier part of the period, particularly for burials, but their principal habitations seem to have been small villages along the river valleys. In the second half of the period such settlements are also found on higher ground, and the geographical area in which this culture was dominant had extended into areas to the south, such as the provinces around Valencia. It subsequently spread further inland, into the province of Alicante. What is particularly distinctive about these Urn-Folk is that they used, and were the first to introduce into the Iberian peninsula, the practice of cremation. The ashes of the burnt bodies were preserved in the distinctively shaped pottery urns from which the culture as a whole takes its name. These urns were generally buried in large numbers, accompanied by a wide variety of grave goods. It has been suggested that such a major change in funerary practice must have been prompted by the emergence of new ideas on death and the afterlife, differing from those of earlier societies and from those of their contemporaries, such as the Las Cogotas people, who were still practising inhumation. What those ideas were cannot be known, but it has been suggested, due to the similarities in such funerary rites with those of other peoples beyond the eastern Pyrenees, that the Urn Folk were the first Indo-European people to enter the peninsula, and in particular represented the first wave of Celts to start colonizing Spain. As with some of the preceding Early Bronze Age cultures, there are numerous variations between areas linked by some common features. Thus while cremation is common to all of this society there are marked variations in the nature of the burials. For example, in the Catalan coastal zone the urns were buried directly in the earth, with no containing or protective structures. Such cemeteries thus took the form of fields of buried urns with no known surface markings. Further inland the urns were buried in stone cists, and small mounds or tumuli of stones were raised over them above ground level.

The Impact of Mediterranean Traders: Phoenicians, Greeks, and the Iberians

The Early Iron Age (c.700–c.200 BC)

The next major revolution in metal technology was the working of iron. The uses found for it gradually grew, supplementing and then eventually replacing bronze in the manufacture of weapons. Knowledge of how to make iron may well have been a direct import into the south of the peninsula from the eastern Mediterranean, mediated through a new group of settlers, the Phoenicians. They were also responsible for the introduction of writing (employed in inscriptions but not, as far as is known, in any literary or documentary fashion) and the use of the wheel in the making of pottery into the Iberian peninsula. Although the name by which we know them is Greek, they were a Semitic people, occupying much of the coastal plain of Lebanon and ethnically and culturally linked to the Canaanites. Tyre and Sidon were amongst their principal ports, and from the 12th to the 8th cent. these and other towns of the region were the centres of independent kingdoms. In Phoenicia the transition from the Bronze to the Iron Age is thought to have taken place during the period c.1200–c.1050 BC. The first evidence of iron production in Spain dates to the 8th cent. BC, and is contemporaneous with the definite establishment of Phoenician settlements in the south.

These settlers came from Tyre and from the recently founded Tyrian colony of Carthage in North Africa (traditionally said to have been established in 814 BC, but not demonstrated archaeologically before c.750 BC). In legend, retold in the work of writers of the Roman period, such as Strabo and Velleius Paterculus, Gades (modern Cádiz) was the earliest and most important of these foundations, and their stories imply that it was established around 1100 BC. No archaeological evidence exists to support such a date, and the earliest finds from the immediate vicinity come in the form of some burials datable to the 6th cent. BC. However, at the nearby site of CASTILLO DE DOÑA BLANCA evidence of occupation by the early 8th cent. has been found, and this corresponds to the dating that has been established for several of the other Phoenician settlements along the south coast (see ALMUÑECAR, PHOENICIAN SETTLEMENTS, Sexi). While evidence of earlier settlement may yet emerge, at the moment the 8th cent. is the earliest point at which a Phoenician presence in Spain can be proved.

The purposes to be served by these Phoenician settlements in Spain remain uncertain. Older views, deriving from the classical sources, presented them as colonies with extensive territories, enslaving indigenous populations and exploiting local mineral resources directly. However, these have now given way to new interpretations, presenting the settlements as small trading centres or *emporia*, that bartered with local populations for their mineral wealth, thereby indirectly exercising economic and cultural control over nearby indigenous communities. A recently discovered site near MÁLAGA, on the Cerro del Villar, may lead to some further modification of opinion, and could even reverse some of the new orthodoxy. This site, close to the mouth of the river Guadalhorce, constitutes the largest Phoenician settlement so far found in the peninsula, with a population possibly well in excess of 1,000 people, and dates to at least the 8th cent. BC. Its size would seem to make it more than just the simple trading station envisaged in present interpretations of the Phoenician settlements on the south coast. Ongoing excavations here will no doubt yield even more interesting results over the next few years.

Whatever the direction that future arguments take over the nature of the Phoenician presence, it is clear from a wide range of finds, such as the tombs at TRAYAMAR (*c*.650–600 BC), that a wide range of luxury items were imported into southern Spain via these coastal settlements, with a direct impact on the art and material culture of some of the indigenous populations of the inland regions. This involved cultural influences from Egypt as well as from the Phoenician homeland. The period of direct Phoenician involvement in Spain was relatively short, due to political upheavals in the Near East. The Assyrian Empire that had been the Phoenicians' main market for imported metal ores was overthrown by the Babylonians in 612 BC. The Babylonians then began to extend their power into Phoenicia itself, and Tyre, the last independent kingdom, fell in 573. These changes and the growing power of the now independent Phoenician settlement of Carthage (near Tunis) seem to have led to the abandonment or destruction of most of these trading stations in Spain by the middle of the 6th cent. BC. Thus, the settlement of Toscanos, the modern Vélez Málaga, which seems to have been settled by the Phoenicians around 750 BC, had clearly expanded considerably in size by 650 BC, only to be abandoned *c*.550 BC.

With the Greeks, who represented the second major external cultural influence on the Iberian peninsula in the first millennium BC, trade may have preceded settlement. Despite various claims in later classical sources, it seems most likely that there were no Greek towns in southern Spain.

However, around 600/580 BC a trading station of the Phocaeans, who also established themselves at Massilia (Marseille) at the same time, had been created on an island off the Catalan coast. This was the Palaiopolis or 'Old City' of AMPURIAS. Within a generation this had expanded to include the new settlement of Emporion on the mainland opposite. Finds of pottery associated with this town, as well as other Greek ceramics that it may have imported, are widely distributed along the eastern seaboard of Spain, and serve as testimony to its far-flung commercial activities. Its influence may also have been felt in building styles, as some of the settlements on the Mediterranean coast of the Levante show possible Greek as well as Phoenician architectural features. (See EL ORAL and SANTA POLA.) Good relations seem to have existed between these Greeks and the local indigenous population, who had a settlement of their own, called Indika (see ULLASTRET), very close to Ampurias. Although Greek commercial and cultural influence declined from the 4th cent. BC, Ampurias remained important, and, faced with a rapidly growing Carthaginian threat to the south, threw in its lot with Rome in the Second Punic War (see below) in 218 BC.

Out of the various eastern Mediterranean influences on the Iberian peninsula, that were at their height during the period *c*.650–*c*.550 BC, there emerged the indigenous Iberian civilization. The geographical area of this culture extended from the Guadalquivir valley in the south up to the eastern Pyrenees. Strong eastern Mediterranean influence on the Balearic islands in the period *c*.550–450 brought them also within its orbit, and by the mid-4th cent. BC, when it reached its greatest extent, Iberian culture stretched further up the Ebro valley and across the Pyrenees into southwest France. In general it ran parallel to the Mediterranean coast, where the Phoenician, Punic, and Greek settlements and trading stations had been or were located. Iberian society never enjoyed political unity, being made up of a number of competing kingdoms and small states. The 4th cent. BC in particular is marked by evidence of destruction from a large number of Iberian settlement sites, indicative of an endemic state of warfare. The Iberians may not even have had a single language, but the material culture of the upper levels of their society throughout the whole of the area shows remarkable similarity and a common debt to the influences of the eastern Mediterranean commercial settlements on the coast. Eastern ideas and styles also seem to have had a powerful impact on Iberian religion.

The early Iberian state with which the Phoenician settlements would primarily have come into contact in the Spanish Late Bronze Age was that of the Tartessians, whose sophistication was remembered and probably exaggerated in later Greek literary sources. It was their control of mineral resources in their territories, not least silver and copper, that lay behind the fabled wealth of Tartessus. These metals were sought by the Phoenicians for export to their markets in the Near East, especially

Assyria. A number of indigenous settlements contemporary with those of the Phoenicians have been located, especially in the Guadalquivir valley. The cultural impact of the eastern Mediterranean on this society is particularly marked. This influence was by no means exclusively Phoenician: Greek objects, and pottery in particular, are found in southern Spain from about 600 BC onwards. Additionally, there are significant finds of ceramics and metal items of Italian manufacture, produced by the Etruscans and by the recently founded Greek colonies in southern Italy. Building styles deriving from eastern prototypes have also been recognized. One of the most famous examples is the structure uncovered at CANCHO ROANO, whose oriental antecedents have been generally accepted, while the nature of the building remains highly controversial. It has been separately identified as being a temple, a palace, a great altar, and some form of factory. Generally, the development of more complex, rectilinear forms of housing in the indigenous settlements in this period is taken as another facet of the external influences then being felt in the southern and eastern half of the Iberian peninsula.

The political changes in Iberian society that took place in the middle of the first millennium BC are not easy to understand because there are no contemporary sources of information. What may be known has to be deduced from the accounts given by later classical authors, such as the Greek geographer Strabo (c.63 BC–AD 19). The extensive kingdom of Tartessus, as described briefly by Herodotus (writing c.484 BC), clearly gave way in the 5th cent. BC to a more complicated pattern of smaller tribal kingdoms and city states. This may have been a period of rapidly changing fortunes for different regions, perhaps reflecting the fluctuating military and political success of local ruling families and individual war lords. Certain sites indicate periods of intense local prosperity followed by equally sudden decline. The 4th cent. BC especially can be shown archaeologically to have been a period of considerable violence, reflecting inter-kingdom, or even more localized conflicts. For example, the important settlement site of ULLASTRET seems to have been burnt around 400 BC. In the second half of this century the level of destructiveness appears to rise, and this has been related to a treaty made in 348 BC between Rome and Carthage. This defined the respective areas of influence between the two powers, but may actually have served to create more intense competition between them in trying to win the support and build up the power of the rulers of potential client states amongst the Iberians. In due course it would be the open conflict between Rome and Carthage in the Second Punic War at the end of the 3rd cent. BC that would lead to the political subjugation and cultural decline of Iberian society.

While Iberian culture dominated most of the south and east of the peninsula in the period c.600–c.200 BC, its other regions were subject to different influences. A second wave of Celtic immigration took place in the 6th cent. BC. The Celts entered the peninsula via the western Pyrenees and established themselves across the northern and western regions, along the Bay of Biscay, and all down the Atlantic coast. These Celtic tribal societies were responsible for the building of the *castros*, which were oval, fortified settlements containing round houses, which are particularly widely distributed across the north-west of Spain and in northern Portugal. These were very different from the eastern-Mediterranean styles of architecture and town planning of the Iberians. In their material culture these Celts can be clearly associated with the La Tène culture known elsewhere in western Europe at this time. However, evidence from funerary inscriptions, pottery, and (in the later stages) coins indicate elements of both Celtic and pre-Indo-European languages being used in these northern and western regions of the peninsula, especially in Lusitania and Galicia. This would suggest the continued survival of some features of the pre-Celtic cultures of those areas.[13] As can be seen elsewhere in this period, Celtic society was highly stratified, with a very competitive warrior aristocracy at its apex. This Celtic society may have dominated a largely non-Celtic subject population.

Another area with a separate cultural identity in this period was the region that classical authors called 'Celtiberia', which, as the name suggests, was marked by a fusing together of Celtic and Iberian elements.[14] Celtiberia was centred on the upper Ebro valley and Aragón, but also extended southwards towards the centre of the peninsula and northwards to Cantabria. Here, as in the Iberian south, contacts with civilizations from outside the peninsula led to the development of more complex forms of political organization and settlement. By the 4th cent. BC what have been seen as genuine towns, with public buildings and a structured layout, had clearly emerged in the Celtiberian area (but not amongst the Celts further west). These settlements varied in size, and some of the smaller ones are referred to as villages, but the basic pattern of the rectangular houses with small courtyards are common to all of them. In the tributary valleys of the Ebro they were numerous and in close proximity to each other. See CABEZO DE ALCALÁ and CASTRO DE LA CORONILLA.

SPAIN AND ROME

Carthage, Rome, and the Iberians (237–19 BC)

Carthage was a Tyrian foundation that took on aspects of the indigenous culture of North Africa to produce a hybrid Punic society. It came to dominate the former Phoenician settlements of the south coast of Spain, following the decline of Tyre in the 6th cent. New Punic foundations developed, and the older trading stations vanished beneath larger

Carthaginian towns. It was not until the defeat of Carthage in the First Punic War (247–241 BC) with Rome, which was fought over control of Sicily, that the Carthaginians became seriously expansionary in a territorial sense in the Iberian peninsula. They sought to make up for their recent losses by augmenting their empire in Spain. Under the leadership of Hamilcar Barca, who established himself at Gadir (Cádiz) in 237 BC, the Carthaginians launched themselves into a series of campaigns of conquest of their Iberian neighbours in the south. Although Hamilcar was killed in the siege of an Iberian town in 229 BC, his son Hasdrubal founded 'New Carthage' (CARTAGENA) in 228 BC, and continued the process of expansion northwards up the Mediterranean coast. Following his murder in 221 BC, his brother Hannibal continued to extend Carthaginian rule towards the Ebro valley. This led rapidly to the outbreak of the Second Punic War, which was initiated in 218 BC by a Carthaginian attack on the town of Saguntum (SAGUNTO), which was protected by treaty with Rome. The first Roman army landed at Ampurias. Although the most famous feature of this war was Hannibal's remarkable but ultimately unsuccessful campaign in Italy, the bulk of the fighting took place in Spain, where, despite some initial disasters, Rome was ultimately victorious by 207 BC, and in the terms of the peace treaty of 201 BC was able to force Carthage to abandon all its possessions in the Iberian peninsula.

There followed almost two centuries of intermittent warfare, during which Rome came to establish direct rule over the whole of the Iberian peninsula. The final stage of this process was concluded by the hard-fought Cantabrian wars of 27–19 BC in the northern mountains. It would be misleading, however, to think of this unusually protracted period of conquest (compared for example with Caesar's pacification of Gaul in less than a decade) as being caused by the stubborn resistance of the indigenous population. It was more a reflection of the peculiar political construction of Roman republican government. In Rome the urban magistracies had become essentially military by this time, and it was necessary to find areas in which at least one of the two consuls and several of the six praetors, all elected annually, could exercise their authority. All hoped to further their own political careers and personal profit through military ventures. The complex pattern of tribal conflicts in Spain and the astute, if occasionally mendacious, diplomacy of Rome meant that there were almost always possibilities of warfare in the peninsula in which Roman armies could take sides. This is particularly marked in the periods 218–178 BC and 155–133 BC. Simply put, it was in the interests of individual Roman politicians and also to the financial benefit of the state to keep an endemic state of conflict in the Iberian peninsula. By the 1st cent. BC, when Rome itself was torn by periodic periods of political uncertainty and civil wars, these came to be reflected in Spain too. Thus in 82 BC, Quintus Sertorius, a partisan of the popular general Gaius Marius, led a revolt in Spain against the supporters of the dictator Sulla. He was able to gain control of most of the two provinces into which Spain had been divided by Rome, and established his headquarters at Osca (HUESCA). He attracted the support of many of the most powerful indigenous tribes, and won a series of victories over Roman armies, but his position was eventually weakened, and in 72 BC he was murdered by one of his own generals. Under Pompey's command savage reprisals were inflicted on his indigenous allies. Their settlements on the sites of the later Roman towns of CLUNIA, HUESCA, TIERMES and UXAMA were all destroyed, as was CABEZO DE ALCALÁ. The Civil War of 49–45 BC between Pompey and Caesar also had its Spanish dimension, due to the presence of important Roman military units in Spain, which took sides in the conflict. With the restoration of relative stability elsewhere in the Mediterranean, Augustus, the first Roman emperor, undertook the campaign to bring Cantabria under control in 27/26 BC, though in part this may have been a reflection of his need to establish his credibility with a successful military operation. Although the war was in theory concluded in 22 BC, it was not until the suppression of a final revolt by the Cantabri in 19 BC that the peninsula was finally entirely pacified and all its parts incorporated within the empire.

Spain in the Early Roman Empire (19 BC – AD 285)

The conclusion of the Cantabrian Wars by 19 BC ended a period of nearly two centuries of wars of conquest and the suppression of indigenous revolts by Rome, and was followed by a major administrative reform that integrated the Spanish provinces within the new governmental structures of the empire. As with some of the earlier wars but on an even greater scale, it also led to the foundation of new settlements in Spain for veteran legionaries. Amongst the most significant of these were Emerita Augusta (MÉRIDA) and ITÁLICA. As settlements of Roman citizens these were granted the status of *coloniae*, which gave their inhabitants the highest level of legal privilege. Other towns founded or redeveloped by the imperial government for groups of the indigenous population, such as MUNIGUA, were made *municipia*, whose inhabitants received the lesser status of Latin citizenship. With the passage of time more and more *municipia* were transformed into *coloniae*. In some cases this was a deliberate reward to mark a special event or particular display of loyalty by the inhabitants, such as the Emperor Galba's grant of *colonia* status to CLUNIA, where he had been taking refuge when called to the throne in AD 68. In other instances the significant physical and economic expansion of a settlement, or the occasional need for a conspicuous display of the emperor's patronage could lead to such a promotion. The distinction ceased to be of legal significance, in terms of the status of the individual inhabitants, when the Emperor Caracalla (211–17) extended the privileges of Roman citizenship to all non-servile inhabitants of the empire.

Many Roman towns in Spain have been excavated, often on more than one occasion, in the course of the 20th cent. The sites of others are known, and extensive programmes of study are in progress in many of them. In some instances a Roman settlement lies below a modern one, such as BARCELONA, CÓRDOBA or TARRAGONA, and in consequence only small sectors of the site are accessible for excavation. In all the above-named cities, and many others, such as MÉRIDA and ZARAGOZA, important features of the Roman settlement have, however, been unearthed and made accessible. In some cases, as for example ASTORGA, BARCELONA, LEÓN and LUGO, significant Roman features, in these cases parts of the walls, still stand to something like their original height. In others important structures, previously buried, have been extensively restored. A fine balance, both academic and financial, needs to be maintained in such cases between the value of recreating imposing and attractive buildings to arouse the visitor's interest, and the dangers of anachronism and the destruction of other features of the site. Few buildings of Antiquity and the Middle Ages in their final state contained only work of a single period, and the complexity of their constructional history can easily be lost in trying to restore them to their assumed condition at one particular point in time.

Roman town sites, such as AMPURIAS, CLUNIA or ITÁLICA, that did not enjoy continuity of settlement into later periods and are not built over by modern structures, obviously offer considerable opportunities for extensive excavation; though it must be admitted that modern farming methods can be as destructive as later building of archaeological sites buried under shallow topsoil. However, it is worth emphasizing that in no case has an entire Roman town site been excavated. ITÁLICA probably comes nearest to this, but logistic and financial limitations make such an undertaking exceedingly difficult. So, while attention has been focused as far as possible on the major public buildings and centres of urban life such as the Forum, it is not possible to make categorical statements about the physical, let alone economic and social, state of entire settlements. Some indications can be found and judgements formed, but they have to remain provisional.

This is worth stressing in the light of some of the most striking features that appear to be common to the towns of Roman Spain in the early imperial period. First, what has emerged not least from the extensive recent study of the Forum areas and their related temples, civic law courts (basilicas) and local council halls (*curiae*) and also of places of major public entertainment, such as theatres, amphitheatres, and hippodromes or circuses, is that most of the larger and the medium-sized settlements owe almost all their architectural finery to imperial patronage. The periods at which this was principally expressed vary from town to town, but almost all tend to fall within a range extending from the reign of Augustus (27 BC–AD 14) up to that of Hadrian (117–38). There are a few examples of such patronage in Spain in the Severan period (193–235), a dynasty which is better known for its interest in the cities of North Africa. As with Lepcis Magna in Libya, whose Severan founder was a native of the town, an imperial birthplace could be a special beneficiary of an emperor's munificence. ITÁLICA was thus enormously extended and enhanced by Hadrian, who was born in the city, but the programme faltered after his death and a substantial part of his new development had to be abandoned by the end of the 2nd cent., probably due to problems of subsidence.

As well as the almost exclusive debt to imperial patronage for the funding of public works and the construction of civic buildings and places of entertainment, what has emerged strikingly from comparative study of sites across Spain is how rapidly these central areas and public buildings began to go out of use. While normally thought to be a phenomenon of the later empire or of the politically and militarily troubled 3rd cent., urban decline, neglect, and abandonment of great public buildings, together with the growth of large deposits of rubbish in former communal centres, can be documented from much earlier periods. Even by the Flavian period (AD 69–96), a time of expansion for some Spanish towns, others were showing clear symptoms of decline, especially marked in the case of AMPURIAS. This is where it is necessary to recall the reservation made above. Decline in the previously most significant foci of public life does not necessarily imply complete urban collapse. Other areas may be rising to greater prominence in consequence. This is certainly the case in the later empire with the development of urban ecclesiastical centres, consisting of complexes of churches, baptisteries, and episcopal palaces. It is also necessary to note the variations between towns in terms of the periods in which signs of decay can be detected, and even between different types of buildings within a single settlement. Moreover, the evidence is far from evenly distributed. Hippodromes (race tracks), which take up a larger area of land than any other form of public building but require much less in the way of construction, are very poorly represented, with significant examples to be found only in MÉRIDA, TOLEDO, and TARRAGONA. While hippodromes may have continued to play a very important role, as the site for political ceremonies as well as for public entertainments, right through the Visigothic period, it would be hard to draw broad conclusions on the survival and use of such buildings in Roman Spain just on the evidence of these two poorly preserved examples.

Spain suffered relatively little in the disturbed 3rd cent. Politically it tended to follow Gaul, through which land-based communication with the rest of the empire ran. Thus, the Spanish provinces formed part of the breakaway Gallic Empire of Postumus (260–9), but reverted to allegiance to the legitimate emperor in the time of his successor Victorinus

(269–71).[15] Invasion of the peninsula by Germanic peoples, such as the Franks and the Alamanni who breached the Rhine frontier in the 260s and again in the 280s, was of limited duration and geographical extent. Sometimes this is invoked, almost like a *deus ex machina* to explain archaeological findings equally capable of other interpretations. Thus, evidence of destruction by fire in the Forum and surrounding sections of CLUNIA, datable to the late 3rd cent., could as easily be the result of accident as of a barbarian sack of the town. Economic problems of this period will inevitably have affected the Spanish provinces as much as other parts of the empire, and can be best seen in the large hoards of highly debased silver coins (*antoniniani*), dating from the middle of the 3rd cent., that have been found buried in various parts of the peninsula. Many of these can be seen in museum displays.

While urban sites are amongst the most interesting features of Roman Spain, a number of significant rural villas exist, as well as important traces of the once extensive network of Roman communications. Such traces include a number of bridges, some of which still serve their original function, and some short stretches of road. Especially impressive architecturally and aesthetically are the bridges at MÉRIDA and ALCÁNTARA in Extremadura. In a few places parts of the water distribution network to nearby settlements may be seen in the countryside. Close to TARRAGONA, ITÁLICA and MÉRIDA may be seen sections of the aqueducts that transported water to the cities, and in the case of MÉRIDA the Roman reservoir, with its dam and water tower that fed one of its main aqueducts, still functions and may be visited. The finest aqueduct still to be seen in Spain is, however, in the very heart of the city of SEGOVIA.

Late Roman Spain (285– 409)

The reign of Constantine I (306–37) saw the emperor's conversion to Christianity in 312 and the beginning of a transformation of the role of the Church within the Roman world. Starting with the imperial constructions in Rome, a specific Christian architecture was developed, matched during the later 4th cent. by a new iconography. New types of buildings, in the form of churches, baptisteries, and martyrial chapels, came into being to meet the requirements for places of worship and for the performance of specific liturgical ceremonies. Before this time, when Christian communities faced intermittent persecution, as in the reigns of Trajan Decius (249–51) and Diocletian (285–305), it was necessary for their meeting places to be inconspicuous, and they normally took the form of a specially designated room in a private villa.

In some cities the decline and eventual abandonment of the former civic and religious buildings associated with the forum may well have been matched in the 4th and 5th centuries by a corresponding concentration of interest in and patronage of church building and the development of episcopal complexes.[16] Unfortunately, where continuity of occupation has been more or less maintained from the medieval period onwards, not only have earlier buildings tended to be replaced, often more than once, by newer structures, but there is also much greater difficulty in gaining archaeological access to still inhabited areas. Thus, for example, the first cathedral and attendant buildings that are assumed to have existed in the upper city of TARRAGONA on the site of the previous temple to the imperial cult, must be located under the present, larger, late medieval cathedral, and only some small access to these earlier levels has been achieved via excavations in its cloister garden. It is not possible in Spain to find the equivalents to the excavations of substantial parts of early ecclesiastical complexes such as those of Lyon or Geneva. TARRAGONA, MÉRIDA, and AMPURIAS provide very interesting examples of Roman Christian cemeteries clustered around the presumed burial place of an early martyr, over whose relics a *martyrium* or shrine was erected.

Certain forms of entertainment went out of fashion in the Late Roman period, in some cases due to Christian hostility. Thus gladiatorial fights declined and were eventually forbidden, while chariot races grew in popularity, and the hippodrome became an important political centre as well as place of sport. There is some evidence of imperial patronage in Late Roman Spanish towns, as for example the refurbishment of the hippodrome at MÉRIDA by Constantine II (337–40), but in general the indications of urban decline both in terms of size and the nature of town life, that begin in the earlier empire, continue in the later. Finds of burials of the Late Roman and Visigothic period in previously residential areas (see the House of the Amphitheatre in MÉRIDA) indicate the physical contraction of even the most important of the cities.

As well as in the evidence of ecclesiastical building, the Late Roman centuries are notable in Spain for a number of very substantial rural villas. Of these, one at least (CARRANQUE) is associated with a powerful family closely linked to the imperial family, and another (CENTCELLES) contains an extraordinary mausoleum that has been suspected of being the burial place of the Emperor Constans (337–50).[17] Others are interesting not only for their scale and sumptuousness but also, in some cases, for the presence of a church within the residential area, as for example in both FRAGA and Pedraza. In both these cases rooms around the main atrium of the villa were transformed into churches, which were developed and continued in use after the residential sections of the house had been abandoned. It is possible that, following a fashion that developed from the later 4th cent. onwards, these became house monasteries, in which the families who owned them and like-minded friends lived, together with various dependants, and followed an ascetic life-style under rules of their own devising. In such a context a place of worship could well be created out of part of the villa. Lacking institutional continuity, and subsequently rather disapproved of by the Church, such private-house monasteries declined, but their churches might be preserved for worship while the villas themselves were abandoned and despoiled. Other sites, such as that of SAN MIGUEL DE ESCALADA, where traces of a Late Roman villa and of a church of 6th–9th cent. date have been found in layers below a 10th-cent. monastery, may have had similar histories. In general, while a few villa sites display continuity of occupation into the early 6th cent., there is hardly any evidence that they were still in use in the Visigothic period proper. However, this does not mean that such semi-palatial residences were not being built at that time, as recent excavation on a very impressive fortified rural villa of probably 7th cent. date at PLA DE NADAL have shown.

Roman rule in Spain came to an end in stages in the 5th cent. 409 saw the passes over the Pyrenees being betrayed to migratory armies of a confederacy of the Alans, the Sueves, and the Vandals, who overran most of the peninsula. Although much of the eastern seaboard was recovered for Rome in 418, and the Vandals moved on to conquer the Roman provinces of North Africa in 429, a Suevic kingdom developed that came to rule virtually all of the west and the south. The Visigoths under Theoderic II (453–66), who had established a powerful kingdom in south-west France, centred on Toulouse, conquered most of the former Suevic kingdom in 456. The remaining Roman territories in the east were taken over by Theoderic's brother Euric (466–84) in the mid-470s. When the Visigoths were themselves defeated by the Franks in 507, they gave up most of their lands north of the Pyrenees to establish themselves in Spain. The vestigial Suevic kingdom in Galicia was finally eliminated by them in 584. Their acceptance of orthodox Christianity (as opposed to the heretical Arian form they had been converted to in the 4th cent.) in 589 led to closer ties with the indigenous Hispano-Roman population. A relatively stable Visigothic kingdom thus emerged to control most of the peninsula until the Arab conquest of 711.

THE VISIGOTHIC KINGDOM (409–711)

The first thing to be said about this period is that archaeologically the label 'Visigothic' is essentially a chronological one, and is certainly not intended to indicate that all or indeed any of the items found in sites datable to this period or which can be ascribed to it on stylistic or other grounds were necessarily made by or for the use of the Visigoths. The Visigoths formed a small, if politically dominant, section of the population during the period from 456 to 711 when much of the Iberian peninsula was ruled by kings of Visigothic origin. Under them the Spanish Church, led by a series of outstanding bishops, such as Isidore of Seville (d. 636) and Julian of

Toledo (d. 690), was the most intellectually active of any in Christendom, and a series of major ecclesiastical councils were held at TOLEDO throughout the 7th cent. Numerous civil and ecclesiastical laws, as well as a substantial body of liturgy, were produced at this time and, under the direction of the bishops of Toledo, large-scale programmes of reform and doctrinal and disciplinary uniformity were introduced. Unfortunately, there was little historical writing, so the personalities and the political history of much of this period remain obscure. Once prevalent interpretations of the late Visigothic kingdom as being decadent and demoralized are now discounted.

Not many years ago it would have been possible to say that the Visigothic period was represented archaeologically by four almost complete churches and a quantity of architectural fragments, metal items, and ceramics. The last twenty to thirty years have seen a substantial increase in the number of sites either attributed directly to this period or containing some elements datable to it, such as the numerous Visigothic burials found in earlier Roman town and villa locations. At the same time, much greater uncertainty would now be expressed about an exclusively Visigothic period for the churches. For example, it has been argued that, of one of them, SANTA COMBA DE BANDE, only the ground plan of the building belongs to this period, and that the extant structure dates from a radical reconstruction in the time of the Asturian kingdom. This is not a view universally accepted. Similarly, argument has continued for some time now as to whether the extant chancel of the otherwise ruined church of SANTA MARÍA DE QUINTANILLA DE LAS VIÑAS is 7th or 10th cent. in date. Arguments about the chronology of two or more distinct phases of construction to be seen in the buildings continue to make it difficult to make categorical statements about other churches of this period, including SAN PEDRO DE LA MATA, SAN JUAN DE BAÑOS, and SANTA LUCÍA DEL TRAMPAL. On the other hand, the imposing and well-preserved church of SANTA MARÍA DE MELQUE has now been firmly dated to the Visigothic period, having previously been regarded as 10th cent. in origin. For a final type of complication also applicable to aspects of other sites, the radical reconstruction of the church of SAN PEDRO DE LA NAVE, following its removal from its original site in 1931, raises serious doubts about the authenticity of its present appearance. While such debates and uncertainties, which are unlikely to be resolved to the satisfaction of all participants, may be the despair of the visitor making first acquaintance with a site, there is no use concealing the fact of their existence or in pretending to a certainty that does not exist.[18] However, they do not detract from the inherent interest of these sites with their striking variations in decorative styles. To the complete or partially preserved churches of this period should also be added some fine fragments of destroyed buildings, notably those to be seen in the Visigothic Museum and *Alcazaba* in MÉRIDA and in the Museo Arqueológico Nacional in MADRID.

Ecclesiastical buildings do not by any means represent the sum of Visigothic archaeology. Quantitatively they are far outstripped by funerary sites, which include a substantial number of burials in former Roman towns and villas. The grave goods of the period are limited, and hardly ever include weapons. A good representative display of finds from burials in a single necropolis may be seen in the Museo de los Concilios in TOLEDO. The interpretation of the large cemeteries, of which this one is an example, is also contentious. It used to be assumed that these were the burials of the Visigoths themselves. The material culture was so poor, though, that the argument was refined by suggesting that these graveyards were those of a Visigothic 'free peasantry', relegated to the less desirable lands of the Meseta (the high plains north of the Sierra de Guadarrama and south of the Asturias), while the nobility and their followers established themselves in the richer river valleys of the south. However, in part this became a self-fulfilling prophecy, with archaeological attention being concentrated almost exclusively on the regions where such finds were expected. That finds were not made to any degree elsewhere in the peninsula was more a product of the pattern of the search than of the real distribution of the evidence. Secondly, allowing for some regional stylistic variation, the material culture of these burials was essentially similar to that of other regions of the western part of the former Roman Empire. It thus seems more reasonable to see these burials, mostly dated by stylistic analysis to the late 5th and 6th cents., as those of rural communities of the indigenous Hispano-Roman population.

More distinctively, Visigothic art, in the sense of being that of the ruling élite, may be seen in the treasures that have been found dating to this period. The most famous is that found at Guarrazar near Toledo in 1849, much of which is displayed in the Museo Arqueológico Nacional in MADRID. This was discovered by some peasants who sold their find to a Frenchman, who secretly transferred the treasure to Paris before announcing its discovery. Most of it was returned to Spain during the Nazi occupation of Paris in the Second World War, apart from a small number of pieces still to be seen in the Musée de Cluny in Paris. Small parts of other lesser treasures, that hint at once having items of the scale and quality of that of Guarrazar, may be seen in the archaeological museums in both BARCELONA and CÓRDOBA.

Where Visigothic archaeology is becoming particularly exciting now and breaking new ground is in a number of settlement and fortress sites. In particular, the town founded in the 570s by King Leovigild and called Reccopolis after his second son seems to have been located (see ZORITA DE LOS CANES). Recent work on it has produced interesting evidence of continuity of occupation across the Arab conquest, though with a modification of use setting in that led eventually to the transfer of the settlement to the present village. In Catalonia a late 7th-cent. fortress has been excavated at PUIG ROM, as has a village, probably of the same period (see below). Other sites of the Visigothic period or with a significant Visigothic phase are still being worked on or are awaiting publication. These will probably include the Roman town site of Ercávica and a Visigothic settlement at Tolmo de Minateda (near Hellín in the province of Albacete).[19] It is still too early, though, to generalize about the nature of urban life and its distribution in Visigothic Spain. The appearance of names of bishoprics in the acts of the church councils held in TOLEDO throughout the 7th cent., and the use of town names on the reverse of the small gold *tremisses* that were the only form of coinage minted at this time imply the continued occupation of several formerly Roman towns, but so far little archaeological evidence has emerged to put any detail on this. A small section of Visigothic BARCELONA is included in the excavation of an earlier Roman street that may be visited near the medieval royal palace. MÉRIDA, which is the subject of an important and substantial literary account of its 6th cent. bishops, is starting to reveal something of its Visigothic past archaeologically as well. Recent excavations of a substantial site by the river Guadiana have demonstrated how high status Roman houses came to be broken up into numerous small occupational units in this period.

ISLAMIC AND CHRISTIAN STATES IN SPAIN

The Umayyad Amirate and Caliphate of Córdoba (711–1031)

It is surprisingly rare for a historical event, usually of limited duration whatever its longer-term consequences, to be reflected clearly in the archaeological record. The Arab conquest of Spain is one such instance, in which a single site seems to preserve the imprint of the dramatic happenings of that period. The Visigothic village site of EL BOVALAR in Catalonia was abandoned in haste by its inhabitants, apparently leaving most of their worldly goods behind, including an unusual number of gold coins of the short-lived King Achila (710–13), who ruled in this area. These, which provide strong chronological indications, and the fact that the site seems to have been destroyed by fire, have led to the quite permissible conclusion that this settlement was destroyed in the course of the Arab conquest of the region around the year 714.

This is not the only site which has important evidence relating to the period of the Arab conquest and the subsequent imposition of their authority on much of the Iberian peninsula, though it is the one with the most immediacy. A number of interesting indications of compromise and continuity have emerged from recent studies. Thus, the presence in the Visigothic graveyard at SEGÓBRIGA, where the basic form of burial was for the body to be placed on its back in a tomb oriented on a west–east axis, of some interments employing the Islamic practice of placing the body on its side in a north–south oriented grave, implies that either the Muslims took over a Christian cemetery or that the two communities shared it. The same phenomenon has been reported in graveyards found at ALCALÁ DE HENARES, Casa Herrera, Simancas, and elsewhere. Similarly, there are some interesting indications of Muslims, again probably in the 8th cent., taking over Christian churches for their own use. This is indicated by small but significant modifications, such as the creation of a small niche in a south wall to serve as a *mihrab*. The small Visigothic churches of Casa Herrera and El Gatillo (in the province of Cáceres) are examples of this. In a similar case the Late Roman mausoleum of LAS VEGAS DE PUEBLA NUEVA (province of Toledo) was found to have such a later niche, only about 1.5 m. wide, inserted in its southern wall.[20] This gives greater credence to the story in some of the Arab historians that ʿAbd al-Rahmān I took over half the church of St Vincent in Córdoba, to serve as a place of worship for the Muslims. This arrangement ended when the ruler took over the whole church and destroyed it to use the site for the first phase of the famous Mezquita (see CÓRDOBA). A similar but even more short-term transitional arrangement was the creation of a gold coinage, to replace that of the Visigothic monarchy, that employed both Arabic and somewhat garbled Latin inscriptions. This rapidly gave way to a predominantly silver coinage on the pattern already used elsewhere throughout the Arab empire.[21]

The conquest itself, commencing in 711, is reminiscent in many ways of that of the Anglo-Saxon kingdom by the Normans in 1066. In the traditional, but relatively late, Arab accounts the issue was settled by a single battle between the Visigothic King Roderic (710–11) and the Arab and Berber forces commanded by Tariq, a Berber freed slave of Mūsā ibn Nusayr, Arab governor of *Ifrīqiya*, North Africa. The reality, as recorded in the near contemporary Spanish Christian text called the *Chronicle of 754*, may have been rather messier, with a civil war over the succession to the throne having broken out amongst the Visigoths in 710, and several rather than one battle being needed to settle the issue. However, as in 1066, the defeat and death of the king and the rapid fall to the invader of the capital, the city of Toledo in this case, led to a paralysis in the administration of a relatively complex governmental system and the inability to produce a new leader to co-ordinate resistance. The relative speed with which most of southern and central Spain fell to the Arab armies (mostly consisting of Berbers recruited in recently conquered North Africa) is testimony more to the sophistication of the Visigothic monarchy than to the decline and decay that historians once thought were its hallmarks. The Arab conquerors' willingness to make treaties with towns and regional rulers, the Visigothic counts, guaranteeing freedom of local self-government and of religion in return for regular tribute and non-resistance is another feature that explains the speed and rapid success of the conquest. Over the following decade, this was followed by the imposition of new administration. The conquest itself was extended north into the Ebro valley in 714 and across the Pyrenees in 721, eliminating a vestigial Visigothic kingdom in south-west France.

Frankish and Aquitanian resistance is associated with the battle of Poitiers in 732 or 733 in which the Frankish Mayor of the Palace, Charles Martel (d. 741), defeated an invading Arab and Berber army. Resistance was assisted by the outbreak of civil war between the Arab and Berber invaders in the 740s which put an end to further expansion. The conflicts paralleled and were influenced by those taking place in North Africa and were a consequence of the political upheavals in the Near East at this time. These ultimately involved the overthrow in 750 of the ruling dynasty of the Arab Empire, the Umayyads. One member of this family called ʿAbd al-Raḥmān managed to escape the purge initiated by the new rulers, the ʿAbbāsids, and, after a period in hiding in North Africa, he crossed to Spain in 756. He was proclaimed ruler by the former supporters of his house and by those opposed to Yūsuf ibn ʿAbd al-Raḥmān al-Fikrī, who had been *de facto* independent ruler of Al-Andalus, as the Arabs called their territory in Spain, since 747.

Military victory over Yūsuf established the Umayyad Amirate or kingdom in Al-Andalus, which lasted until 1031 (though with an enhancement in status in 929 when ʿAbd al-Raḥmān III took the title of Caliph, which gave him religious as well as secular authority). The history of this period is complex, in that even within the boundaries of Al-Andalus the power of the Umayyads fluctuated continually for much of their rule. It took ʿAbd al-Raḥmān I (756–88) until 780 to impose his authority on the Ebro valley, and he had had to bring Toledo and much of the centre of the peninsula into subjection before doing so. He faced local rebels and also attempts by the ʿAbbāsid caliphs, ruling in Baghdad, to overthrow his regime. His son Hishām I (788–96) and grandson Al-Ḥakam I (796–822) faced civil wars on their accessions against rival members of the dynasty and periodic local revolts, even in CÓRDOBA, their capital. In the later years of Al-Ḥakam and under his son ʿAbd al-Raḥmān II (822–52) the authority of the rulers was more firmly established. The period was also marked by the growing import of ideas and aspects of the material culture from the now flourishing ʿAbbāsid Near East. Under both ʿAbd al-Raḥmañ II and his son Muḥammad I (852–66) extensive programmes of fortification were undertaken both on the frontiers and in some of the more volatile settlements in the south. These can still be seen from extant town walls and fortresses such as those of MADRID, MÉRIDA, BUITRAGO and TALAMANCA. In the later 9th cent. problems of local order became far worse, and in the reign of ʿAbd Allah (888–912) the authority of the Amir (king) at times extended no further than the confines of the valley of the Guadalquivir. His grandson and successor ʿAbd al-Raḥmān III (912–61) reimposed Umayyad rule across the whole extent of Al-Andalus and began to expand his interests into North Africa as well. His reign and that of his son Al-Ḥakam II (961–76) marked the apogee of Umayyad Al-Andalus, both militarily and culturally. The power of the state was in many ways enhanced during the ascendancy of Al-Manṣūr (d. 1002), who in the post of *Hajīb* or Grand Vizier effectively ran the government in the name of the ineffective Hishām II (976–1009), but conflicts between his sons and other political and racial tensions led to an intense period of civil wars and usurpations that culminated in the collapse of Umayyad rule and the abolition of their caliphate in 1031.

The period of Umayyad rule in southern and central Spain has benefited more than any other from a virtual revolution in archaeology in the peninsula. Not long ago, there was quantitatively and qualitatively hardly any Spanish Islamic archaeology, beyond what a few enthusiasts, often architects by training, could undertake. The leader in the field was Leopoldo Torres Balbás (d. 1960), who contributed regular reports to *Al-Andalus*, the main, indeed sole, scholarly journal to concern itself at all with the subject.[22] Over the last ten to fifteen years a very wide range of excavations of Islamic sites of all periods has been carried out, and the study of the institutional and social organization of the Hispano-Arab states has benefited enormously from the wider deductions that have been drawn from this flurry of archaeological activity.[23] Responsibility has been shared largely between Spanish and French scholars, the latter primarily associated with the Casa de Velázquez (the French academic institute) in Madrid, and the range of journals or series of publications in which reports on this work, full or provisional, may be found has expanded rapidly. Indeed, it is not easy to keep track of all that is going on, as much publication is highly localized, reflecting the financial backing provided by the relatively new autonomous and other regional governments for the study of the particular past of their own area. Conversely, the broader patterns that emerge from the excavations can be limited geographically according to whether or not provincial government is willing to put money into archaeological research. Thus, some provinces appear to be full of Islamic sites, while neighbouring ones seem to be totally deficient in them. In some cases, too, money seems more readily available for reconstruction, maximizing tourist appeal of relatively well-known and accessible sites, than for the excavation of new ones.

It cannot be said, however, that any form of consensus exists as to the wider deductions to be drawn from this explosion in Islamic archaeology, much of which has concentrated on the Levant. The interpretation of individual sites can be debatable enough, whatever the period, but the drawing of generalized conclusions on the basis of a range of sites is bound to be even more controversial. Particular attention has been given to the fortresses, of varying scale and function, that are attributed to this period, following on the rise in scholarly interest in the phenomenon of

Early Medieval 'incastellamento' (castle-building) in Italy.[24] Studies of particular areas, such as the Alpujarras in the Province of Granada and much of the Levant, have revealed what appears to be a regular pattern of fortifications (*ḥuṣūn*). It is possible, though far from proven, that such an even distribution of a hierarchy of fortresses, towers of refuge, and watch towers (*ḥiṣn/burj/atalaya*) extended over most of Al-Andalus in the Umayyad period, matching the probable growth of a regular pattern of administrative units known as *quras*. If this were to be the case, it would be a mark of the considerable sophistication of the state, unmatched since the fall of Rome, in planning, undertaking, and financing such a widespread campaign of public works. Uncertainty remains about the dating of some of the key fortresses, but this is a fast growing area of research.

In general, however, it has to be said that the study of medieval castles across the whole of Spain is distinctly in its infancy. There has not been the equivalent of central government interest in bringing such buildings into public control and maintenance that has been marked in Britain for many decades. In consequence, some Spanish castles are almost entirely neglected and in danger of further decline (as well as being hazardous to visitors), while others have been appallingly restored in the interests of making them appealing, without proper study and in a way that is destructive of their archaeological record. However, a number of important fortresses of the Umayyad period have survived, and can be viewed. Amongst the most significant are BALAGUER, BAÑOS DE LA ENCINA, EL VACAR, and GORMAZ. Close to Córdoba, in the heart of the small town of Bujalance is a fortress built by ʿAbd al-Raḥmān III in 935.[25] For a good example of a local tower of refuge see BUJARRABAL and some of those in the vicinity of BALAGUER. *Atalayas* of a later period are frequent in the regions around Granada, but for some Umayyad ones close to Madrid see TALAMANCA.

The Umayyad period has left two very important urban sites of 10th and early 11th-cent. date. One, known as LOS VASCOS, is difficult of access, but is a unique survival of a small fortified town, probably inhabited by Berbers of the Nafza tribe, and mainly concerned with metal-working. It was almost certainly abandoned in the immediate aftermath of the Castilian conquest of TOLEDO in 1085. Only a small part of the site has so far been excavated, but it already has provided interesting information on housing and town planning in the late Umayyad period. At the other end of the social scale is MEDINA AZAHARA the palace city built close to Córdoba for ʿAbd al-Raḥmān III (912–61), which was destroyed in a civil war in 1010. Here evidence of the opulence and sophistication of the late Umayyad court has emerged from continuing study and reconstruction of the destroyed buildings of the palace and administrative areas of the city. Another site that is only just beginning to be developed, but which may have important evidence of the late Umayyad and Taifa periods of occupation, is CALATRAVA LA VIEJA.

According to the Arab geographer Ibn Ḥawqal, who visited Al-Andalus in 948, the majority of the rural population were then still Christian. Literary sources also record the presence of Christian villages and monasteries in the Sierra Morena north of Córdoba, and in the Montes de Málaga. Some of these may well have been involved in the long-standing revolt of ʿUmar ibn Hafṣūn (d. 918), whom Arab histories claim converted to Christianity in the course of it. His principal fortress and the site of a church he is reported to have built may be located at the site now called BOBASTRO. There are grounds for doubts as to the certainty of this identification, but if this site is not that of the historical Bobastro, it is certainly that of a Christian settlement of Umayyad date. Another such settlement, that had a subsequent Islamic phase, has been extensively excavated and studied at Marmuyas in the Montes de Málaga.[26] As well as by previous migration northwards into the kingdom of León (see below), the survival of Christian communities in the south was dealt a fatal blow in 1126 when the Almoravids began a wholesale deportation of such populations to North Africa, following their collaboration with Aragonese raids into Al-Andalus earlier in the decade. One effect of this is the higher level of discontinuity of occupation in rural settlements in the south as opposed to other parts of the peninsula.

The Asturian and Leonese Monarchies (718–1037)

Following the Arab invasion and the collapse of the Visigothic kingdom, a small Christian realm emerged in the Asturias, in the northern mountains of the peninsula. Traditionally, this resulted from the victory of a Visigothic noble called Pelayo over an Arab army at the battle of Covadonga in 718. This developed a substantial legendary patina in later centuries. Pelayo (718?–37) was eventually succeeded by his son-in-law Alfonso I (739–57), who was the founder of a dynasty that lasted until 1037. From small beginnings the kingdom grew, at first laterally into Galicia in the west and into the Basque territories in the east. Under Alfonso II the Chaste (791–842) a permanent capital was established at OVIEDO. Under his successor Ramiro I (842–50) a palace complex was developed on the nearby hillside of MONTE NARANCO. Together, these two contain the best collection of buildings belonging to the period of the Asturian kingdom. Other Asturian churches, mainly datable to the reign of Alfonso III the Great (866–910), are located within easy distance of Oviedo, and include Santa Cristina de Lena, which has interesting decorative parallels with one of the churches on MONTE NARANCO, San Pedro de Nora (by 905), Santa María de Bendones, and San Salvador de Valdedíos (consecrated 893).[27]

Military expansion southwards across the mountains and onto the high plain of the Meseta developed under Ordoño I (850–66) and his son Alfonso III, assisted by a period of political weakness and fragmentation in the Umayyad Amirate in the south. In consequence, following Alfonso III's deposition by his sons, the royal residence was moved south, first to Zamora and then, under Ordoño II (913/14–24), to LEÓN. His son Ramiro II (931–51) established Leonese control over the Duero valley and most of the Meseta, defeating the Umayyad Caliph ʿAbd al-Raḥmān III (912–61) at the battle of Simancas in 939. A period of intermittent civil war and regional unrest under Ramiro II's successors, up to the time of his grandson Vermudo II the Gouty (982–99), did not, however, lead to a restoration of direct Umayyad rule north of the Sierra de Guadarrama. Even the series of devastating raids led by the dictator Al-Manṣūr (d. 1002), which include the sack of the Galician sanctuary and supposed burial place of the Apostle James at SANTIAGO DE COMPOSTELA in 992, did not lead to a reduction in the extent of the Leonese kingdom.

However, during this period the local aristocracies of the frontier districts of Galicia (in the north of modern Portugal) and of Castile (centred on Burgos) became increasingly independent. The counts of Castile of the dynasty of Fernán González (d. 970) developed family ties with the ruling house of the neighbouring kingdom of Pamplona of Navarre. Under the Navarrese king Sancho III the Great (1004–35) Castile was thus absorbed into his kingdom, and in 1032 he overran much of León. Although the last Leonese king of the founding dynasty, Vermudo III (1027–37), retained the Asturias and was able to recover León on Sancho's death, he faced a challenge from one of the latter's sons, Fernando, who had inherited the County of Castile in 1035. In the decisive battle of Tamarón Vermudo was defeated and killed by Fernando (who was also his brother-in-law and who as Fernando I (1037–65) established a new ruling dynasty over the joint kingdom of León and Castile).

The short chronicles written in the Asturian kingdom in the late 9th cent. (two versions of the *Chronicle of Alfonso III* and the *Chronicle of Albelda*) claim that under Alfonso I and his son Fruela I the Cruel (757–68) much of the Meseta had been overrun by the kings and deliberately depopulated; in effect creating a *cordon sanitaire* between the Asturian kingdom and the Umayyad state of Al-Andalus. This process then had to be reversed in the period of the Leonese monarchy, to repopulate the recently reconquered areas. While this remains the orthodox view, doubts have been expressed about the extent of the 8th cent. depopulation. Recent excavations in Avila, for example, indicate continuity of settlement there right across this period, and there are features to be seen in SEGOVIA that support such a view. It is clear from documentary records, however, that there was a significant migration from the Basque regions into Castile in the 9th/10th cents.[28] Another migratory component that contributed to the repopulating of the Duero valley in the Leonese period came from the south, in the form of the so-called Mozarabs. Although this term was originally used by Arab authors to refer to indigenous converts to Islam who had become culturally Arabized, it is now normally employed of southerners who, while adopting many features of Arab material culture, retained their adherence to Christianity. The growth of religious conflict in and around Córdoba from the mid-9th cent. onwards and the major regional conflicts of the reigns of Muḥammad I (852–86), al-Mundhir (886–8), and ʿAbd Allah (888–912) let to a migration north-wards of members of this community. Particularly well represented in the northern documents are groups of monks who fled from the south and established new communities, often with royal or comital backing, in the frontier zones of the Meseta. The exact extent of this phenomenon is hard to evaluate, in that it is not clear how many members of the laity may have accompanied the monks. Recent research has shown that the use of Arab or Islamicized names in some peasant communities in the north is not a reliable indicator of their origin in the south.

What is clear is that very distinctive styles of art and architecture developed in and around León in the 10th cent., markedly different from those found north of the mountains in the Asturias. Tenth century monas-tic churches, such as SAN MIGUEL DE ESCALADA (consecrated 913), San Cebrián de Mazote (near Tordesillas, Valladolid: c.915), Santo Tomás de Ollas (in the town of Ponferrada in the Bierzo: c.931), and Santiago de Peñalba (near Ponferrada: c.937)—all worth visiting—contain elements in their plan, such as the use of scallop-shaped apses and transepts, and in their decoration, notably in their aniconic capitals and horseshoe arches, that are immediately reminiscent of Umayyad architecture.[29] Similar features in miniature can be seen in manuscripts associated with such monasteries, which also have very distinctive ways of treating perspective and the depiction of natural forms. Particularly notable in this respect are a series of manuscripts of the *Commentary on the Apocalypse* of the Asturian monk Beatus (c.786) containing numerous illustrations and diagrams in this Mozarabic style. Good examples of these are on perma-nent display in the cathedrals of El Burgo de Osma (dated 1086), Gerona (dated 975 and painted by, amongst others, a woman called Ende), and Seu d'Urgell (c.970), the library of the monastery of El Escorial (c.950/5), and in the British Museum (dated 1109). Amongst others that may not always be on show are those in the Biblioteca Nacional in Madrid, the Pierpoint Morgan Library in New York, and the library of the University of Valladolid.[30]

Some of these monasteries were founded on sites previously occupied by churches of probable Visigothic date, as can be deduced either from references in foundation charters or inscriptions (e.g. San Pedro de Montes in the Bierzo, consecrated in 919 on the site of a monastery founded by the Visigothic bishop Fructuosus in the mid-7th cent.) or from the reuse of earlier elements such as columns and capitals in their construction (e.g. in San Cebrián de Mazote). Some of the monasteries founded in the kingdom of León in this time subsequently languished; much to our good fortune, as this meant that they were not rebuilt at later periods in more modern styles. Others, such as Eslonza (see SAN MIGUEL DE ESCALADA) were taken in hand by the international monastic orders that were encouraged to establish themselves in the kingdom from the time of Alfonso VI (1072–1109) onwards, and were entirely reconstructed in the current fashions of western European architecture, leaving few if any traces of their original buildings. An unusual exception here is the Galician monastery of Celanova (see SANTA COMBA DE BANDE), which has retained a perfect 10th-cent. chapel in its interior. The Mozarabic style, which some have argued was not so much an alien import from the south as a development of the Leonese region itself, was patronized by the monarchy itself. This may be seen from the slight remains of the royal monastery of San Salvador del Palat de Rey in LEÓN, built by Ramiro II, which also served as his burial place and that of his sons Ordoño III (951–6) and Sancho I the Fat (956–8, 959–66).

The Kingdom of Pamplona, and the Catalan Counties (801–1147)

A significant role in the history of the Pyrenean regions in this period was played by the Frankish Carolingian Empire. The Franks had had ambitions of expanding their power into the Ebro valley ever since the 6th cent., and may have controlled some of the upper end of the valley and the city of Pamplona in the early 7th. In the confused conditions of the late 8th cent., while the first Umayyad ruler was trying to consolidate his authority in the peninsula, local Arab leaders appealed to the Frankish ruler Charlemagne (768–814) for aid. His expedition to the Ebro in 778, culminating in a failed siege of ZARAGOZA, was a disaster, and his rearguard was massacred by the Basques on the ensuing retreat. However, in 801 his son Louis (then king of Aquitaine, and later emperor, 814–40) was able to capture BARCELONA, and establish a Frankish county centred on it. This survived an Umayyad onslaught in 827, and gradually a more complex administrative pattern developed as the area between the Pyrenees and the Río Llobregat was resettled, not least by refugees from the south and the descendants of those driven across the Pyrenees in the 8th cent. Further counties were established to supplement those of Gerona (captured by the Franks in 785) and Barcelona. The rank of *Marchio* or March Warden (hence Marquis) was held by the principal royal officer on the frontier, which itself was called the *Marca Hispanica*, or Spanish March. (It did not come to be called Cataluña until the 11th cent.) In 878 nearly all these counties, together with the title of *Marchio*, were granted to Wifred I the Hairy (d. 897/8), a member of an important local family.

His descendants, while remaining subject to the Carolingian and then the Capetian kings of France, continued to hold all the secular and most of the principal ecclesiastical offices south of the Pyrenees. The marriage of Ramón Berenguer IV, Count of Barcelona, to Petronilla (1137–62) daughter of Ramiro II of Aragón (1134–7) led to their son Alfonso II (1162–96) obtaining the Aragonese crown and uniting the Catalan counties to it.

While the political development of the eastern end of the Pyrenees grew from Frankish involvement and subsequent loyalty to the French crown, the western end presents a contrary picture. Having destroyed the walls of Pamplona on the retreat from his failed Ebro campaign in 778, Charlemagne left it vulnerable to recapture by the Umayyads. However, a successful local revolt in 799 led to its return to Frankish rule in 806. At least one other royal expedition was necessary to maintain its loyalty before a Frankish army was defeated by the Basques in the Second Battle of Roncesvalles in 824. It was in consequence of this that an independent Basque kingdom came into existence in Pamplona under the rule of Iñigo Arista. A second dynasty came to power, following the abdication or deposition of King Fortún the Monk in 905, under whose rule the kingdom had expanded southwards into the Rioja, with Nájera established as a second capital. These monarchs had marriage ties with the powerful Banu Qāsī, a family of indigenous origin but converted to Islam, who ruled much of the Ebro valley, occasionally independently or otherwise as viceroys for the Umayyads. The apogee of the kingdom came with the reign of Sancho III the Great (1004–35), son of García III the Tremulous (995–1004), whose power briefly extended over much of the kingdom of León and also over the Duchy of Gascony, north of the Pyrenees. On his death the realm was divided between his sons, leading to the emergence of separate kingdoms of Navarre and Aragón, as well as an independent Leonese–Castilian monarchy. The attempt of Navarre to retain a predominant position came to an end with the battle of Atapuerca (see GRAN DOLINA) in 1054, in which García Sánchez III (1035–54) of Navarre was defeated and killed by his brother, Fernando I of León-Castile. The subsequent success of the León-Castile monarchy and of that of Aragón in extending their territories southwards cut off Navarre from the expanding frontier against Islam and left it isolated, until eventually absorbed by Castile in 1514 (apart from Basse-Navarre north of the Pyrenees, which was united with the French kingdom in 1589).

Although Basque archaeology may be said hardly to have existed, not least for political reasons, before 1975, there has been quite a lot of attention given to Roman sites in the Basque areas and Navarre. Pamplona, the Roman Pompaelo, has benefited from various excavations, and there is an important villa site nearby at LUMBIER. Recent excavations have also revealed the existence of a Roman port, in use until at least the 4th cent., at IRUN, on the modern coastal frontier with France. In the Basque province of Alava there is also a Roman town site, with evidence of late imperial occupation at Iruña. Finds are on display in the archaeological museums in Pamplona and Vitoria. On the fringes of the Basque regions, in southern Alava on the edge of the Ebro valley, have been located a series of caves, several of which have been carved into the rough form of churches, with chancel screens, niches, and subsidiary chambers cut out of the rock. In some of these graffiti have been found, consisting of religious inscriptions as well as crosses and a small variety of figures. The alphabet used can be equated with that employed in documents of the Visigothic period, and it is to that time that the construction of at least the cave churches should be dated.[31] Some of the caves could well have been occupied at much earlier periods, and it is possible that the churches and dwelling caves continued in use for quite some time after the end of the Visigothic kingdom. Moving chronologically and geographically, recent excavations have uncovered something of a group of depopulated medieval villages, including their churches, in the valley of the lower Urraul (Urraul Bajo), an area about 20 km. south-east of Pamplona.[32] Occupation of these sites has been shown in some cases to be as early as the 9th cent., and they mainly continued in use until at least the 14th. These villages, apart from sections in some of them that serve as modern settlements, were abandoned and have left only traces of their foundations. An early village church, though, has been largely preserved at AISTRA, and gives some indication of what these others would once have been like.

The South: From the Taifas to the Castilian Conquests (1031–1248/1492)

The disintegration of the Umayyad caliphate led to the emergence of a series of regional kingdoms, varying in size and power and in the ethnic origins of their ruling dynasties. Some of these, such as the Zirid monarchs of GRANADA, were Berbers; others, such as the ʿAbbādids of SEVILLE, were Arabs, and yet others, like the Mujāhadids of Denia, were Ṣaqāliba, which is to say the descendants of slaves, often of Slav ancestry, who had been sold to the Arabs of Al-Andalus by the Vikings and others. The ensuing period is known as that of the Mulūk at-Ṭawāʾif or 'Party' (in the sense of faction rather than entertainment) Kings. Their realms are normally called the Taifa kingdoms. In its way this was a vigorous period of urban growth and intellectual advance, with the provincial towns, which had been starved of government resources by the Umayyads in favour of Córdoba, enjoying something of a cultural and economic renaissance. Amongst the most powerful and sophisticated of these kings were the rulers of SEVILLE and ZARAGOZA, some of whom were themselves noted poets. Intellectually, it was a more adventurous period too, with considerable literary productions and scientific writings to its credit.

However, the political fragmentation and the fluid frontiers of the newly created realms led to frequent conflict, with the larger Taifas gradually absorbing the weaker ones. However, these internecine struggles and the generally disunited state of Al-Andalus in this period gave the Christian rulers of León-Castile and Aragón the opportunity to extort annual payments or *parias* from the Taifas as the price of peace. A number of devastating raids and well-applied Christian support for one side in a conflict made it clear how necessary such payments were, even though their economic effects can only have become increasingly deleterious to the Islamic kingdoms.

A breach of the *status quo* came, however, in 1085, when Alfonso VI of León-Castile (1072–1109) captured the enfeebled Taifa and city of TOLEDO. As the former Visigothic capital, Toledo was a valued ideological prize for a monarchy that in many ways depicted itself as the heir to the Visigoths. The rulers of the other Taifas in the south (one of whom was the author of an extant autobiography that is the best source for this period[33]) responded by appealing to Yūsuf ibn Tāshufīn (1061–1106), founder of Marrakesh and ruler of most of the western half of North Africa.

He was the leader of a fundamentalist confederacy of Berber tribes, whose members called themselves the *al-Murabitūn*, or 'dwellers in the fortress-monasteries' (i.e. *ribats*: see GUARDAMAR); probably better known by their Hispanized name of the Almoravids.[34] Crossing the Straits of Gibraltar, he defeated the recently victorious Alfonso VI at the battle of Zallaqa or Sagrajas, near BÁDAJOZ. A second Almoravid intervention in Al-Andalus, commencing in 1089, was, however, directed at eliminating the Taifa rulers and bringing their kingdoms under Yūsuf's rule and also imposing his strict religious revival. The southern Taifas were eliminated by 1091. Valencia, which had previously been captured by the ruthless Castilian adventurer and mercenary Rodrigo Díaz de Vivar (d. 1099), known as El Cid, fell in 1101 and ZARAGOZA was taken by Yūsuf's son Alī b. Yūsuf (1106–42) in 1109.[35] This marked the limits of Almoravid expansion, and Zaragoza fell decisively to Alfonso I the Battler of Aragón (1104–34) in 1118. Little material trace of Almoravid rule can be found in Spain, though constructions such as the 12th-cent. walls of SEVILLE may be of Almoravid date or of Almohad date, and in all probability could contain work of both periods, so close in time and so brief were they. A unique fortified rural villa at MONTEAGUDO that has been attributed to the Almoravids belongs more exactly to the rule of a local dynasty that established its power over parts of the south-east during the time in which Almoravid authority in Al-Andalus was disintegrating.

This disintegration was primarily the result of events in North Africa, where the Almoravid rulers, once known for their fundamentalist rigour, were being accused of heresy by members of a new movement of Islamic revival, known as the *al-Muwahhidūn* or 'those who affirm the unity of

God'.[36] Almoravid power collapsed rapidly, and the fourth ruler of the dynasty, Ishāq b. Ibrahim (1146–7), was killed. The Almohads first entered Spain in 1145, and began to eliminate the local kingdoms that had sprung up in the wake of Almoravid decline. Under Abu-Yūsuf Ya'qūb al-Manṣūr (1184–99) SEVILLE became the capital of the whole Almohad Empire, and a major programme of building and fortress construction began. A victory over the Castilians and their allies at the battle of Alarcos in 1195 seemed to presage a major revival of an Islamic Al-Andalus, but the military verdict was reversed at the battle of Las Navas de Tolosa (see BAÑOS DE LA ENCINA) in 1212, when Muḥammad an-Naṣir (1199–1214) was defeated by a confederacy of the Castilians and the Aragonese, aided by contingents of knights from southern France. This led to a rapid collapse of Almohad power in Spain. Risings in their African dominions led the Almohad rulers to abandon Spain at the end of the 1220s, and even to renounce their distinctive religious teachings. A member of the dynasty, al-Bayyasī, set himself up as independent ruler in Córdoba and Seville in 1224. His brother, who governed Valencia, did likewise, and a local ruler called ibn Hud (d. 1238) established himself in MURCIA in 1228. Aided by this disintegration, the ensuing Christian advance, led by Fernando III (1217–52), who in 1230 had re-united the kingdoms of León and Castile (divided in 1157), was rapid. CÓRDOBA fell in 1236 and SEVILLE in 1248.

Brief as was the Almohad presence in Spain, it has left a surprisingly impressive legacy. Of the great mosque in SEVILLE, the minaret survives almost intact as the cathedral bell tower. It is one of the finest examples of the North African style of Islamic religious buildings, and stands comparison with only a handful of other constructions of this period, such as the minaret of the Kutubiya mosque in Marrakesh. A variety of smaller mosques or parts of them have survived in the structure of later churches that were built to replace them after the Christian conquest. Here again, SEVILLE is well endowed with examples. There are also a number of small bath houses (see item 3 in GRANADA) and other minor constructions of this period scattered over southern Spain. The programme of fortress building undertaken by the Almohads, including the formidable example at ALCALÁ DE GUADAIRA, has perhaps not yet received the scholarly attention that it deserves. This is due in part to a wider neglect in Spain of the study of castles, of which there are many. In some cases they remain physically neglected and are deteriorating in consequence, but in others they have been over-restored. The latter process normally involves rebuilding them to what is taken to be their original height, and often making the addition of Violet le Duc-like extravagances, in the form of pointed roofs, twee turrets, and elaborate ornamental machicolations that could never have provided any defence at all on a battlement—but which look pretty and painlessly pseudo-medieval. The trouble with all this is that, first it may have been done without any regard to the slender evidence relating to the actual nature of the castle's defences and internal buildings, and secondly it invariably damages the archaeological record, preventing the subsequent study of variations in the stonework and other features that might provide clues to the actual, and inevitably complex, construction history of the fortress. These strictures by no means apply exclusively or primarily to the castles of the Almohad period. They relate to all medieval fortresses in Spain that are in danger from the blight of reconstruction or have already been damaged by it before serious study has been undertaken. The reader is requested to sneer disparagingly at all such monstrosities, and to make every effort to visit unreconstructed castles before they too fall victim to this hideous fate.

While the Castilians made headway in the south in the first half of the 13th cent., the Aragonese were advancing down the Mediterranean coast. In 1238 after a two-year siege, Valencia fell to Jaume I of Aragón (1213–76), who had previously conquered the Balearic islands (1230–1). A subsequent Castilian expansion eastwards to the area around MURCIA in the 1240s (first by treaty with the local ruler and then by conquest in the 1260s) cut the Aragonese off from further advance in this direction, but by this time their rulers' attention was being directed overseas, not least towards Sicily.[37] It might have been expected that the kingdom of GRANADA, set up by Muḥammad al-Ghalīb (1230–72), founder of the Nazirid dynasty, would soon fall to the rapid Castilian advance, but from the 1250s onwards it received substantial military aid from the Banu Marinid sultans, who ruled from Fez and had replaced the Almohads as masters of the area of modern Morocco. This was only terminated in 1340 by the crushing victory of Alfonso XI of Castile (1312–50) and Afonso IV of Portugal (1325–57) over the Marinid sultan Abu-l-Hāsan ʿAlī (1331–48) at the battle of the Río Salado. However, the civil war between the sons of Alfonso XI and the political weakness of the ensuing Trastámara dynasty saved Granada from serious threat for several decades. Not until the 15th cent., and then intermittently, did a significant Castilian advance into the Nazirid realm resume. ANTEQUERA fell in 1410, but the process of conquest was slow, and only gained real impetus with the unification of Castile and Aragón under Isabel (1474–1504) and Fernando (1479–1516). MÁLAGA, an occasional alternative capital for the increasingly divided Nazirid dynasty, fell in 1487, and Granada surrendered to Fernando and Isabel on 2 January 1492.[38]

While relatively few sites of this period have been investigated in detail, some of the frontier fortresses have received attention (e.g. GAUCÍN and TEBA), and the finest buildings of the period, in the form of the Nazirid palaces of the Alhambra in GRANADA, stand more or less in their original form.[39] The palace at MÁLAGA, although heavily restored and with little of its original beauty, gives something of the feel of the Nazirid period, as well as containing sections from earlier periods. The Nazirid lustre-ware pottery, with its distinctive gold/brown colouring and some pieces of exceptional size, is well worthy of attention. Some of the best examples can be seen in the Museo Nacional de Arte Hispano-Musulman in the Alhambra, and there is a smaller selection in the Museo Arqueológico Nacional in MADRID. Some fine weapons and armour of Nazirid manufacture have also survived, and various pieces, including items said to have belonged to the last Nazirid king, Muḥammad XI (1482–3 and 1487–92), and captured from him at the battle of Lucena in 1483, are displayed in the Real Armería in the Palacio del Oriente and in the Museo del Ejército (Calle Méndez Núñez, 1) in Madrid.

[1] For the dinosaur eggs see the reports in *Nature*, **376** (1995), 781, and in *Current Archaeology*, **146** (1996), 66.

[2] For surveys of some of the current arguments over human evolution see R. Leakey and R. Lewin, *Origins Reconsidered* (London, 1992), and for the history of the subject J. Reader, *Missing Links: The Hunt for Earliest Man* (2nd edn.; London, 1988).

[3] *Evolución humana en Europa y los yacimientos de la Sierra de Atapuerca* (2 vols.; Valladolid, 1995).

[4] Although the site offers little in itself, the finds from various campaigns of excavation may be seen in the Museo Paleontológico at Ambrona (On the N II from Madrid to Barcelona turn left (north) to Torralba, just after the 146 km. marker. 5 km. on pass through the village of Torralba and continue for another 3 km. to the museum.)

[5] B. Sykes *et al.*, 'Paleolithic and Neolithic Lineages in the European Mitochondrial Gene Pool', *American Journal of Human Genetics*, **59** (1996), 185–203.

[6] As the great majority of these cave sites are either inaccessible or require the services of a specialized guide, they are not included here.

[7] To preserve these vulnerable paintings, access to the cave is restricted, and permission must be requested at least six months in advance from the Museo y Centro Nacional de Investigación de Altamira, located 2 km. outside Santillana del Mar (Province of Santander, Cantabria), which also contains important collections of finds. The cave and its paintings have been reproduced in the grounds of the Museo Arqueológico Nacional in MADRID (which also has important Stone Age collections in the museum proper).

[8] The entry to this site is 5 km. SE of Montefrío, in the Province of Granada, when approaching on the GR 222 from Illora; it is signposted.

[9] G. Delibes *et al.*, 'El poblado de Almizaraque' in *Actas del Congreso: Homenaje a Luís Siret (1934–1984)* (Seville, 1986), 167–77.

[10] P. Bahn, 'The Neolithic of the French Pyrenees' in C. Scarre (ed.), *Ancient France* (Edinburgh, 1984), 184–223.

[11] Relatively little is to be seen beyond some foundations of defensive walls and houses, as well as some of the tombs. On the N 340 88 km. NE of ALMERÍA, and about 4 km. after passing Vera, turn S on the AL 821. The site is about 1 km. down the road, on a hill to the left, just before crossing the Río Antas into the town of the same name. For the rich finds from the site visit the Museo de Almería (Carretera de Ronda, 13) in Almería.

[12] R. Chapman, *Emerging Complexity: The Later Prehistory of South-East Spain, Iberia and the Western Mediterranean* (Cambridge, 1990).

[13] María Cruz Fernández Castro, *Iberia in Prehistory* (Oxford, 1995), 349–67.

[14] The poet Martial (*c.* AD 40–104), who came from BILBILIS, spoke of himself as 'born from the Celts and the Iberians' (*Epigrammata* x. 65).

[15] J. F. Drinkwater, *The Gallic Empire* (Stuttgart, 1987); not least for the revised chronology for these reigns.

[16] For a good African example and general discussion see T. W. Potter, *Towns in Late Antiquity: Iol Caesarea and its Context* (London, 1995).

[17] Dimas Fernández-Galiano, 'The Villa of Maternus at Carranque', in P. Johnson, R. Ling, and D. J. Smith (eds.), *5th International Colloquium on Ancient Mosaics* (Ann Arbor, 1994), 199–211; Helmut Schlunk, *Die Mosaikkuppel von Centcelles* (2 vols.; Mainz, 1988).

[18] See C. Godoy, *Arqueología y liturgia. Iglesias hispánicas (siglos IV al VIII)* (Barcelona, 1995), 187–339.

[19] L. Abad Casal *et al.*, 'El proyecto de investigación arqueológica Tolmo de Minateda', *Arqueología en Albacete* (Madrid, 1993), 145–76.

[20] T. Hauschild, 'Das Mausoleum von Las Vegas de Pueblanueva', *MM*, **19** (1978), 323, 339; L. Caballero Zoreda, 'Pervivencia de elementos visigodos en la transición al mundo medieval. Plantamiento del tema', *III Congreso*, **i**. 111–34, especially pp. 122–7.

[21] Anna M. Balaguer Prunés, *Las emisiones transicionales árabe-musulmanas de Hispania* (Barcelona, 1976).

[22] Conveniently collected in his *Obra dispersa* (7 vols.; Madrid, 1981–3). He also wrote a monograph on the Islamic towns: *Ciudades Hispano-musulmanas* (2nd edn., Madrid, 1985).

[23] For an enthusiastic survey see T. F. Glick, *From Muslim Fortress to Christian Castle* (Manchester, 1995), 13–37. It may be hoped that this book disproves his too hasty assertion on p. xiii.

[24] Glick, *From Muslim fortress*, 13–37 and 105–13. For the Italian phenomenon see *inter alia* Chris Wickham, *Il problema dell'incastellamento nell'Italia centrale* (Florence, 1985).

[25] Located just south of the N 324, 44 km. east of Córdoba. See also Cañete de la Torre 9 km. further east down the N 324, which has a re-used Umayyad fortress tower in its Plaza Mayor.

[26] Inaccessible and so not included here, but for a recent account of it see S. Fernández López, 'Marmuyas (Montes de Málaga): analisis de una investigación', *I Congreso*, **iii**. 163–80.

[27] M. Nuñez Rodríguez, *San Salvador de Valdedíos* (Oviedo, 1991).

[28] R. Collins, *The Basques* (Oxford, 1986), 163–71.

[29] M. Gómez-Moreno, *Iglesias mozárabes* (2 vols.; Madrid, 1919; reprinted Granada, 1975); or more briefly J.-F. Rollán Ortiz, *Iglesias mozárabes leonesas* (León, 1983).

[30] J. Williams, *The Illustrated Beatus*, **i** and **ii** (London, 1994); three further volumes are projected.

[31] A. Azkarate, *Arqueología cristiana de la Antigüedad Tardía en Alava, Guipúzcoa y Vizcaya* (Vitoria/Gasteiz, 1988), 133–498; and L. A. Monreal Jimeno, *Ermitorios rupestres altomedievales* (Bilbao, 1989).

[32] Carmen Jusué Simonena, *Poblamiento rural de Navarra en la Edad Media* (Pamplona, 1988).

[33] Amin T. Tibi (trans.), *The Tibyan: Memoirs of 'Abd Allah b. Buluggin, Last Zirid Amir of Granada* (Leiden, 1986).

[34] On their origins and the history of the movement and its rulers see Jacinto Bosch Vilá, *Los Almorávides* (Granada, 1990); and Vincent Lagardère, *Les Almoravides* (Paris, 1989).

[35] On El Cid see Richard Fletcher, *The Quest for El Cid* (London, 1989).

[36] The Almohads have not attracted as much recent research as the Almoravids, but see A. Huici Miranda, *Historia política del imperio Almohade* (2 vols.; Tetuan, 1956–7).

[37] T. N. Bisson, *The Medieval Crown of Aragón* (Oxford, 1986), 58–103.

[38] For the history of this period, primarily from the Islamic perspective, see M. A. Ladero Quesada, *Granada: historia de un país islámico (1232–1571)* (2nd edn.; Madrid, 1979); and L. P. Harvey, *Islamic Spain 1250 to 1500* (Chicago and London, 1990).

[39] Not being strictly archaeological sites these palaces have not been treated here, although some excavations in other parts of the Alhambra have been described, as have some sites in other parts of the city of GRANADA. On the palaces see J. D. Dodds (ed.), *Al-Andalus: The Art of Islamic Spain* (New York, 1992), 127–71.

A–Z Guide to Archaeological Sites in Spain

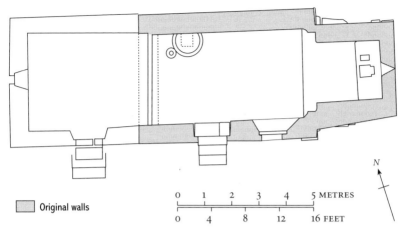

0   1   2   3   4   5 METRES

0   4   8   12   16 FEET

N

▲ Aistra: church of Saints Julian and Basila (after Arbeiter)

Aistra   10th/11th cent. church

*From Salvatierra (between **Vitoria/Gasteiz** and Altsasu) take the A 3016 north-*
wards; after 2 km. turn right onto the A 3018 to San Millán and Zalduendo village
(c.5 km.). Continue on a short distance through Zalduendo to Aistra.

First brought to notice in 1970 as the oldest church in Alava, the church of
Sts Julián and Basila was initially considered to belong to the Visigothic
period. However, subsequent analysis has led to its being re-dated to the
10th–11th cents. In its simple rectangular shape it is similar to a number
of other churches of this period whose ground plans have been recovered
in excavations of deserted villages in Navarre.

Alange   Roman baths

Head south from MÉRIDA on the N 630/E 803 for 12 km. before a small road to the
left leads for another 12 km. to Alange.

Parts of a Roman spa bath house, in the form of three domed rooms with
heated pools, entered by steps, continue in use in the town to the present.
The castle, of Almohad origin, was entrusted to the Order of Santiago
after it was taken in 1230. Alfonso IX (1188–1230) also defeated an
Almohad army near Alange when it was trying to raise his siege of
Mérida, which fell soon after.

Alava   Dolmens

Some of the grave goods recovered from the dolmens mentioned above
may be seen in the Museo Provincial de Alava in Vitoria/Gasteiz. Note also
the Museo de la Sociedad 'Amigos de Laguardia' being established in the
former palace of the Condes de Salazar in the Calle Mayor of Laguardia.

This will replace an earlier museum of the same name, where many of the finds from these tombs were first exhibited.

Dolmens

Neolithic burial mounds, dating from c.2500–1500 BC, dolmens would originally have consisted of a series of large inward-pointing stones, so arranged as to produce a roughly shaped chamber between them. A single large stone was placed on the top to cap the structure, and the whole covered with earth to produce a prominent round or oblong hump in the ground. In the course of time the earth has often been eroded away leaving the stones exposed, but in some cases the mound has remained, and it has been possible to excavate the burial. In the 19th cent. this could be done by smashing through the top with sledge-hammers, with disastrous consequences! In the best examples the cap stone remains balanced on top of three or so of the uprights, but in others the whole or part of the structure has collapsed at an earlier point. Although relatively numerous, it should be assumed that such burials were reserved for a limited number of high-status individuals. Grave goods, in the forms of ceramics and items of personal adornment, would have accompanied the burials.

A selection of the best of these that can be seen easily, grouped in three areas:

Around Laguardia

Alto de la Huesera (Laguardia) *Leaving Laguardia, head 1 km. north on the A 124/N 232, before turning east towards Elvillar, on the A 3228/CV 140. Then take a small road to the left, not more than 1 km. along the road to Elvillar. This leads about 700 m. to the location of the dolmen, on a slope to the right.*

This dolmen was discovered and excavated in 1948. The chamber consists of six stones, with the cap stone having collapsed between them. Flints and a large quantity of human bones were found in this site.

Return to the A 3228 to continue to:

Chabola de la Hechichera (Elvillar) *On the A 3228/CV 140 heading east towards Elvillar from Laguardia, just after passing the sign marking the 68th km. and when Elvillar has come into view, the sign to the dolmen will appear on the left of the road.*

Excavated in 1936, and again in 1974. The cap stone is in place and the chamber is made up of nine large slabs. After the original construction, the mound was reused for burials in at least two later periods. Fragments of a splendid Late Neolithic round-bottomed bowl with stamped decoration belong to the first of these, but there are also pottery and metal finds indicative of Bronze Age and Celtiberian use of the site.

Continue on to:

El Encinal (Elvillar) *From Laguardia take the A 3228/CV 140 east to Elvillar, and continue through the village in the direction of Cripán, before taking the second turning on the right. Stop on the right at the next crossroads along, where a sign will indicate the path to the dolmen.*

Human remains, some stone tools and shards of pottery were recovered here in 1951. The cap stone is missing.

For two other major dolmens in this area and for a Neolithic and Celtiberian village just north of Laguardia, see **La Hoya***.*

To the east of Vitoria/Gasteiz

Sorgiñetxe ('House of the Witches') *On the N1, heading from Vitoria/Gasteiz towards Alsasua/Altsasu, turn off at Salvatierra/Agurain on to the A 2128 heading south towards Opacua. Around 4 km. on, a small road leads right to the village of Arrizala, where the path to the dolmen is signposted.*

This is a particularly fine, and probably early example, made up of six stones, with the cap stone *in situ*. Its earth mound seems to have been lost early on, as no trace has been found of it archaeologically. Human remains and a flint arrow head were found in an excavation in 1890.

Aitzkomendi *On the N1, continue 5 km. east from the bypass around Salvatierra/ Agurain* (late 15th-cent. church) *to Eguilaz, where the dolmen may be seen on the left of the road.*

This is a particularly large and complex example, with a fully capped chamber formed by ten stones. The rectangular chamber is approximately 3×2 m., rising to a height of 3 m. Around it stands most of the original earth tumulus. About one-quarter of this earth mound has been removed, but the rest has been retained, showing the substantial size of the original monument. It continued to be dug into for burial purposes in later periods. Burials of the Late Neolithic and Bronze Age were found in the central chamber, and Iron Age cremation urns were discovered buried in the earth mound.

The Cuartango/Koartango Valley

On the A 68 from Zaragoza to Bilbao, on the section heading north from Miranda de Ebro, turn off onto the A 3314 that runs parallel and to the east of it for much of this section. About 5 km. north of Zuazo de Cuartango/Koartango Zuhatsu is the village of Catadiano/Katadiano. Here the way to a group of four dolmens is signposted.

The two most substantial, known as 'San Sebastián' North and South, were excavated in the 19th cent., as was one of the other pair, 'Gurdipe' South. 'Gurdipe' North, of which little remains, was only discovered in 1955 and excavated in 1962. Neither of the San Sebastián dolmens retains its capping, but they are otherwise good examples. The southern one retains much of its irregularly shaped earth mound.

Alcalá de Guadaira Islamic fortress

20 km. east of SEVILLE on the N334

This is one of the most impressive (and picturesque) fortresses in Andalucia; one moreover that has so far been spared the horrors of a modern restoration. The negative consequences of this benign neglect are that little serious study has been made of the site, and there is hardly any information available on it, least of all in the town itself. The castle is also not properly looked after, and is potentially unsafe in certain areas. Although located next to a popular small plaza, it should be avoided outside the hours of daylight.

Although the full building history of the site is not clear, the differences in building styles give good clues as to the general phases of construction. An origin in the Almohad period seems likely, when the stretches of the main curtain wall built in *tabiya*, together with the towers of identical construction, were probably erected. Restorations and repairs, together with new works, entirely built of ashlar should belong to a second phase of refortification after the Castilian capture of SEVILLE in 1248. This may have taken place as late as the mid-14th cent. when the area was the centre of feuding between the noble families of the Duques de Medina and the Marqueses de Cádiz. Some further repairs were carried out by the French during the Napoleonic period (1808–13), when they garrisoned the castle to protect the vital bridge below it. There are two baileys, with a wall containing three large towers dividing them. The central tower is clearly of later construction than the other two. There is also a lower outer wall around part of the enceinte, and various storage pits and cisterns, as well as traces of vaulting, can be seen within the ruins. Stretches of wall also run eastward from the castle to defend the upper part of the town.

Alcalá de Henares Roman and Islamic town

Located just south of the N II/E 90 from MADRID to ZARAGOZA, 35 km. from the former, it is also easily accessible by frequent local trains from the capital. The Roman archaeological site is located to the west of the town, between the old road to Madrid and the Río Henares. Two other Roman villas and a bath complex have been found east of the town, just south of the old road to Guadalajara. There is another villa site due south of the town on the Camino del Puente, which follows the line of a Roman and later medieval road to the Puente de Zulema. The Islamic site of Alcalá la Vieja is situated south-east of the town, across the Henares, and may be approached by the Camino Virgen del Val from the south-east corner of the Ciudad Universitaria. The chapel of San Isidro, to the north-east of the present town, may mark the site of the medieval Jewish cemetery.

The first site chosen for Roman Complutum was a flat-topped hill south-west of the present town on the far side of the Río Henares, which was occupied from the 1st cent. BC until the end of the 1st cent. AD, when the settlement had been relocated into the valley below, and north of the Henares. The new town seems to have been prosperous, to judge by the houses that have been uncovered, dating from the 3rd to 5th cents. and by the quality of the **mosaics** found in a number of them. The two best depict a tipsy Bacchus being supported by his tutor Silenus and a satyr in an apsed *triclinium* in the villa which has been christened 'the House of Bacchus', and a scene of Leda and the Swan (Jupiter in animal form to whom Leda bore four children) in 'the House of Leda'. No public buildings have yet been located, though some of the channels for the water supply may be seen. Complutum was the seat of a bishopric throughout the Visigothic period; the last known incumbent was Bishop Spassandus, who signed the acts of the Sixteenth Council of Toledo in 693. It did not have a mint. In the mid-7th cent. a monastery was established in or near the town by Bishop Fructuosus of Braga, the best-known monastic founder of the Visigothic period (*Vita Fructuosi*). A Visigothic necropolis has been located to the east of the present town, between it and the two rural Roman villas.

Vita Fructuosi

The most substantial saint's life written in the Visigothic period, this anonymous text gives an account of the career of Fructuosus, metropolitan bishop of Braga (656–c.665), who was also abbot of Dumio and the most active founder of monasteries at the time. Two extant monastic rules are attributed to him, as well as a letter to King Reccesuinth (649–72).

Following the Arab conquest, a new settlement was established on an entirely different site, which came to be called al-Qalat ʿAbd Salam, while the Roman and Visigothic town was abandoned. Around a fortress on a hill overlooking the river, at least two suburbs seem to have developed. No traces of these are visible, but two ruined towers and part of the wall of the fortress may be seen.

The town survived the Castilian conquest of Toledo in 1085, but it and its territory were finally taken by the forces of Archbishop Bernard of Toledo in 1118. Finds of medieval pottery suggest that under the rule of the archbishops the former Arab town initially expanded, but in the 14th cent. yet another new settlement was developed on the site of the present town, eventually replacing Alcalá la Vieja. The (much restored) **medieval walls** on the northern and western sides of the present town were built for Archbishop Tenorio in 1389. The fortified **archiepiscopal palace** (now an archive) was begun in 1209, rebuilt in 1375, and completed under Archbishop Contreras in 1422–34, but it was badly damaged in 1940. Cardinal Cisneros founded a university here in 1508, which, retaining the name 'Complutense', was transferred to Madrid in 1837. Cisneros died in 1517; his tomb is in the chapel of the Colegio Mayor de San Ildefonso (1498; rebuilt 1543–83). Devotees of Don Quixote will be interested to

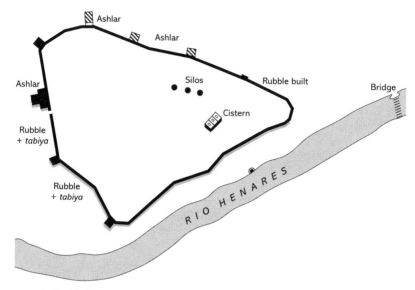

Ashlar

Ashlar

Ashlar

Silos

Rubble built

Bridge

Rubble + tabiya

Cistern

Rubble + tabiya

RIO HENARES

▲ Alcalá de Henares: the Arab fortress (Alcalá la Vieja)

note that the town was the birthplace of Cervantes (1547–1616), and has a small museum devoted to him.

An archaeological museum for the town is being developed in the 16th-cent. Dominican Monasterio de la Madre de Dios (Calle Santiago).

Cardinal Cisneros (d. 1517)

Francisco Jiménez de Cisneros was born at **Torrelaguna** in 1436, and became cardinal archbishop of Toledo in 1495. Responsible for the wholesale destruction of Arab manuscripts in the former kingdom of **Granada** in 1499, he founded the University of **Alcalá de Henares** (where he is buried) in 1508. At the university he also patronized the preparation of the famous six-volume polyglot Complutense Bible (1514–17). He led the expedition that conquered Oran in North Africa in 1509, and served as regent of Castile and Aragón after the death of King Fernando in 1516.

Alcalá la Real Arab fortress and houses

The town lies on the N 432 between GRANADA *and* CÓRDOBA, *52 km. north of Granada.*

Alcalá belonged to the *qura* or administrative district of Elvira (Granada) in the Umayyad period, and became an important cultural centre in its own right in the time of the Almohads. It was known in Arab sources under a variety of names, including Qalat Yaḥṣib and Qalat Bani Saʿīd. The castle, now called the 'Fortaleza de la Mota', is built on a flat-topped hill that dominates the town and the surrounding countryside, and covers an area of *c*.4 ha. This would have been the nucleus of the Arab town, which extended to include some 3 ha. more in a suburb in the vicinity of the church of Santo Domingo. Although recently over-restored, the central part of the **fortress**, in the form of two towers linked by two short stretches of curtain wall, has at least 11th-cent. origins. A horseshoe-arched doorway in the larger of the two towers is clearly of late Umayyad or Taifa date, although much of the rest of the structure belongs to a later rebuilding, probably in the 14th cent. With the fall of Córdoba in 1236, Alcalá became a vital Nazirid frontier fortress facing the Castilian-controlled Guadalquivir valley. It was probably in response to this new role that the defences were strengthened, notably by the addition of new structures protecting the access to the summit of the hill. A *torre albarrana*, or free-standing tower attached to adjacent walls by a fortified bridge extending from its upper level, was built across the road up the hill, creating a powerful gateway. At the foot of the main tower of the fortress on the summit and extending from it eastwards to the edge of the hill, foundations of 11th- to 14th-cent. Arab houses have been uncovered.

Captured by Alfonso XI of Castile in 1341, Alcalá then became the Christian outpost nearest to Granada, and its fortifications were repaired and restored at various points thereafter, until the final conquest of the Nazirid kingdom in 1492. A fine but now ruinous church of Santa María was built in the late 15th cent. south-west of the early fortress. There is also what is thought to be a Roman mausoleum in the north-east sector of the town, and a 16th-cent. abbot's residence.

*It is worth deviating from the N 432 at **Piños Puente** (12 km. north of Granada) to see the 10th-cent. fortified bridge, and to turn off again to the right about 1 km. further north, to go to **Moclín** (15.5 km.), where you can visit the substantial remains of an Arab castle. Returning to the N 432 at Puerto López (4.5 km. west from Moclín), you will pass a good example of one of the many late medieval watch towers that guarded the frontiers of the kingdom of Granada. Alternatively, 2 km. north of Piños Puente the N 432 curves westwards to avoid the hill known as **Cerro de los Infantes***.

Cerro de los Infantes was the site of a battle in 1319 in which two uncles of Alfonso XI of Castile were killed in a failed invasion of the Nazirid kingdom. Excavations in the late 1970s revealed structural evidence of Late Bronze Age and Iberian occupation of the hill, with a pottery sequence extending from the Neolithic to the time of the Roman Empire.

Alcántara (province of Cáceres)   Roman bridge

From CÁCERES head west for 13 km. on the N 521 (towards the Portuguese frontier), and then turn onto the C 523, which leads, after 50 km., to the town of Alcántara. The bridge is just over 1 km. further on.

One of the finest extant examples of Roman bridge-building, this continues to bear traffic across the Tagus (Río Tajo). The name comes from the Arabic *al-Qanṭara* ('the bridge'). Built of granite and constructed without mortar, it consists of six arches, and the total length is 204 m. It was built in AD 105–6 by Caius Iulius Lacer, and dedicated to the emperor on behalf of the local indigenous populations: the Igaeditani, the Lancienses, the Arabrigenses, and the Banienses Paesures. In the centre is a triumphal arch dedicated to the Emperor Trajan (98–117). At the western bridge-head are remains of a small temple also honouring the emperor. There is also an inscription recording the builder's name and that of his associate Curius Laco (*CIL* ii. 2559). One arch had to be restored in 1543, and another, the second from the east side, was destroyed in 1809, and its wooden replacement again in 1836. The whole bridge was restored in 1860.

The town of Alcántara was taken from the Almohads by Fernando II of León (1157–88) in 1166, but lost in 1174. When regained in 1214 by Alfonso IX (1188–1219), it soon became the headquarters of the military **Order of Alcántara** (1218). There is an impressive castle in the town, but this is of late medieval date. The site of the original castle of the Order, now almost entirely destroyed, lies 1 km. away. Tombs of some of the earliest Masters of the Order of Alcántara are preserved in the 13th-cent. church.

A return may be made back down the C 523 for 26 km. and then onto the C 522, which leads for 25 km. (via Garrovillas—worth a look) to the N 630/E 803 (Cáceres to Salamanca via Plasencia). At Alconétar, 14 km. north up this road, is a ruined 2nd-cent. AD Roman bridge. The C 526 from here leads 34 km. to the Roman site of **Coria**, *passing the castle of* **Portezuelo** *at 10 km.*

The **Alconétar bridge** was originally nearly 300 m. long; only about half remains. It is said to have been destroyed by the Almohads in the early 13th cent. to prevent the Castilian advance on Cáceres. A fortress existed at **Portezuelo** in the Umayyad period. Its garrison raised Alfonso III's siege of Coria in 877. Like the castle of Alcántara, Portezuelo was taken by Fernando II in 1166 and given to the Templars. The Almohads retook it in 1174, and when regained in 1212 it was given to the Order of Alcántara (the cause of dispute with the Templars). It is a simple but powerful fortress with a rectangular double enceinte and two semi-circular towers.

Almedinilla (Córdoba) Roman villa

The village of Almedinilla is located on the C 336 10 km. east of Priego de Córdoba and 17 km. west of ALCALÁ LA REAL.

This is a rural villa that was probably the centre of an agricultural estate, but its plan is close to that of Roman town houses. The building has a

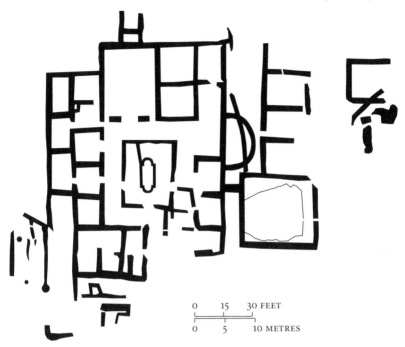

0   15   30 FEET

0   5   10 METRES

▲ Almedinilla: the Roman villa

central rectangular atrium with central oval pool, placed within a peristyle off which open the principal rooms.

Elements of its decoration, not least parts of a bronze statue of Hypnos, give further evidence of the sophisticated tastes of its owners. The villa was probably first built in the second half of the 1st cent. AD, and it seems to have been enhanced and maintained with a high level of care throughout the 2nd cent. This was not kept up in the 3rd cent., although there are no grounds for thinking that it was abandoned at that time. In the late 3rd or the 4th cent. a substantial restoration and rebuilding took place. The building seems to have been abandoned and systematically demolished in the middle or late 5th cent. A Late Roman and Visigothic cemetery associated with the site testifies to continued occupation of the area, though no longer of the villa.

Hypnos

Hypnos was the Greek god of sleep, whose brother was *Thanatos* (Death). He was said to live in a cave on the island of Lemnos, with his sons, the *Oneiroi* (Dreams).

Almería   Arab town

Some pre-Roman ceramics have been found in the town, and there has been considerable argument over whether or not this was the site of a Roman harbour called Portus Magnus. That there was once a fish-salting factory here was established by the discovery of salting vats in a location on the Calle de la Reina. Substantial quantities of late imperial pottery, including imported North African lamps, were found in the *Alcazaba*. Of the ensuing Arab settlement of Al-Mariya or 'the Watchtower', little is known until the town was developed in 955/6 by ʿAbd al-Raḥmān III (912–61) as a naval base, both in response to some isolated Viking raids and as part of his wider military and commercial interests in North Africa and the western Mediterranean. The town expanded further in the 11th cent.; it was for a time the centre of a Taifa kingdom (1013–38 and 1052–91, then it fell to the Almoravids). It was also briefly conquered by the Taifa kingdom of Valencia. It was taken by Alfonso VII in 1147 but he was unable to hold it. It was taken by Fernando II of Aragón in 1488, following an earthquake the previous year, and its Muslim population was expelled in 1490.

The *Alcazaba*

The impressively sited *Alcazaba* has been in part so horrendously restored that it looks as if it were built for a film set. A devastating earthquake in 1522 destroyed much of the original building, as well as most other parts of the city, and it was largely abandoned and neglected thereafter. A re-fortification took place in the 19th cent., which is particularly apparent in some of the battlements and the circular tower in the south-west of the first section of the fortress. The modern restoration began in the 1950s and has extended over several decades.

The *Alcazaba* divides into three sections, approached from the east. The first of these, entered via a steep path from the foot of the hill, is the largest and comprises an area of almost 13,500 sq. m. It lacks major internal structures, and probably served in the Umayyad period as the defended encampment for mobile forces (cf. GORMAZ) and/or a place of refuge for the civilian population. There are a number of towers, including the **Torre de los Espejos** (8 × 8.5 m.), which dominates the entry. At the eastern tip of the fortress stands the much restored (1975–80) *Baluarte del espolón* 'fort of the spur', a polygonal battery of Vaubanesque type, that incorporates some original masonry. In the centre of the court there is a three-aisled cistern. In the north-west corner of this section, adjacent to the wall that divides it from the central portion, is a late Nazirid (15th cent.) tower, with a *mirador* or viewing pavilion on top of it.

The central part of the *Alcazaba* is rectangular (122 × 85 m.; c.10,500 sq. m. in area), and is filled with the ruins of a series of buildings. Most of these belong to a **palace** that in present form largely dates from the first half of the 14th cent. This replaced an earlier one, known from literary sources, built by the Taifa ruler Abu Yaḥyā Mu'izz al-Dawla (1052–91). Some traces of this survive, for example in the form of some ruined arcading of late Umayyad style close to the north wall and lying between the 'public' **bath complex** (reconstructed in 1975) and the palace proper. Another bath house has been identified within the private part of the palace, and also some separate houses—probably for leading members of the court—on the eastern side. Two of these houses, assumed to date from the 11th cent., were reconstructed in the 1970s to give some sense of their original character. Little of any of the other parts of the domestic buildings of the *Alcazaba* survives above ground (though there is no telling where the mania for reconstruction might someday lead), but it is possible to use the plan to get orientation and some sense of how the various buildings that stood here once were related.

Its western end, the highest part of the fortress, is triangular, and many of its principal features, particularly the round towers, derive from a refortification from 1492 to 1534, following the earthquakes of 1487 and 1490. There is a double-aisled cistern under the central section of the courtyard.

The Town

A wall with rectangular towers runs north from the centre of the *Alcazaba* to the adjacent hill of San Cristóbal. This may be Umayyad in origin, or possibly early 11th-cent. On the hill itself there are series of circular towers, of clearly different, late medieval, construction. There is also a monument here to mark a chapel built by the Order of the Temple during the brief Castilian occupation in 1147.

The **cathedral church of San Juan** (Plaza Catedral), first erected in 1490 and then rebuilt in 1524 after the earthquake, stands on the site of the principal **mosque**. This was of Umayyad origin from the second half of the 10th cent., and was enlarged by the Taifa ruler Khayrān al-Ṣiqlabī (1013–28). Recent study shows that the present building still incorporates much of the fabric of the *quibla* of the mosque; this now forms the south wall of the church. The arcades that jut out from the wall into the nave were added in the 17th cent. Towards the western end may be seen the *mihrab*. This was given a plaster decoration in the Almohad period, but this has in part disintegrated to reveal the original caliphal work, the only contemporary parallel to that of the Mezquita in CÓRDOBA. Excavations have also uncovered some of the 11th-cent. second phase of construction elsewhere in the church. Literary sources record that further embellishment was added to the mosque later in the Taifa period and under the Almohads. A particularly fine and important collection of mainly 11th- and 12th-cent. Arab inscriptions from a necropolis has been found here.

Finds from the *Alcazaba*, especially of Islamic ceramics, together with items from the Punic **necropolis** of Villaricos (on the coast 15 km. north of the Parador at Mojácar), from the Copper Age site of Las Herrerías, and from the Bronze Age settlement of **Los Millares** (see below) may be seen in the Museo de Almería (Carretera de Ronda, 13).

Head north for 12 km. on the N 340 to Benahadux, and then 4 km. further on the CN 324 to Gador (enquire at the Ayuntamiento *here for the key or advice). The* **Los Millares** *site is to the right of the road 3 km. further on.*

Los Millares is regarded as the most important of all the Copper Age sites in south-east Spain. It was occupied from *c*.2600 to 1800 BC. The site contains foundations of some circular houses and traces of up to four lines of defensive walls, at least one of which has semicircular towers and dwellings built into it. Despite the fortifications, little evidence of warfare has emerged. There is also an important necropolis of the beehive tombs that are typical of this period, as well as burials in artificial caves.

Almonaster la Real   Umayyad mosque

Travelling south on the N 435 from Zafra towards HUELVA, *11 km. south of the intersection with the N 433, which is near Jabugo (noted for its hams), turn west onto a small road that leads 7 km. to Almonaster.*

The Arab name *Al-Munastir* implies the previous existence on the site of a Christian monastery, which in this part of Spain could only have been of Visigothic date. Fragments of Roman and Visigothic stonework in the fabric of the church that dominates the site testify to this and to earlier phases of occupation. Located within the ruined walls of the small Arab hill-top fortress, this church also retains much of the prayer hall of a mosque of Umayyad date (10th cent., or possibly 9th), including the brick *mihrab* projecting on its southern side. The prayer hall consisted of a central nave with two aisles on either side, the breadth of each decreasing proportionately. The nave and aisles are divided by brick arcades, supported on rough rectangular stone pillars or reused Roman columns, and at least one re-employed Roman Corinthian capital. Other simpler fluted capitals are contemporary with the building. The original entry was in the north bay of the east side. A small courtyard was cut out of the rock in the north-east corner, and contains a pool once used for ritual ablutions. The detached rectangular minaret on the north side has been recast as a bell tower. The eastern apse and sacristy and western porch were also added when the building was turned into a church. Sixteen undated graves were discovered under the prayer hall.

Returning north, take the N 433 eastwards for 16 km. to **Aracena**. *1 km. further on is the abandoned village of El Castillo.*

El Castillo is surrounded by the ruined defences of an Almohad fortress, captured by the Knights Templar, who also repaired it. The late 13th-cent. church of Nuestra Señora de los Dolores reuses much of a mosque of the same period, as can be seen from the horseshoe arcades in the interior and the minaret converted into a bell tower.

Almuñecar Roman and Phoenician town

Located on the coastal highway between Málaga and Almería, 21 km. west of Motril.

The Phoenician and then Carthaginian settlement of Sexi (see South Coast: PHOENICIAN SETTLEMENTS) that once occupied this site is represented by a **necropolis** containing 94 Phoenician and Punic graves at Puente de Noy, and by some chambers carved out of the rock in the Cueva de los Siete Palacios. Some Egyptian alabaster jars bearing cartouches with the names of some 9th-cent. BC kings were found in this area, but they were discovered together with a variety of Greek pottery items dating to about 700 BC. This collection must therefore have been deposited in the 8th cent. BC.

Slightly more may be detected of the Roman settlement here. In the middle of the town, in a site labelled as *Factoría de Salazones* ('Salted Fish Factory'), you can see a series of rectangular tanks carved from the bedrock, which once formed the centre of a Roman **fish-curing factory**. Part of a ruined **Roman aqueduct** may be seen up the Río Seco, 1 km. north of the town.

*At **Torrecuevas** (4 km. north of the town) two further sections of the same aqueduct may be seen. On the hillside 3 km. up the road from Almuñecar to Torrecuevas (signposted as 'Columbario Romano') there is a small rectangular Roman family tomb, of early imperial date, containing twenty-six niches for funerary urns.*

Ampurias Greek and Roman town   ★★

*Off the N II or the parallel A 7/E 15 between **Gerona/Girona** and **Figueras/ Figueres** the GE 513 runs 20 km. eastwards to La Escala/L'Escala. A turning to the north just before entering the town leads 2 km. to the site.*

Emporion (whence the English word 'emporium') developed as the principal Greek trading settlement in Spain. There are essentially three distinct settlement sites here. The oldest, the original Greek settlement or *palaiapolis* ('old town'), is located under the present village of Sant Martí d'Empúries. This area was originally an island, and the land between it and the newer Greek town, or *neapolis*, about 500 m. to the south was covered by a bay of the sea, forming a natural harbour. The new settlement was built on the southern end of the bay, with its eastern side fronting directly onto the sea. A stone breakwater (sometimes misleadingly called a 'wharf') was built on an outcrop of rock on the beach to protect the town against damage by the sea during storms. The much larger Roman town was built just under 200 m. inland. Although a Rhodian colony was established at **Rosas**, the establishment of major Hellenic settlements in Spain was primarily the work of Greeks from Phocaea and took the form of colonizing ventures from already established Phocaean towns in the west, notably Massalia (Marseilles: founded *c.*600 BC) and Alalia (Aleria in

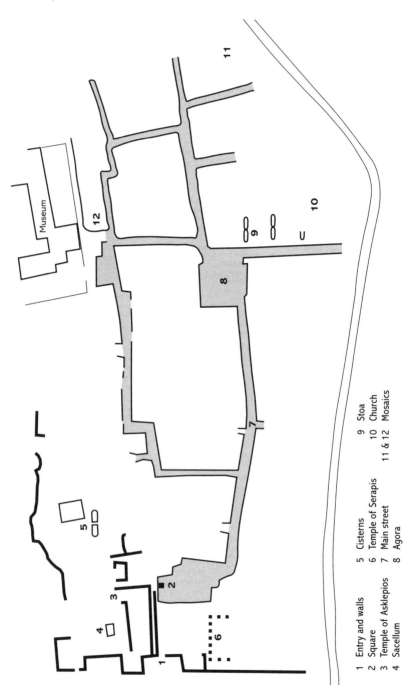

1 Entry and walls
2 Square
3 Temple of Asklepios
4 Sacellum
5 Cisterns
6 Temple of Serapis
7 Main street
8 Agora
9 Stoa
10 Church
11 & 12 Mosaics

▲ Ampurias: the Greek town of Neapolis

Corsica; abandoned after a war with Carthage in 540 BC). The first Phocaean presence at Ampurias may date to 600–580 BC, as a trading station rather than a full-scale settlement. The island may have also housed an indigenous population, established in the 7th cent. BC.

Difficulties of excavating in the modern village have limited what may be known of this site. Excavations have revealed a wall probably of the 4th cent. BC, and the claim that the village church (built 1507) stands on the site of a temple is based on the discovery in the vicinity of two sphinxes (now in the Museo Arqueológico in BARCELONA). A necropolis belonging to the early settlement, located to the south of the *neapolis*, was found and looted in the 19th cent. The Greek settlement on the mainland, which developed into the new town of Emporion, may date to the mid-sixth cent. The subsequent commercial success of the Greek town, evidenced not least by finds of its pottery exports at many sites on the Spanish Mediterranean coast, led to the growth nearby of an indigenous Celtic settlement (see **Ullastret**). In the conflicts between Rome and Carthage the Greek colonists sided with Rome, and the first Roman army to arrive in the Iberian peninsula disembarked in Ampurias in 218 BC. From then on the town was under Roman political hegemony, although retaining local self-government. In 49 BC Caesar established a *colonia* for veteran legionaries who had fought with him in Spain in the Civil War. The Roman town soon eclipsed the Greek one, though there are traces of occupation in the latter until the 3rd cent. AD.

However, it is in the Greek rather than in the Roman town that the most important early Christian monument is located, in the form of a ruined **basilica** surrounded by burials. As with many such buildings, it may have been constructed over the burial site of an early martyr (cf. the basilica of SANTA EULALIA in MÉRIDA and the cemetery basilica in TARRAGONA), which like all pre-4th-cent. Roman cemeteries had to be outside the town.

A church, of Carolingian or possibly Visigothic date, once stood on the site of the present church in **Sant Martí**, as an inscription still to be seen records that the church was rebuilt by Count Gauzbert in 926. Excavations close to the present church found evidence of occupation in the Late Roman and Visigothic periods. It is possible, though not certain, that the political upheavals of the 5th cent. AD led to a major resettlement of the more easily defended island, and abandonment of much of the mainland town. Following the Frankish conquest of Gerona in 785 and of Barcelona in 801 this region came under Carolingian rule, and a County was established in the 10th cent. This continued in existence until the early 15th cent., when it was annexed to the Crown by Martin I of Aragón.

Most of what is visible in the Greek *neapolis* dates from the later Hellenistic and Roman Republican periods (3rd–1st cents. BC), though traces of a 5th-cent. BC sanctuary that then stood outside the town and of some indigenous dwellings have been found in the area of the later temple of Asklepios (see below). The surviving section of the town wall, around the entry to the site on its southern side, dates from the 3rd cent. BC. Through the entry is a small square, with bases for a statue (probably of a Roman emperor) and a fountain. To the left is the site of the **sanctuary of Asklepios,** the Greek god of healing. (The statue of the god found here may be seen in the archaeological museum in BARCELONA; a copy has been put up *in situ*.) An adjacent temple may have been dedicated to Hygeia. Between the temples and the outer wall was a *sacellum* or open-air

Hygeia

Hygeia (Health) was one of the daughters of Asclepius, the Greek god of healing (hence modern 'hygiene'). Her sisters were Panacea (All Healing), Iaso (Cure), and Acesis (Remedy).

location for the performance of religious rites. On the other side of the temple complex may be seen some of the town's fresh-water cisterns. To the right of the square by the entry is another temple, dedicated to **Serapis,** a divinity of Alexandrine origin, whose cult was a Hellenistic development. In front of this begins the principal street of the town, with

Serapis

Serapis was composite divinity, first recorded in the reign of Ptolemy I Soter (305–285 BC). His attributes were composed of both Egyptian and Greek elements. The centre of the cult was the Serapeum in Alexandria, which was eventually destroyed on the orders of the Emperor Theodosius I in AD 391. Isis, although hitherto a purely Egyptian goddess with a distinctive place in the indigenous pantheon, was regarded by devotees of Serapis as his consort.

private housing on either side. The street ends in the central square or *agora,* which probably once had porticoes around it. Another street crosses the *agora* on the far side. Its right hand branch leads past the site of the *stoa* or principal market. Further down this street and set in from the *stoa* may be seen the **4th-cent. church,** built out of a former Roman bath house. Around the basilica may be seen a large number of tombs dating to the Visigothic and Carolingian periods. In this quarter of the town it is also possible to see some simple floor mosaics, including a few with Greek inscriptions. One of these (close to the Museum) reads: ΗΔΨΚΟΙΤΟΣ: 'sweet dreams'! A **site museum** has been established in a former monastery of the Servites (abandoned in 1835). This contains some helpful models, as well as a variety of finds from the Greek and Roman towns. Other items may be seen in the archaeological museum in BARCELONA.

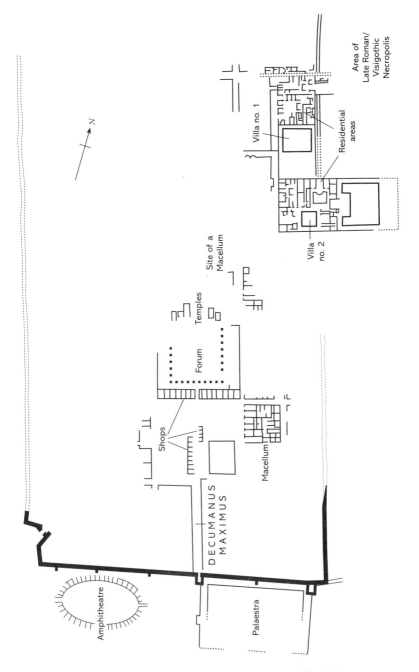

▲ Ampurias: excavated part of the Roman town (after Ripoll Perelló)

The **Roman town** is less fully uncovered than its Greek predecessor, but its layout is easier to comprehend. Its area was roughly 350×800 m., and it was defended by a rectangle of walls, of which a substantial section survives on the south side. Outside the wall in the south-west you can see the remains of an amphitheatre, of which the rubble supports for the seating survive, and in the south-east there was an open-air *palaestra* or gymnasium, the outline of whose walls can be made out. There was a gate in the middle of the town hall, reinforced by a later tower, giving access to the *Decumanus Maximus*, the main street, which led directly to the **forum** in the centre of the site. The area of the forum had previously served as the site of the *praesidium* or headquarters building of the Roman fortress erected in the 2nd cent. BC, traces of which have been found outside the north-east corner. The final section of the *Decumanus* is flanked on both sides by equal-sized *tabernae* or shops, and the south side of the forum was also flanked by shops, which backed onto it. In one of these was found a large millstone for grinding cereals, so it may have been a bakery. Another contains a possible dyeing vat. To the right of this final section of the *Decumanus*, and level with the south-east corner of the forum, is a *macellum* or market, with a variety of separate sections and different-sized stalls.

After the founding of the civilian settlement in the late Republican period the area was transformed by the creation of a large **temple** with surrounding portico in the middle of the north end of the forum plat-

▼ Ampurias: a Roman villa

form, and the creation of the shops at its southern end. These initially seemed to have opened northwards, facing towards the temple. In the reign of Augustus this direction was reversed, and a new portico around the southern, eastern, and western sides of the forum was created, linking with that already built around the temple. A basilica and a curia or possibly a small temple to Augustus (*aedes Augusti*) was erected to the east of the main temple. A single-aisled *macellum* or market of two facing rows of stalls was also built adjacent to the north edge of the forum. Other small shrines seem to have been built parallel to the temple in the late 1st or early 2nd cent. However, by this period decline had already set in, with the collapse of parts of the Republican porticoes on the north and east side of the temple. Recent study has shown that the whole area of the forum was in decay and falling out of use before the end of the 2nd cent. AD. Although there is evidence of use of the area in the 3rd cent., it was totally ruinous by the beginning of the 4th.

Beyond the forum towards the north-east corner of the town may be seen two substantial early imperial **private villas**, with well-preserved if not very inspiring floor mosaics. The one nearer to the Museum, known as the 'Casa Villanueva', is entered from the street, and is organized around an atrium with central pool (*impluvium*), which also served as a collecting point for water for the house's cisterns. The public rooms are on the northern side of the atrium. Those on the south, including a large porticoed garden or peristyle with semicircular exedra in the centre, served as the private quarters of the family that owned the villa. Under the portico of the garden was a store chamber, entered via a small stairway. On the far side of the garden were yet other rooms, with mosaic floors. There was a bath house in the north-west corner of the villa. The other house, on the south side of the first one, is slightly smaller, but was equally luxurious, with mosaic floors and stuccoed walls. Under the *impluvium* in the centre of the atrium around which the villa is organized is a cistern.

Antequera Dolmens and Islamic fortress ★
(Visit together with BOBASTRO)

On the eastern outskirts of Antequera are some of the finest, and most accessible dolmens in Spain (NB: normal visiting hours only). Two of these are situated in a small park 1 km. down the road leading from the centre of the town to the N 331 to MÁLAGA.

The older of the two dolmens, 'La Menga', dates to *c*.2500 BC and consists of a large covered passage 25 m. × 6.5 m., with its roof supported by huge stone pillars. There are some carved figures (not all of which are ancient) on the last stone on the left. The other dolmen here, 'Viera', takes its name from that of the two brothers who discovered it in 1905. This consists of a roughly circular vault (nearly 2 m. wide × 2 m. high) approached via a

▲ Antequera: interior of a dolmen

19 m. long passage. The stones used are smaller and also better cut than those of 'La Menga', arguing for a somewhat later date, towards 2000 BC. The third dolmen, 'Romeral', is located about 3 km. further down the same road, near its junction with the N 331. Its construction differs from that of the other two in that, while large slabs are used for its roof, the walls are built of much smaller stones and bricks made of earth. The round vault is over 5 m. wide, rising to a height of nearly 4 m. It is approached via a passage 20.5 m. long and roughly 1.5 m. wide. From the main vault a smaller passage leads to a second chamber. This tomb has been dated to c.1800 BC, owing to its greater complexity.

Of the Roman town of Anticaria little is known, but excavations began in 1988 on a bath complex found next to the Colegiata of Santa María la Mayor (c.1550), on the hill near the **Alcazaba**, which is the main legacy of the period of Arab rule. This rule lasted until the town fell in 1410 to the Castilian prince Fernando 'el de Antequera', who later became king of Aragón (1412–16). This siege is said to have provided the first opportunity for the use of gunpowder in Spain. Of the fortress there survive some stretches of restored walls and rectangular towers that do not exceed the height of the wall, together with the massive '**Torre Mocha**', a much larger square tower (with an incongruous baroque belfry on the top of it), located in a vital corner of the defences. It is linked by a wall with two small towers to another, narrower square tower that rises to almost the same height as itself. It has been dated to the 13th cent. The 'Torre Mocha' and adjacent walls are built on top of earlier walls, that can be seen below and in front of them. These have a different construction, with layers of thin stones interspersed with the larger ones. It has often been suggested that these are of Roman date, but this has never been satisfactorily established.

There is an excellent small archaeological museum (Museo Municipal) in the Palacio de Nájera (Plaza Guerreo Muñoz), which contains a fine Roman bronze statue of a boy, known as 'the ephebe of Antequera', a fine if damaged bust possibly of the period of Gallienus (253–68) and some Visigothic decorated tiles (from burial vaults).

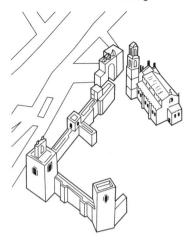

▲ Antequera: the fortress

*From Antequera the road past the dolmens leads via the N 331 to the N 321 Seville to Granada motorway. A turning south 4 km. down this road leads in 3 km. to **Archidona**.*

Archidona was the site of an early Phoenician settlement (8th cent. BC) called Escua, which passed into Carthaginian hands, before being conquered by Rome around the end of the 3rd cent. BC. Under the Umayyads the town was the capital of the *qura* or administrative district of *Rayya*. A **fortress of Arab origin**, subsequently held by the Order of Calatrava, perches on top of the hill above the town. In the **chapel of the Santísima Virgen de Gracia** on the summit is preserved part of a small 15th-cent. Nazirid mosque. This was briefly the centre of an independent kingdom ruled by the Nazirid king Abū Naṣr Saʿd (1453–64), who made himself ruler of Granada in 1455.

Astorga Roman walls

The town is situated 36 km. west of LEÓN, on the N 120, which bypasses it to the south and west.

Astorga, like LEÓN and LUGO, is fortunate in preserving substantial sections of its Roman walls. Argument exists as to whether there was an indigenous settlement on the site, but no archaeological trace of this has been found. On the other hand, traces of a large fort discovered recently support the view that Asturica was one of the main Roman military bases in Augustus's Cantabrian War (26–22 BC). It was made into a *municipium* following the end of the war, and given Augustus's name. The creation in the same reign of the 'Camino de la Plata' linked it with MÉRIDA and SEVILLE in the south, and other roads led to Braga and LUGO. In AD 1 it became the centre of a *conventus*. Agreements apparently made with some of the indigenous population of the surrounding area in AD 27 are

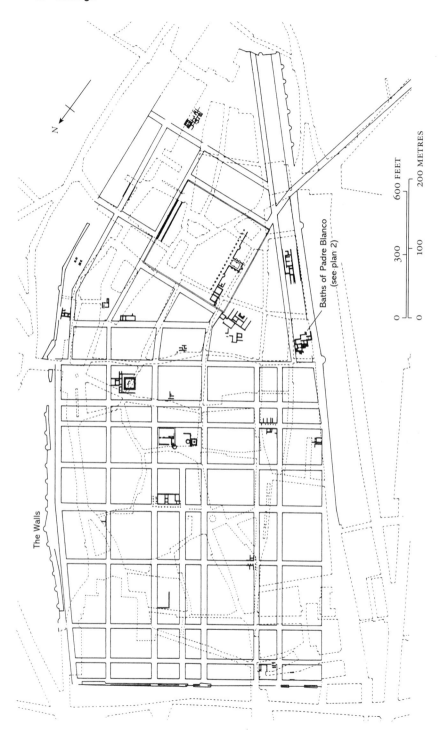

N

The Walls

Baths of Padre Blanco
(see plan 2)

600 FEET

300

0

200 METRES

100

0

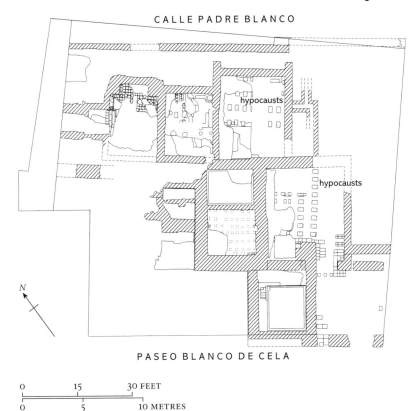

CALLE PADRE BLANCO

hypocausts

hypocausts

N

PASEO BLANCO DE CELA

0   15   30 FEET

0   5   10 METRES

▲ Astorga: plan of the small public baths discovered in the Padre Blanco street (after García Marcos and Vidal Encinas)

◀ Astorga: the Roman town superimposed on the modern street plan

recorded in an extant bronze inscription (*CIL* II. 2633), though its authenticity has recently been challenged. The town, as the centre of an important mining industry, seems to have prospered in the early imperial period, at least until the mid-3rd cent. Under the administrative reorganization in the reign of Septimius Severus (193–211) it became the capital of the new *Provincia Citerior Antoniniana*. Over fifty sites in the town have been studied in the last decade, often in consequence of rescue excavations, and something of a picture of the **Roman settlement** is emerging from this. A few of these sites are being preserved for inspection (enquire at the *Ayuntamiento* or the *Oficina del Turismo*). Part of a basilica, probably of Julio-Claudian date and of exceptional length (over 90 m.), has been discovered; it filled the southern side of the forum. Sections of it may have housed the *Curia*, as well as serving as a temple of the imperial cult (an *Aedes Augusti*), and as the normal lawcourts. The northern edge of the forum has been defined by the remains of a *cryptoporticus*, though what stood above this has not yet been established. A large public-bath complex has been found, as well as traces of a small one that probably served a defined sector of the town. The subterranean water supply of the town has been fairly extensively explored, though this has revealed little of the way water was brought into the settlement. The layout of some of the porticoed streets has also been deduced. Some of a number of houses of the 1st and 2nd cent. contained parts of mosaic floors and columns and walls painted to imitate marble. One villa built in the 2nd cent. had part of its structure built over by the town walls, indicating that the latter did not include all the area once filled by the early imperial town.

These **walls**, now to be seen along much of the northern edge and in the south-east sector of the town, were constructed in the late 3rd or early 4th cent., at a time when similar construction was being undertaken in many locations in Spain.

The later imperial period is not so well documented from recent excavation, but a number of features of it are clear, and cohere with those found elsewhere in Spain. In particular, public buildings appear to go out of use, with rubbish pits being found in a number of such locations. The larger and grander houses of the early empire were frequently modified, their rooms being remodelled and reduced in size. Construction work of this period also involved much reuse of earlier materials, including inscriptions and decorative items. Substantial quantities of pottery, especially of locally produced Spanish *terra sigillata*, have been found. Of the subsequent Visigothic period little is known archaeologically.

The existence of a Christian community in the town is recorded in AD 254, in a letter of Bishop Cyprian of Carthage (*Ep.* 67). A bishopric came into existence in the 4th cent.; this was still functioning at the time of the sixteenth Council of Toledo in 693. In 456 the Suevic kingdom of Rechiarius (448–56) was destroyed following a defeat by the Visigoths on the Río Orbigo, 12 (Roman) miles from the town (probably close to where the N 120 now crosses the river). Astorga was itself sacked by the troops of the Visigothic king Theoderic II (453–66) in 457. After the Arab conquest, according to the *Chronicle of Alfonso III* (see MONTE NARANCO), the town was evacuated by the Asturian king Alfonso I (739–57), and reoccupied and refortified by Ordoño I (850–66).

The town was besieged in 1810 by a French army under Marshal Junot; the 3rd–4th-cent. walls continued to provide successful defence.

Roman and medieval finds from the town can be seen in the Museo de los Caminos (Glorieta Eduardo de Castro), owned by the Diocese of Astorga.

There is also a late medieval cathedral (1471–1559), with a baroque west portal (1693).

Enthusiasts for the work of the Catalan architect Gaudi will be delighted by the episcopal palace, which was completed in 1909 to his designs.

Bádajoz Arab fortress

The Alcazaba *or fortress of Bádajoz stands at the highest point in the old city.*

Although evidence has been found of earlier Bronze Age, Roman (then called *Pax Augusta*), and Visigothic occupation of the site, Bádajoz is first known to have been fortified in 875, in the course of a local rebellion against the Umayyad Amir Muḥammad I. In the Taifa period it became the capital of one of the largest of the kingdoms, falling into the hands of the Almoravids in 1094–5. The Almoravids had previously won the

▼ Bádajoz: the Alcazaba (after Valdés Fernández)

THE ALCAZABA

Rió Guadiana

Torre de Espanteperros

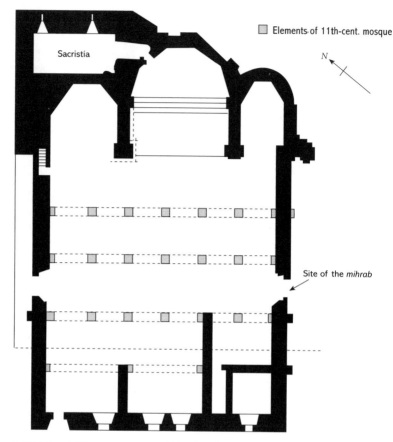

Sacristía

Elements of 11th-cent. mosque

N

Site of the *mihrab*

▲ Bádajoz: 11th-cent. mosque within church in the Alcazaba

battle of Zallaqa or Sagrajas just north-east of the city against Alfonso VI of León-Castile in 1086. A substantial refortification of the town and its *Alcazaba* took place under the Almohads in 1168–9. Bádajoz was captured by Alfonso IX of León in 1230.

A substantial amount of the medieval wall of the *Alcazaba*, mainly dating from the 12th and 13th cents., has been preserved. Various sectors of the site, both inside and outside the walls, were excavated in the late 1970s. Although now relatively empty, the size of the site and its continuous previous occupation, most recently by the army, has limited the results achieved. A museum to house finds has been opened in the 16th-cent. palace of the Duques de Roca (previously employed as a barracks). One particularly deep trench was able to identify traces of a probable Bronze Age occupation. Greek, Roman, and 18th-cent. objects, as well as Islamic ceramics, have been recovered from a number of the locations dug. The most obvious pre-Islamic elements to be seen now are some reused

Visigothic carvings, mainly to be found decorating the Puerta del Capital and the Puerta de Carros. A particularly conspicuous pilaster located in the latter is clearly related to those found in the cistern in the *Alcazaba* in MÉRIDA. Within the fortress the former chapel of the Military Hospital has been shown to preserve some elements of an 11th-cent. **mosque** (with probable dimensions of about 18 sq. m.), notably in the lines of internal arcading, which would originally have run at right angles to the *quibla*, producing five parallel aisles. The central one, with a width of over 3.5 m., was broader than the others (under 3 m. each), and leads directly to the present south door, which thus takes the place once occupied by the *mihrab*. At the highest point of the site, approached by a small street off the whitewashed Plaza Alta, is an octagonal tower, known as the Torre de Espanteperros, built by the Almohads around 1150, with similarities in design to the Torre de Oro in SEVILLE.

Recent excavation of the *Alcazaba* has been concentrated on two areas: (1) around the main entry on the north-western side of the fortress, and (2) to the south-east, in a zone lying between the walls and the River Guadiana.

1. Work on the *Alcazaba* proper has concentrated on the defences around the principal entrance and on an adjacent area within the walls. Sections of a lower outer wall immediately paralleling the main inner one have been uncovered to the north of the entrance, showing the continuation of this feature of the defences from the better preserved section south of the gate. Within the walls, to the left of the gate, trial trenches uncovered a small section of housing, probably 11th-cent., including also the contents of a rubbish dump, containing cattle bones.

2. The second main area excavated has emerged as being the location of a walled suburb, marked by the presence of a group of houses, built of poor-quality materials and belonging to a single short period of construction. The lack of evidence of a 10th-cent. level of occupation and a remark in the text of the Arab geographer al-Idrīsī have led to the conclusions that this area was developed as a commercial suburb early in the 11th cent. but was abandoned around 1100, following the overthrow of the Taifa monarchy by the Almoravids in 1094.

Note also some reused Visigothic capitals (whitewashed over) in the colonnade to the south side of the Plaza de San José adjacent to the west wall of the *Alcazaba*.

Note also the cathedral of 1232–84 in the Plaza de España at Bádajoz. Bádajoz suffered several sieges in the Peninsula War and a horrendous sack in 1812 at the hands of the Duke of Wellington's army. Some of its 18th-cent. Vaubanesque defences may still be seen on both sides of the river.

Baelo   Roman town   ★

Going westwards on the E 5/N 340 from Algeciras to **Cádiz***, 15 km. west of the turning to* TARIFA *a small road on the left leads 7.5 km. directly to the site, now known as Bolonia, lying below the Sierra de la Plata and close to the sea shore.*

A small Roman coastal town, subsisting amongst other things on tuna-fishing, sauce-making and olive oil-pressing industries, and according to Strabo (*c.* AD 17) serving as the main port of embarkation for Tingis (modern Tangiers), this site has been extensively excavated over many decades by French archaeologists from the Casa de Velázquez in Madrid (initially from 1914 to 1921 and then ever since 1966). They have uncovered quite a lot of the town, especially at its southern end. It is thus one of the best and most complete Roman urban sites in Spain, displaying good examples of the main features of town planning of the early imperial period, but also some unusual elements. The outline of much of the walls can be deduced, and some small sections of it are visible on both east and west. Two towered gateways have been located on either side, though little remains visible. These parallel entries were linked across the width of the town by the *Decumanus Maximus*, the principal thoroughfare. On the northern side of this street, and more or less centrally placed, lies the most significant part of the site to be uncovered, in the form of the paved forum and the buildings related to it, many of which have been dated to the reign of the Emperor Claudius (41–54), in whose reign Baelo became a *municipium*.

Earlier structures appear to have been removed at this time to make way for a major campaign of public building. The new **forum** (45 × 33 m.) was surrounded on its southern, western, and eastern sides by porticoes, linking it to other buildings, some of whose foundations have been uncovered. The large rectangular building (36 × 20 m.) on the southern side, whose eastern end overlaps the east portico of the forum, was arcaded internally. Built under Claudius, its location and the discovery of a very large, and probably locally carved, statue (reusing the body of an earlier Julio-Claudian imperial figure) of the Emperor Trajan (98–117) in the eastern end suggests this served as a basilica or lawcourts. The 1st-cent. AD structures, including a small building with two staircases, between the basilica and the *Decumanus* have not been identified. One of them may have served as the municipal archive, where not only public documents but also private deeds were lodged. The three buildings on the western side of the forum are very unequal in size, but all front directly onto the portico. The largest of them (9.5 × 18 m.) is centrally placed, and enjoyed a grand entry across the portico. In plan they look like temples, and the central one may have been devoted to the imperial cult. Recent excavations have led to the suggestion that there were at least two periods of building here, a Julio-Claudian phase being entirely replaced by a 2nd-cent. one, probably in the reign of Trajan, that is represented by the

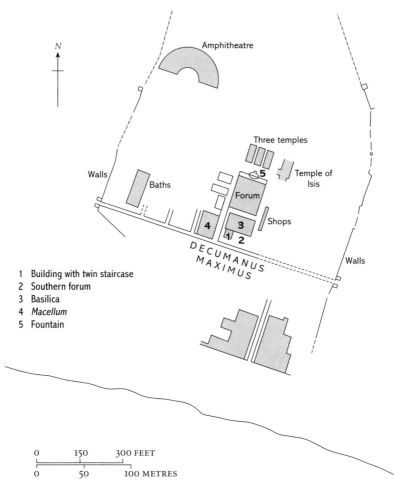

▲ Baelo: plan (after Sillières)

1 Building with twin staircase
2 Southern forum
3 Basilica
4 *Macellum*
5 Fountain

buildings now visible. This indicates a surprising amount of building and rebuilding in a relatively short period. The southernmost of the three buildings may have gone out of use in the early 3rd cent. AD, and the other two may have been abandoned in the 4th cent.

On the northern side of the forum, instead of a portico there was a **raised podium**, that curved around a hemispherical fountain or pool in the centre of it. Behind this, on the podium itself, stood an altar. This podium served as the location for the main **temple complex** of the town, and was approached up steps at the northern end of both the eastern and western porticoes. Immediately behind the fountain and its altar stood three parallel and identical tetrastyle temples, facing southwards over the forum. They are likely to have been dedicated to Jupiter, Juno, and Minerva. The western two, like the forum, were probably built in AD 50–60. The third was a later addition, probably of early Antonine date. The concept of the triple temples dominating the forum probably owes much to Roman North African town-planning, such as may be seen at Sufetula (Sbeitla) in Tunisia. To the east of the three temples, and not directly related to them, stood a fourth, dedicated to the Egyptian goddess Isis, dating from AD 80–100. Its foundations are less well preserved. A small lead cursing tablet was found in the temple requesting the goddess to punish the thief who had stolen all of the worshipper's bedclothes.

Immediately to the west of the basilica, and fronting onto the *Decumanus Maximus*, can be seen the *macellum*, or **market**; the outline of its ten individual stalls has been preserved around the central courtyard. This was probably built in the late 1st cent. AD, replacing a fish-salting factory. Four shops across the front of the building faced directly onto the street. This complex may have gone out of use by the late 3rd cent. AD. Further west and a little north of the *Decumanus* a large **public bath complex** of the 3rd cent. has been uncovered. Due north of this, across an area not fully explored, are the remains of the theatre, whose western edge overlooked the town wall.

Jupiter

Jupiter was the principal Roman god. The cult was of Etruscan and Italic origin, and he was seen primarily as a sky divinity, one of whose attributes was the sending of thunderbolts and lightning. This deity was identified with the very similar Greek god Zeus.

Juno

Originally the Etruscan goddess of women, her cult was adopted by the Romans, and was equated with that of the Greek goddess Hera, the wife of Zeus. As Juno Lucina she was venerated as the goddess of childbirth.

Minerva

Like many Roman cults the worship of Minerva was of Etruscan origin. She was the patron goddess of craftsmen, and was also held to be the keeper of the city of Rome (in the way that her Greek counterpart, Athene, was the special protectress of Athens).

On the eastern edge of the forum are the foundations of some shops; these seem to have given way to a large unidentified building by the end of the 1st cent. AD. Their function may have been taken over by the *macellum*, thus leaving the forum area exclusively for religious and governmental purposes. Other structures have been uncovered in the south-east of the site, between the modern buildings and the beach. These belonged to a **factory** for the manufacture of *garum*, a piquant sauce made from decomposing salted fish heads, guts, and blood, of which the Romans were fond. Outside the town two extramural Roman **necropolises** have been excavated. Some of the burial practices, as in the necropolis of CARMONA, indicate the survival of Punic traditions into the early Roman imperial period.

In the late imperial period centralized planning and interest in public buildings appear to have declined sharply. The *Decumanus Maximus* began to accumulate rubbish, and by the end of the 4th cent. had been built over by a series of small, poorly constructed dwellings. By this time the basilica was probably no longer used, any more than the temples around the forum. The theatre, too, seems to have been abandoned by this time, and became a rubbish tip, before being re-employed for an intramural cemetery; the practice of burial within the walls of a settlement became normal under the Late Empire. Whether the town still continued in occupation in the Visigothic period has not been determined.

Although finds from excavations were initially taken to the Museo Arqueológico Nacional in MADRID and to the Museo Arqueológico in **Cádiz**, where they may be seen, an annexe of the Cádiz museum has been opened on the site itself.

Balaguer   Arab fortress

Recent study has revealed that the fortress belongs to two phases. The first, which may be compared with other fortifications of the same period such as the *Alcazaba* of MÉRIDA of 835, is Umayyad of the pre-Caliphal period. The major frontier fortification established here in the 9th cent. was probably built by Lope ibn Muḥammad, one of the Banu Qāsī family, who maintained a large measure of local autonomy in the Upper March throughout the 9th cent. Victory over Count Wifred the Hairy of Barcelona in 897 may have prompted the construction of the fortress, which guarded a route towards LÉRIDA, 30 km. to the south-west. The second phase of construction is attributable to the Taifa period in the 11th cent., when a substantial and luxurious **palace** was placed within the earlier defences, some of which may have been restored at the same time. The palace was probably built for Yūsuf al-Muzaffar, a member of the Banu Hud dynasty of Zaragoza, who ruled independently from Lérida from 1046–7 to 1067. The town was then reintegrated into the Taifa kingdom of Zaragoza by his brother Aḥmad ibn Sulaymān (*c.*1049–82). In 1102 Balaguer was captured by the Castilian count Pedro Ansúrez, and it subsequently became a stronghold of the counts of Urgell. In 1319 it was the birthplace of King Pedro IV the Ceremonious (1336–87) of Aragón. The **fortress** is on a hill overlooking the Río Segre in the north of the town and is roughly rectangular (*c.*140 × 70 m.). An Arab bridge may

▼ Balaguer: the Arab fortress (after Ewert)

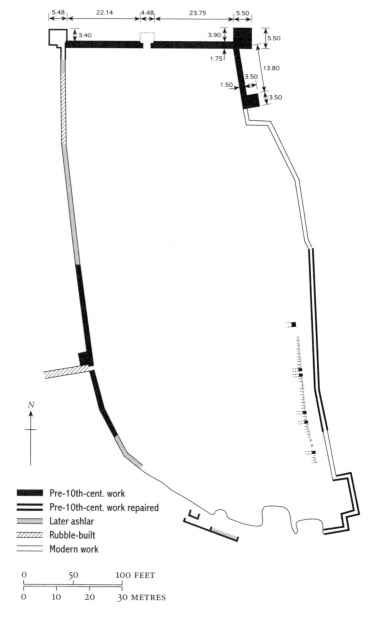

Pre-10th-cent. work
Pre-10th-cent. work repaired
Later ashlar
Rubble-built
Modern work

0   50   100 FEET
0   10   20   30 METRES

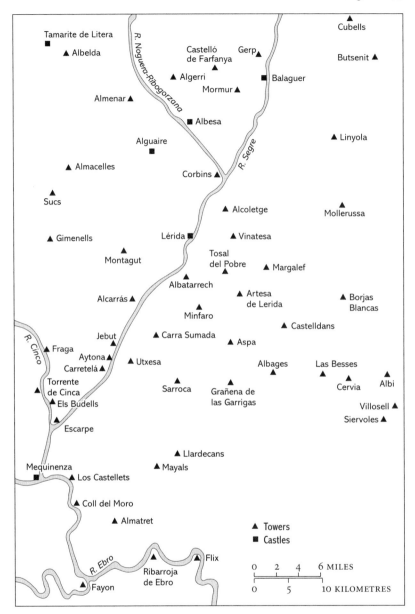

▲ Balaguer forming part of the defensive network around Lérida (after Scales)

have crossed the river below the site. The northern sector of the wall, with the square tower in the north-east corner, is almost entirely attributable to the late 9th-cent. original phase of construction. A tower in the middle of

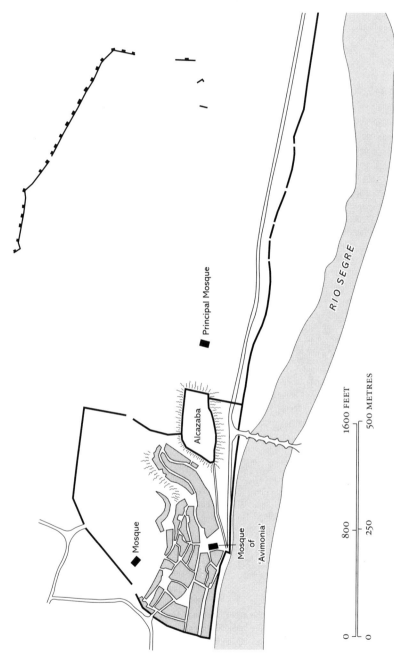

RIO SEGRE

Principal Mosque

Alcazaba

Mosque

Mosque
of
'Avimonia'

1600 FEET

500 METRES

800

250

0

0

▲ 11th-cent. Balaguer

the north wall was destroyed subsequently to open up a gateway. In addition the tower to the south of the north-east corner tower and the wall joining them, and a section and small tower in the centre of the west wall, have been ascribed to this period. Much of the rest of the eastern wall may belong to this first phase of construction, but most of it has clearly undergone repairs and restoration at various later stages. The same applies to the north-west corner tower. Of the palace building only decorative fragments have survived, uncovered in excavations in 1967. Comparison with comparable material from the **Aljafería** of ZARAGOZA enabled the nature and date of the structure to be deduced. Fragments of pottery from the Umayyad phase were also recovered.

By the 11th cent. Balaguer formed part of a complex system of defences around Lérida (see plan B), of larger and smaller fortifications. The small ones took the form of either a *hiṣn* (a fort strategically located both for defence and the oversight of a rural district) or a *burj* (a tower or fortified enclosure serving as a local place of refuge). In the area of Balaguer a good example of a *hiṣn* (plural; *huṣūn*) may be seen at **Ager** (35 km. north of Balaguer on the L 904) which has a square tower and section of wall, once thought to be Roman but now reassigned to the Umayyad period, showing marked similarities to the defences at Balaguer, and which from the evidence of literary sources must have existed by 922. Other *huṣūn* have been identified at Os de Balaguer, Camarasa, Rubió, Alòs de Balaguer, and Sant Llorenc (all around the Río Segre above Balaguer). There are traces of a *burj* at **Gerb** (4km. due north of Balaguer). **La Rápita** (2km. south-east of Balaguer—visible from the fortress in Balaguer) is a privately owned castle, whose corner tower, although much restored and repaired at later periods, is of clearly Umayyad date. The name itself indicates the presence here of a *ribat* (an Islamic fortress-monastery), whose origins may go back as early as the 8th cent.

Recent excavation in the town of Balaguer itself has concentrated on the development of the **Islamic city**, whose original nucleus has been located in and around the Pla d'Almata, just north of the fortress. The principal mosque was almost certainly located on the site occupied by the later medieval church of Santa María d'Almata. By the 11th cent. a lower town, to the south of the fortress and on the flatter ground adjacent to the river bank, had begun to develop. There are traces of two mosques in this zone. This district had expanded still further southwards by the 14th cent., under Catalan rule.

Baños de la Encina   Arab fortress

On the N IV–E 5 from MADRID to CÓRDOBA, Bailén is bypassed 100 km. north-east of Córdoba; from the centre of Bailén a small road leads 11 km. directly to Baños de la Encina on top of the long hill, the easternmost edge of the Sierra Morena, which flanks the western side of the main road between Bailén and La Carolina. Approaching from the north, the J 504 leads westwards to the site from the N IV at a point 23 km. south of the turn-off for La Carolina.

This large and imposingly sited castle was probably begun by the Caliph al-Ḥakam II in 968, as may be inferred from an inscription in the Museo Arqueológico Nacional in MADRID (see 'Sources', p. 316) which records the completion of one of the towers in August of that year. It dominates the important route between Córdoba and the Central March that lies at its feet, as well as keeping a controlling eye over the hill country to the west. Its dimensions are approximately 100 m. long by 46 m. wide, and the wall is reinforced by fifteen towers; one of these was clearly restored in the later Middle Ages. It is constructed of stone and rises conspicuously above the level of the other towers. These and the walls are built of rammed earth (Arabic *tabiya*), in the same way as those of the fortress of EL VACAR and the outer walls of TURÉGANO. There is a horseshoe-arched gateway, flanked by towers. Some of the interior has been reused for the village cemetery.

*Approximately 2 km. north of the last turn-off to La Carolina the N IV–E 5 passes by the village of **Las Navas de Tolosa**, close to the battle site.*

In the battle of Las Navas de Tolosa in 1212 Alfonso VIII of Castile, with Aragonese and Navarrese help, decisively defeated the Almohad army of Muḥammad ibn ʿAbd-Allāh al-Naṣir (1199–1214).

Baños de Valdearados   Roman villa

From Aranda de Duero take the BU 910 north-east for 15 km.; a turning to the right leads to the village. The site is located on open ground immediately west of the village. If the mosaics have not been restored to their original location, ask for their whereabouts at the Ayuntamiento.

This is one of a number of substantial Roman villas to be found on the Meseta, the Castilian plateau. It is unusual in apparently having been first built under the Late Roman Empire, and also in preserving some fine specimens of mosaic decoration of that period relatively intact. It has been dated to the 4th cent., with occupation continuing across the 5th and possibly into the early 6th cents. It is conceivable that an earlier villa may be located close by, but so far no traces of Early Imperial occupation of the site have been found, save for one coin of Augustus (27 BC–AD 14) and another of Trebonianus Gallus (251–3). On the eastern side of the site 21 tombs have been excavated, of which at least 7 are those of children. A number of funerary practices are represented in this **necropolis**, including burial directly in the soil and in cists made of thin flat stones. The tombs are oriented in a west–east direction, and the arms are in most cases folded across the bodies. Some of the tombs are located within a sector of

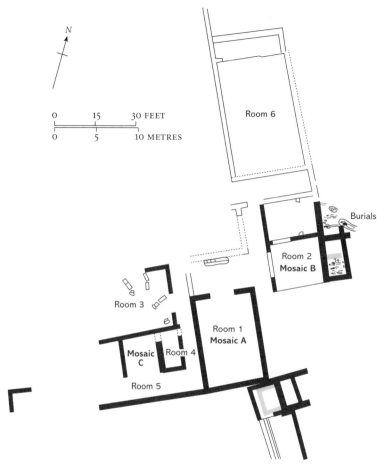

N

0   15   30 FEET
0   5   10 METRES

Room 6

Burials

Room 2
Mosaic B

Room 3

Room 1
Mosaic A

Mosaic
C   Room 4

Room 5

▲ Baños de Valdearados: the Roman villa (after Argente)

room 2 of the villa, which had clearly ceased to function by the time of these burials. Although some of the evidence might suggest a date as early as the mid-7th cent. for these inhumations, the excavators consider that they probably should be assigned to the 9th to 11th cents.

Only a portion of the villa, corresponding to what may have been its south-east corner, has been excavated. There was no central atrium or garden, or at least none has been discovered; this makes it difficult to assess the general plan of the building, or to see how its conception may have differed from the norms of earlier Roman rural villas. About half a dozen rooms have been located, together with a right-angled section of corridor linking some of them. Three substantial **mosaics** have been recovered:

Mosaic A (*c*.10 × 6.5 m.; in room 1) has an elaborate geometric border, incorporating small panels of decoration. Of these the four square ones in the corners are filled with stylized busts. On each of the longer sides there are two rectangular hunting scenes and on the shorter sides one. Each of these depicts one animal being chased by another. One of these panels on each side also contains the name of the appropriate wind: EURUS (actually wrongly located in the north-east rather than the south-east), BOREAS (North), ZEFYRUS (West), NOTUS (South). In the centre of the mosaic, below a band of stylized vine-leaf and a cornice-shaped decoration surmounted by two peacocks, there are two large panels. In the lower, which is bordered on three sides by a frieze of vine leaves, is a depiction of Bacchus/Dionysus, bearing a vine and a wine jug, travelling in a biga, which is a chariot drawn by two animals: in this case, tigers. He is accompanied by a pipe-playing satyr and a bacchante holding a crater (a Greek wine vessel). Above in another panel, partly damaged on its left side, is another depiction of Dionysus, in a bacchanalian scene, with an arm around Ampelos and holding Ariadne (his wife in some myths) by the wrist, surrounded by revellers. On the right may be seen the bearded Silenus and a donkey. Argument as to the dating depends upon the deductions to be made from a corpus of mosaics of related style from both Spain and North Africa, but the first half of the 5th cent. seems the most probable. It should occasion no surprise to find such explicitly pagan themes being used decoratively in this period, when the empire had been officially Christian since 392; compare the 4th-cent. Bacchus mosaic in the 'House of Bacchus' in Complutum (ALCALÁ DE HENARES). The size of the room and the nature of its decoration would imply this was the *triclinium* or dining-room of the villa.

Dionysius (or Bacchus) and Ariadne

The god of ecstasy and, in particular, of wine, he was also called *Liber* by the Romans. Ariadne was the daughter of the Cretan king Minos and she helped Theseus to kill the Minotaur. Different versions of the story exist of why he then left her on the island of Naxos, where she became the wife of Dionysius. Her cult would seem in origin to be that of a nature goddess, probably peculiar to Naxos.

Mosaic B (*c*.6 × 5 m.; in room 2) has been partly damaged by the later burials on the eastern edge of this room. Only a section of a head remains from the unidentifiable scene of the central portion of the mosaic, which was framed within an eight-pointed star, formed by two overlapping squares. This in turn is framed by a variety of geometric shapes, formed by the intertwining of lines of twisted rope decoration. The panels thus formed contain geometric shapes, vessels, busts (in the corners), birds, and running animals (one in the centre of each side). All this complex pattern is itself contained within a rectangular outer border of separate square and rectangular panels of either geometric or highly stylized floral designs, interspersed on two sides with depictions of equally stylized wine jugs. This mosaic has been dated to the 4th cent.

Mosaic C (in room 5). This T-shaped room would once have been filled by four rectangular panels of fine mosaic (the three on the south side forming a continuous rectangular space about 11.5 × 2.5 m.). However, apart from the thick twisted rope border, the whole of the easternmost panel has been lost. So, too, has the north-west corner of the west mosaic, which was made up of a series of geometric shapes. Between the two mosaics already mentioned was a third; this has also suffered some damage to its central section, which is comprised of an illusionist's pattern of cubes, sandwiched between lines of wave-like patterns. Best preserved and most impressive is the fourth panel (4.5 × 4 m.), immediately to the north of the central one. Like the other three it lacks any figurative depiction, i.e. it is aniconic in its design, apart from the use of two large stylized jar shapes in the central section. All the mosaics in this room are dated to the 4th cent.

A fine bronze brazier decorated with lions' heads and many potsherds, including several of late *terra sigillata*, have been uncovered on the site, as well as a few 4th- and early 5th-cent. coins.

Barcelona Roman and medieval site ★

The historic centre of Barcelona, representing the area of both the Roman settlement and the medieval city, is located at the heart of the much larger modern city, between the cathedral and the harbour (where a replica of Columbus's ship the Santa María may be seen).

Founded under Augustus (27 BC–AD 14) for veterans of the Cantabrian wars, Roman Barcino was given the status of *colonia* but, forming part of the *Conventus Tarraconensis*, was less important than TARRAGONA throughout the Roman and Visigothic periods. Its port was used for the export of wine and the city was also celebrated for the quality of its *garum*, the Roman fish sauce, by the late 4th-cent. poet Ausonius. The Visigothic king Ataulf was murdered here in 416, as was one of his successors, Amalaric, in 531. After the Arab conquest Barcelona became the principal garrison town in the region, before being captured by the future emperor Louis the Pious in 801. Under Frankish rule it was the centre of the most important county in the March. Its ruling family, the descendants of Count Wifred the Hairy (d. 897/8) came to dominate the whole of Christian Catalonia, and the marriage of Count Ramón Berenguer IV to the daughter of King Ramiro II (1134–7) led to their acquisition of the crown of Aragón. Barcelona remained the administrative and economic centre of Catalonia throughout the Middle Ages, retaining distinctive legal and political rights within the Aragonese kingdom.

The Roman settlement was roughly oval in shape, enclosing an area of 10.5 hectares, with centrally placed entries on the four main sides. Its southern side lay close to the sea, which was about 200 m. inshore of the site of the present harbour in the first millennium AD. The location of the forum will have been where the principal roads (*Cardo Maximus* and *Decumanus Maximus*) that ran from these gateways intersected. However, continuous occupation of the city and much development of the area from the Middle Ages onwards has prevented substantial excavation of the presumed area of the forum, and thus little is known of its dimensions and components, other than for the probable presence of a temple in the north-east corner. Something of the Roman street plan has been recovered, though it is far from complete or uncontentious.

Some of the **outer walls** remain the most tangible features of the city's Roman past. Although restored and rebuilt at various times, substantial stretches of these may be seen, particularly of the northern and eastern sections. Part of the **northern gateway** stands immediately to the east of the entry to the medieval cathedral (begun 1298). Aqueducts also once approached the city at this point. The dating of the first building of these walls is highly debatable, with proposals ranging from the Republican period to the early 4th cent. AD. The towers certainly seem to be Late Roman in style, and thus most probably 4th-cent.

In the north-east corner of the old city, close to the site of the medieval palace of the kings of Aragón and the Museu d'Historia de la Ciutat, excavation of part of a **Roman residential area** has proved possible. Entry to this is via the museum. Part of a street of 2nd-cent. AD houses, some of which contain large storage jars, may be seen below the present street level. A bust of the Emperor Antoninus Pius (138–61) found in the site is to be seen in the museum. Under the present cathedral has been found part of one of its predecessors: a **basilica**, with attached baptistery probably of the 5th cent. The baptismal font, located inside an octagonal arcade, stood within a rectangular building, abutting directly onto the western end of a triple-aisled basilica. The eastern end of the basilica has not been recovered. On the southern side of the church and baptistery have been found parts of other attached buildings that would once have composed the main ecclesiastical complex in the city. About 100 m. further south is part of a colonnaded building, in whose construction a number of Roman tombstones were reused; this has been described as a *palatium* (palace) of Visigothic date. If so, given the ecclesiastical buildings nearby, this may have been episcopal rather than regal.

The fine, if austere, Romanesque church of **Sant Pau del Camp** (west end of the Carrer de Sant Pau) retains two Visigothic decorated imposts and capitals in its entry portal. The monastery itself was founded by

Count Wifred II (897/8–911), who was buried in it, and the inscription over the portal has been dated to the 10th cent. Located outside the walls of the city, the original buildings were probably destroyed in Al-Manṣūr's sack of Barcelona in 985, and further destruction was wrought by the Almoravids in 1114. Most of the present church and cloister, with its carved capitals, dates from a 12th-cent. rebuilding.

The **Museu Arqueològic** contains substantial collections of materials ranging from the Palaeolithic to the Visigothic period. As well as Greek and Roman finds from AMPURIAS, there are important items from Barcelona itself, notably a series of mosaics and sarcophagi. There are excellent collections of painted Greek vases, primarily imports from southern Italy, Roman glass, inscriptions, and portrait busts. The Visigothic materials, while few in number, are generally of high quality, and include some items from the **Torredonjímeno Treasure** (found in the province of Jaén). That this originally included at least one liturgical crown, of like quality to that of King Reccesuinth in the Guarrazar treasure (see MADRID), is proved by the presence of some pendant letters, but nothing more of this has survived.

From Barcelona local trains can be used to get to the important monastery of **Montserrat**, home of a boys' choir with a very distinctive tradition of singing, whose origins go back to the 13th cent., and to **San Cugat des Vallès** and **Tarrasa**.

Bilbilis—Cerro de la Bambola   Roman town

*From **Calatayud** take the N 234 northwards in the direction of **Soria**. After less than 2 km. it turns sharply to the north-west. At this point a small road leads directly to the site, about 3 km. further on.*

Of the substantial Roman town, birthplace of the poet Martial (*c*. AD 40–104), relatively little remains. The main interest lies in the temple complex around the hill of Santa Bárbara, which dominates the site. An earlier Celtiberian settlement, which had been faithful to Rome in the Sertorian Wars and had supported the Caesaran party in the Civil Wars, was turned into a *municipium* in the reign of Augustus and lavishly endowed. Following inadequate excavations earlier in the century, new campaigns of digging were carried out in 1971, 1975, and 1980 on the temple sector, which have made possible an understanding of its original form. The **temple** itself, on an elevated platform, was dedicated to the imperial cult, and is testimony to the special favour with which the town was regarded and the patronage extended to make its physical appearance match its new enhanced status. In front and on either side of the temple platform an artificially flattened terrace was created. The western extension seems to have been in the form of a portico, terminating in a fountain, possibly the site of a *nymphaeum*. On the eastern side of the temple there was a paved ramp, providing access to the terrace. Below this, and running alongside the eastern edge of the terrace, was another open portico. On the level of the terrace itself a similar portico ran across the full width of the southern end, facing the steps up to the temple platform and the entry to the temple itself. This was entered at both its eastern and western ends by staircases leading up from the lower level. Beneath this southern portico have been found traces of a barrel-vaulted underground passage or a *cryptoporticus*, which may have served as a storage area for the temple. The western edge of the terrace seems to have remained open. Of the temple itself only slight evidence of its foundations may now be seen. A bust, probably of the Emperor Claudius, was found in the vicinity of the temple in 1664, and is now in the Museo Arqueológico in Zaragoza. The 1980 excavation uncovered part of a dedicatory inscription to Tiberius, dated to AD 28, which would have accompanied a statue of this emperor. The later history of Bilbilis is obscure. It was not the site of a bishopric in the Late Imperial or Visigothic periods, nor of a mint. Its close proximity to **Calatayud** ('The Fortress of Ayub'), said by Arab sources to have been founded in the 8th cent., might suggest that a settlement of some sort had continued to exist at Bilbilis until that time.

Bobastro Mozarabic church

(Visit together with ANTEQUERA)

From ANTEQUERA take the C 337 SW for 37 km. to the turn (to the right) to Alora. Take this and continue for about 15 km. towards El Chorro. At the dam at the entry to the Desfiladero de los Gaitanes take the road left and ascend the mountain. There are signs but not at the site itself!

Whether this site really is the Bobastro of the Arabic sources is open to question, although the identification is now widely accepted. There is a danger that separate historical and archaeological evidence is being forced to conform in a single context, which only succeeds in distorting both. The Bobastro of the literary sources was the principal base of the rebel leader 'Umar ibn Hafṣūn, who made himself ruler of much of southern Al-Andalus up to his death in 918. His sons were unable to maintain his power and Bobastro fell to 'Abd al-Raḥmān III in 928 (Ibn Hayyan V. xxiv). Textual references would seem to locate this fortress further to the south-east of this site. The identification has been made largely thanks to the presence of a church, which being partly cut out of the rock has survived at least half intact. Ibn Ḥayyan records that a church was found in the fortress when Bobastro fell, proof than Ibn Hafṣūn and his family, who were originally Muslims, had apostatized from Islam. However, the church and the small fort on this site are quite distinct, and it is unlikely that the latter would have proved the unassailable redoubt that the literary texts make of Ibn Hafṣūn's headquarters. It is more probable that the church belonged to one of the numerous rural Christian communities

Ibn Hayyan

Ibn Hayyan (987–1076) is the author of the most substantial surviving narrative history of the Umayyad period, including important sections from the otherwise lost works of earlier Arab historians. Only parts of this work, the *Muqtabis*, survive, relating principally to the years 912–42 and 970–4.

that survived in Al-Andalus, at least until the depopulation undertaken by the Almoravids in 1126.

On the summit of the mountain (be wary: the road ends abruptly at the edge of a precipice!) may be seen traces of the foundations of a small stone-built fort, located on the highest point, about 50 m. from the road. The views are spectacular, but little else may be seen.

About 1 km. back down the road, on the left while ascending, a path leads up the face of a large rock (unsignposted). Follow this and after about 200 m. a wall crosses the path; there are also traces of building. Follow the path that leads downwards, directly to the site. Although in theory fenced in, the gate had been destroyed when last seen. (Warning: there is an open well head in the middle of the site, flush with the surface level, with the possibility of a precipitate and fatal drop into a cavern below.) A square of low walls may mark the site of a tower or building, but the main interest lies in the church. Most of its southern side was carved directly from the bedrock and has survived, including some arcades of the nave. Most of the northern side will have been built up of stones, which have long since been removed. To judge by the style of the arcading, the church should date from the 9th or 10th cents. Beneath the church is a cave. If in the Visigothic period this had been used by a hermit of renowned sanctity, the existence of a local cult could explain why a church was

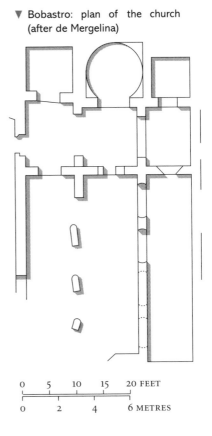

▼ Bobastro: plan of the church (after de Mergelina)

0   5   10   15   20 FEET

0   2   4   6 METRES

built on the site at a later period. Such a process can be documented in the case of the Visigothic hermit-saint Aemilianus and the medieval monastery of **San Millán de la Cogolla** (*18 km. south-west of Nájera in La Rioja*). The elimination of the Christian presence in Al-Andalus also served to obliterate any such local saints' cults in the region.

Bonete   Mesolithic, Iberian, and Arab site

The village of Bonete is located just south of the N 430, 49 km. east of Albacete. The site itself is on top of a hill (visible from the N 430) 1 km. west of the road linking Bonete to Montealegre del Castillo.

The village was located on the flat top of the hill, which covers an area of 977 × 53 m. Little is to be seen although structural traces, in the form of foundations of houses, were found in the south-eastern sector. These have been identified as probably belonging to the Iberian settlement called Ello. It was probably destroyed in the period of conflicts with Rome in the first half of the second cent. BC. A previous, Late Bronze Age, occupation of the site, dating to around 800 BC, was established from pottery finds.

*Montealegre del Castillo, 10.5 km. south of Bonete, is notable for the Iberian site of **Cerro de los Santos** (see Madrid: Museo Arqueológico Nacional).*

Above the village of Montealegre del Castillo (*10.5 km. south of Bonete*) stands a ruined castle of Arab origin, with a cistern. Destruction of the castle is said to have occurred in the civil war between Pedro I the Cruel (1350–69) of Castile and his half-brother Enrique II de Trastámara (1369–79).

*On the N 430 11 km. west of Bonete, the AB 860 leads 10 km. to **Alpera** (where the key can be obtained at Calle de Seda, 1). 1 km. north of Alpera, turn right onto the AB 871, and just under 2 km. further on a small road to the left leads another 3 km. to the site (which is signposted) of **Cueva de la Vieja**.*

Here there are Mesolithic rock paintings of human figures and animals, dating from *c.*8000 BC onwards.

*Continue on the N 430 23 km. west of Bonete and then just south of the road to **Almansa**.*

Here is a castle of Arab origin, later belonging to the Templars and substantially rebuilt in the 15th cent. Now horribly over-restored, it does at least house a small *parador*.

Botorrita   Roman town

*Head south from ZARAGOZA on the N 330 for 21 km. before turning left onto the A 2101. Botorrita is 1 km. down the road, while the Roman site is about 2 km. north-east, and is approached via a track to the left just over the **Río Huerva** and immediately before the entry into the modern town. As the site is fenced, it is necessary to obtain the key from the Ayuntamiento in Botorrita.*

Not much is known of the history of the Celtiberian settlement here. As part of the war against Viriathus and his allies, Quintus Caecilius Metellus captured it in 143 BC; though many of the inhabitants had already fled to refuge in NUMANTIA and TIERMES. A new building programme in Roman style clearly took place here in the 1st cent. BC, but nothing is known of the town under the Empire.

Little remains of the Celtiberian and Roman settlement of **Contrebia Belaisca**. The main visible structure is part of a large building made of mud brick, divided into a series of small chambers, some of whose walls still stand to a height of over 2 m. The building was originally fronted with a marble colonnade, now collapsed. Several of the drums of the columns may be seen, as well as some of the capitals. The style of the latter has enabled the construction to be dated to the Late Republican period, but the purpose of the building is not know.

The most significant find made on this site is that of a bronze inscription, known as the *Tabula Contrebiensis*, recording the intervention made in 87 BC by Valerius Flaccus, governor of the province of Hispania Citerior, in a dispute over the construction of a watercourse, involving the Celtiberian tribes of the Salluienses, the Sosinestani, and the Allavonenses. The matter was to be adjudicated by the senate (i.e. the town council) of Contrebia.

Bruñel Roman villa

*Turn south off the N 322 (Albacete to Bailén) at **Torreperogil**, 10 km. east of **Ubeda** (Museo Arqueológico in the Calle Cervantes), and proceed down the J 314 (which becomes the C 323 at Peal de Becerro) towards **Quesada**; 7 km. south of Peal de Becerro turn left at a signpost to the site, which is a further 4 km. on. A sign near the villa gives instructions for obtaining the key at a local farm.*

The Roman villa at Pago de Bruñel, excavated in the 1960s, is a good example of the lavish rural villas that were built in various parts of Spain in the 4th century. Here, an already substantial courtyard villa of that period was rebuilt in even grander style later in the same century. A 50 m.-long **hall** with apsed ends was constructed over the southern half of the earlier **atrium**, with a new peristyled **court** (34 x 23 m.) being built to the south of it, from which opened a series of rooms of larger proportions than those of the earlier villa (some of the foundations of which can be seen to the north of the later hall).

Particularly notable are the fine **mosaics** preserved in several of the rooms of the later villa.

*The C 328 leads 14 km. east from Peal de Becerro to **Cazorla**. Here and at the neighbouring village of **La Iruela** (1 km. north-east) may be seen two powerfully sited castles of 12th-cent. origin with later rebuilding and restoration. In 1179 the Treaty of Cazorla prevented further Aragonese expansion into Andalucia, leaving Castille a free hand in that direction.*

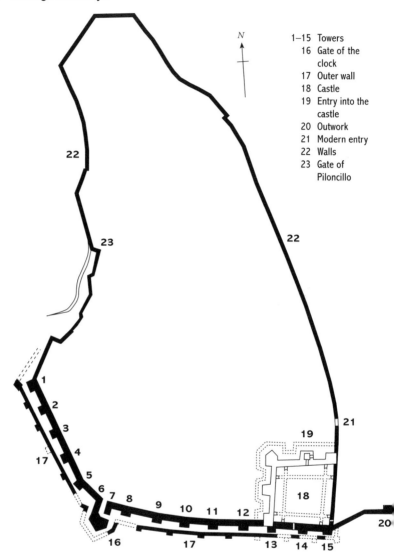

N

1–15 Towers
  16 Gate of the
      clock
  17 Outer wall
  18 Castle
  19 Entry into the
      castle
  20 Outwork
  21 Modern entry
  22 Walls
  23 Gate of
      Piloncillo

▲ Buitrago de Lozoya (after Laina and Terrasse)

Buitrago de Lozoya   Arab fortress town

On the N 1, 66 km. north of MADRID.

Together with TALAMANCA DEL JARAMA, Buitrago was constructed in the Umayyad period as a fortress protecting the route northwards from TOLEDO to the Pass of Somosierra. Although there are no earlier literary references to it, its role is clear from its capture by Alfonso VI in 1085 as the prelude to his taking of Toledo, and from the survival of elements of Arab construction in its extant medieval defences. The town was given a new Christian population in 1169, and became a property of the church of Toledo.

The **curtain wall** is roughly triangular, with its southern stretch forming the hypotenuse. This was the most vulnerable part of the enceinte, and in consequence the most heavily defended, with a lower outer wall paralleling the main one, which here included fifteen towers. A late 13th- or early 14th-cent. **castle** was added in the south-west corner, incorporating part of the town wall. It was modified to make a more palatial residence in the 15th cent., when in the ownership of the Marqués de Santillana. Of the towers of the southern wall, the five to the east of the main gate are partly constructed in *tabiya* and almost certainly date from the period of Arab rule. The towers to the west of the **Puerta del Reloj** has been dated to the late 11th or early 12th cent. Both sets of towers have been subject to subsequent restorations and repairs, up to the present. The Puerta del Reloj itself was originally a simple gate set between two rectangular flanking towers, but the addition of a pentagonal outer section attached to the eastern one gave it a new, more complex, right-angled approach. This modification, together with the construction of the whole outer wall, has been dated to the 12th or 13th cent.

Bujarrabal   Arab tower

*Take the C 114 eastwards from **Sigüenza** (12th-cent. cathedral and 14th-cent. episcopal castle with few traces of earlier phases, now restored as a* Parador*). After 22 km. take the turning to the left on to a minor road, signposted to Bujarrabal. The tower lies about 100 m. north of the church on the edge of the village, beside the fields.*

Only parts of three of the walls of this squat rectangular tower still stand. It was identified on the basis of its method of construction, and represents a good example of an Arab *burj* (hence the Buj- in the toponym) or local defence tower, put up by the Umayyads in the 10th cent. as a refuge for the population.

*Continue on the same road, which leaves the village in a westerly direction, heading back to Sigüenza; 6 km. on lies the village and castle of **Guijosa**. Fragments of an earlier partly Arab castle are located 2 km. north on a hill called 'Castilviejo' (Old Castle).*

Guijosa castle itself, to the west of the village, is a small noble stronghold mainly of the late 14th cent. It is 365 m. square, originally with a tower in each corner. Two and a half of these still stand, as does much of the rectangular keep (probably datable to the mid-14th cent.) in the centre of the courtyard. This has fortified balconies on each side at the second-floor level, and the original entrance lies on the first floor with a cistern or storeroom below. The arms of Don Iñigo de Orozco may be seen over the entry in the outer wall.

Cabezo de Alcalá (Azaila) Celtiberian town

On the N 232 from ZARAGOZA to Castellón 58 km. from Zaragoza and 1 km. after passing the village of Azaila, a turning to the right (west) leads directly to the foot of the hill, about 1.5 km. further. The hilltop site dominates the lower valley of the Río Aguas Vivas.

Study of this site began in 1868–72, with important excavations being undertaken at various points from 1919 to the 1960s. As a result virtually the whole of the hilltop has been excavated. The interpretation of the history of the site, based on the material finds, has been controversial. Juan Cabré suggested in 1943 there was a pre-Celtiberian phase of occupation, followed by two periods of Celtiberian settlement, the second and last of which ended *c.*27 BC. A. Beltrán postulated in 1964 the existence of three chronologically distinct phases of Celtiberian occupation, the first extending from *c.*500 BC to the Second Punic War, followed by a reconstruction *c.*195 BC which lasted until a second destruction at the end of the Sertorian Wars (in the 70s BC), and a final short stage ending with the third destruction of the town in the aftermath of the battle of Ilerda (LÉRIDA) in 49 BC. In 1984 M. Beltrán, revising earlier opinions of his own, argued for no more than two phases of occupation: one by a pre-Celtiberian population in the Early Iron Age (*c.*700 BC), and secondly a

▼ Cabezo de Alcalá: the largest of the houses (after M. Beltrán)

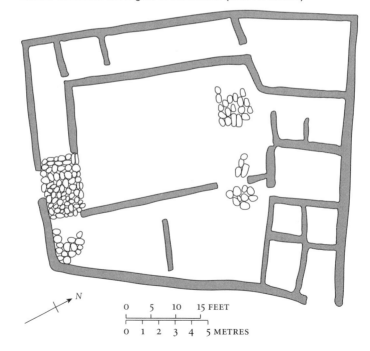

N

0   5   10   15 FEET

0   1   2   3   4   5 METRES

Celtiberian phase that came to an end with the destruction of the settlement in the Sertorian Wars. This represents current orthodoxy. The main significance of this site is the evidence it provides of how Roman ideas of town planning and domestic architecture were starting to influence Celtiberian settlements such as this one in the Late Republican period.

There are two distinct sections: a **lower settlement** to the east, located down on the plain, and an **acropolis** on the hill, which has been the primary focus of archaeological interest. The town fell to Roman attack, probably around 72 BC, and part of an assault ramp (75 × 26 m., rising to a height of 4 m.) built by the besiegers up the side of the hill is visible on the south-east side. This was identified as such by M. Beltrán in 1984; previously it had been classified as a gigantic Celtiberian tomb. Much of the upper part of the town remains visible, with walls standing in parts up to 2 m. high. In the **lower town** a stone street with domestic houses on either side can be seen close to the assault ramp. An unusual element, indicative of strong Roman cultural influence, is the seven-roomed bath house (only limited traces of this are visible) at the foot of the hill of the acropolis on the north-east and close to the principal northern entry to the town. These baths, which include a large circular room for a bath-tub, have been dated to the late 2nd cent. BC, and are thought to be located in the commercial sector of the town. The large quantity of loom weights (about 400) recovered from the site also indicate the presence of a considerable weaving industry in the town.

The acropolis covers an area of about 246 × 132 m., and served as residence for the more important families, religious centre, and fortress. The western side, which is irregularly shaped, falls away precipitately. The eastern side was defended by a ditch (c.6 m. deep and 4 to 11 m. wide) around the base of the hill, and access to the top was gained via a series of ramps on this side. On the inner side of the ditch was a wall, and another ran around the edge of the acropolis on the brow of the hill. Both walls were about 80 cm. thick, and in general the defences do not appear very strong. On top the street pattern can easily be made out. Up here the houses are larger and more spacious than in the lower town, and there are a number of public buildings, including a temple located at the crossroads of the two major streets, with its façade facing the principal entry to the acropolis from the south-east. The vestibule or *pronaos* (1.20 × 3.56 m.) is floored in *opus signinum*, as is the first section of the interior. Here was found a stone altar. The inner section is raised on sandstone blocks 80 cm. above the lower, to provide a platform for the display of bronze statues of the gods. The walls of the whole of this inner chamber (6.5 × 4 m.) were painted in stucco, of which traces were found. The remains of a catapult, of the type called *scorpio* ('scorpion'), were found in the ruins of the temple, and another was found in one of the houses. Of the houses, the largest (290 sq. m.) was located in the very centre of the acropolis. It has a single entry, with a central courtyard, around which are disposed a series of irregularly shaped rooms, of very unequal size. Smaller houses (as little as 45 sq. m.) were much simpler, with entry off the street into a narrow court around which on the ground floor might be no more than three rooms, including a kitchen.

To the south-east of the acropolis, between it and the road, may be seen the Celtiberian necropolis, marked by a number of stone-built round burial chambers. An earlier Iron Age necropolis of the preceding Celtic phase of occupation of the site is located south-east of the Celtiberian one, and is bisected by the road.

Ceramic finds from the site, including imported Campanian wares, may be seen in the Museo de Zaragoza (Plaza los Sitios, 6).

Castillejo de la Romana, 7 km. due east of Cabezo de Alcalá, is another Iberian town site on a flat-topped hill (209 m. high). About 1.5 km. north of Azaila a small road runs east from the N 232 towards the village of La Zaida, passing the foot of this hill after about 8 km.

The site was excavated in 1975, and a settlement was found, dating from the 3rd to 1st cent. BC and consisting of a central street with houses on both sides. Burials of four children were discovered under one of the dwellings. In general the site had suffered extensively from erosion and agricultural use.

Cáceres   Roman, Arab, and medieval town   ★

A Celtiberian settlement on this site was taken over by Rome in 54 BC. Although it has long been assumed that the ensuing Roman settlement was founded by Julius Caesar, it now seems more probable that it was the work of C. Norbanus Flaccus, proconsul in Spain *c.*34 BC, from whom the new town took its name. Of Roman *Colonia Norba Caesarina* the most tangible remains are parts of the defensive walls around the old town. In particular the gate in the south wall, the Puerta del Cristo, may be of late Republican construction. Little is known of the history of the settlement, and its almost continuous occupation has limited the amount that may be recovered by excavation. The six square or rectangular towers that are built out from but are connected to the north wall have been attributed to an Almohad refortification of the town, possibly around 1180. These are classic examples of *torres albarranas*. Construction in *tabiya* or rammed earth distinguishes these and a few other towers in the enceinte from those that were built in stone after the Leonese conquest of the town in 1239. The complex building history and the reuse of earlier elements, especially well-shaped Roman stones, makes it difficult to disentangle the construction history of the various sectors of the walls.

In November 1165 the town was taken by a Portuguese adventurer called Geraldo the Fearless, who created a virtually independent principality for himself in Extremadura, but was forcibly dispossessed by

Fernando II (1157–88) of León in 1169. With King Fernando's encouragement, the military Order of Santiago was founded here on 1 August 1170 to defend the town against an expected Almohad attack. It received its distinctive name as one element in an agreement, made in 1171 with Archbishop Pedro of Santiago, that it would also defend his church's town of Albuquerque, in return for a banner of St James and the rents from various properties. However, the Almohad ruler Abu-Ya'qūb Yūsuf I retook Cáceres in 1174. Fernando II nearly regained Cáceres in a siege in 1184. The town eventually fell to Alfonso IX of León on 23 April 1229.

The archaeological sections of the **Museo de Cáceres** (Plaza de las Veletas) are located in a 17th-cent. noble's house, the Casa de Ovanda-Mogollón, which also contains a fine *aljibe* or cistern of the Almohad period. It is thought that this once formed part of the Almohad citadel or *Alcazaba*. Amongst the archaeological collections may be seen the foundation inscription of the Visigothic basilica of **Ibahernando** (see MONTÁNCHEZ for the site). There are also various Roman inscriptions, including a milestone of the Caesar Constantius I (296–305), and pottery of various periods. Opposite the museum is the **Palacio de las Cigüeñas**, with a fortified tower dating to 1477. Amongst the many other fine examples of late medieval and 16th–17th-cent. noble residences is the **Palacio de Toledo-Moctezuma** (in the north-east corner of the walled town), once owned by descendants of the Aztec king Moteuczoma II (1503–20), better known as Montezuma, and the **Casa de Ulloa**, which houses a *Parador*.

About 3.5 km. north from Cáceres on the C 524 to Plasencia via Torrejón el Rubio, the road passes the site of 'Cáceres el Viejo' on the left.

This was a Roman legionary camp, probably destroyed by Sertorius early in his revolt (*c*.78 BC). It was excavated, but the site is on private land and was covered over again following the dig. Items found may be seen in the Museo de Cáceres (see above).

Calatalifa   Arab fortress and deserted medieval village

*Located on private land within the boundaries of **Villaviciosa de Odón**, on the left bank of the Río Guadarrama. Villaviciosa is approached on the M 501, which runs west from the N V/E 90 15 km. from the centre of MADRID.*

> In Villaviciosa is a castle built in 1582, to which Fernando VI retired after the death of his wife in 1758 and where he himself died in 1759. It now houses the airforce archives.

This **fortress** was located on two major lines of communication in the Umayyad period: one that ran down the valley of the Río Guadarrama from the passes of Fonfría and Balatomé in the Sierra de Guadarrama

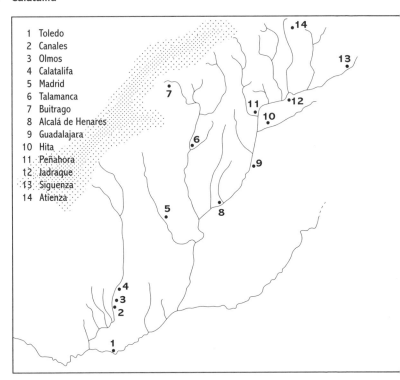

1 Toledo
2 Canales
3 Olmos
4 Calatalifa
5 Madrid
6 Talamanca
7 Buitrago
8 Alcalá de Henares
9 Guadalajara
10 Hita
11 Peñahora
12 Jadraque
13 Sigüenza
14 Atienza

▲ Arab fortresses between Toledo and the Sierra Guadarrama (after Rubio Visiers and Paloma López del Álamo)

towards Toledo, and the other that went from Talavera eastwards towards the valley of the Jalón and the route to the Ebro (see MEDINACELLI). The name derives from Arabic *Qalat Khalīfa* ('fortress of the Caliph'), which seems to indicate a foundation in the time of ʿAbd al-Raḥmān III (912–61), the first Umayyad Caliph. However, the fortress clearly was in existence by 939, when ʿAbd al-Raḥmān witnessed an eclipse of the sun here on his way to the campaign that ended in the battle of Simancas (Ibn Hayyan). Following that defeat he is recorded as refortifying the site in 940. It probably fell into the hands of Alfonso VI around 1083–5, but there are few references to it until 1118, when it is recorded as belonging to the church of Toledo. It was given to the *Concejo* or town council of Segovia in 1161. An attempt to repopulate it was made in 1270. The last recorded reference to it is dated 1404.

The **medieval village** (approx. 4 ha.) was established on a small plateau in a naturally defensible site, with ravines on the north and south and the Río Guadarrama on its western side. Excavations have revealed two walls, using different types of construction, and the base of a tower on the vulnerable eastern side. All that remains visible of the fortress now are two *aljibes* or cisterns. One of these, the larger one situated on the side of the hill by a watercourse, consists of two chambers separated by an arch. This cistern, like the smaller rectangular one in the middle of the site, is constructed of reddish brick. About 90 per cent of the pottery finds from the site belong to the period of Islamic occupation. Two of the four groups of these Islamic ceramics have been dated to the 9th and early 10th cents, indicating a pre-Caliphal origin for the site. Like OLMOS and MADRID, it may well owe its creation to Muḥammad I (852–86). These excavations have also probably disposed of earlier arguments that sought to locate the site of Calatalifa around the 13th- to 16th-cent. castle of **Batres** in the province of Toledo.

Calatrava la Nueva Castle   ★

Take the CR 512 south from Ciudad Real for 40 km. before turning right onto the CR 504. Just over 6 km. down this road, a turn to the right leads up to the castle. This road was partly created to facilitate the visit to the castle by Felipe II (1556–98) in 1560.

Following the battle of Alarcos in 1195, the Order of Calatrava lost their original headquarters, the fortress town of CALATRAVA LA VIEJA (see this entry for earlier history of the Order). The knights re-established themselves first in the castle of Ciruelos and then in 1198 in that of Salvatierra (see below), but lost the latter to the Almohads in 1210. They then moved to the castle of **Zorita** (see RECCOPOLIS). However, following the Castilian victory at **Las Navas de Tolosa** in 1212 and the definitive abandonment of Calatrava la Vieja in 1216, the newly constructed fortress that came to be called Calatrava la Nueva was made the centre of the Order. As the Order was founded by Raimundo, abbot of the Cistercian house of Fitero, it combined monastic and military practices perhaps more closely than any other. Thus a castle such as Calatrava physically combined the components of fortress and monastery in a unique way, as can still be seen from the ruins.

On an imposing site, this powerful and well-preserved **castle** dates primarily from two periods: the 13th and 15th cents. There is a double enceinte, with a third wall on the eastern side. Within the inner curtain wall are a number of different structures. There is a massive fortress or keep that is the most imposing feature of the entire complex. Nestling below it on the northern side is the church, on the eastern side the monastic buildings, and on the western side the *Campo de los Martires* ('Field of the Martyrs'). This was the cemetery of the Order, and it took its name from the presence of relics of those brothers of the Order who had been massacred at Calatrava la Vieja when it fell to the Almohads in 1195. On the instruction of the eighth Master, Martín Fernández de Quintana, their remains were transferred, together with those of the seven earlier Masters

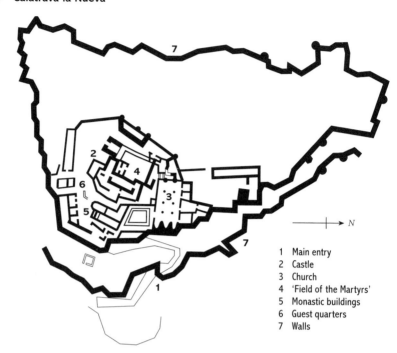

1 Main entry
2 Castle
3 Church
4 'Field of the Martyrs'
5 Monastic buildings
6 Guest quarters
7 Walls

▲ Calatrava la Nueva

of the Order, to this location in 1217. To the south, across the courtyard, are the remains of the guest quarters and other domestic buildings.

The **church** (with restored roof), whose west front presents a partly fortified appearance, was built in the early 13th cent. and is typical of Cistercian architectural austerity, but it had a large rose window inserted over the west door in the reign of Fernando and Isabel of Aragón/Castile (1474–1504), when much rebuilding took place in the castle. There is a three-aisled nave, terminating in an apsed chancel, with parallel chapels on either side. On the north side of the nave are a series of irregular shaped funerary chapels built by various Masters. On the south side a door communicates with the now much ruined **cloister**, which, from the evidence of a shield bearing the arms of the last Master, must have been rebuilt in the late 15th cent. To the south of the cloister was the kitchen and parallel to it the refectory (dining hall), which was also restored in the late 15th cent. East of the cloister was the great trapezoidal '**Torre de Vela**', which served as the bell tower of the monastery-fortress. In the lower level a chamber served as the **Chapter House** of the Order, where the knights met under the presidency of the Master. Above this was the **Library**. Off the south-eastern corner of the cloister, and adjacent to the refectory, was the courtyard of the **Parlour**. This latter building (between the courtyard and the outer wall), which combined a south-facing view and stone benches along the walls, was the only place outside the chapter house where the members of the Order could speak, and even this privilege was not gained until four years after their admission. South of the Parlour is the much ruined site of the **dormitories**, in which the knights slept.

As the **keep** is founded on a rocky emplacement in the centre of the inner bailey and stands higher than the surrounding buildings, it is entered via a stairway leading up to its ground floor. Here there is a lower hall opening onto the central courtyard. The quarters of the Master and the main hall of the keep were on the next floor up, approached by a stair from the central courtyard. On the level above this there was once the archive, in a room built entirely without use of wood, against the danger of fire. A cistern below the Master's bed-chamber provided the keep with an independent supply of water.

A programme of restoration of the castle commenced in October 1991; this may not be good news, as in practice *restauración* can mean 'make it look as if it were only built yesterday'!

On the other side of the CR 504, about 1 km. due east of Calatrava la Nueva, and before the turning for the castle, you will pass the ruins of the slightly earlier Castillo de Salvatierra.

This was given to the Order in the late 12th cent. There are also traces of earlier fortification, of possibly Roman date.

Calatrava la Vieja   Arab town and Christian fortress   ★

*Head east from **Ciudad Real** (there is a fine Mudéjar gate of 1328 on the north side) on the N 430 for 9 km. to Carrión de Calatrava, where a minor road heads northwards. On this take the right-hand fork about 1 km. north of Carrión, leading to La Encarnación. A track leads on from the village to the castle, about 500 m. to the west.*

Situated on a small plateau, bounded on the north by the Río Guadiana, this site has several natural defensive features. An Iberian settlement here represents the earliest occupation so far known. No reports have been made of subsequent Roman or Visigothic phases, though these may yet be found. Located on the main route between CÓRDOBA and TOLEDO, an Arab town was in existence here by 785, which was destroyed in the course of an uprising in Toledo in 852. It was refounded by Muḥammad I the following year. Under the Almoravids it became one of their principal fortresses, threatening the Castilian hold on Toledo. In 1147, with the support of Ibn Ḥamdin, a local ruler in Córdoba who opposed the Almohads, Alfonso VII of Castile (1126–57) took Calatrava. Charters he issued show that the Castilian ruler tried to repopulate the town with Christians. He entrusted it to the Templars, but they eventually felt they could not hold it against an expected Almohad attack and returned it to King Sancho III (1157–8). Raimundo, Cistercian abbot of Fitero, offered to hold it for the king, and developed a new military order, that of

▲ Calatrava la Vieja: castle of the Order of Calatrava

Calatrava, to hold the fortress. The rule of the Order, which was spiritually subject to the monastic Order of the Cistercians, was approved by Pope Alexander III in 1164. The Almohads took the town in 1195 after their victory over the Castilians at the battle of Alarcos. In 1212 it fell to Alfonso VIII of Castile and Pedro II of Aragón, following the battle of Las Navas de Tolosa. However, the headquarters of the Order had by now moved further south (see CALATRAVA LA NUEVA), and the fortress and town of Calatrava la Vieja were definitively abandoned in 1216. Various excavations have been conducted here since 1984, though to judge by the little so far published, attention has concentrated primarily on aspects of the outer defences. The area within the walls may prove to be one of the most interesting early Islamic town sites in Spain.

The town was defended by a single wall containing forty-two towers and a barbican across the ditch on the south side. Some of the latter has been exposed by excavation but little of the wall, other than for a short sector on the south side, remains. It seems probable that the masonry was deliberately removed, possibly to provide for the fortifications of Ciudad Real, which was founded by Alfonso X of Castile in 1252. It has been suggested that the flow of the Río Guadiana was regulated so as to surround the town with water. Part of this hydraulic system can be seen in the form of a dam extending northwards from the north-west sector of the town wall to the Río Guadiana. This incorporated four defensive towers, the most northerly of which has been dated to the 10th cent., by comparison of its structure with that of other similar constructions. A shorter, less well preserved dam has been found reaching to the river from a tower in the north wall of the *Alcazaba*. The *Alcazaba* was located at the eastern end, and is the most substantial feature of the site to be seen today. It was refortified in the Almohad period and by the Order of Calatrava. A double wall with two centrally placed towers flanking a gate divide it from the town. A large pointed quadrilateral tower on the east end (flanked by a smaller equivalent to the north) is reminiscent of that to be seen in the castle of **Zorita** (see RECCOPOLIS), and probably dates from the Almohad occupation of 1195–1212. There are two *torres albarranas* on the southern side. Although there is some argument about the chronology of the development of these distinctive forms of tower, they seem to belong to a late stage in the fortification and may date from the 12th or 13th cent. Within the *Alcazaba*, the main structural survival is part of the church, rebuilt after 1212.

> Archaeological materials from various sites in the province may (in theory at least) be seen in the Museo de Ciudad Real (Calle Prado, 4) in Ciudad Real, which also has a cathedral (1490–1528).

Cancho Roano   Roman town and Iberian palace

In the village of Zalamea de la Serena (Bádajoz). On the C 413 heading south-west from Castuera in the direction of Llerena, after 13 km. a small road leads due south 2 km. to Zalamea. Alternatively, from MEDELLÍN *go 9.5 km. east to Don Benito, and then continue 43 km. to the south on the BA 624 (which turns into the BA 632 at Quintana de Serena).*

Of the Roman town of Iulipa the principal trace is a tall thin mausoleum that dominates the Plaza Mayor. One and a half Roman columns, with a Corinthian capital, have been reconstructed rather picaresquely on top of it. The church contains reused Roman columns, probably from a small temple, and there are remains of a castle of Arab origin, captured in the 13th cent. by Pedro Yañez, Master of the Order of Alcántara. However, the most significant discovery made here in the course of extensive excavations in the 1980s was that of a unique Iberian construction that has been variously interpreted as being a palace, a temple, or a factory. No agreement has yet been reached on its identification. It has been dated to the 6th cent. BC, and is centrally located within the traces of the settlement, with a necropolis to the north-east. The building was found to be roughly square and surrounded by a terrace 2 m. wide and about 2.5 m. high. Access was gained from the east side, where a lower patio broke the otherwise square layout of terrace and building. Entry was via the wing of the building to the north and thence along a corridor that ran the whole length of the eastern side. Off this lay groupings of rooms. If the identification of the site as a palace be accepted, analysis of the location of finds has suggested that the four chambers in the north-west were the living

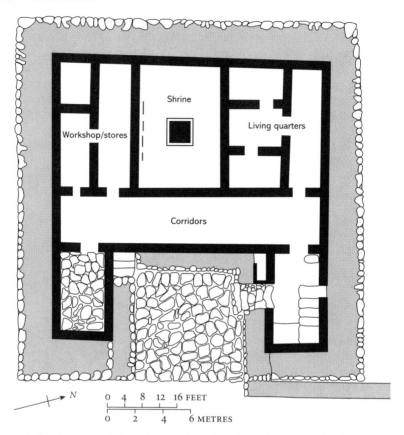

▲ Cancho Roano: 6th-cent. BC Iberian palace (after Almagro-Gorbea/ Domínguez/López-*Ambite*)

quarters of the ruling family. A large central hall of 10 × 7.5 m. is taken to be a throne room or a sanctuary. The three rooms to the south-west were probably storerooms or workshops. The nearest parallels with this building are Near Eastern. It appears to have been destroyed by fire in the late 5th cent. BC. From this last period in the history of the site dates a fine bronze figure of a horse.

Caparra   Roman town

*Heading southwards on the E 803/N 630 from **Salamanca** to CÁCERES 16 km. north of Plasencia (and 40 km. south of Béjar) a small road leads west for about 10 km. to the ruins of the town. A more adventurous approach could be essayed by leaving the E 803/N 630 about 25 km. south of Béjar, taking the road that leads westwards for 5 km. to **Abadía**, which contains a fortress once belonging to the Order of the Temple, and which was subsequently turned into a Cistercian* *monastery. There is a fine (restored) 13th-cent. cloister of horseshoe arches. Two alternative roads lead on to the village of Zarza de Granadilla, whence it is possible to follow a track to the fortified but now deserted medieval village and castle of* **Granadilla***. The un-towered walls are of Arab origin, but the castle is late 14th-cent. From Zarza a road leads south-west towards the village of Guijo de Granadilla. About 10 km. along this road a left turn will lead 5 km. to Caparra.*

The Roman town of Caprera was one of a number of settlements along the Camino de la Plata that led from Hispalis (SEVILLE) and Emerita (MÉRIDA) northwards via Salmantica (Salamanca) to the silver mines in the Asturias. Some of the road itself can be seen on the hillside and on the bridge over the Río Hervas near Baños de Montemayor (14 km. south of Béjar on the E 803/N 630).

The entire line of the walls of the town has been established, and substantial sections remain visible. Within the site the most significant remains are those of a temple, which from an inscription on a statue found within it was probably dedicated to Jupiter, and of a large four-sided arch that gave access to the forum. Of the temple little more than the lowest levels remain, but, other than for the decoration of its upper section, the whole of the unusual arch, including its vaulting, has been preserved. An extant inscription shows that it was erected, probably in the 2nd cent. AD, by a local citizen called Marcus Fidius Macer. Part of a wall adjacent to the arch and forming part of the periphery of the forum still stands to a considerable height. The foundations of a rectangular building between the arch and the temple of Jupiter probably belonged to another temple, dated to the 1st cent. AD, though with no indications of its dedication. There are traces of a large circular building outside the walls to the south, which could have formed part of a largely wooden amphitheatre. There is also a small but well-preserved Roman bridge over the Río Ambroz on the northern side of the town, about 100 m. from the line of the walls.

Finds from the site have included various inscriptions (some now in the palace of the Duque de Arión in Plasencia), a milestone of the Emperor Nero (54–68), a fine bust of the Emperor Antoninus Pius (138–61), and other sculptures. Another milestone, of the Emperor Severus Alexander (222–35), was clearly defaced as part of the official *damnatio memoriae* that took place under his successor Maximinus I; this involved the destruction of statues and the obliteration of the emperor's name on all official inscriptions. An inscription (on the base of a lost statue) erected to the Caesar, or junior emperor, Decentius (350–3) is the best evidence so far of the continued existence of the town in the late imperial period.

About 5 km. due south of Caparra, an altar stone (76 × 73 cm.), probably Visigothic, has been found in the village of **Oliva de Plasencia** (*next turning to the south off the E 803/N 630—about 15 km. by road*); it is kept in the presbytery. A milestone of Trajan (98–117) and other Roman inscribed stones are also to be seen reused in the village.

Carmona   Roman and Arab town

Bypassed by the N IV/E 5 38 km. east of SEVILLE.

The earliest archaeological evidence relating to this site is a late Neolithic dolmen found buried early this century in the area of the Plazas de San Fernando and del Mercado. It had a roughly circular central chamber (3.5 m. in diameter) and a corridor 17 m. long, partly cut into by the construction of one of the walls of the *Ayuntamiento*. Small finds of ceramics have established Bronze Age occupation of the area, and by the later Iron Age this was a Tartessian settlement, which had been subjugated by the Carthaginians by the time of the Second Punic War. In 206 BC Scipio Africanus won a victory close to the town over Hasdrubal and an army of Iberian and Numidian allies. Subsequently the town became tributary to Rome; for this purpose it minted a coinage bearing its name of Carmo. In the early Umayyad period the town had an important Arab community, and ʿAbd al-Raḥmān I was besieged here in 763 by supporters of the Abbasid dynasty. In 914 it was held by rebels against his descendant ʿAbd al-Raḥmān III. In the Taifa period it formed part of the kingdom of Seville. It fell to Fernando III of Castile in 1247.

The Puerta de Sevilla, at the west end of the town walls, is of Carthaginian origin, probably dating from the 230s to 220s BC. The Carthaginian core of the central bastion is not visible because the gate was rebuilt in the Roman and Umayyad periods and has undergone modern restoration. The principal remains of the Roman town are the site of the amphitheatre and, above all, the important necropolis next to it. *The latter are located towards the western edge of the town, where the C 432 to* ALCALÁ DE GUADAIRA *diverges from the road leading to the N IV*. Recent rescue excavations have also thrown a little light on the forum and temple of Augustus, probably both constructed around AD 20. The **amphitheatre** is an example of an early type that used stone initially only for the supports of the wooden seating. This particular one was subsequently rebuilt entirely in stone, probably in the 2nd cent. AD. Relatively little of it may now be seen.

The **necropolis** is located between the amphitheatre and a Roman road that parallels the modern road that leaves Carmona in the direction of SEVILLE. It was work on the site of the Roman road that led to the discovery of the necropolis in 1869. Major excavation began in 1884. Within the necropolis zone, which has its own museum containing items found in the tombs (which amongst other things provide evidence of the continued use of Punic names here well into the Roman period), there are twelve major burial monuments as well as numerous minor ones. Something like 800 burials have been discovered in all, and there are still about 250 of these in the area to be visited. They vary in period from the late 1st cent. BC to the 4th cent. AD. It seems likely that the necropolis went out of use with the Christianizing of the Empire in the 4th cent. The area

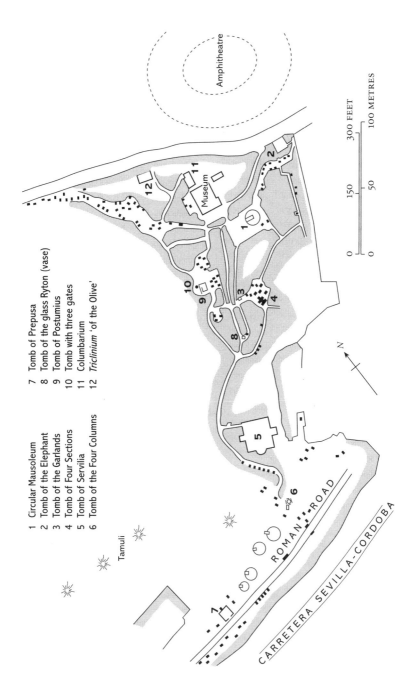

1 Circular Mausoleum
2 Tomb of the Elephant
3 Tomb of the Garlands
4 Tomb of Four Sections
5 Tomb of Servilia
6 Tomb of the Four Columns

7 Tomb of Prepusa
8 Tomb of the glass Ryton (vase)
9 Tomb of Postumius
10 Tomb with three gates
11 Columbarium
12 *Triclinium* 'of the Olive'

▲ Carmona: Roman necropolis

was reused for burials in the Visigothic period. These took the form of inhumations, unlike the earlier Roman ones which were cremations. Most of these tombs are family ones, containing the remains of several cremations. These tombs normally consist of chambers, in some cases retaining traces of their original painted decoration, with niches in their walls to contain small stone boxes holding the ashes of the dead. Thus in the 'Tomb of the Four Sections' there are four chambers opening off a central hall, with five niches for urns in each.

In particularly grand examples, space is also provided for the Roman custom of families gathering to take commemorative meals on the anniversaries of the deaths of their ancestors and relatives. Some also add opulent, even ostentatious, extra features. The largest of the tombs (38 × 34 m.) is that of Servilia (so called from the name on a statue found in it). This incorporates a colonnaded atrium, approached via a covered gallery where the statue had stood. In the opposite far corner of this patio is the entry to the tomb chamber proper. Even this is preceded by an extraordinary trapezoid vestibule carved out of the rock with the appearance of ribbed vaulting. At the apex there is a hole to allow light in from above. The level above the vestibule and the tomb chamber was also used, probably as a ceremonial *triclinium* or dining-room, thus making this into a two-storey tomb. Traces of figurative painting can also be seen in various parts of this tomb. A hoard of coins of Pedro I of Castile (1350–69) was found in the tomb, which may also have been robbed in Antiquity.

Another such *triclinium* may be seen in the 'Tomb of the Triclinium of the Olive', excavated in 1885. This consists of a trapezoidal patio

▼ Carmona: Tomb of the Elephant (after A. Losa)

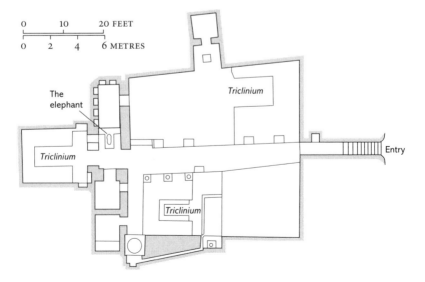

(10 × 7 m.) entered via a stair. Around three sides sixteen niches for urns have been cut out of the rock in two rows. In the centre of the patio there would once have been a table, surrounded by benches. In the end not used for the urns, at a level three steps below the rest, you can see a well and remains of the kitchen where the funerary meals were prepared. The roof over the tomb was held up by two pillars, the square supports for which can be seen. One of the most striking tombs is that 'of the Elephant', so called from the figure of one discovered in a well in the tomb, and now reinstalled on a pedestal. Entry is via nine steps into an open court (11 m. long), at the far end of which some chambers have been hollowed out of the rock. One of these on the right has a series of funerary niches, but the large central one set back behind the others will have served as a *triclinium*. Surprisingly, there are indications of two other *triclinia* in the courtyard. One, to the right as you descend the stairs, seems linked to two small chambers hollowed out of the rock beside it. The other is on the left in the opposite corner of the court, and has its own fountain (much damaged) linked to a well in the cooking area. The presence of three such *triclinia* has led to the suggestion that this tomb served for a *collegium* of three families, using the tomb in common but with their own reserved areas.

All the tombs are different and worth inspection, and together they represent one of the finest Roman provincial funerary complexes.

The Alcázar de Arriba, at the upper end of the town, was converted into a palace by Pedro I of Castile but was ruined in an earthquake in 1504. Some of it has been usefully converted into a *Parador*.

Carranque (Toledo) Roman villa

From the N 401 the TO 432 leads west 36 km. south of Madrid (or 36 km. north of Toledo). After nearly 6 km. it changes name (to the TO 431) but not direction at Ugena. Carranque is 2 km. further down the TO 431. From the village, the site is another 3 km. away by footpath, involving a fording of the Río Guadiana. (Quite shallow!) Get advice locally on the approach to the path and on parking.

A site still in course of development, this consists of the fairly substantial remains of a luxurious villa of late imperial date. Excavation commenced in 1983. Its location is not easy of access, requiring a lengthy cross-country walk. The villa itself came into existence around the middle of the 4th cent., and is of unusual design. The capitals carved from porphyry, a striking purple stone quarried in Egypt and normally reserved for use in imperial residences and sarcophagi, imply that the owners of the villa enjoyed direct imperial patronage. The mosaics found within the villa have been dated to the second half of the 4th and first half of the 5th cent. The name Maternus in the damaged inscription flanking the principal mosaic recalls that of Maternus Cynegius, a Spanish aristocrat and friend of Theodosius I, who served as Praetorian Prefect of the East (384–8). The *triclinium* (dining-room) mosaic itself (5.5 × 4.5 m.) is generally well preserved, except for one corner. It consists of a central roundel, flanked by four semicircular panels and (originally) four square ones in the corners, all of which are contained within a large geometric border. The three surviving corner figures are easily recognized as Athena, Diana, and Hercules. The subjects of the scenes in the semicircular side panels have been identified as 'The Bath of Diana', 'Neptune and Amymone', 'Pyramus and Thisbe', and 'The Rape of Hylas'. The identity of the central figure is less certain, but it has been suggested that it may be Fortuna. The subject matter of some of the panels has raised the possibility that the ultimate inspiration for the mosaic, which as the damaged inscription indicates was the product of a named workshop, was the *Metamorphoses* of Ovid. The pagan nature of the figures depicted might argue against a direct association of the villa with Maternus Cynegius himself, as he was responsible for the closing down of many temples in the East during his time in office, but the use of classical motifs in domestic decoration is no sure indication of pagan beliefs.

Of the structure of the villa, a series of rooms around the central atrium may be seen. In the north-west corner a section of outside wall with the beginning of the internal vaulting of the room of basilican shape that it served still stands to a height of 4 m. or more. This portion of the villa may have continued in use as a church after the rest of the building had fallen into decay and been despoiled of its stone. On the way to the villa you pass a well-preserved Roman mill at the point where you ford the Guadiana. It is on the east bank.

Cartagena Roman town

It is on the Mediterranean coast, approached from the north by the N 301 from Murcia (62 km.) or the N 332 from Alicante (109 km.)

The particularly well-sheltered natural harbour has made this town an important port and naval base throughout much of its history. There were ancient silver mines in its hinterland, and in the Roman period it became known for its exports of esparto grass, for which it received the nickname of *Spartaria*. Founded in 228 BC by Hasdrubal as 'New Carthage' this was the centre of Barcid rule in Spain until Hasdrubal's murder in 221. It was besieged by the Romans in 210 BC, and its surrender to Scipio Africanus in 209 BC led rapidly to the end of the Second Punic War in Spain. Over the next two centuries it was transformed into a typical Roman town. It was besieged by Gnaeus Pompey in 46 BC during the Civil War, and around 45 BC it was made into a *colonia* by Julius Caesar, under the name of Colonia Victrix Julia Carthago Nova. By the Flavian period (69–96) it had become a *conventus* capital. The city was made the centre of the province of Carthaginiensis in the reorganization carried out by

Diocletian (285–304). This also led, by the 5th cent., to its bishop becoming the Metropolitan of an ecclesiastical province of the same name. Little is known of its later history until it was taken by the troops of the Emperor Justinian I in 551. It then became the administrative centre of the small Byzantine enclave along the south-east coast of the peninsula and site of a mint, until the region was finally reconquered by the Visigoths around 624. Surprisingly little is recorded of it under Arab rule, when it served primarily as the port for MURCIA. In the Reconquista it was taken by Fernando III of Castile-León in 1243, and a diocese of Cartagena was established.

This rather dilapidated town, as well as having a number of small Roman sites within it, has recently become famous for the discovery of **one of the oldest known Roman theatres**. Located in the Cierro de la Concepción, in the centre of the city and near the cathedral that was ruined in the Civil War, it may date from no later than 4 BC. This has been suggested by inscriptions from the site referring to Augustus's appointment in that year of his grandsons Gaius Caesar and Lucius Caesar (who died in AD 4 and AD 2 respectively) as his intended successors. The theatre was built out of the slope of the hill, and may have seated around 6,000 spectators. Structurally it seems to be of pure Roman form, rather than representing the earlier Graeco-Roman style that is to be seen in the theatre at MÉRIDA (built in 16 BC). Roman theatres proper had a strictly semicircular *cavea* or seating area, with a covered colonnade around the highest level, and balconies flanking the stage that were reserved for imperial or local dignitaries. The only other early examples of this tradition that are known are the theatres of Pompey (55 BC) and of Marcellus (13 BC) in Rome, but in contrast to that of Cartagena only very limited traces of these have survived. Excavation of this site is still in progress, but the lowest level of the seating, the orchestra, and the foundations of the stage have already been uncovered. More discoveries may be expected here.

Roman inscriptions have been found reused in the hill-top fortress known as the Castillo de la Concepción, which was rebuilt by Alfonso X after 1266, and traces of the Roman amphitheatre have been located beneath the modern bull-ring. The 4th- and 5th-cent. Christian cemetery of San Anton has also been excavated. The period of Islamic rule is represented by traces of a lighthouse by the port.

Three separate **archaeological museums** can be found in the town, owned respectively by the state, the town council, and a local savings bank. These are, first, the Museo Nacional de Arqueología Maritima (Apartado de Correos, 72), which contains items from a variety of subaquatic excavations from all round the Spanish coasts, together with models of ancient ships. Secondly, the Museo Arqueológico Municipal (Calle Ramón y Cajal, 45), covers a wide range of local finds of different periods. The third museum, the Colección Arqueológico of the Caja de

Ahorros del Mediterráneo (Calle del Duque, 28) houses in its basement part of a Roman street discovered below the present building as well as various items found on the site.

Carteia Roman town

On the N 430/E 15 between Algeciras and Marbella, turn onto the N 351 at San Roque, heading towards Gibraltar. A turn to the right after about 2.5 km. leads towards Puente Mayorgo. Continue on this road through the town and across the Río Guadarranque. The site is located in the midst of a series of oil refineries.

In origin an Iberian settlement of the Turdetani, the town was occupied by the Carthaginians in 228 BC, before being captured by Rome in 206 BC. It was resettled in 171 BC as a *colonia* for 4,000 sons of Roman legionaries and local women (Livy 43. 3), and was one of the last refuges of the supporters of Pompey in Spain in 45 BC. It was a centre of export of local wine, as evidenced by finds of kilns for the making of large amphorae, and for the manufacture of *garum*, the notorious Roman sauce made from decomposing fish entrails.

Livy

Titus Livius (59 BC–AD 17) wrote a history of Rome from its foundation up to AD 9 in 142 books, of which only thirty-five survive, being concerned mainly with the period 218–167 BC (Books 20–45). There are also a few fragments of other books and some later brief summaries of the whole work.

Excavations in 1971–4 revealed part of a bust of the Emperor Augustus and a headless togate statue of the 1st cent. AD, as well as a variety of inscriptions, including a dedication to the Emperor Hadrian (117–38). Finds of coinage extending from the Republican period to the later 4th cent. AD indicate the continued existence of the town into the time of the Late Empire, but nothing is known of it in the Visigothic period. Little major structural evidence has been unearthed, but in a large and somewhat unkempt site traces may be seen of a theatre, a bath complex, some walls, and the area of the forum. The foundations of an early Christian basilica with attendant necropolis have also been located. You can see finds from the site in the Museo Histórico Municipal in San Roque (Calle San Felipe, 7).

Casas de Reina Roman town

*From Llerena, 35 km. south-east of **Zafra** on the N 432, take the C 432 for about 6.5 km., passing through the town of Casas de Reina. The fortress is on the hillside to the left of the road. A track leads to the left over the railway line to the theatre.*

Late Neolithic or Copper Age settlement in this area has been established by excavations in 'la Huerta de Dios', which have included the discovery of two stone idols.

Roman *Regina* stood a little over 1 km. east of the present town. Excavations since 1978 have uncovered the seating of a small theatre, built into the slope of a hill in the north-west sector of the town, which has been tastelessly restored with modern steps. Nothing remains of the *scaenae frons* beyond some fragments to be seen lying around the site. This building seems to have gone out of use in the late imperial period. The Arab fortress, of Almohad date, contains some reused fragments of Visigothic decorative carving, probably coming from a church. This might imply that the hilltop became the focus of settlement in the Late Roman or Visigothic period, at the expense of the more vulnerably sited town below.

The C 432 continues south-east to Guadalcanal (c.20 km.) and on for 11 km. to **Alanis**, *where ruins of an Arab fortress, of Almohad date, may be seen.*

Castillo de Alba Asturian fortress

In the upper valley of the Río Bernesga; take the N 630 north from LEÓN *for 25 km. and turn west onto the C 626, which leads 4 km. to Sorribos de Alba.*

This is probably the *castellum* of 'Alva' that Alfonso III (866–910) is said (by the chronicler Sampiro) to have built around 874 in the territory of León. Unlike the other two such fortresses, at Luna and Gordón, which were substantially rebuilt in succeeding centuries, Alba seems to have remained little altered from its original 9th-cent. state until destroyed by Alfonso VIII (1158–1214) of Castile in 1196. These castles were all built on the southern edge of the mountains (the Corderilla Cantábrica) dividing the Asturias from León and the Meseta, and were part of the process of expansion of the kingdom into and the repopulation of the latter area. The castle, of roughly rectangular shape (approx. 150 × 50 m.), was built with dry stone walls, made out of large limestone blocks. There are two rectangular towers (6 × 4 m. and 4 × 3.5 m. respectively) at either end. The larger of the two, in the north-west, has a doorway in its south wall and a small wall in front of the tower cuts it off from the rest of the castle, forming a separate defensible zone. Gateways into the fortress from without have not yet been located. Towards the centre of the site there is a probable cistern (12 × 4 m.), and there may have been an area of domestic buildings between it and the wall.

Castillo de Doña Blanca Punic/Carthaginian settlement

Take the N IV northwards from **Cádiz** *towards Jerez de la Frontera; 2.5 km. after leaving the northern edge of El Puerto de Santa María, a road leads right towards El Portal; 3 km. down this road a turn to the right leads directly to the site.*

Excavation of this site, located beside what would once have been a significant river port on the Río Guadalete, began in 1979, and has revealed

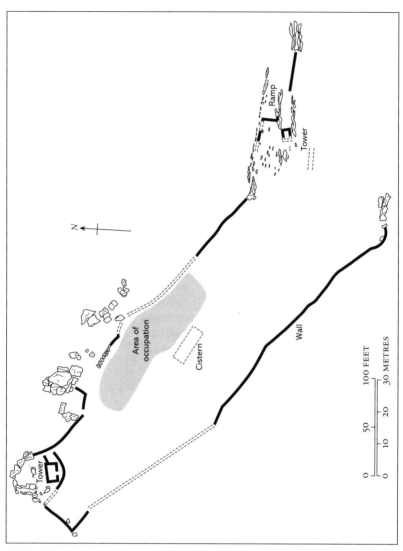

▲ The castle of Alba (after Gutiérrez González)

traces of an early Phoenician settlement, dating to the 8th cent. BC, which in turn developed into a Carthaginian town that survived into the 3rd cent. BC. Traces of houses have been uncovered, as well as two necropolises. Artefacts discovered include items showing commercial contacts with the Greek colonies of the western Mediterranean, There are indications of an earlier settlement, dating from the Late Neolithic, in the vicinity.

Castro de la Coronilla Celtiberian settlement

*Located within the boundaries of the village of Chera. On the N 211 in the direction of Monreal del Campo, 7 km. east of **Molina de Aragón** take a small road south to the village of Prados Redondos (5 km.), whence a road leads 2 km. north-east to Chera on the Río Gallo. Access to the hilltop is by ramps up the northern side. (NB This site is on private land. Enquire in the village.)*

The site is located on a flat-topped hill some 30 m. high. The northern half of it was excavated between 1980 and 1986, when three separate levels of occupation were uncovered. The earliest and deepest has been dated from the Early Iron Age, while the later two corresponded with phases of Celtiberian occupation. Problems with the Carbon-14 dating make the unique record of the earliest phase provisional, while no satisfactory readings have been achieved for the more recent ones. The temporal division between the two Celtiberian periods was clearly brief, and the distinction would seem to represent a period of rebuilding and restructuring of a continuously occupied site. On the other hand, there was a period of abandonment between the Iron Age settlement and the Celtiberian re-occupation, when the flattening of the top of the hill was carried out, to expand the habitable area. From the more recent period have come most of the visible traces of buildings, including silos and storehouses, some of which were erected on earlier Iron Age foundations. Material finds have enabled the early phase of occupation to be related to the Urn Field culture, attested to elsewhere in Aragón. Finds of Iberian coins on the site, from the mints of Sekaisa, Bolskan, and Calagurris (Calahorra), have enabled the two more recent levels of occupation to be dated to the later 2nd and the 1st cents. BC. It is probable that the Celtiberian reoccupation of the defensible site around the middle of the 2nd cent. BC, after centuries of abandonment, is a reflection of the endemic warfare in the peninsula at that period. Of particular interest have been the disproportionately large finds of fragments of imported Italian pottery from the site.

Castulo Roman and Iberian town

This is a 40 ha. site, located on a flattened hilltop immediately west of the Río Guadalimar, with its eastern boundary being defined by the Arroyo de San Ambrosio.

The earliest settlement was that of an Iberian people known as the Turdetani. As with many such sites, it was extensively remodelled following the Roman conquest, and the main features date from the imperial period.

In the **town house of 'Olivar'** a number of rooms have been uncovered, together with part of a bath house that pertained to the villa. Two rooms of the bath house are partly preserved, with some of the hypocausts of the underfloor heating system still visible in the more northerly one. A number of small rooms have been located between the bath complex and what would once have been the central patio or atrium of the villa. It is approximately 9 sq. m. A hoard of forty-seven bronze coins of the period 378–88 was found hidden under the roots of an olive tree in this patio; its date of deposit has been put around the year 400. Vast quantities of pottery fragments have been uncovered from this site, the greater part of which date to the 4th cent. AD.

Parts of the **wall of the town** are visible along the south-eastern flank on the edge of the steep slope down to the Río Guadalimar. Another section was uncovered at the opposite end of the site, to the north-west.

A number of **cemeteries** were excavated in the early 1970s. In the area of the north gate of the town sixty tombs were excavated. The dating of this cemetery has proved controversial. One of its excavators has placed it in the 1st cent. BC to 1st cent. AD, on the grounds that the great majority of the burials are cremations, a practice that became increasingly unfashionable from the Flavian period onwards. On the other hand it has also been dated to the 4th cent. AD on the basis of the finds of coins and ceramics, which virtually all appear to belong to that period. The quality of the latter, including a large number of amphorae, is generally poor, and this has been taken as further proof of the economic decline of this settlement in the Late Roman period.

In the early 1980s excavations on a site called **La Muela**, situated in the valley between the south-eastern lobe of the hill on which Castulo stands and the Río Guadalimar, revealed four phases of occupation, ranging from the Late Bronze Age to the 4th cent. BC. The main structural discovery was of part of a sanctuary that was certainly functioning in the 6th cent. BC, and pottery finds indicated strong Phoenician cultural influence on Castulo in that period.

For finds from the site visit the Museo Arqueológico in Linares, located at Calle General Echagüe, 2, which is devoted primarily to Castulo.

Centcelles Roman villa and mausoleum

Immediately north of the A 7, about 1 km. east of Constantí, and 7 km. from the centre of TARRAGONA. *The site is in a farmyard, some of whose buildings overlie the unexcavated parts of the site. (If approaching on foot beware of the farm dogs: personal experience!)*

The relatively modest early imperial villa (late 1st/2nd cent.) is dwarfed by the great mausoleum built in the heart of it, overshadowing its domestic quarters. The burial for which this was built will have been in the now empty crypt in the middle of the floor (visitable via a flight of steps). There is a four-lobed chamber to the west that can only be entered through the main room of the mausoleum, whose purpose is unclear but which must belong to the same phase of construction. The square

▶ Centcelles: Roman villa and mausoleum

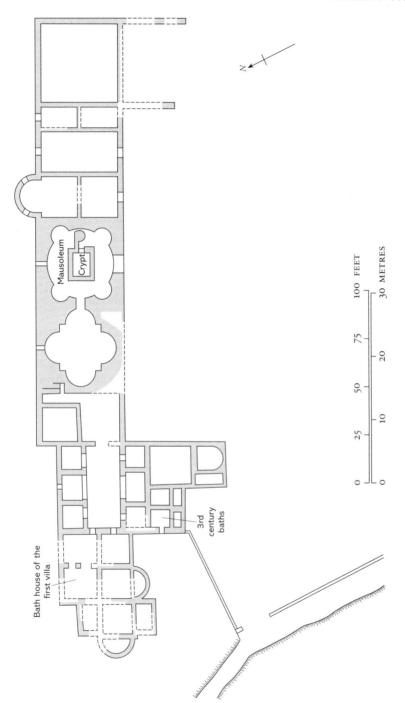

Bath house of the first villa

3rd century baths

Mausoleum

Crypt

N

0	25	50	75	100 FEET
0	10	20	30 METRES

mausoleum with polygonal upper storey is striking, not only for its size, but even more for the survival of part of its original **mosaic decoration** in the cupola. Although badly damaged, enough of this has been preserved to allow a reconstruction of some of its main components to be made, and for the work to be clearly dated to the 4th cent. In particular, the lowest of the three concentric rings of decoration is relatively well preserved and can be seen to display a succession of images of hunting. Amongst the images in the next ring, which is divided into sections by depictions of columns, may be seen a ship (Jonah and the whale?), Daniel in the lions' den, and the three Israelites in the burning fiery furnace. The innermost ring is poorly preserved, other than for two male figures, one of whom carries a bunch of grapes. They may have been part of a set of depictions of the Four Seasons. The central roundel is almost entirely lost. Why a mausoleum of such size and magnificence should have been constructed here and in such a dominant position in an otherwise unexceptional rural villa has always aroused discussion.

In the church of the impressive Cistercian **monastery of Santes Creus** you can see a porphyry sarcophagus, reused as part of the tomb of King Pere II (see below), which is said to have been brought from the villa at Centcelles. Such sarcophagi were only used for imperial burials (cf. the examples preserved in the Vatican and in Istanbul). The only probable candidate for such a burial in this region and in this period is the Emperor Constans (337–50), who was killed at Elne, near Perpignan, fleeing from the usurper Magnentius (350–3) (Zosimus II. 42). The name of the adjacent town of Constantí may help support such an identification, which has, however, been questioned by some scholars.

Zosimus

A 6th-cent. historian, probably writing in Constantinople, his truncated work in five books is of value for its inclusion of information from earlier writers whose work is otherwise lost.

The original **villa**, built around a central courtyard, appears to have been redeveloped in the late 3rd cent., with many of the earlier structures being covered over by larger-scale and more grandiose new ones. To this phase belongs the apsed chamber immediately east of the mausoleum (which has revealed traces both of the earlier villa and of medieval use of the site) and the bath house to the south-west of the main line of this wing of the building. Traces of the previous baths can be seen at the westernmost edge of this wing. These features might suggest the villa was either part of an imperial estate or belonged to a family prominent amongst the supporters of the Constantinian dynasty (293–363).

*To see **Santes Creus** take the N 240: 21 km. north from Tarragona to the inter-section with the C 246; 7 km. east along the latter, just after the turn to the A 2, another turning to the left leads due north along a minor road for 7 km., to the right-hand turn to the monastery (less than another km.).*

Although damaged in the secularization of 1835, this is still one of the finest medieval monasteries in Catalonia. Established on this site in 1158, it preserves a church (1174–1221), a cloister (1163), monastic buildings, and the palace of Pere II (1276–85) and Jaume II (1291–1327), both of whose tombs may be seen in the church.

Cieza Arab town

Head north for 44 km. from MURCIA *on the N 301 to Cieza. The site is on the hill-side opposite, south of the river. A small bridge crosses the river south-east of the town. Approach to the site itself is on foot.*

Near to the present town of Cieza, high on a southern hillside overlooking the valley of the Segura, is a deserted settlement. Excavation has revealed that this was the site of the Arab town of *Siyasa*, gradually abandoned by its Muslim inhabitants after the Castilian conquest of 1243. It was a walled town, with an *alcazaba* at the highest point, in the north-west corner, and a **cemetery** has been located on a subsidiary hill to the south, just within the probable line of the walls. Just below and on the west side of this cem-etery is the likely site of the main entry to the town. Excavations have been concentrated in a small part of the eastern sector, and much of an area of domestic buildings has been uncovered. The main mosque and other public buildings have yet to be found. Four streets have been located, together with seventeen **houses** clustered together, each built around a small courtyard, with kitchen, stores, and latrines (linked to subterranean pits) leading off. Each has some form of reception room; in some cases with an adjacent smaller chamber that may have served for sleeping. The largest of the houses has two such reception and sleeping rooms. Like several of the others it also has some form of stable. At least two houses have their own cisterns. Steps can be seen in some houses, leading to an upper floor. Although closely packed together, two distinct classes of housing can be seen here: eight of the seventeen are of a poorer and simpler kind, with an area no more than 61 sq. m.; some less than 36 sq. m. They are also more or less uniform in their plan and show few if any traces of decoration. The nine larger houses range in size from 119 to 146 sq. m., have much greater variety in their organization, and show evidence of a range of decorative styles. The latter extend from those of the late Umayyad period up to that of the early Nazirids. The bulk of the evidence, however, seems to relate to the 12th and early 13th cents. and the site is a rare and important source of information on Islamic town life in this period.

Finds from the site are kept in the Centro de Estudios Arabes y Archeológicos 'Ibn Arabi' in MURCIA.

There is a restored fortress of Arab origin near the village of Blanca: 10 km. south of Cieza on the N 301 turn right (eastwards). The 'castillo moro' is about 6 km. down the road.

Clunia   Roman town   ★

*On the N 234 heading south from **Burgos** (passing turnings to both* QUINTANILLA DE *LAS VIÑAS and **Santo Domingo de Silos**) towards Soria, 76 km. from Burgos (11 km. south of Salas de los Infantes) a right turn onto the C 111 leads south-west for 20 km. before a small road to the right leads 1 km. to the village of Peñalba de Castro. Keep on for a further 1 km. to the site of Clunia.*

An earlier Celtiberian settlement may have been located on the nearby hill of Alto del Cuerno. The Marian leader Sertorius was besieged here in 75 BC, and the town was subsequently sacked by Pompey as an act of reprisal.

The Roman settlement on the flat-topped Alto de Castro was founded in the reign of Tiberius (14–37), probably as part of the administrative reorganization of the north-west in the aftermath of the Cantabrian Wars. Clunia seems to have received the status of *municipium* at the same time, as testified to by its local coinage. This was raised to the higher level of *colonia* by the Emperor Galba (68–9), who was taking refuge in the town when called to the imperial throne. It also served from the reign of Claudius (41–54) until the Severan period as the capital of the large *Conventus* of *Hispania Citerior*. A fragment of a bronze inscription recording the town's municipal laws has been found. Layers of ash found in some of the buildings in the centre of the site seem to indicate a major destruction by fire around the year AD 284—whether the result of accident or sack is not known. Following rebuilding the town seems to have continued to function until the middle of the 5th cent. No evidence so far has emerged of continuity of occupation of the urban settlement into the Visigothic period; nor was it the seat of a bishop. A Visigothic necropolis, containing bodies and some lyriform belt buckles of 7th-cent. date, has been discovered around a later (still extant) chapel adjacent to the forum; this has also been dated by the presence of a coin of the period of the joint reign of Kings Egica and Wittiza (692/4–702), from the mint of Evora.

Excavations in 1959–60 located the **Forum** (140 × 100 m), one of the largest in Spain, of which only the eastern section has so far been excavated. This forum, probably built on the site of an earlier Julio-Claudian one, dates from the time of the Flavian dynasty (69–96). All its northern end was taken up by a rectangular three-sectioned basilica with internal arcades. Extending northwards from and at right angles to this basilica was a rectangular structure, of which only a little of its much decayed podium survives. Along the eastern edge has been uncovered a series of **shops** opening onto a portico, conceivably matched by a similar range on the west side. Pere de Palol, who excavated the site, believes, on the basis of the traces of decoration and of the objects found in them, that the larger

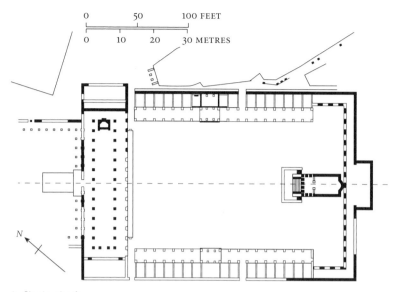

▲ Clunia: the forum

chambers in the middle of the rows of shops should be classified as shrines. At the southern end, within the open space of the forum itself, was a large **temple** on its own platform, facing directly towards the enigmatic structure that extends northwards from the centre of the basilica. The roof height of the temple, perhaps matched by that of the basilica, would have been above that of the porticoes and shops flanking the forum to east and west. Suetonius (*Galba* IX. 2) records the existence of a temple to Jupiter in Clunia, which may be this one. Inscriptions indicate the existence of a temple devoted to the imperial cult. Although this has not been located archaeologically, Professor Palol has speculated that this might have been the function of the building that once stood on the podium attached to the basilica.

> ### Suetonius
>
> Gaius Suetonius Tranquillus (c. AD 69–140) was the author of *The Twelve Caesars*, completed around AD 121. It comprises brief and frequently scandalous biographical accounts of Julius Caesar and the emperors of Rome from Augustus to Domitian. His work on the lives of prominent Roman authors has largely been lost.

A **shrine** of the 1st cent. AD, dedicated to the phallic divinity Priapus, was discovered in 1981 in the innermost part of an underground gallery over 600 m. long, associated with subterranean springs north-east from the forum and about 300 m. west of the theatre. The cult site may be linked to the presence of the stream that created this series of natural galleries. Phallic and Priapic statuettes were found, as well as names carved on the walls by some of the votaries.

Outside the east wall of the forum, in a triangular *insula*, has been found an unusual **bottle-shaped building** (48 × 30.5 m.), entered via an arcaded portico at the 'neck', closest to the forum and probably containing a colonnaded central space (34 × 21 m.). This has been dated to a period later, albeit undetermined, than the forum, and identified as a possible *macellum* or market. Beyond its southern end began a series of *insulae* containing private residences and a small **bath complex**. A triangular house can be seen in the angle between these 'Baths of the Forum' and the forum itself. Evidence of late 3rd-cent. destruction has been found throughout this area The *Decumanus Maximus*, the principal road across the breadth of the town, intersects the *Cardo* near the north-east corner of the forum. It leads thence to a theatre cut out of the natural rock on the edge of the hillside. Little remains of this beyond some of the lower levels of the seating, carved from the rock, and part of the *scaenae frons*.

Traces of two **public bath houses**, known as 'Los Arcos I and II', have also been uncovered close to the *Decumanus*, between the forum and the theatre. The outline of their walls has been restored and their plans are easily seen. Traces of mosaic may be seen, particularly in 'Los Arcos I', which also retains much of its large communal latrine. This bath complex seems to have been built early in the 1st cent. AD and it was substantially reconstructed in the 2nd cent. (to which phase the mosaic and *opus sectile* floors belong). Evidence of late 3rd-cent. destruction has also been found here. The site appears to have been in use once more by the mid-4th cent., but no longer as a bath house. Some of the original rooms were subdivided and finds of late Spanish *terra sigillata* have led to the suggestion that it may have served as a ceramic factory, until final abandonment in the mid-5th cent. Less is to be seen of 'Los Arcos II', which has been dated to the late 1st and 2nd cents. AD.

A large **urban villa** to the north-east of the forum, built in the 1st cent. AD, occupies a whole *insula*. It had both winter and summer diningrooms (*triclinia*). Traces of 2nd-cent. mural paintings may be seen. The mosaics date from a 4th-cent. rebuilding (there is another one from this site to be seen in the Museo Arqueológico Nacional in MADRID). A hoard of coins from the reigns of Gallienus (253–68) to Carinus (283–5) was found in the villa.

The town served as a major centre of pottery-making in the early imperial period, producing both *terra sigillata* and painted wares. The *sigillata* tradition continued, with different designs, into the late imperial centuries. Finds in this site of large numbers of coins of Claudius II (268–70), as opposed to those of Victorinus (269–70), help confirm the recovery of Spain by the legitimate emperor from the independent 'Gallic Empire' at this time.

Córdoba Roman and Islamic remains ★★
(Visit together with MEDINA AZAHARA)

Corduba Patricia was established as a Roman *colonia* in 152 BC by Marcus Metellus, on the site of a former Iberian settlement. After the provincial reorganization of 27 BC it was made the capital of Baetica. A Christian community existed in the city in the 3rd cent., and one of the first known bishops, Ossius (d. 337), was an adviser to Constantine I (306–37), the first Christian emperor. Little is known of the history of the later imperial city, but a revolt against the Visigothic King Agila (549–54) led to a period of local independence until this was crushed in 572 by Leovigild (569–86). Following the Arab conquest of 711, Córdoba soon replaced Seville as the administrative capital of Al-Andalus. It retained this position when the Umayyad dynasty established itself in Spain in 756, and the city benefited considerably from their patronage. The civil wars of the period *c.*1010–31 marked the end of a long period of prosperity, and following the abolition of the Umayyad caliphate in 1031 power in the city and its hinterland were taken by the dynasty of the Banū Jahwar (1031–75). Córdoba passed into the hands of the rulers of Toledo and then of Seville, before coming under Almoravid and then Almohad rule. It was captured by Fernando III of Castile (1217–52) in 1236.

Roman Palace of the Tetrarchic Period

Travellers arriving in Córdoba on the AVE, the high-speed Madrid to Seville train, may be pleased and disturbed to know that their mode of transport caused both the discovery of one of the most important Roman palace sites in Europe and its destruction. Work on the new rail terminal revealed a large Roman and early medieval site, first hinted at in 1922, which was made the subject of rescue excavations during 1991. Only a small section of the site may now be seen immediately to the north of the railway track, close to the station. On top of a villa of the mid-2nd to 3rd cent. were uncovered the substantial foundations of a major palace of Tetrarchic date that seems to have been built in a single phase of construction. A fragment of an inscription has been interpreted as referring to the Caesars Constantius and Galerius (293–305), and creation of the palace has been attributed to the senior emperor Maximian (286–305, 306–8), at the time of his campaign in Spain in 297/8. The palace was articulated around a semicircular *cryptoporticus* with a diameter of 109 m. Radiating off this were a series of halls and of passageways leading to other structures, including a bath complex. The *porticus* terminated at each end in tri-conch halls, and across its front ran a wall, pierced only in its centre by a gate flanked by two large military-style towers. This gate faced the city and was aligned with the central and largest hall of the complex, which with its apsidal end is reminiscent in size and construction of such Tetrarchic throne halls as that of Constantine in Trier, that of the villa of Maxentius on the Via Appia, and the Piazza Armerina palace in Sicily. Despite such similarities the actual plan of the palace is unparalleled. The techniques of construction differ from those used on other Roman buildings of Córdoba. Although much of the site seems to have gone out of use in the mid-6th cent., the northern tri-conch hall was reused as a church, and a Christian cemetery, a role it continued to play until the early 11th cent. A funerary inscription of a bishop, Lampadius, dated to 549, was found being reused as a 10th/11th-cent. tombstone. Suggestions that this church may be identified with the Basilica of St Acisclus, the principal patron saint of Córdoba, are now thought less probable.

Other Roman Sites

The loss of much of this site is all the sadder given the paucity of other Roman remains in Córdoba. A 'reconstructed' (or more accurately 'brand new') **temple** in the centre of the city contains little more than two genuine capitals. On the other hand, the 250 m.-long bridge over the Guadalquivir south of the **Mezquita** (see below) is Roman in origin. It was repaired by the Arab *wali* or governor Al-Samh in 719/20, following damage by flooding, and again in 971 by the caliph Al-Ḥakam II, but still retains much Roman stonework. The small **fortress** that defends its southern end, the *Calahorra*, probably dates from the Almohad period (*not* Umayyad, as once thought). It was used in 1369 by Enrique II of Castile as a prison for members of the nobility, and since 1987 has housed an Islamic audiovisual and model exhibition.

The Alcázar and Walls

Probably 9th-cent. walls along the south-west flank of the city, including an extension south-west to the Puerta de Sevilla, were restored in the Almohad period, and probably at various points after the Castilian conquest of 1236. In the south-west extension these walls incorporate the former **Alcázar** (undergoing restoration). This is a rather muddled complex, incorporating some formal gardens and part of a **fortified palace** built for Alfonso XI (1312–50). Within the latter are several rooms belonging to an Arab-style bath complex built in 1328. Some Roman items, including a number of small mosaics, found in the site are also displayed in the building. Of particular note is an extremely fine mid-3rd-cent. sarcophagus, in the form of a **tomb house**. It was probably made in Rome and shipped to Córdoba, where the lifelike bust of its owner was then carved on the deliberately unfinished body.

The Synagogue

Just inside the western wall, and south of the Puerta de Almodóvar, lay the medieval Jewish quarter, of which a rather damaged small **synagogue**

(Calle Maimonides) may still be seen. It was rebuilt in the 14th cent., and after the expulsion of the Jews in 1492 became a hospital for sufferers from rabies. In 1588 it was taken over by the Confraternity of Saints Crispin and Crispinian, whose members were the city's shoemakers. It was restored in 1900 and further in 1928. There are a number of Hebrew inscriptions, mainly scriptural, but including one (the largest; on the east wall of the prayer hall) dated to 1314/15 in the name of Ishaq Moheb, son of Efraim, that seems to refer to the rebuilding of the synagogue. There is a small museum in the adjacent 16th-cent. house.

Bath Houses

In the Plaza de los Mártires in front of the entry to the Alcázar may be seen the roofs of a small 9th/10th-cent. bath complex, probably once forming part of the Umayyad palace. This has been neglected and is normally unguarded; it may be entered. Descending the steps, you come to a group of interconnected chambers, whose vaulted ceilings have small star-shaped openings. These would once have served as steam baths. There is also a small vestibule. Part of another bath house, probably dating from after the Castilian conquest, can be visited (for a fee) in a private house in the Calle de Santa María, leading off from the north-east corner of the Mezquita. The first room entered served as the *tepidarium* or warm bath Its arcading, decorated in imitation of that of the Mezquita, is supported on reused columns and capitals. A small barrel-vaulted *caldarium* (steam bath) beyond has a set of rectangular vents in the ceiling. Twenty other caliphal or Mudéjar bath houses have been located in the city.

The Mezquita

Despite the presence within it of a 16th-cent. Christian cathedral and an earlier chapel, the Mezquita remains the most substantial and most impressive relic of the Islamic presence in Spain. In architectural terms, it is the third largest mosque ever built (22,250 sq. m.: exceeded only by two ruined 9th-cent. Abbasid mosques at Samarra in Iraq). According to Arab tradition it is built on the site formerly occupied by the church of St Vincent. If so, the reused Visigothic capitals and altar-stone, to be seen particularly in the north-west corner of the present building, may derive from that earlier structure. The story that ʿAbd al-Raḥmān I (756–88) bought the half of the church that had not been requisitioned for Muslim worship at the time of the conquest is too reminiscent of the story told of the origins of the Umayyad mosque in Damascus to be entirely credible, but whatever the truth of that, it was late in his reign that the present building was begun. It was dedicated in 786.

The expansion of the mosque over the next two centuries is testimony to the growth of the Muslim community in Córdoba. Starting from ʿAbd al-Raḥmān I's original section, comprising the present north-west corner (73.5 × 37 m.: in twelve aisles north–south by 11 cross aisles east–west),

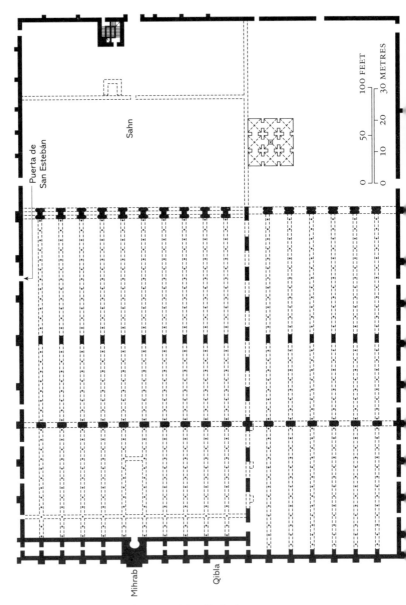

▲ Córdoba: the Umayyad mosque (after Grabar)

the building was almost doubled in size by ʿAbd al-Raḥmān II (822–52), who extended it southwards by another eight cross aisles, and then it was extended again by twelve new cross aisles to its present southern limit in 965/6, under Al-Ḥakam II (961–76). A massive extension by eight aisles eastwards was carried out under the regime of the military dictator Al-Manṣūr (d. 1002). The earlier sections of the prayer hall are notable for their reuse of Roman and Visigothic columns and capitals. (A particularly fine Visigothic altar may be seen free-standing in the north-west corner.) This was a typical feature of early Islamic religious buildings, and rather than representing a response to shortage of materials it should probably be seen as the product of deliberate ideological motivation, emphasizing both the triumph of the Muslims and the superiority of their faith. Al-Manṣūr's extension is constructed entirely out of new materials. His columns also lack pediments, and no opportunity seems to have been taken for self-aggrandizement. The whole of this section is much more utilitarian than its predecessors. Other rulers had also contributed in varying degrees to the creation of the mosque. The doorway known as the Puerta de San Esteban, on the west side of the prayer hall, is dated by an inscription to 855/6 in the reign of Muḥammad I (852–86). The great minaret, partly preserved in the present bell tower, was built in 952 under ʿAbd al-Raḥmān III (912–61). It was badly damaged in a storm in 1589 and the present upper section was added between 1593 and 1618. The original masonry was given an outer casing 1.58 m. thick around 1650–64. The Patio de los Naranjos on the north side was once the *sahn*, where Muslims would have performed ritual ablutions before entering the prayer hall. The Puerta de Perdón, which gives entry to it from beside the bell tower, was built in Mudéjar style in 1377. It seems certain that the arcades, now filled in, that divide the *sahn* from the prayer hall would originally have been open, thus making the interior much lighter than it seems to the modern visitor.

The *maqsura* fronting the *quibla* of the second phase of the building, that of ʿAbd al-Raḥmān II, is in part still to be seen in the Capilla Villaviciosa, but the greatest achievement has been the preservation of almost all of the *quibla*, with its original mosaic decoration, of Al-Ḥakam II's extension. It has survived thanks to its having been bricked up after the Christian conquest of 1236; it was only discovered in the 19th cent. The initial adaptation of the building for Christian use involved the creation of chapels within it (see the present Capilla Villaviciosa of 1371; restored in 1892), but not the wholesale destruction of the building that was the norm elsewhere (e.g. SEVILLE). In 1523 the cathedral chapter determined to build a bigger church within the structure of the former mosque, and despite some opposition created the present Renaissance-style structure in the centre of the building (completed in 1607). This involved the removal of sixty of the Umayyad columns. The resulting stylistic disharmony of the building is said to have been criticized by Charles V on his visit to the city in 1526.

The Mezquita was once connected by a passage, built in the reign of ʿAbd Allāh (888–912), at its south-west corner to the Umayyad palace, which extended westwards from the Calle Torrijos to the Plaza de los

Mártires and the city walls. Apart from the bath house previously mentioned, the only other visible trace of this complex may be seen in the form of a tower, one face of which is preserved in the Casa de Expósitos (once an orphanage and currently serving as a tourist information office), adjacent to the 15th–17th-cent. episcopal palace.

Other Islamic Sites

Recent rapid excavation in the western part of the city has uncovered traces of 10th-cent. housing and possibly of a sectional mosque, but these were rescue digs prior to redevelopment, so none of this remains visible and little has been published. Some of the other mosques that served different sections of the Umayyad city have been partly preserved in having their minarets transformed into bell towers for the churches that were built in Córdoba after the Christian conquest. Of these the most striking and probably the earliest is the 9th-cent. tower of San Juan (Calle Lope de Hoces), with a now blocked double horseshoe-arched window in its upper stages. A 10th-cent. minaret is re-employed in the church of Santiago (Calle Agustín Moreno), as is another of the same period in the Convento de Santa Clara (Calle del Rey Heredia). A section of the east wall of the city is partly incorporated into the buildings on the west side of the Calle de San Fernando, whose line marks the formal limit of both the Roman and the Arab city in this direction. Excavations have been taking place in this area, which may reveal more of the organization of the numerous suburbs that surrounded Umayyad Córdoba.

The Archaeological Museum

The **Museo Arqueológico**, housed in the 16th-cent. noble palace of Jerónimo Páez (Plaza Jerónimo Páez), is particularly rich in both its Roman and its Arab holdings, but also has a smaller but important Visigothic collection, including items from the Torredonjímeno Treasure (see also BARCELONA) and a unique column with attached capital with defaced depictions of the four evangelists. On the first floor there is also a notable collection of items, including inscriptions and the inscribed bronze bell of abbot Samson (dated to AD 925), pertaining to the Christian population of Umayyad Córdoba. Not least is this evidence for their continued use of Latin into the 12th cent. Here too are some Arab funerary inscriptions and items from MEDINA AZAHARA.

Dueñas (Palencia) Roman villa

Located 3 km. south-west of the Visigothic church of SAN JUAN DE BAÑOS, *between the rivers Carrión and Pisuerga, and just east of the main railway line from* **Valladolid** *to* **Burgos**, *this site is on enclosed private property adjacent to the Trappist monastery of San Isidro.*

The importance of the villa of Cercado de San Isidro lies in the quality of the mosaics found in it and in its proximity to the royal foundation of San

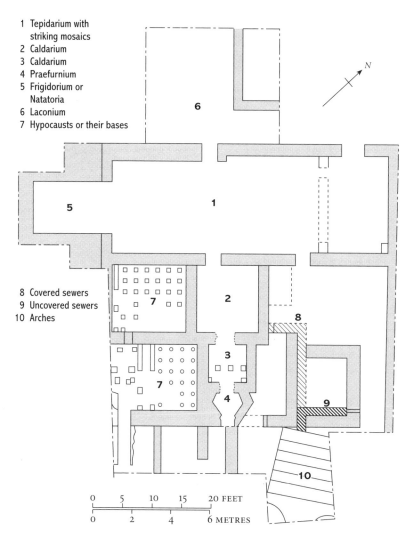

1 Tepidarium with
   striking mosaics
2 Caldarium
3 Caldarium
4 Praefurnium
5 Frigidorium or
   Natatoria
6 Laconium
7 Hypocausts or their bases

8 Covered sewers
9 Uncovered sewers
10 Arches

0   5   10   15   20 FEET
0   2   4   6 METRES

▲ Roman villa of 'Cerado de San Isidro' (after Revilla, Palol, and Cuadros)

Juan de Baños, erected on the estates of the Visigothic king Reccesuinth (649–72). The site was excavated in 1962 and 1963, and revealed part of the bath house of the villa complex, including a substantial *tepidarium* (11 × 5 m.), two *caldaria*, a *frigidarium*, and the furnace room. Traces of wall painting were found in several of the rooms, but the most striking feature was the **floor mosaic** of the *tepidarium*, which has been dated to the 3rd cent. The central part of this is much damaged, but a separate panel (5 × 2 m.) at the western end, depicting aquatic figures and oceanic deities, was found almost intact. In the larger damaged section of the mosaic the figure of a horse, bearing the legend AMORIS ('Of Love') on its neck, and part of a geometric border have been preserved.

The church of the Convento de San Isidro is partly Romanesque. The first monastery on the site was founded in 911, when it was endowed by King García of León; the area was repopulated around 883, possibly with immigrants from Al-Andalus.

*At 9 km. south of the village of Dueñas (itself 3 km. south of the villa) a right turn onto the VA 902 leads 7 km. to the interesting castle of **Trigueros del Valle**, with double-walled enceinte. Returning to the main road and continuing southwards, left turns off the E 80/N 620 either at the 109 or the 112 km. mark (distances from Burgos) both lead 2 km. to the castle of **Cabezón de Pisuerga**.*

This is another early foundation, and was subject of a famous siege in the reign of Pedro I the Cruel (1350–69).

El Bovalar Visigothic village

From the N II (NB there is no easy access from the A 2/E 90) between LÉRIDA and ZARAGOZA take the C 242 southwards from its junction with the N II about 1 km. east of FRAGA, and follow it past Seròs and across the Río Segre (10 km.). Immediately across the river a track leads left for less than 1 km. to the site. This is enclosed within a metal fence (though the gate has been known to be left wide open!), with a viewing path beside it.

The site is located on a flat hillock overlooking the Segre, with its northern edge falling away steeply to the river bank. The presence here of a **church** of Visigothic date was first recognized in 1943 and this was excavated in 1967. The building survives only to the height of little more than 1 m. above its foundations, but its layout is fully preserved. Its rectangular shape, with a chancel enclosed between two small flanking chambers, and with a small rectangular baptistery at the western end, can easily be made out. The plan of the church dates it probably to the 6th cent. A section of wall with a column base at the end of it coming in from the north wall towards the centre of the building indicates that there was once a small crossing dividing the chancel from the nave. The equivalent wall on the southern side is missing. A section of the chancel screen was found *in situ*. Unfortunately, it was also left there and was subsequently stolen. The whole of the church, other than the chancel and the small chamber to its left, was used as a place of burial, and stone sarcophagi of various sizes can be seen buried in the sub-soil throughout most of the building. A variety of bronze and ceramic liturgical items, including a fine incense burner, were discovered on the site, and removed for exhibition in the archaeological museum in LÉRIDA. Also located and now reconstructed in the museum was the surround of the baptismal pool from the west end of the church, together with its covering six-columned baldachino.

▲ El Bovalar: 6th-cent. church and late 7th-cent. village (after Palol)

In 1976 another series of excavations was initiated under the direction of Professor Pere de Palol, with a team from Barcelona. As well as completing the work to be done on the church, this campaign involved an exploration of the area immediately adjacent to the building on its southern side. Here was found a group of rooms arranged around two courtyards, one of which was right next to the church. The full report of these excavations has yet to be published, and only very brief summaries are currently available. The excavators have described the group of interconnected buildings attached to the southern side of the church, and a smaller related set of chambers on the north side, as a **village**. This assessment is based more on the nature of the numerous small finds made on the site than on the plan of the structures, which is quite unlike that of other early medieval villages known in western Europe, where the separate and distinct nature and location of the different buildings is in marked contrast to the plan of the structures seen here. Nor is it easy to explain their envelopment of the church.

A verdict on the nature of this complex must await the publication of a comprehensive report, but it seems clear that the buildings around the church date from over a century after its construction. It has been stated that a wide range of personal items and domestic utensils were located by the excavators throughout the village site, illuminating many aspects of rural life in the late Visigothic period. The dating of the site has been based on the discovery of a scatter of gold coins, again throughout the buildings, in the form of *trientes* of the last Visigothic kings. The earliest date to the sole reign of Egica (687–692/4) and the latest to that of King Achila (710–13). This includes the first ever discovery of a coin of the latter monarch struck by the mint of Caesaraugusta (ZARAGOZA), thus providing proof that his regional kingdom in Catalonia and the eastern Pyrenees also extended up to the middle of the Ebro valley. Again, the numerous gold coins reported throughout this site raise questions about its identification as a village. They and the other finds were apparently scattered as if dropped or abandoned in haste, and evidence of burning has also been found, though there are no human remains. The reasonable deduction has been made that this establishment, whatever its character, was abandoned suddenly and destroyed in the course of the Arab conquest of the Ebro valley in 714.

El Oral (San Fulgencio, Alicante)   Iberian settlement

*On the south-east side of the Sierra de El Molar, a small massif overlooking the Mediterranean south of **Alicante**, at a height of about 40 m. above sea level. The N 332 passes immediately to the east of the Sierra on its way from Guardamar to SANTA POLA at La Marina del Pinet.*

The possibility that the Vega or plain north of the mouth of the River Segura was covered by the sea in the 1st millennium BC, leaving the Sierra de El Molar as an island, has been suggested but not proved archaeologically. If not actually submerged, the area is likely to have been extremely marshy. All known settlements of this time have been located on the higher ground south of the river, on El Molar or on the slopes of the Sierra de Crevillente.

Recent excavations have uncovered part of the small settlement on the upper slope of the hillside, surrounded by a perimeter defensive wall with small square towers. It is typically Iberian in being organized in roughly

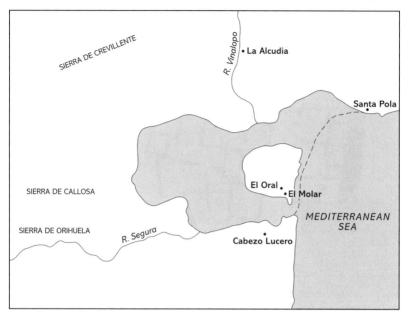

▲ Mouth of the River Segura with hypothetical coastline (after Shefton)

rectangular groups of contiguous houses, often consisting of just two rooms, clustered around a central courtyard, with a system of streets dividing these conglomerations into separate blocks or *insulae*. However, the regularity of the planning and the relatively large size of the houses mark this off from most other known Iberian villages. (For another unusual settlement in this area see SANTA POLA.) Twenty-one houses have been identified, comprising a total of fifty-one rooms between them. A few larger houses of five or six rooms could have their own central court-yard, while still forming part of the block. The earliest phase of occupation of this site dates to the second half of the 6th cent. BC, but it appears to have been abandoned by *c.*450 BC. The initial establishment of this and the other early Iberian settlements in this area may owe something to the presence of a Phoenician trading post in the dunes of GUARDAMAR, at the mouth of the Río Segura. Ceramic finds also indicate that in the 5th cent. BC the dominant material influence had become that of Greek pottery from AMPURIAS. Other Iberian settlements located in this area include **La Picola** (see SANTA POLA), La Escuera (*c.*4th–2nd cent. BC; also on the southern flank of the Sierra de El Molar), and Cabezo Lucero (5th–3rd cent. BC). Necropolises have been found associated with all three, as well as with El Oral, whose burial place was the site known as El Molar. Here further finds of Attic pottery of the late 6th/early 5th cent. were made. An Iberian sanctuary, of which no material remains have been found, may

Defensive outer wall of settlement

STREET

STREET

Houses around a central court

▲ El Oral: excavations of houses and outer wall (after Abad Casal)

have stood on the site of the present Castillo de GUARDAMAR, as terracotta votive statues have been uncovered there.

El Vacar Arab fortress

On a low hill to the left of the road when travelling northwards along the N 432, 30 km. north of CÓRDOBA.

This fortress (whose name comes from Arabic *Akabat al-Bakar* 'Mountain of the Bulls') has attracted surprisingly little attention, despite its accessibility and the unusual nature of its design. It is rectangular (60 × 50 m.), with a single entry and relatively low walls, and with solid square towers, of the same height as the wall, in each corner and in the centre of each wall. These towers extend only 2.5 m. out from the walls. The walls are 1.5 m. thick, and the construction is of *tabiya*. Its plan is very like that of a Late Roman fort, or a smaller-scale version of some of the fortified residential or palace sites built by the Umayyad dynasty in Syria (661–750). It has no equivalent in Spain, but has several parallels in the Near East. Although no proper study of it has been undertaken, these features alone would suggest that its origins should be placed early in the period of Arab rule in Al-Andalus, probably during the Umayyad Amirate (756–912). Its location, on the principal road leading directly north from Córdoba through a valley in the Sierra Morena, and enjoying a commanding view over the surrounding countryside, gave it particular importance. A battle took place here on 22 May 1010 between two rival claimants for the Caliphate,

Sulaymān al-Mustaʿīn (1009–10 and 1013–16) and Muḥammad II al-Mahdī (1010). In 1134 it was the scene of a Castilian victory over the Almoravid ruler ʿAlī ibn Yūsuf (1106–42). In 1237 it was given to the town of Córdoba by Fernando III of Castile.

*The castle of **Bélmez**, 50 km. further north on the N 432, is built on a rock beside the town (NB: very dangerous ascent).*

It consists of a large square three-storeyed tower, standing to a height of 10 m., with an adjacent curtain wall containing three small round towers. From here the castles of Fuenteovejuna and Névalos were in sight, and it is likely that they formed an intercommunicating group, serving as watch towers and first line of defence against Christian raids during the Almohad period. Bélmez was restored and garrisoned by the French in 1809.

Fontanarejo   Early Berber settlement

Located on a small hill, called El Moro del Castillejo, on the north side of the Arroyo del Castillejo, within the parish boundaries of and about 2 km. south-east of Fontanarejo: take the CR 731 north-west from Ciudad Real for 32 km. to Porzuna, and continue in the same direction for nearly 3 km. on the C 403, before turning left onto the CR 722. Continue on this for 32.5 km. to Alcoba de los Montes. On the far side of the village a left turn leads about 8 km. to Fontanarejo.

Slight traces survive of an early Islamic fortified settlement, which from its location was most probably of Berbers, and which can be dated from ceramic finds to no later than the 9th cent.; it may well have originated in the 8th. It continued in occupation until the Castilian conquest of the area in the late 11th cent. Other pottery fragments show that a Christian settlement existed on the site in the 13th and 14th cents., but it appears to have been abandoned by the end of the 14th cent. Twenty fragments of Bronze Age wares indicate occupation of this site at that period too.

The site is about 150 m. long, but quite narrow. The only structural remains now to be seen are two walls. One of these (5 m. long × 1.5 m. wide × 1.5 m. high) formed part of the defensive outer wall of the settlement, and it contains in itself a narrow postern gateway (80 cm. wide). The other section of wall (about 1 m. long × 80 cm. high) formed part of the structure of a house. The piles of stones around the site once formed the structure of the other dwellings and the rest of the outer wall, which were unmortared.

Fraga   Roman villa, and Bronze Age and Islamic settlements   ★

On the N II, 27 km. west of LÉRIDA and 115 km. east of ZARAGOZA.

The site of an Iberian settlement, dating to the 4th cent. BC, is located 3.5 km. north-west of the town on the A 1234. (It is signposted.) Only its rather neglected **necropolis** may be seen, on the hillside descending from the hilltop towards the river. Fraga was the site of an important fortress town in the early Islamic centuries, which formed part of the ring of defences around LÉRIDA in the Taifa period. It was taken by the Almoravids in 1104, and in 1134 one of their armies inflicted a major defeat on Alfonso I (1104–34) the Battler of Aragón, when he was trying to besiege the town. It fell to Count Ramón Berenguer IV (1131–62) of Barcelona in 1149. Little is known archaeologically of the Arab phase in its history, but recent excavation of a site called Zafranales, about 1 km. from the centre of the present town, has yielded some indications. This site is located on a naturally defensible small hill (30 × 18 m.; 62 m. above the height of the river) with steep sides, on the left bank of the Río Cinca. Excavation of an area where two sections of wall were seen to join produced evidence, first of Mid- to Late Bronze Age occupation, and secondly of a medieval phase. Part of a room was uncovered together with clear indications, in the form of charred wood and cinders, of its having

▼ Fraga: the villa of Fortunatus

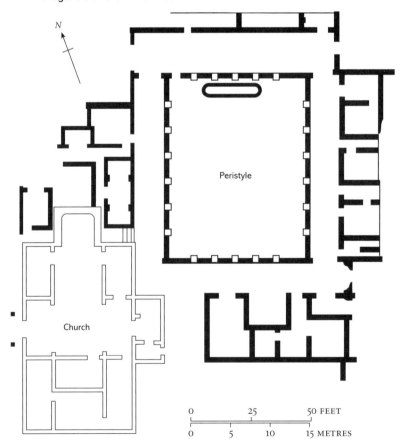

N

Peristyle

Church

| 0 | | 25 | | 50 FEET |
| 0 | 5 | 10 | | 15 METRES |

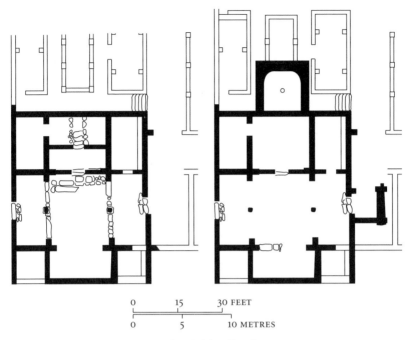

0   15   30 FEET

0   5   10 METRES

▲ *(left)* Fraga: the early 5th-cent. church (after Tuset)
  (right) Fraga: the late 6th-cent. church (after Tuset)

been burned. Few minor finds were made, but the pottery fragments have been dated to the late 11th cent.

The most important site in the vicinity of Fraga is the Late Roman **Villa Fortunatus** *(Located just under 5 km. north-west of the town on the A 1234. The site is signposted; it belongs to an adjacent farm from which admission is gained—most reasonable hours.)* First excavated between 1925 and 1936 by Serra y Rafols, the site was reinvestigated by Professor de Palol in 1980. Of the villa a series of rooms on the southern, eastern, and western side of a central peristyled courtyard (20.5 × 17 m.) have been preserved, together with much of their geometric mosaic flooring. On the south side one room has been identified as a possible *tablinum*. Its mosaic floor decoration (6 × 4.5 m.) includes an inscription containing the name of Fortunatus, the probable owner of the villa and commissioner of the mosaic, and the Christian symbol of the Chi-Rho (the first two Greek letters of *Christos* combined to make a monogram). Other familiar symbolic images from the Late Roman Christian repertoire, such as peacocks and doves, feature in this mosaic, which is of the 4th cent.

In the south-west corner of the court the original structures of the villa were altered to create a small **church**. Three phases of building have been detected here. In the earliest, dating to the 4th cent., this area formed part of the principal domestic quarters of the villa, and may have been the *triclinium* or dining-room, entered via a small vestibule. The floor was covered by a single mosaic, parts of which were buried in the second phase, in which the eastern end (previously the vestibule) was transformed into a tripartite chancel. In the central section of this a section adjacent to the end wall was dug out, probably to serve as a depository of relics below an altar. A new entry was also created in the south wall, leading into the peristyle of the villa. This process of transforming the area into a small church, similar in plan and scale to that of EL BOVALAR, took place in the early 5th cent., from the evidence of pottery finds no later than *c.*420/30. In the later sixth century (probably) a further transformation occurred. A rectangular apse (semicircular internally) was added to the east, and a large stone altar, held on a pillar created from a single stone, was set up. (This may previously have stood over the relic pit in the previous chancel.) A small ante-chancel that had been created in the western part of the central section of the previous chancel was also removed at this point. At the same time a room at the western end was transformed to serve as a baptistery. By this period the residential sections of the villa seem to have been abandoned, as may be seen from the wide scatter of graves covering much of the area around as well as inside the church.

*Leaving Fraga on the N II in the direction of Zaragoza, after 2 km. take the C 1310 northwards for 7 km. to the **Ermita de San Valero**, which is within the bounds of Velilla de Cinca.*

Although the present chapel dates from the early 13th cent., finds from the site indicate that it probably replaced a church of Visigothic origin, which in turn was located in the vicinity of a Late Roman villa.

*Just off the C 1310 to the left, at about 40 km. north-west of Fraga, is the partly restored convent of **Sigena**.*

The convent was established by Queen Sancha of Aragón in 1183. The chapel of San Pedro off the north transept of the church contains the tomb of Pedro II (1196–1213). The chapter house once contained a splendid series of late 12th-cent. frescos, severely damaged in 1936 in the Civil War, of which the remaining traces may be seen in the Museo de Arte de Cataluña in Barcelona. The paintings were made by a group of itinerant English artists, also associated with the extant Winchester Bible.

Fuengirola Islamic fortress

Located on the coast at the southern end of Fuengirola, between the mouth of the Río de Fuengirola and the N 340 Cádiz to BARCELONA highway.

Fuengirola may have been the site of the Phoenician settlement of *Suel*, but its principal monument is the castle. It once formed part of a defensive

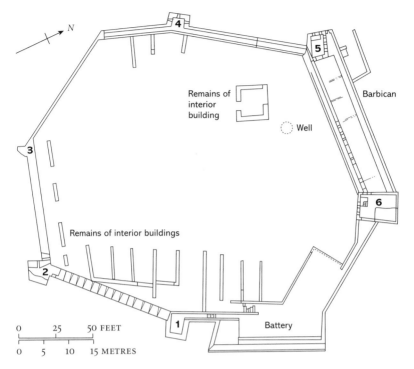

N

Remains of
interior
building

Well

Barbican

Remains of interior buildings

0   25   50 FEET
0   5   10   15 METRES

Battery

▲ Fuengirola: the castle (after Román Riechmann)
1–6. Towers

system of fortresses (including Estepona, Marbella, MÁLAGA, Torre de Mar, and Nerja) and watch towers along this coast, that existed in the Nazirid period and was continued and extended after the Castilian conquest of Fuengirola in 1485, principally in response to the threat of pirate raids from North Africa. In origin the castle of Fuengirola may have been a *ribat*, or fortress monastery of Almoravid date (early 12th cent.), though its excavator could not rule out it being an early Nazirid construction (13th/14th cent.). Literary references indicate the existence of a fortress here by 923/4 (Ibn Hayyan), but, apart from one tower, none of the present structure could be dated that early.

Six **towers** have been preserved of which four are of the same height as the circuit of walls (*c*.11 m.). The main form of construction of most of the walls and all but one of the towers involved an upper part made of *tabiya* (rammed earth) built on top of a lower section (about 4 m. high) of masonry, both being covered with a layer of white plaster. The exceptions to this pattern consist of the large battery on the east side, which was built by the Conde de Tendilla in 1553, and a section of thin wall on the southwest, which was entirely rebuilt after 1812. The largest of the towers, of which only the bottom section is original, once served as an angled entry. It was rebuilt in the 16th cent. One of the towers (no. 3) may be earlier than the others and represent the reuse of a 10th-cent. watch tower, whose existence here is recorded by Al-Rāzī. All the towers show signs of restoration and repair and two were heightened in the 16th cent., at which time the **barbican** was also constructed. Some niches uncovered in the northeast of the inner wall, in an area known from a plan made in 1785 then to have been occupied by a church, may have once belonged to a mosque or open air prayer hall (*musalla*). Much of the castle was damaged in a fire in 1653, and it was rebuilt in 1730, with the addition of barrack blocks in the courtyard. There were further repairs made in the 19th cent.

Al-Razi

A 10th-cent. Arab geographer and historian whose work has only partially survived in the form of a 15th-cent. Spanish translation of a lost Portuguese translation of c.1300 by Gil Pérez of the Arabic original.

*On the N 340 4 km. east from Fuengirola, in the coastal village of **Carvajal**, is an early imperial villa site.*

The villa is known as 'Torreblanca del Sol', and its bath complex has been excavated. It may, wholly or in part, have been turned into a fish-preserving factory in the 4th cent., when salting tanks were added. A badly damaged, partly visible, Visigothic necropolis of at least thirty-two burials around this site indicates that the villa/factory had entirely gone out of use by the 6th cent.

Gaucín   Islamic fortress

Located on a ridge (688 m.) above the C 341, 37 km. south-west of Ronda.

Earlier occupation of this area can be seen from the Roman villa site of 'Casas del Abrevadero' (8 to 10 km.) and the Visigothic necropolis at Loma del Enmedio (4 to 5 km.). A fortress existed here in the Umayyad period, certainly by 914 (Ibn Hayyan). It was taken by ʿAbd al-Jabbar, son of Al-Muʿtamid, the former Taifa ruler of Seville, as part of his revolt against the Almoravids in 1095. It subsequently became a frontier fortress of the Nazirid kingdom, and Alonso Pérez de Guzman 'el Bueno' (see TARIFA) was killed here in 1309 leading an expedition to counter raids into Christian territory. Together with other castles and towns in the region Gaucín surrendered after the fall of Ronda in 1483. The castle passed into the hands of the Duques de Medina Sidonia, descendants of Guzman el Bueno, who appointed castellans to run it. It appears to have been deserted by the early 18th cent., but was refortified and in use in both the Peninsular War and the First Carlist War of 1836–9. It was restored

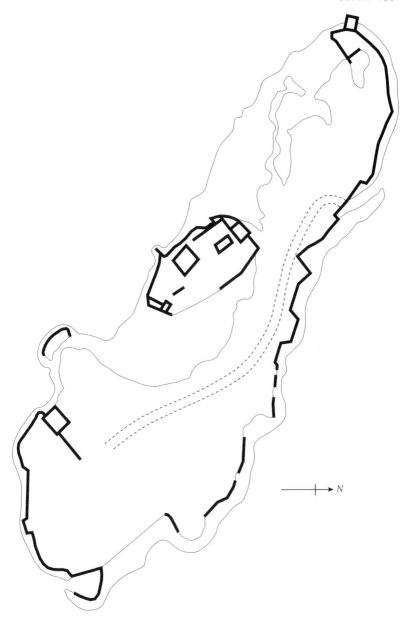

▲ Gaucín: the castle (after Peral Bejarano)

again immediately after the latter, and in 1842 held a garrison of forty
men and six cannon, but was deserted once more by the end of the decade.
The long history of the occupation of the fortress makes the disentangling

---

First Carlist War (1833–9)

On the death of Fernando VII (1808–33) the throne passed to his daughter Isabel II (1833–68), but her right to succeed was challenged by her uncle Don Carlos (d. 1855), who proclaimed himself king as Carlos V. The main areas of Carlist support were in the north, especially in Navarre and the Basque region, but the divisions also ran along political lines, with Liberal opinion favouring the queen and her mother, the regent Cristina. The Carlist revolt collapsed in 1839, due to military defeat and internal divisions, but the pretender's grandson, also called Carlos (d. 1909), revived the movement in the 1870s, provoking the Second Carlist War (1873–5). Carlism survived to play a role in the politics of the Second Republic (1931–6) and the Spanish Civil War of 1936–9.

---

of its component elements particularly difficult. A variety of Islamic pottery fragments, dating from the 10th cent. onwards, have been recovered from the site.

Gormaz   Arab castle   ★★

On the N 122, within 2 km. of leaving El Burgo de Osma in the direction of Soria, turn right onto the C 116. After approximately 10 km. a road turns off right to Quintanas de Gormaz. The village of Gormaz lies 2 km. beyond the latter. A road through the village leads up the southern side of the hill to the fortress. The castle is visible over a considerable distance.

One of the largest castles in Europe, this 10th-cent. fortress, 366 m. long by between 15 and 52 m. wide, covers the whole of the hilltop on which it is placed, guarding a crossing of the River Duero at its foot and placed in a strategic location between the upland to the south and the rapidly widening valley to the west. This was a vital frontier district in the 10th cent. between the central March of the Umayyad caliphate, centred on MEDINA-CELLI, and the County of Castile. The fortress, probably established around 940, guarded the Arab territories from Christian raids and also served as the base from which periodic expeditions were launched into Castile and Alava, the southern marcher regions of the kingdoms of León and Navarre.

It is possible that this first Arab castle occupied only the eastern end of the hilltop. A major refortification, including the western end, was carried out in 965 by the caliph Al-Ḥakam II, and in 975 the castle was subjected to a three-month siege by the rulers of León and Navarre. Although the Umayyad relieving army was unable to fight its way across the Duero, the siege was lifted by a surprise sortie from the castle. In 1059/60 the fortress was finally taken by the kingdom of Castile. Its military significance seems to have declined rapidly in the late 12th cent., when the site was abandoned. But in the period of the Castilian civil wars in the 1360s it was reoccupied, probably by the inhabitants of the local village. The eastern end was turned into an independent fortress or *alcazár* by the building of a powerful tower on the inner face of the southern wall and the development of a complicated new entry from the western section of the castle. At some point in the 13th or 14th cent. some of the southern wall, which had been undermined by erosion, was also rebuilt.

Excavations carried out from 1979 to 1981, primarily in an area close to the westernmost gate (NB the caliphal period architecture, but heavily restored during excavations in 1935/6), have revealed the various phases of occupation. A wall in the centre of this site and various post holes have been assigned to a Celtiberian settlement. There are no traces of Roman or Visigothic occupation (though fragments of Visigothic carving have been found reused in a 14th-cent. context in the eastern Alcázar and in the apse of a church in the village below). In the 10th cent. there is little trace of large-scale occupation. A limited permanent garrison must have held the fortress, with tented accommodation being erected to house the periodic expeditionary forces. Most of the visible remains of structures uncovered in the western end belong to the late medieval phases of civil occupation. A hoard of eighty forged coins of Enrique II (1369–79) was uncovered, together with some of the apparatus used to make them, in a layer of destruction by fire, datable to *c.*1380. In the early 15th cent. the site was abandoned permanently.

The once-fortified Recuerda Bridge over the Duero (*due south of the castle*) may be Roman in origin, but in its present state it shows evidence of 10th-cent. construction, especially in its central and

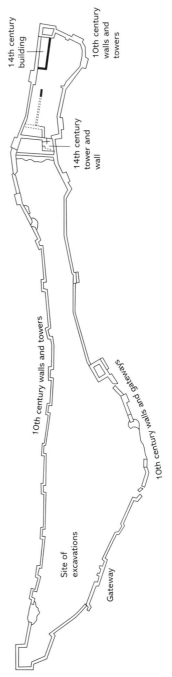

▲ Castle of Gormaz

▲ The Castle of Gormaz (10th-cent.)

northern parts. It was restored in the Late Middle Ages. It was defended by two towers at the northern end, still visible in the late 18th cent.

Gran Dolina cave (Atapuerca) Palaeolithic site

Atapuerca is located 14 km. east of Burgos; approach via the N 1 (Burgos to Miranda de Ébro) and turn south onto a small road at Quintanapalla, which leads 4 km. to the village. A local guide is needed to obtain safe access to the cave.

This cave site yielded evidence of early human occupation, including bones from at least four individuals, initially dated to around 400,000 years ago on the basis of palaeometric readings. However, this chronology has recently been revised. Indications of the last major reversal of the Earth's magnetic field have been found in the readings from this site, and as this event has been dated to around 780,000 years ago, these findings would require the hominid occupation to be put back to that period.

This would support the interpretation of the species found as being an early form of *Homo heidelbergensis*. However, it has also been suggested that the fragments of bone and teeth belong to a hitherto unknown hominid species, provisionally named *Homo antecessor*, that was ancestral to both *Homo sapiens* and Neanderthal man. This argument, together with an even more recent claim that the finds are indicative of cannibalism, remains highly controversial. This discovery, together with recent evidence of even earlier hominid occupation of a site near ORCE, also appears to undermine the argument that adverse climatic conditions prevented any human settlement in Europe before about 500,000 years ago.

Atapuerca is also the site of a crucial battle in 1054 between García of Navarre (1035–54) and his brother Fernando I of Castile (1037–65). The defeat and death of King García, possibly the result of treachery, put an end to a period of Navarrese domination in northern Spain and led to the kingdom's territorial decline.

Granada Islamic city   ★★

In the Roman period the principal settlement in this area was the town of Illiberis or Elvira, whose precise location has been a matter of scholarly controversy. This was the site of a bishopric in the Visigothic period and also under the Umayyads. It was in the Taifa period that Granada was developed to replace the earlier town, but even then the heart of the new settlement was on the northern hill, the Albaicín, which had once been the site of an Early Iron Age settlement. The Alhambra, for which Granada is now most famous, only became the royal residence and administrative centre of the kingdom under the Nazirids (1236–1492). Their once powerful realm, which shrank rapidly in size in the course of the 15th cent., was lost with the surrender of Granada to Fernando and Isabel of Aragón and Castile on 2 January 1492.

In the Nazirid period there were technically two cities here: the palace city of Medina al-Hamra and the much larger, if less prestigious, city of Medina Garnata that lay at its feet and on the opposite hillside to the north. It is not easy to recover the sense of the Alhambra as a settlement in its own right, and it is important to recall that areas that now seem empty or lightly occupied were once filled with the houses of those who served the rulers in their palace complex, and with the shops, baths, and other necessities that they required. Something of these parts of the palace city have been recovered by excavation of empty spaces on the southern side of the site. Five houses, in addition to those in the *alcazaba* (see below), have been found under the gardens in this area around the Calle Real. They are generally structured around a central courtyard with a small pool, off which the principal rooms opened.

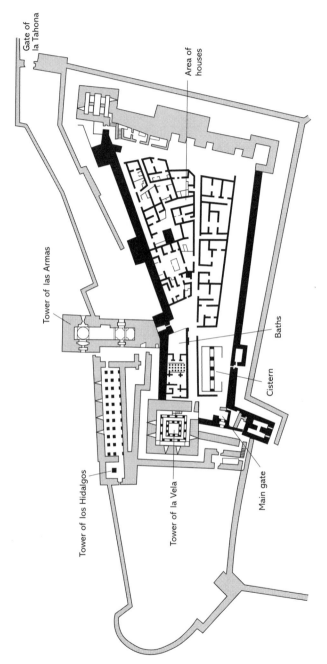

▲ Granada: Alcazaba of the Alhambra (after Pavón Maldonado). Walls outlined in black are 11th-cent. structures, others are of the Nazirid period.

The *Alcazaba*

This is the most substantial survival from the pre-Nazirid periods in the Alhambra. Both the main northern and southern walls, with their towers, and the entry in the south-west corner date from the 11th cent. So too do the various foundations of domestic buildings that fill the intervening space, and a cistern near to the main gate. While less dramatic than the great Torre de la Vela at the western end, let alone the palaces in the main part of the Alhambra, this section of defences and housing is worth attention as a product of the period in which the city was ruled by the Berber Zirid dynasty (1013–90). The Nazirid fortifications in the *alcazaba* mainly date from the reign of Muḥammad I (1230–72), the first ruler of the new dynasty.

The *Hammam al-Yawza*

A bath house located on the Carrera del Darro is of Zirid date. (Its roofs with distinctive star-shaped openings to admit light may be seen from above from the Torre de las Armas in the *alcazaba* of the Alhambra.) Subsequent reuse of the site has made the internal organization of the baths unclear, though an arcaded steam room, preceded by a vestibule, and an adjacent section that once contained plunge pools can be seen. A little to the west, heading down the Carrera del Darro towards the city centre, you can see on the other side of the stream the springing of a ruined 'Bridge of the Qadi', also possibly of Zirid date.

Bath Complex

A hitherto unknown bath complex dating to the Almohad period (12th/13th cents.) and located in the former Jewish quarter of the city began to be studied and excavated in 1984. It is located in a site previously occupied by the 18th- and 19th-cent. buildings of a school run by the Mercedarian order in the Plaza de los Tiros. It was immediately established that the central part of the bath complex, consisting of its *al-bayt al-wastani* or *tepidarium* with its hypocausts, had been preserved, and was dated by the surviving capitals. Further investigation has shown that virtually all sections of the baths, including service areas and *al-bayt al-sajun* or *caldarium* with its plunge baths, have also to some degree been preserved, and a programme of continuing excavation and restoration has been launched. We know, too, that a district mosque, that of Ibn Gimara, was located next to the baths. In the same district a collection of capitals of the Almohad period have been found reused in the Casa de los Girones, as (in 1983) have some carved wooden friezes with 13th-cent. Cufic inscriptions in the Casa de los Tiros.

The Maristan

This public hospital of Granada (Calle de Buñuelo) survived as a building until demolished in 1843, and is the only example of such a structure

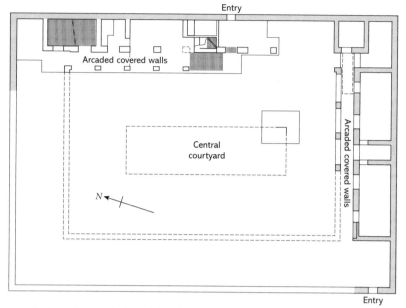

Entry

Arcaded covered walls

Arcaded covered walls

Central
courtyard

N

Entry

▲ Granada: the Maristan (after Salvatierra Cuenca)

known from Al-Andalus. Excavations begun in 1984 have recovered something of the outline of the building (38 × 26.5 m.) and features of its internal layout. Two lion-shaped fountains that feed a garden pool in front of the Torre de las Damas in the Alhambra are said to have been brought there from the Maristan.

The Albaicín

The site of the earliest settlement in Granada, it dates back to the 7th cent. BC. Evidence of structures of this period was found in a rescue excavation in the Calle María la Miel. These took the form of square houses built of mud brick, similar to those better documented in the **Cerro de los Infantes** site (see ALCALÁ LA REAL). No trace has yet been found here of the early Iberian culture of the 6th and first half of the 5th cents. Two necropolises seem to document use of the area in the later 5th and 4th cents. In the Early Roman Imperial period in the first two cents. AD there is evidence for pottery factories in this area (one in the Cartuja and the other at the eastern end of the Carmen de la Muralla in the Albaicín). One kiln has been found in the latter and it seems to have been devoted to the production of *terra sigillata*. The northern flank of the Albaicín retains much of a line of walls and towers (visible from the west end of the Cuesta de la Alhacaba and from the steps up the side of the hill, but not easy to approach closely). These are thought to be of Zirid origin, as the expansion of the city in the Nazirid period led to the extension of its walls much further to the north. (Part of these later walls may be seen running west from the Puerta Fajalauza.) Remains of two mosques have been incorporated in the churches of El Salvador and San Juan de los Reyes (both otherwise 16th-cent.). Another 16th-cent. church, San José, in the southwest corner of the Albaicín, has a horseshoe arch in its south wall, probably of the 11th cent. The Albaicín remains the most attractive part of Granada for casual wandering, and for the views it affords.

Museums

There is a Museo Arqueológico in the Carrera del Darro (no. 41), displaying a wide range of objects from prehistoric to Islamic times. A Museo Nacional de Arte Hispano-Musulmán was opened in 1962 in the Alhambra (entered through the Palace of Charles V), which is particularly rich in Nazirid items, especially ceramics.

Guardamar   Islamic ribat

*On the N 332 from **Cartagena** to **Alicante**, Guardamar lies between the road and the sea 37 km. south of the latter. The turning to the dunes is about 1 km. further south.*

The incidence of Spanish place names incorporating the element *rabit*, which is the Spanish form of the word ribat, such as the monastery of La Rábida near Huelva or the resort of La Rábita near **Adra**, suggests the previous existence on these sites of *rabitun*, fortress 'monasteries', to which men withdrew for periods of time of their own choosing, both to lead an austere Muslim lifestyle and, in some cases, to fight for Islam. While many of these were therefore located in frontier districts, others were built on coastal sites to provide defence against maritime raiders, who from the 840s could include Vikings. However, no traces have been found of the structures themselves in locations bearing such names. A number of these buildings survive virtually intact in North Africa, notably at Sousse and Monastir in Tunisia. However, excavations begun in 1984 have uncovered the first clear example of such a foundation in Spain, in a grove of pine trees amongst the dunes at Guardamar del Segura (province of Alicante). Surprisingly, its plan is quite unlike that of the North African equivalents, which take the form of high-walled square or rectangular fortresses built around a central courtyard.

At Guardamar what has emerged is a series of individual chambers strung out in three roughly parallel lines, divided by narrow streets or passages. The buildings were constructed of rammed earth erected on lower courses of stonework. Each individual cell has its own *mihrab*, and the lines of buildings are oriented to face south-west towards Mecca. Traces have been found of a defensive perimeter wall around the whole site. In the central line of buildings, towards its eastern end, there is a two-aisled mosque. Elements in its construction have led to its being dated to

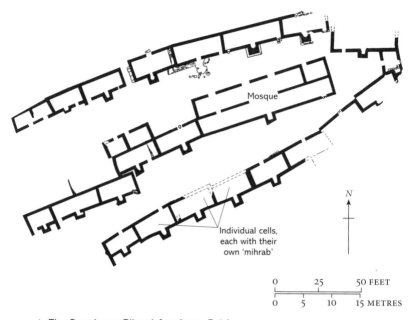

▲ The Guardamar Ribat (after Azuar Ruiz)

the 9th cent. An inscription found on the site, however, records the completion of a mosque in 944; this may refer to a subsequent restoration or enlargement of the building, possibly the construction of the second aisle or hall. Ceramics, inscriptions, and traces of painted wall plaster have emerged from the excavations.

For Phoenician settlements and necropolises in the Segura valley, immediately north of Guardamar, see EL ORAL.

Huelva Phoenician, Tartessian, and Roman settlement

Capital of the province of the same name, 88 km. west of SEVILLE on the E1/A 49.

Traces of a Phoenician settlement, dating from the 8th to late 6th cent. BC, have been found in the course of recent excavations at Calle del Puerto, 8–10. An Iberian settlement belonging to the kingdom of Tartessus occupied the site after the Phoenicians. From this period comes the **cemetery** on the hill of **La Joya**, within the modern city boundaries, that was excavated in the 1970s. Nineteen tombs have been uncovered, and four of these contained particularly rich assemblages of grave goods in gold, bronze, and alabaster. One of them (no. 17) contained a two-horse chariot. None of the burials appears to have been marked by structures above ground. Both inhumation and cremation were practised, and each tomb is quite distinct in terms of the items buried in it. What is especially notable is the wide diversity of these grave goods, and the very clear evidence that they virtually all provide of strong eastern Mediterranean cultural influences. This has made La Joya one of the key sites in the understanding of Tartessian culture. Of the succeeding Roman town of Onuba much less is known, but local archaeological collections from all these periods are housed in the Museo de Huelva at Alameda de Sundheim, 13. Here may also be seen finds from the Phoenician and Roman copper mines of **Tharsis**. The town was captured by Alfonso X of Castile around 1262. On the northern edge of the town is a good (and unusual) example of an Arab aqueduct. Traces of the mosque that previously occupied the site may be seen in the church of San Pedro.

Slag heaps from the ancient mines may be seen at Tharsis, 47 km. north of Huelva up the C 443.

Huesca Arab fortifications

Capital of the province of the same name, easily accessible by road and rail.

The layout of the medieval city of Huesca can easily be deduced from modern town plans, and is defined by the oblong area within the Coso Alto, the Coso Bajo, the Ronda de Montearagón, and the Calle Costa. Along the inner side of both of the latter considerable stretches of the **medieval walls** may be seen. Although, like most medieval town walls, these were repaired at various times, they date back to the Arab occupation of the city that was ended by its conquest by the Aragonese king Pedro I in 1096. The construction has been dated to the period around 875. In particular, the foundations of a series of shallow rectangular towers along the Calle Costa show clear relationship with the 9th-cent. fortifications of such sites as BALAGUER and MADRID. Much detail on the interior of the Arab city can be recovered from the post-conquest documentation, especially of the cathedral and of the fortress monastery of Montearagón, when a major redistribution of property occurred. The approximate locations of six suburbs, five of which possessed mosques, and of four intramural sectional mosques have been deduced from this evidence. The present cathedral (1497–1515), replaces an earlier one of 1278 on the site of the main mosque.

The Museo Arqueológico Provincial is located in the Plaza de la Universidad, and forms part of the Museo de Huesca. The oldest section of the building dates to the 12th cent., when it formed part of the palace of the kings of Aragón.

Near Huesca may be seen the fortress monastery of **Montearagón** (7 km. east on the N 240) and the very impressive 11th–13th-cent. castle of Loarre (14 km. west on the A 132 to Esquedas and then 13 km. north-west on the A 1206).

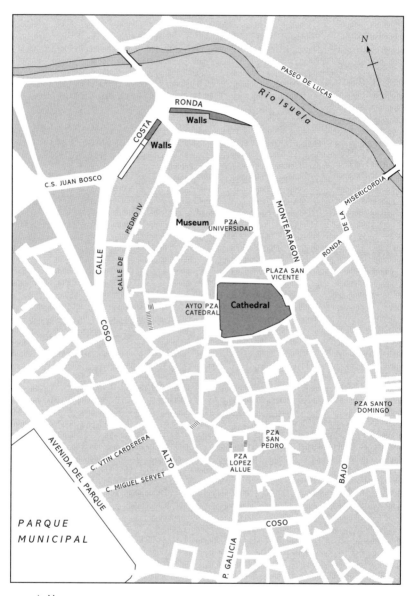

▲ Huesca

Ilduro   Iberian village

Located by the village of Cabrera de Mar, which may be reached by the N II from BARCELONA *to **Gerona/Girona**. About 24 km. north of Barcelona, and 4 km. before reaching Mataró, a small road leads inland for 4 km. to Cabrera.*

On the southern slope of the hill culminating in the castle (see below), this was the site of the Iberian town of Ilduro, occupied according to the evidence of pottery finds from the 6th to the beginning of the 1st cent. BC. It was replaced by the Roman town of Iluro, on the coast at Mataró, where the earliest phase of construction has been dated to the late 2nd cent. BC. The first excavations here began in 1885. The town was triangular in shape, and displays similarities in its planning to that of the more sophis-

▼ Ilduro

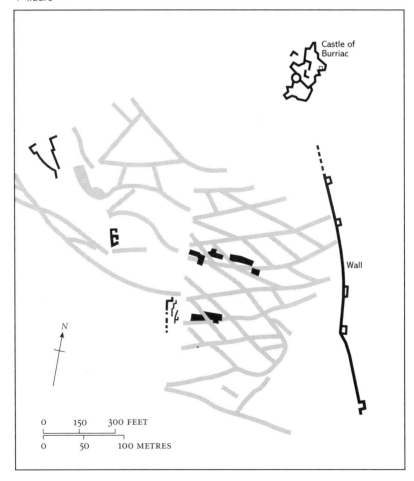

ticated settlement at ULLASTRET. The eastern defensive wall and sections of streets and houses can be seen.

Four **tombs** were found here, dating to c.300–250 BC. They were all in the form of small holes, about 1 m. in diameter and 80 cm. deep. Each contained two upright amphorae, with their pointed bases dug into the earth. One of these was used to hold the incinerated ashes; the other probably contained a liquid. Two of the tombs were of warriors, and contained swords, shields, and lances, together with a large variety of high-quality Hellenistic pottery. One of the two burials also included the ashes of a second individual. The other two tombs lacked both weapons and luxury ceramics. It also seems likely that items of clothing were included in the burials.

See also the castle of **Burriac**, on the summit of the hill, of which the keep and four ruined walls remain.

Pottery finds, especially of Hellenistic and Roman Republican origin, together with coins from the site can be seen in the Museu de Mataró (Calle Carreró, 17–19—in Mataró: see also TORRE LLAUDER).

Irún Roman town

Excavations in the frontier town of Irun carried out in late 1992 and early 1993 have uncovered traces of a Roman settlement, which may well prove to be Oiaso, whose existence was recorded in literary sources but whose precise location had never been established. A trench sunk next to the church of Juncal, in the Calle Santiago, revealed wooden remains from a quayside 3 m. below the present street level, establishing the existence here of a Roman harbour, datable from a coin find to the 2nd cent. AD. In addition a stairway, founded on large stone blocks, and part of the foundations of a building were exposed. These are dated to the 4th cent. There were also finds of glass and ceramics, including *terra sigillata*. A thick layer of black mud over the site has preserved many perishable items, such as a leather shoe. The level of the sea here in the Roman period was about 1.5 m. below the present.

A Roman necropolis has also been discovered and excavated around the chapel of Ama Xantalen. As the burials include those in amphorae, a Late Imperial date seems likely.

Itálica Roman town   ★★
(Visit together with SEVILLE)

The N 630/E 803 from SEVILLE to MÉRIDA heads northwards on the west bank of the Guadalquivir; 8 km. north of its divergence from the E 1/A 49 (Seville to Huelva motorway) a small road turns left to Santiponce and the ruins of Itálica (signposted). There is also a regular bus service from the centre of Seville directly to the site (enquire at the Oficina del Turismo).

The earliest Roman settlement in Spain, Itálica was founded in 205 BC (Appian 38) for veteran legionaries, following the defeat the previous year of the Carthaginians at the battle of Ilipa (Alcalá del Río) in the Guadalquivir valley. Part of the site chosen had previously been used for an indigenous settlement of the Turdetani, dating from the later 4th cent. BC. The status of *municipium* was probably acquired in the reign of Augustus (27 BC–AD 14), and this led to the issue of a local bronze coinage. The town itself seems to have been extensively remodelled under Augustus and his successor Tiberius (14–37).

Appian

A Greek, living as an imperial official in Alexandria in the mid-2nd cent. AD, he compiled from earlier sources a history of Rome from its foundation up to the reign of Trajan (98–117) in twenty-four books, of which eleven survive. Book 6 relates to Roman wars in Spain.

The real fortune of Itálica lay in the fact that it was the birthplace of the Emperor Trajan (98–117) and home town of his cousin Hadrian (117–38), the first Roman emperors of provincial origin. Under Hadrian, who was actually born in Rome but whose family came from Itálica, the size of the city was greatly extended, and a radical programme of public and private building instituted, centring on a ritual complex dedicated to the cult of his predecessor. The settlement was also elevated to the status of *colonia* under the new name of Colonia Aelia Augusta Italica.

Both the size and the wealth of the city apparently dropped in the 3rd cent. and a new wall, encompassing a reduced area, was erected in the late 3rd or early 4th cent. While some public buildings, including the temple of Trajan, were abandoned, there is evidence that some substantial private residences were still being built in the 4th cent. Of Itálica's later political history little is known until 583, when the city, which then formed part of the kingdom of the rebel Hermenegild (579–84), was besieged and taken by his father Leovigild (569–86). In the 7th cent. it was eclipsed in political, social, and economic importance by nearby Seville (Hispalis), but remained the seat of a bishopric. The last known bishop of Itálica attended the sixteenth Council of Toledo in 693. Probably by the early Islamic period the inhabited parts of the settlement had shrunk to little more than the area of the present village of Santiponce. Settlement of a much reduced kind appears to have continued here until as late as the 12th cent.

The Turdetanian settlement, like the later Roman town, was located in the area of modern Santiponce (constructed in 1603). This **Iberian settlement** seems to have been quite small (*c.*13 ha.) and made up of buildings erected of mud-brick on stone footings, with clay floors. Indications of metal-working and pottery-making have been found. Of the earliest **Roman town**, of Republican date, which may have been essentially a continuation of the Turdetanian one, little is known beyond

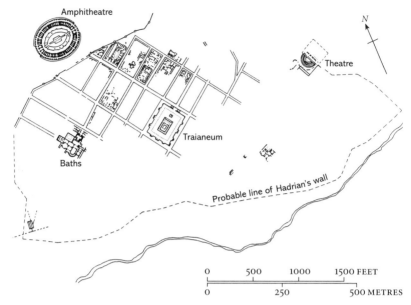

▲ Itálica: plan

a site containing a building with two large rooms on the hill of Los Palacios. By the time of the Civil War (49–45 BC), the settlement was enclosed within a defensive wall (*BC* xx. 6). Inscriptions and recent excavation have proved more informative about the rejuvenation the town seems to have enjoyed under Augustus and Tiberius. The forum and a probable temple of Apollo of Augustan date have been located in the area of the village, and the theatre, still visible in Santiponce, was built in the reign of Tiberius (see below). Despite the substantial westwards extension of the city in the 2nd cent., this seems to have remained the site of the forum and the principal civic buildings. However, most of what can be seen in the main area of excavations belongs to the new city of Hadrian's reign, and this will be described first.

The first monument encountered on entering the site is the ruined **amphitheatre**, one of the best-preserved examples in Spain (see also MÉRIDA and TARRAGONA) and the fourth largest known from any part of the Roman Empire, once capable of seating 40,000 people. Most parts of the vaulted galleries that ran underneath the tiers of seats have survived, as have the subterranean passages and central rectangular space beneath the floor of the arena. These passages were used to transport and retain animals and other participants in the spectacles, unseen by the spectators. Although their covering is now lost, you can still see the pillars of the central area; these would once have supported a wooden floor, and probably a variety of trapdoors giving access to the surface. The seating is

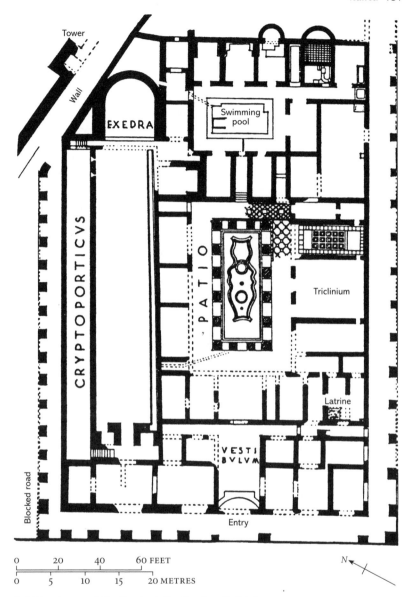

Tower

Wall

EXEDRA

Swimming pool

CRYPTOPORTICVS

PATIO

Triclinium

Latrine

VESTI BVLVM

Blocked road

Entry

| 0 | | 20 | | 40 | | 60 FEET |
| 0 | 5 | 10 | 15 | 20 METRES |

N

▲ Itálica: house of the Exedra (after García y Bellido)

poorly preserved, except at the lowest levels, having been quarried for its stone, but the layout of the rows and the location of the magistrate's box in the centre of the northern side may be clearly distinguished. The amphitheatre lay just outside the **walls of the city**, which were defended by regularly placed rectangular towers and date from the reign of

Hadrian. You can see a small section of the walls, including one of the principal gates, between the amphitheatre and the rest of the site, which lies within their circuit.

A regular grid plan of square or rectangular building plots (*insulae*) separated by broad rectilinear streets is typical of Roman town planning, and is well illustrated here. Immediately through the walls facing the amphitheatre lay a district of large houses, which was the focus of the main campaigns of excavation. Fine 2nd-cent. mosaics have been discovered in a number of these houses. Although the site was, in the main, not built over in subsequent periods, planting, animal foraging, and also antiquarian enthusiasms have led to a number of these sustaining damage or being lost following their discovery. Several of the best have been transferred to the Museo Arqueológico in Seville, but a satisfying number can still be seen *in situ*. Passing along the road from the amphitheatre, the first *insula* on the left is a small triangular space (because of the lie of the walls) with traces of the columned portico that fronted the whole of the street still visible, but little else of note.

The second *insula*, however, is taken up by one very large and luxurious structure, known as '**The House of the Exedra**', which is built around a rectangular atrium, in the centre of which is a complex curvilinear pool (*impluvium*). A series of rooms once opened onto the atrium from three sides. In the south-west corner there is a large latrine; you can see part of its black and white mosaic floor, which depicts pygmies fighting on the backs of ostriches. The dining-room or *triclinium* was in the middle of the southern side of the atrium; the room adjacent to it on the east and parts of the two porticoes adjacent to it have preserved sections of polychrome marble pavement in *opus sectile*. To the east of the atrium, approached via a short flight of steps, another set of rooms surrounds an open swimming bath. Hypocausts in one of the rooms on the eastern outer wall suggest that this whole area may have been some kind of bathing complex. The villa receives its name from the unusual arrangement on its northern side. Here a long open patio (40 × 9 or 10 m.), entered via a suite of rooms on its western end, is flanked by a *cryptoporticus* to the north and a semicircular apse or 'exedra' to the east, calculated to have reached to a height of 20 m. The purpose of this area is not obvious, but it may have been a gymnasium or *palaestra*. There are indications that some parts at least of this house rose to a height of three storeys. While it has long been assumed that this building is an unusually large and luxurious private residence, its scale and some of the peculiarities of its structure and organization have led more recently to the suggestion that it was a *collegium* of some sort, possibly for adolescents (*iuvenes*).

Down the second street on the right from the main gate (and facing the corner of the 'House of the Exedra') lies a substantial public bath complex, approached up an unusually broad street (8 m. wide, with colonnaded pavements 4 m. wide on each side). On the way towards the baths you can see the outline of a house on the left, with mosaics in some of the rooms closest to the street. There is a latrine in the south-west corner. The bath house, known traditionally as '**Los Baños de la Reina Mora**' (Baths of the Moorish Queen), was first excavated in 1861. The central feature is a large swimming pool (21 m. long) with an apsidal western end. This was surrounded by a number of square chambers and atria. On the northern edge of this site there is a large vaulted underground area, whose purposes are not clear. Recent geophysical surveys of the area have revealed something of the sections of the baths no longer visible, and including a probable gymnasium across a street to the south. Extending over four *insulae*, this bath complex appears to have been the largest known in Roman Spain. To the south-west of the bath house and adjacent to the westernmost corner of the outer wall are the remains of a *castellum aquae* which served this complex, as well as other parts of the city. Water was led into the city from the north-west along an aqueduct starting in hills to the west of Gerena. This 1st-cent. aqueduct was amplified by Hadrian, and seems to have gone out of use in the mid-4th cent. Slight traces of this system survive where it crosses the Cortijo de las Dueñas, the Cortijo Villadiego, and the Cortijo de Conti.

Continuing along the street leading from the gate, the next *insula* after that containing the 'House of the Exedra' has revealed little of the outline of the buildings that once filled it, but traces of a number of mosaics may be seen, especially from the side street that separates it from the next *insula* to the south. The latter is better endowed with foundations of buildings, including the so-called '**House of the Peacocks**', which would originally have been entered off the main street. To north and south of a rectangular central atrium, which had a central cistern feeding two fountains, you can see the floor plans of two sets of rooms. The *triclinium*, boasting a fine mosaic depicting peacocks, is in the middle of the north side. The kitchen was probably located in the group of rooms flanking the main entry, as a large oven is located in one to the left of the vestibule. To the east of the atrium a wall shields the private quarters of the owners, built around a second atrium and a *piscina*. A small recess with mosaic floor in the east wall of the main atrium served as the *Lararium*, the shrine of the household gods (*Lares*). Within the domestic suite, a series of fine mosaics may be seen in the rooms of the south-eastern corner. Less can be seen of the house immediately adjacent to the east, which takes up the rest of the *insula*, but there are mosaics in rooms next to the outer walls on both the northern and southern sides.

The next *insula* to the south has suffered from having the cemetery of Santiponce located across its western half (and over the street into the eastern end of the *insula* opposite). Although the cemetery has now been moved, its presence was fatal to the structures that lay below it. The building that once filled the eastern half of this *insula* (it is likely but not certain that a different dwelling lay under the cemetery section) has come to be called '**The House of Hylas**', from the subject of one of its numerous surviving mosaics. This offers the best collection of geometric mosaics still *in situ* in Itálica. To the east of it, across the street, the western end of another house has been excavated, including one small mosaic. The rectangular chambers opening onto the colonnaded pavement in its north-west corner, lacking access to the rest of the building, may well have been shops. Continuing up the road that runs between the last two buildings described to the next *insula* on the right, you can see the east end of another house of this same, 2nd-cent., period; this is constructed around an atrium with curved *impluvium*.

Another broad road ran east–west on the far side of this *insula*. Recent excavation has revealed that it led to the central feature of the whole of Hadrian's 'new city' of Itálica, the **temple complex** of the cult of Trajan or *Traianeum*. This appears to have been demolished and despoiled, probably in the later imperial period, by when the size of the city was drastically reduced. Fine marbles and other stonework from this site were reused elsewhere in the city. The walled precinct, with semicircular and rectangular *exedrae*, was approached via facing stairways and a tetrapylon on its eastern side. Within the precinct a colonnade surrounded an octastyle temple and a large external altar facing the steps up to the temple. There seem to have been four pairs of statues between the colonnade and the temple on both of its longer sides.

Geophysical surveying has recently yielded information on some of those parts of the city that have not been excavated. Strikingly, this has indicated that a number of the *insulae* in the north-west of the city, while laid out for building on, never had any constructions on them. This, together with indications of 3rd-cent. decline and the abandonment of much of the area between the temple of Trajan and the northern wall, suggests that the Hadrianic flowering of the city was short-lived. Subsidence may have caused abandonment of some buildings, but wider political and economic factors may be the true explanation: the end of the notional Antonine dynasty (created by adoptions more than ties of blood) in 192 and the rise of that of the Severans marked an end of imperial support for the city.

There is a small site museum containing finds from the excavations, located at the entry near the amphitheatre. While the main site is primarily Hadrianic, and this period has received the lion's share of attention, recent excavation has been devoted to the earlier and later phases of the settlement's long history, and much of this has been concentrated in and around the village of Santiponce.

Just west of the village, and close to the line of the southern wall of the Roman city, lies another public bath complex, originally excavated in the 19th cent., and called misleadingly '**Los Palacios**' (The Palaces). Like the Baños de la Reina Mora, whose dimensions it seems to match, its central feature is an apsed swimming pool, but little more of it can be made out. It dates from the reign of Trajan (98–117). In the north-east corner of the village itself may be seen the (now over-restored) remains of the theatre, built under Tiberius (14–37), but refurbished with newer-style decoration in the 2nd cent., possibly under Hadrian and again in the reign of Septimius Severus (193–211). Immediately to the east of its *scaenae frons* (back wall of the stage) was a large porticoed square (44.5 × 39.5 m.), similar to that located in an identical position beside the theatre at MÉRIDA, of which the theatre wall provided the western side. There was a large ornamental pool in the centre, and a small shrine to the goddess Isis (identified from inscriptions) has been located off the middle of the southern colonnade. This area is currently being excavated, and arguments over its dating, ranging from the time of Tiberius to the 2nd cent., may thus be resolved. Town walls of the same period have left visible traces on the southern and south-eastern edges of Santiponce; in the fields to the north of this area pagan and Christian burial grounds have been located.

Isis

She is an Egyptian goddess of great power, wife of Osiris and mother of Horus. Her cult, linked to that of the Hellenistic divinity Serapis, became popular in Rome by the Late Republican period.

The best of the sculptures from Itálica, including busts of Augustus (27 BC–AD 14), Nero (54–68), Vespasian (69–79), and Marcus Aurelius (161–80), may be seen in the Museo Arqueológico in SEVILLE, together with many other small finds. Other items from the site, including sculptures and mosaics, became part of the collection of Doña Regla Manjón y Mergelina, Condesa de Lebrija (1851–1938). These may be seen in the Palacio de Lebrija (C/Cuna 8), but only by previous appointment. There are also Arab and medieval items of interest in this collection, as well as in the Museo Arqueológico. In the Museo Arqueológico Nacional in MADRID may be seen the Itálica *Oratio*, found in 1888. This consists of part of a bronze inscription giving the text of a speech made in AD 176/7 by a senator, whose name is lost, decrying the large rewards paid to gladiators. This oration was delivered in opposition to one previously given by the future emperor Marcus Aurelius Commodus (180–92), and its publication in this form was ordered by a *senatus consultum* or decree of the Senate.

Jerez de la Frontera Almohad mosque

This was probably Roman Asido Caesaris, and is now known principally as the home of sherry. The town was taken by Alfonso X of Castile in 1264.

The 'de la Frontera' element in the name, first recorded in 1380, refers to the frontier with the Nazirid kingdom of GRANADA. The 17th-cent. **church of San Salvador** is on the site of the Friday Mosque or *jami*, whose minaret influenced the detached location of the present bell tower. The architectural history of the **Alcázar** has not been easy to deduce. Fortifications of Almohad date may constitute rebuilding of earlier structures, and they were themselves repaired and restored at various times after the Castilian conquest. In the Alcázar, the present **Capilla de Santa María la Real** incorporates most of an unusual late 12th-cent. Almohad mosque. This has a brick-built prayer hall approximately 10 sq. m. topped by an octagonal dome. The entry on the north-west side was through three arches, leading from a small courtyard containing a central pool, a well with a ceramic head, and a minaret in the northern corner. On the south wall of the prayer hall is a rectangular *mihrab* under a now restored domed ceiling, matched by two other small domes in either corner. The reduced dimensions and unusual plan indicate that this was not a congregational mosque; it is better seen as a private or palace chapel for the commander of the fortress.

The Museo Arqueológico Municipal, containing local collections, is being rehoused in Plaza Julián Cuadra, 12–13.

La Hoya Neolithic and Iron Age settlement

From Laguardia (province of Alava) take the N 232/A 124 nothwards (direction of Samaniego). Where it is joined by the CV 140/A 3228, about 1 km. north of the town, a narrow road leads directly to the site, which is signposted from the main road.

This site was discovered in 1935, and was further excavated in 1950 and from 1973 onwards. The earliest level of occupation has been dated to the 15th cent. BC, with a second phase coming about 200 years later. A Celtiberian settlement site, though, from around the 4th cent. BC, provides most of what can be seen today.

A rectangular area has been uncovered, within which a prow-shaped central section, forming a block of dwellings around two central courtyards, is delineated by streets on all three sides. On the outer edges of these streets the foundations of further structures are visible, and more sections of housing probably lie under the areas not yet excavated. A narrow entry into the settlement faces the tip of the triangular block of houses, and the stone defensive wall of the village ran off on either side.

The earliest Neolithic dwellings traced under the Celtiberian levels were simple wooden post-built structures, and a wooden wall probably ran around the settlement. The second Neolithic phase was marked by increased use of stone, both in the lower levels of the rectangular houses and in a new defensive wall. The Celtiberian houses and defences were more substantial in the breadth of their walls and in the size of stones employed. Pottery from both the Neolithic and Iron Age occupation has been recovered, together with Celtiberian iron tools and weapons. Bronze ornaments and fastenings from the latter period have also been recovered, together with a number of small bronze cult objects. Additionally, there are some carved horn pieces that may have been used as whistles, and an interesting set of weights. The finds have been divided between a small museum on the site and the Museo Provincial de Alava in Vitoria/Gasteiz. Further excavation of this site is being undertaken.

A number of dolmens may be seen in this immediate area, including one known as **San Martín** and another called **El Sotillo**, *both situated on the A 124/N 232 on the 4 km. stretch of road from Laguardia north to the Sanatorio (hospital) de Leza. Both are indicated by road signs.* For three dolmens to the east of Laguardia see ALAVA.

La Pedrosa de la Vega Late Roman villa

*From PALENCIA head north on the C 615 for 40 km. to **Carrión de los Condes** (two Romanesque churches) and on for a further 19 km., when a turn to the left leads 2 km. to the site (signposted).*

A remarkably fine example of a Late Roman rural villa, no doubt then linked to a large agricultural estate, this dates from the 4th cent., and seems to have continued in use until destroyed by fire in the 6th cent. The villa was discovered in 1968 and first excavated in 1969–70.

▼ Pedrosa de la Vega: Roman villa (after Keay)

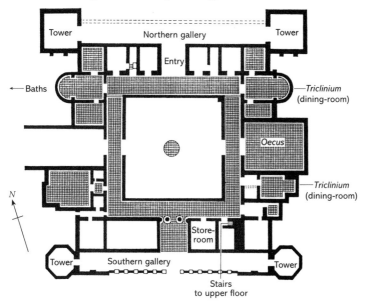

It would have presented a fortified appearance, with towers in each corner of the central section, which is articulated around a large square courtyard. Entry from either the northern or southern sides was through ornamental galleries (the northern one is lost) placed between the towers. Two *triclinia* or dining-rooms have been detected in the eastern wing, opening onto the peristyle around the central court. These flank a large rectangular room, thought to be an *oecus* or reception hall. Slight traces of a bath complex have been found to the west of the main section of the villa, but hardly any of this can be seen. Extremely fine 4th-cent. mosaic floors, not least of spirited hunting scenes, can be seen in the portico around the court and in the rooms on the east and west sides.

Finds from the site are on display in the Museo Monográfico de la Villa Romana de la Olmeda (Iglesia de San Pedro, Plaza de San Pedro) in **Saldaña**, opened in 1984. There is also a castle of 11th-cent. origin to be seen in this village.

*At **Quintanilla de la Cueza**, 17 km. west from Carrión de los Condes on the N 120, just beyond Cervatos de la Cueza, is another villa (signposted) on the edge of the village.*

This smaller Roman villa, of the 1st–4th cent. AD, contains some fine if simple early imperial mosaics.

Lacipo Roman town

The site occupies the northern end of a steep-sided hill located between the village of Casares (province of Málaga) and the Río Genal; there is no road access (and not really much to see). Casares is approached via the MA 539, which runs between San Luís de Sabinillas, on the coast 11 km. south-west of Estepona, and GAUCÍN. Almost equidistant between the two, a road leads eastwards for less than 2 km. to Casares, which houses a ruined late medieval castle.

Situated on a naturally defensible site, this was once a settlement of the Iberian people called the Turduli. Little is known of its history beyond references in Pomponius Mela (II. 94) and Ptolemy but, after the founding of the Roman town, it formed part of the *conventus* of Gades (Cádiz). Campaigns of excavation in 1975 and 1976 were directed at two sectors of the site, in both cases revealing the outlines of interconnected rectangular rooms, probably once forming parts of private residences. These have been dated to generally between the 1st cent. BC and the 1st cent. AD. No traces of public buildings emerged. Pottery found in 1976 confirmed the previous Iberian occupation. A Visigothic necropolis was discovered in the zone excavated in 1975, which seems to have come into being after the earlier Roman buildings had been abandoned. Occupation of the site in the Visigothic period thus seems probable, but the nature and scale of this cannot be gauged. Of Late Roman or other medieval phases nothing is known.

Las Médulas Roman mines

*Proceed for 25 km. south-west from **Ponferrada** (the centre of a much more recent coal-mining industry and notable for its restored Templar castle) on the N 536. Just before entering the village of **Carucedo**, a small road to the left leads south for about 4 km. to Las Médulas.*

An impressive Roman gold-mine can be seen about 300 m. to the east of the village of Las Médulas, where a great quarry-like scar in the land represents the site of a gold-bearing hill collapsed to release its ore. This is thought to have been worked between the 1st and 4th cent., with the use of slave labour at least in the early imperial period. Water was brought to the mines by six **aqueducts** and stored in two huge **tanks** on the eastern edge of the collapsed hill. This was used to wash out the ore from rubble created by undermining the hillside with tunnels and causing it to collapse. The particles of gold were retained in heather placed in wood-lined canals into which the water was directed once it has passed through the rubble. The heather, once dried out, was then burnt to release the tiny pieces of gold. This was collected and sent to ASTORGA and thence south to MÉRIDA and SEVILLE. Over 230 Roman gold-mines are known from the area of the modern provinces of the Asturias and LÉON, and Pliny the

▼ Las Médulas: Roman gold-mine (after Bird)

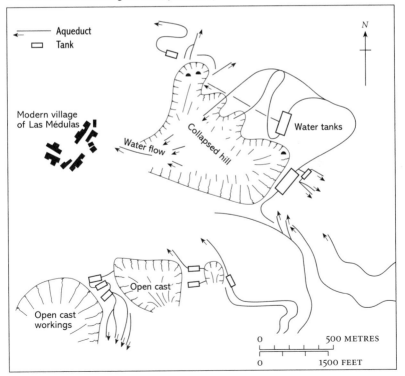

Elder (d. AD 79) recorded that the Spanish mines yielded up 20,000 (Roman) pounds of gold a month for the imperial government. There are also three smaller **open-cast mines** about 600 m. south of the village.

Las Vegas de Puebla Nueva Roman Mausoleum, Visigothic Church, and Early Islamic Mosque

*Head south from **Talavera de la Reina** on the TO 742 for 9 km. before a left turn leads for about 11 km. down a small road to **La Pueblanueva**. Continue through the village northwards for 5 km. before a left turn leads westwards to Las Vegas de Pueblanueva. Here a track runs north for about 250 m. before a left turn leads 1.5 km. to the farm of El Alamo. The site is in a field 200 m. south-west of the house.*

▼ Las Vegas de Puebla Nueva: reconstruction of ground plan of Late Roman mausoleum (after Hauschild).

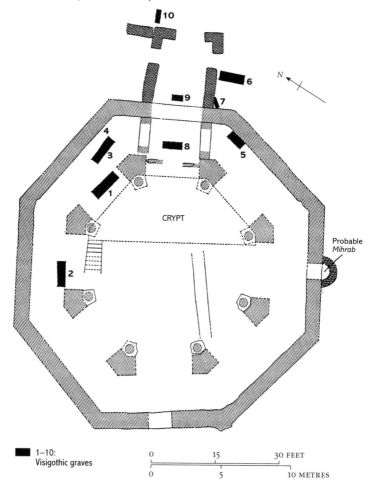

CRYPT

Probable Mihrab

1–10: Visigothic graves

0   15   30 FEET

0   5   10 METRES

The foundations of a Late Roman **mausoleum**, probably dating to the mid- to late 4th cent., were excavated here in 1967 and again in more detail between 1971 and 1974. The building itself was octagonal with a total diameter of *c*.22 m., containing a higher central chamber (15 m. in diameter) supported almost certainly on an octagonal arcade paralleling the outer walls, and probably supporting a domed roof. The subterranean **crypt**, in which the burials took place (cf. the mausoleum at the villa of CENTCELLES, has survived, together with the L-shaped stair that gave entry to it. It occupies less than half the space of the central chamber that would have stood above it. Three **sarcophagi** (or stone coffins) were built on to the flat west wall of this crypt, and a number of fragments of Late Roman and Visigothic pottery were found in it. One marble sarcophagus from this site, depicting Christ and the twelve Apostles standing in a row on its front, may be seen in the Museo Arqueológico Nacional in MADRID. The heads of all the figures have been removed, though other damage is light. This suggests deliberate mutilation, probably in the Islamic period (see below). Some marble fragments, probably from the same sarcophagus, were found in 1967, and these included part of an inscription with the letters HOL, possibly part of the name Bartholomeus.

The 1970s excavations revealed a number of burials of Visigothic date around the outer rim of the building, and a quantity of pottery that was dated to the second half of the 6th cent. It seems very likely that the mausoleum had been converted into a small church by that time. Perhaps even more interesting is the evidence, in the form of a small niche built into the south-east wall at a date later than the original construction, that this building was subsequently reused as a mosque. This phase is probably to be dated to the 8th cent., and is a rare example of the phenomenon of direct reuse of a church as a place of worship for the Muslims.

Finds of pottery dating from the 1st to 4th cent. AD in an area about 500 m. south of the mausoleum indicate the presence there of a small Roman settlement.

León   Roman and medieval town   ★★

Like ASTORGA and Braga (in Portugal), León developed from a legionary fortress of the Early Imperial period, as is reflected in its Roman name, Legio. From the reign of Vespasian (69–79) it was the headquarters of the *Legio VII Gemina*, an association still attested to in the *Notitia Dignitatum*, a listing of imperial military units throughout the empire dating to *c*.400–25. A civilian settlement developed around the fortress, and a Christian community is attested to here in AD 254. Little is known of the town in the Visigothic period, when it was not the seat of a bishop. After the Arab conquest it was depopulated by the Asturian kings in the mid-8th cent. Resettled in the late 9th cent. under Ordoño II (913–24), it became the new capital of the monarchy formerly established in the Asturias (see OVIEDO). It later gave way to Burgos, but again served as capital in the period when the Leonese and Castilian kingdoms were divided (1157–1230).

Of the **Roman fortress** the most substantial survival is of sections of the wall, albeit much restored and repaired in later periods. The best preserved of these runs northwards from the west end of San Isidoro el Real, and retains some of the original semicircular Roman towers. There is another section of similar character running northwards from the east end of the cathedral (see below). It probably dates from the late 3rd or early 4th cent., contemporary with the extant Roman walls of LUGO.

The most powerful of the 10th-cent. Leonese kings, Ramiro II (931–51) created the monastery, now called **San Salvador del Palat del Rey** (located off the east end of the Plaza de Abastos. Access to the church is not easy, as it is no longer in regular use; enquire at the Oficina del Turismo), close to the royal palace, to serve as a pantheon for the royal dynasty. His daughter Elvira, who later served as regent of the kingdom (*c*.967–75), was the first abbess. Ramiro II and his sons Ordoño III (951–6) and Sancho I the Fat (956–8, 959–66) were buried in it, but the original constructions were probably destroyed when Al-Manṣūr sacked León in 988. The palace has not been recovered but part of the church of the monastery has survived, though encased in constructions of much later date. A major excavation of the site has recently been undertaken, though it is not yet published. Much of the original crossing on four piers, with some of the walls of the adjacent semicircular chancel, have been preserved in the later rebuildings. Decorative fragments were also recovered.

Under the succeeding dynasty, which was of Navarrese origin, a new **Pantheon** was developed at the west end of the collegiate church of **San Isidoro el Real**. The church grew out of the monastery of San Pelayo, founded by Sancho I and Elvira *c*.966, to which the relics of the preeminent Visigothic scholar St Isidore of Seville were translated in 1063. The Pantheon (8 × 8 m.) was built under Fernando I (1037–65), and dedicated in 1063. It came to contain his body and those of other members of his dynasty, and the ashes of Alfonso V (999–1027). The church, begun at the same time, was not consecrated until the reign of his great-grandson Alfonso VII in 1149, and is a very fine example of Spanish Romanesque. The magnificent frescos that cover the walls and ceiling of the Pantheon (though recently in urgent need of repair) date to the reign of Alfonso VII's second son Fernando II (1157–88). There is a treasury attached to the church, which contains some important items, including a superb Bible written in Visigothic script in 960 and a copy of it made for Fernando I. There is also a fine 11th-cent. agate chalice and the relic box used to transport the remains of St Isidore, together with the Arab textiles in which they were wrapped.

Isidore of Seville (d. 636)

Brother of Bishop Leander of Seville (d. 599/600), who was responsible for the conversion of the Visigothic king Reccared in 587, Isidore was the most prolific and influential author of this period. His most famous work is an encyclopaedia in twenty books called the *Etymologies*. His works became widely dispersed throughout western Europe. He was also an influential figure politically and in the Spanish Church.

The elegant 13th–14th-cent. **cathedral of León**, built on the site of a Roman bath complex given to Bishop Cixila by Ordoño II, offers such a surprising and overwhelming impression when first entered (especially on a sunny day) that no attempt will be made to describe it here. Just go and experience it!

The **archaeological museum** is housed in the church of the Convento de San Marcos. This was founded in 1168 for the Order of Santiago, but its present buildings date from 1513–49; it is now a very luxurious *parador*.

There are sections of a **small suburban roman villa** of the 3rd–4th cent., with mosaic floors, to be seen at Navatejera (*3 km. north of León on the LE 311; far side of the village*).

Lérida/Lleida Roman and Islamic town

Ilterda was a settlement of the Ilergetes, who also founded Osca (HUESCA). Of Roman Ilerda little is known beyond references in literary sources. A few ceramic and sculptural fragments have been recovered, including a fine Corinthian capital, possibly from a temple, which was erected with a fragment of column as a monument in the Plaza de España in 1880. A Roman necropolis was located near the railway station. It included some burials under roof tiles of Late Imperial date and a late 4th–early 5th-cent. inscription. Of the Visigothic town, which was the seat of a bishop, little has survived beyond a few carved fragments. You can see these, together with the much more impressive finds from EL BOVALAR and Roman and earlier items, in the Museo Arqueológico del Instituto de Estudios Ilerdenses (in the former Hospital de Santa María: Avenida Blondel, 62). Under Arab rule, the most important period in the history of the city was the 11th cent., when it became the capital of a small Taifa kingdom, separated from that of ZARAGOZA in 1046, but reunited in 1067. At this time Lérida was at the heart of a complex system of concentric rings of fortified towns and castles that provided its outer defences (see BALAGUER). It was taken over by the Almoravids in 1094. The town was captured by Counts Ramón Berenguer IV of Barcelona and Ermengol VI of Urgell on

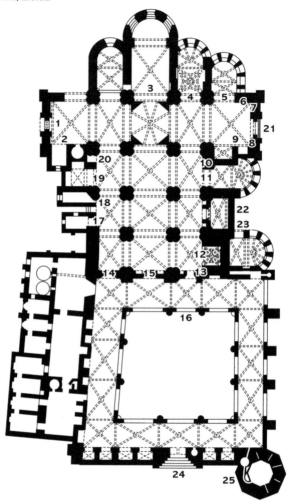

1 Sant Berenguer's Door
2 All Saints Chapel
3 Presbytery, Ground Plan and Dome
4 Chapel of Sant Pere
5 Chapel of the Conception
6 Chapel of Sant Salvador
7 Chapel of Santa Agnès
8 Chapel of Sant Joan the Evangelist
9 Chapels of the Conversion
   of Sant Pau and Santa Llúcia
10 Chapel of Sant Tomàs
11 Chapel of the Epiphany
12 Chapel of Sant Joan the Baptist
13 Chapel of Santa Margarida

14 The Cloister
15 The Portals of the Romanesque
   School – Chief Portal
16 Route through the interior
17 Chapel of Sant Vicenc
18 Chapel of Sant Erasme
19 Chapel of l'Assumpció
20 Chapel of Santa Petronella
21 Visit to the outside of the Cloister,
   The Door of Annunciation
22 Door of Fillols
23 Chapel of Jesus
24 Door of the Apostles
25 The Belfry

▲ Lérida: the Seu Vella

24 October 1149. Following this the seat of the bishopric previously located at Roda de Isábena was moved here, and the principal mosque of the Arab town became the first cathedral.

The most significant building in the town is the **old cathedral or Seu Vella**, on which work began on 22 July 1203. Of earlier, 12th-cent., date is the chapel of Santa Maria l'Antiga on the north side of the cloister. Some of the structure of this survives in the 14th-cent. rebuilding associated with the construction of the cloister. The cathedral was consecrated in 1278, though the bell tower on the west side of the cloister, on which work began in 1364, was not completed until 1416. It stands to a height of 60 m. The tympanum over the great western door into the cloister was finished in 1447. Internally the church is relatively small (113 m. long), but there are numerous chapels, mostly added or refurbished by local noble families in the 14th cent. Despite much damage inflicted during its use as a barracks (1707–1947), the church remains a very fine if decoratively austere example of the transitional style. The unusual placing of the fine 14th-cent. Gothic cloister (begun in the late 13th cent., but mostly dating from after 1334) to the west of the church, and the location of the bell tower are reminiscent of the plan of a major mosque (cf. the Mezquita in CÓRDOBA). That the principal mosque of Arab Lérida stood on this site is confirmed by the presence of decorative fragments, of 10th-cent. date, reused in the Gate of the Annunciation (Puerta de la Anunciata: built 1215) in the cathedral.

On the higher ground on top of the hill to the west of the cathedral stands the remains of the **royal castle** of Lérida, now much restored, which began as an Arab fortress. It was rebuilt in the 13th cent. and extended in 1341. Around it may be seen fortifications added by French engineers during the War of Spanish Succession (1700–12).

The medieval bridge across the Segre is thought to be of Roman origin, and the late 13th-cent. church of Sant Llorenc replaced a mosque on the same site.

Los Vascos Arab city   ★

From the NV E90, coming either from Madrid or from the direction of Bádajoz, turn south at Exit 148 (Oropesa: Parador in the castle, dating from 1366–1402) on to the TO 701, towards El Puente del Arzobispo (15 km.). The road changes name (to TO 702) but not its southerly direction in Puente del Arzobispo (bridge of 1338, built by Archbishop Tenorio of Toledo). About 7 km. further south, near the turning to Navalmoralejo, a farm track to the left leads to the site. The name of the farm is 'Las Cucañas'. NB: access cannot be had from the TO 730 to the north of the site (which is marked on Michelin Map 444). The site is approximately 2 km. east of the TO 702, and lies just south-east of the farmhouse.

Not easy of access, but an important site, subject to a continuing programme of excavation, initiated in 1975. From what has so far been revealed, this Arab city seems to have been founded in the 10th cent. and

▲ Los Vascos: Berber town of the 10th/11th-cent.

abandoned in the 11th, probably following the Castilian conquest of Toledo in 1085. There was some form of Roman settlement on the site, as indicated by finds of *terra sigillata* and roof tiles, but no evidence has yet emerged of continuity into the Visigothic period. The excavator has found no grounds for supporting the view that this may have been Roman Augustobriga, otherwise thought to be located at Talavera la Vieja. The name of the eventual Islamic settlement is not certain, but it may have been the Nafza referred to by Ibn Hayyan in relating events of the year 901. This would make of it a settlement of members of the Berber tribe of that name. Its name may have been changed to Basak (hence modern Vascos), recorded in the 11th cent. as a dependency of Talavera de la Reina, following a possible refoundation by Al-Ḥakam II in 964. Whatever the truth of these arguments, the town itself clearly served both as a centre of metal-working and as a part of the defensive organization of the Central March. As an urban site of this period, never subsequently reoccupied, it is a unique source of information on the organization of town life in late Umayyad and Taifa Spain.

Beyond the recently excavated Islamic cemetery (visible tombs), access to the site is via the southern **wall**, parts of which stand to a height of 3 m. or more. The wall is reinforced by a series of small rectangular towers. There are only two main gates: the one in the south wall and another to the north-west. The western wall and gate may belong to a prior Roman settlement, and the beginnings of a horseshoe arch, visible in the remains of the west gate, may represent an Islamic addition to much earlier structures. The excavator of the site has not given much support to such a view, while admitting that different styles and quality of construction may be seen between on the one hand the eastern and western walls and on the other the walls on the south and north sides. An explanation offered for this would see the work being conducted simultaneously and rapidly by teams trained in different techniques, working on different parts of the defences. The site, which is approximately 8 ha. in area (possibly indicating a population of *c*.3,000 people), is roughly rectangular, with the substantial remains (so far unexcavated) of the *Alcazaba*, or fortress, lying in the north-west corner. No internal buildings of the *Alcazaba* are still standing, but there is a cistern.

▼ Los Vascos (after Izquierdo Benito)

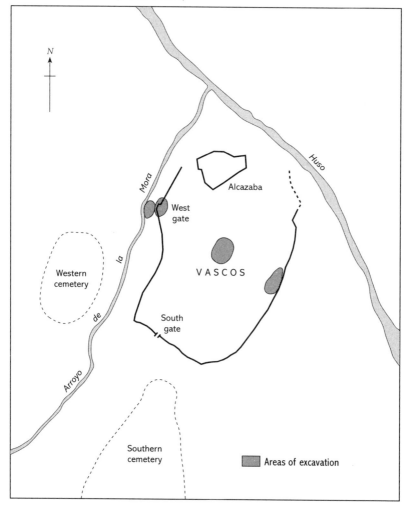

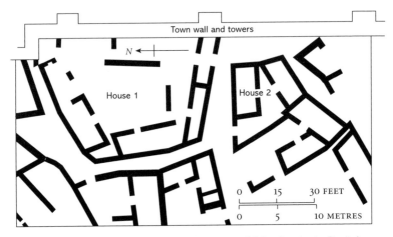

Town wall and towers

N

House 1

House 2

| 0 | 15 | 30 FEET |
| 0 | 5 | 10 METRES |

▲ Los Vascos: excavated houses by the east wall (after Izquierdo Benito)

Four main areas of excavation can be visited, following paths through the rather scrubby undergrowth. In the very centre of the site an area was uncovered in 1979–80 that revealed a large building with its rooms arranged around a central courtyard. This was covered in a second phase by a circular stone pavement. It has been suggested that the large oven visible in one of the rooms was too big for purely domestic use, and that the building may have been a workshop.

More explicit evidence of **metalworking** has emerged from the most recently (1983–8) excavated part of the site, along the inner face of the eastern wall, where several moulds and iron objects have been recovered. Two buildings in particular may be seen, lying alongside the wall. The more northerly is a house with central polygonal courtyard, that expanded to the south in a second phase of building. Immediately south of this, and adjacent to a small postern gate in the wall, is a 'V'-shaped building, with traces of an exterior pavement lying between its two arms. Similar large grey flagstones can be seen in adjacent passages between the buildings. These were almost certainly the very narrow lanes of this industrial quarter.

Towards the northern end of the west wall a small gateway was excavated in 1975–8, together with the area adjacent to it in the interior of the city. Some small, probably domestic or shop buildings were uncovered on either side of the road leading to the gate. Outside this west gate, in 1981–3, a set of vaulted chambers were discovered, identified as the remains of a public bath house. (Good examples of such Arab public baths can be seen in Córdoba, Gerona and Granada.) A changing room, steam rooms, hot and cold baths, and a furnace room have been discovered. The building was probably located in this position because of a nearby stream, known as 'La Mora'. It is possible this area formed a suburb of the main city. A quantity of ceramics, of both fine and coarse wares, has been recovered from the various parts of the site, from which the evidence for dating has been drawn. A programme of further intensive excavation on this site is planned.

*If returning in an easterly direction, i.e. towards Madrid or Toledo, take the TO 714 from El Puente del Arzobispo to Talavera de la Reina (35 km.); here it is possible to see substantial remains of the 10th-cent. Arab walls and towers (**torres albarranas**). If proceeding from Talavera to Toledo, you come to El Carpio de Tajo (48 km.) (located—via a small road—on the river bank, south of the village and just east of the Ermita (chapel) de Ronda); this was the site of a major Visigothic cemetery, some of the finds from here can be seen in the Museo del Arte Visigodo in Toledo.*

Lugo Roman town walls

Capital of the province of the same name, Lugo remains relatively little known to visitors. A Celtic settlement may have existed on the site, but the Roman town developed from a legionary fortress of the time of the Cantabrian Wars (cf. ASTORGA). From epigraphic evidence it had certainly been given the status of *municipium* by the Severan period (193–235); the grant may have been made under the Flavian emperors (69–96). Of Roman Lucus Augusti the most tangible evidence is the late 3rd-cent. AD circuit of walls and towers, which entirely encircles the centre of the city in a roughly oblong shape. These are amongst the best-preserved and certainly the most complete set of Roman town walls to be found in Spain. The town was the capital of the *Conventus Lucensis*, and its bishop exercised authority over the other churches of eastern Galicia. A massacre of some of the Roman inhabitants at the hands of the Sueves took place in 460.

Following the Arab conquest of Galicia around 714, the city may have been abandoned. Late 9th-cent. Asturian chronicles claim it was depopulated by Alfonso I (739–57). The belief that the diocese was refounded around this time by a refugee African bishop called Odoarius depends on documents of dubious worth. By the mid-9th cent. the town was reoccupied and the centre of the local power of King Ramiro I (842–50). By the late 11th cent. it was the site of a royal mint and had market rights.

The **walls** have been repaired at various times, as can be seen from the variety of stonework, both in the size of the blocks and the constructional techniques displayed throughout the circuit. (See, for example, the two distinct layers of construction in the towers flanking the Puerta del Carmen.) The full extent of the walls (which have a broad path on top of them throughout their circuit) is 2,117 m., and they stand to a height of between 9 and 15 m., and are approximately 5 m. wide. Early engravings indicate that some at least of the towers, almost all of which now stand no higher than the walls, once reached to a greater height, having two layers

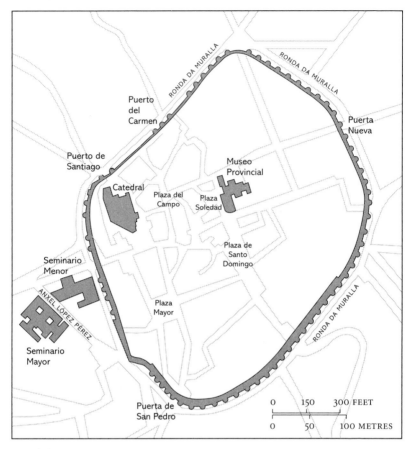

▲ Lugo

of round-arched openings above the level of the wall parapet. You can see a trace of the lower of these in the Torreón de la Mosquera, which retains two such openings. Thirty-one Roman inscriptions (mostly funerary dedications and altars) have been found reused in the walls. Of these twenty-two have been moved for exhibition in the Museo Provincial (Plaza Soledad, 6: the former monastery of San Francisco, with Romanesque cloister), and another four are still to be seen in the inner span of the Puerta Nueva; the others have disappeared.

Rather poorly preserved remains of three rooms of a **bath house** survive between the walls and the Río Miño, below the Puerta de Santiago. These include a vaulted room once containing plunge pools served by natural hot spring water. An arch and section of wall also survive from the probable *frigidarium*, converted into a chapel by the 17th cent. Small excavations have also served to locate the possible site of the forum (Plaza del

Campo) and a probable temple and other structures (Plaza de Santo Domingo and Plaza de Abastos). The old bridge over the Miño from the city is of Roman origin but much rebuilt in the course of the centuries.

The **cathedral** was begun in 1129 by Bishop Pedro III (1113–33/5), and the transepts and chancel were completed by 1177. The nine-bay nave is mainly of 13th-cent. date. The west end and crossing were given three late baroque towers in 1769–84, which obscure the essentially Romanesque nature of the building.

One of the most striking single objects of Late Roman date to be found in Spain is the probably 5th-cent. '**Chrismon of Lugo**'. This is a circular marble tablet with a Chi-Rho with pendant alpha and omega in its centre surrounded by a moralizing inscription: AURUM VILE TIBI EST ARCENTI PONDERA CEDANT PLUS EST QUOD PROPRIA FELICITATE NITES ('Gold is of small price to you; the burdens of silver pass away; it is better that you shine in your own happiness'). This once served as the main altar stone of the Chapel of Nuestra Señora de la Hermida in the valley of Quiroga, before being transferred to the Museo Diocesano (in the Seminario: Calle Angel López, 2); very limited hours of opening.

Lumbier Roman villa

The foundations of one wing of this villa may be seen on the left side of the road immediately in front of the gorge known as the Hoz or Foz de Lumbier, when travelling eastwards on the N 240 from Pamplona/Iruñea towards Jaca, approximately 32 km. from Pamplona and 2 km. before reaching Liédana.

Literary records document the existence of a small Roman town called Ilumberi, but it has not been precisely located geographically. Survival of the place-name, however, would suggest it is in this immediate area. Of the villa a line of rooms about 120 m. long, fronting onto a corridor, may be seen. Excavations of the site in 1921 uncovered a quantity of well-preserved mosaics; one of these, decorated with geometric designs, was said to be about 56 sq. m. The mosaics were recorded in 1928 as being in the possession of two local landowners.

Subsequent excavations, published in 1956, indicated that the original 2nd-cent. AD villa had been massively extended in the 4th cent. As many as 135 rooms have been found belonging to this phase of the villa's existence. Particularly notable are the indications of large-scale agricultural activity. To the north of the original peristyle a substantial, triple-aisled granary was built. Storerooms and wine presses were created on the south side, and a group of forty small rooms in the south-east may have been accommodation for farm labourers.

On the other side of the main road traces of a subterranean water system were found, together with a large number of fragments of a red pottery and twelve small kilns, implying the existence of a ceramic factory. Also located in this zone was a Roman necropolis containing forty burials.

Finds of coins of Marcus Aurelius (161–80) and Maximin I (235–8) help to confirm a 2nd- to 3rd-cent. date for the site.

A hand-axe to be seen in the Museo de Navarra in **Pamplona** (in Room IX) is evidence of Neolithic settlement in this area.

Madrid Islamic fortress   ★★

While the real importance of Madrid stems from the decision taken by Felipe II (1556–98) in 1561 to make it the capital of his empire, the town itself already had a significant past, some of which has been brought to light by recent excavation. A scatter of Palaeolithic and Bronze Age finds, and the reuse of Roman stonework in the second medieval wall (see below) establish the human occupation of parts of the city centre in Antiquity, but no precise settlement sites have been located. The first definite settlement evidence relates to the fortress of Mayrit (hence Madrid), established here in the Umayyad period as part of the defences of the routes leading from the Sierra de Guadarrama to Toledo. As such this needs to be considered alongside BUITRAGO DE LOZOYA and TALAMANCA DEL JARAMA, located to the north-east in the Jarama valley, on the road from the Puerto de Somosierra. (For the parallel route to Toledo, 20 km. west of Madrid, down the valley of the Guadarrama, see OLMOS and CALATALIFA.)

The foundation of the **fortress** on the heights overlooking the Río Manzanares can be dated to the reign of Muḥammad I (852–86). It may have covered little more than the area around the intersection between the Calles Mayor and Bailén, now mostly taken up by the Cathedral de la Almudena, adjacent to the Palacio del Oriente. It has to be said that there is no agreement on the precise dimensions or internal character of the settlement. The existence of three gates has been suggested and partly proved, and the walls were clearly augmented by a series of square towers. A section of this wall, excavated between 1972 and 1975, may be seen in the Parque de Muḥammad I, immediately below the eastern end of the cathedral, on the other side of the road. Although the towers here had been eliminated in a later reuse of the wall, their positions and dimensions can easily be made out. A restoration of these defences in the 10th cent. has also been deduced; this probably followed the sack of the fortress by Ramiro II of León (931–51). Regrettably, and despite serious opposition, work began in 1996 on an underground car park below the Plaza de Oriente, destroying any further archaeological evidence in this area.

A substantial increase in the size (to *c*.24 or even *c*.35 ha.) of the settlement with an expansion of its defences followed some time after Alfonso VI's conquest of Toledo and its related fortresses in 1085. This second town **wall** of Madrid, of 12th-cent. date, had four gates and was marked by the use of semicircular towers. Sections of this wall have been excavated

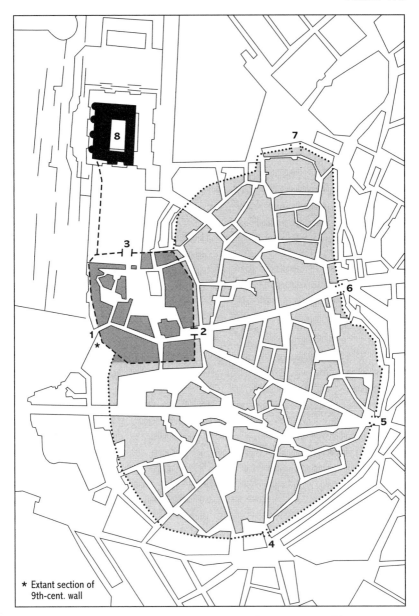

* Extant section of
  9th-cent. wall

▲ Madrid. 1–3. Gates of the Islamic town, 4–7. 12th-cent. gates, 8. The
  Alcazar, * Extant section of 9th-cent. walls.

in the Calle Escalinata, Plaza de los Carros, Plaza de Isabel II, Plaza de Independencia, and several other locations, but such city-centre sites can only rarely be developed into permanent exhibitions. Of the **buildings of the medieval town**, the towers of the churches of San Nicolás (Calle de San Nicolás) and San Pedro (Calle de Segovia) have survived. Both are in the Mudéjar style albeit fairly plain. There has been some disagreement as to their dating, but it seems reasonable to place them in the 12th or 13th cents.

Madrid should not be missed, not only for the Arab wall—and much else of more recent interest—but for the sake of the **Museo Arqueológico Nacional** (Calle de Serrano), which houses very fine collections of prehistoric (in the basement), Iberian, Roman, Visigothic, Islamic, and medieval materials. Of especial note are the Iberian statues known as the 'Dama de Elche' and the 'Dama de Baza', the frieze from the Cortijo de Tixe (Osuna), the male and female figures from the **Cerro de los Santos** site, the funerary monument from Pozo Moro, the Roman mosaics and sculptures, the Visigothic liturgical crowns and other items from the Guarrazar treasure, an original section of the arcading from the **Aljafería** in ZARAGOZA, the ivory crucifix of Fernando I (1037–65) of León-Castile, and the tomb of Alfonso Ansúrez (d. 1093). There are many more items from all of the periods covered here, as well as collections from later periods on the first floor. In the garden is a subterranean reproduction of the **Altamira** cave paintings. There is a substantial research library of archaeology on the first floor. Visiting exhibitions are also housed on this level.

The **Prado Museum** (Paseo del Prado) will no doubt be visited for its phenomenal collections of Spanish and European art, but it is worth noting both the many fine examples of classical sculpture (some bought in Italy by Spanish collectors), which are scattered throughout the galleries, and the exhibition of the extraordinary 11th–12th-cent. frescos from **San Baudelio de Berlanga**. There is also much good late medieval Spanish religious art from Castile and Catalonia.

One of the greatest treasures of Late Antiquity, the *missorium* of the Emperor Theodosius I (379–95), is housed in the Real Academia de la Historia, but may not be seen without a prior appointment. This is a large silver dish made to commemorate the tenth anniversary of the emperor's accession. It displays him enthroned between his co-rulers Valentinian II (375–92) and Arcadius (383–408), and was probably given to a prominent Spanish supporter or relative of the imperial house.

The Instituto Valencia de Don Juan (Calle Fortuny, 43) houses a splendid private collection of Spanish Islamic textiles and ceramics, as well as later medieval items, but can only be visited by appointment and for purposes of study. Another private collection, now open to the public, which includes a selection of medieval minor arts, may be seen in the **Museo Lazaro Galdiano** (Calle Serrano, 122).

Málaga Islamic palace and fortress

Little is known of the earliest phases of occupation in Málaga, which became the site of the Phoenician trading station of Malaca (thought to be located in the area of the *Gibralfaro*—see below) by the end of the 8th cent. BC. After a phase of Carthaginian rule the settlement submitted to Rome at the end of the Second Punic War, and became increasingly Romanized in its material culture. Like many other places along this coast, it became a centre for the making and export of *liquamen*, the Romans' favourite condiment, a sauce made from fish intestines. The town was granted the status of *municipium* under the Flavian dynasty (AD 69–96). Of that Roman town the only monumental trace is the over-restored and now rather neglected **theatre** built into the inland slope of the hill that houses the Nazirid *alcazaba*. Built in the Early Imperial period, this had been abandoned by the end of the 3rd cent. AD. Small finds are more revealing, and include a fragment of a bronze inscription recording the municipal charter granted by the emperor, and a number of statues. Amongst these are two statues of Attis found in the theatre during excavations in 1960, and some badly damaged statues of members of the local nobility of early imperial date, discovered reused in later buildings. These and some Roman ceramics can be seen in the archaeology section of the Museo de Málaga, housed in the *alcazaba*. This includes a larger selection of pieces found elsewhere in the province of Málaga.

Attis

He was a young man who, in Greek mythology, was loved by Cybele the Mother Goddess (in origin a divinity from Phrygia). When he proved unfaithful, she drove him insane and he castrated himself. The priests of the cult of Cybele and Attis were also castrated. Special ceremonies of the cult were performed in Rome between 22 and 27 March each year.

Málaga was the seat of a bishop in the late Roman period, and formed part of the territory conquered by the forces of the Byzantine emperor Justinian I (527–65) around 551. It was sacked by the Visigothic king Leovigild (569–86) in 570 and reintegrated into the Visigothic kingdom by 619. Coins of its mint are known in the reign of Sisenand (630–6). Little is known of it in the Early Islamic period. It was frequently threatened by the rebel leader ʿUmar ibn Hafsun (d. 918), but remained loyal. After the fall of the Umayyads it replaced Archidona (see ANTEQUERA) as the capital of the *qura* or administrative district of *Rayya*, and was the seat of the Hammudid dynasty until the town was taken by the Zirids of GRANADA in 1056. After the end of their kingdom in 1090 it came under Almoravid and

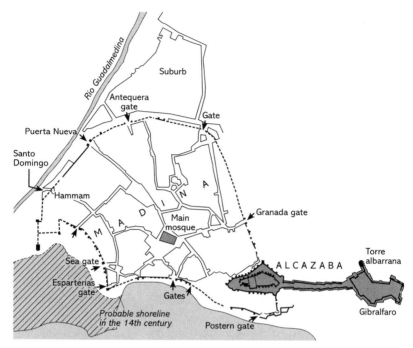

▲ Arab Málaga with probable line of the city walls (after Pavón Maldonado)

then Almohad rule. Following the collapse of the Almohads and the loss of CÓRDOBA to Fernando III of Castile in 1236, Málaga became part of the Nazirid kingdom, probably in 1239. At the end of the Nazirid period it was the seat of a rival court to that of Granada, until it fell to the Castilians in 1487. The remaining Morisco population was expelled in 1568 following a revolt.

There are **two Nazirid fortresses**, both heavily restored, located one above the other on the hill overlooking the eastern end of the city centre. The upper fortress or *Gibralfaro* ('hill of the lighthouse') retains its walls but no buildings. (It also had a rather unsavoury reputation, being poorly policed and far from the inhabited parts of the city.) It is largely the work of the Nazirid king Yūsuf I (1333–54). The lower fortress or *alcazaba* retains a small palace in the centre of it. Some of this, as can be seen from the horseshoe arches on narrow columns (e.g. in the entry to a pavilion overlooking the sea) and from the traces of stucco decoration that have survived on the arches, has affinities with MEDINA AZAHARA, and should probably be dated to the period of Ḥammūdid rule (1010–56). The massive fortified gateway into the palace area may also date from this period. The presence of even earlier buildings here, such as the mosque built by Muʿāwiya b. Ṣāliḥ of Emesa (d. 774), is known from literary records but has not been confirmed archaeologically. The early core of the palace has been overlaid by later buildings and fortifications of a subsequent Nazirid phase of occupation. Notable here are the **pavilions flanking a rectangular ornamental pool**, whose decoration as well as the overall plan is reminiscent in smaller scale of features to be seen in the Alhambra in GRANADA. Some of these halls are used to house the archaeological museum (see above). The buildings, walls, and horseshoe-arched gates of this small complex and its surrounding defences give a sense of the Ḥammūdid and Nazirid palace, but the extensive modern rebuilding weakens the conviction.

Additional archaeological materials, notably from **Cártama**, may be seen in the *Bellas Artes* section of the Museo de Málaga (Palacio de Buenavista, Calle San Agustín, 8).

In 1996 excavations on the hill known as the Cerro del Villar, about 3 km. west of Malaga and close to the mouth of the River Guadalhorce, revealed the existence of the largest Phoenician settlement to be discovered so far in Spain. It dates from no later than the 8th cent. BC and had a population of at least 1,000 people. Excavation is due to continue on the site for some time to come, and further discoveries may be expected.

Marialba Late Roman and Visigothic church

*Leave LEÓN by the N 601 in the direction of MADRID, and after about 1 km., in the village of **Puente del Castro**, turn onto a small road heading south towards **Alija** and **Villarroaña**. The monument is to be found 5 km. down this road, near the village of **Marialba de la Ribera**, located between the road and the **Río Bernesga**.*

This important church was probably built as a *martyrium*, in which the relics of a local martyr(s) were venerated. It is the earliest known church in the north of Spain, and the largest martyrial building in the whole of the Iberian peninsula. It was excavated in 1967–8 by the German Archaeological Institute in MADRID. Nothing survives above floor level, but this is well preserved, and has provided evidence for a complex building history. Three phases of construction have been detected. The first, dating to the earlier 4th cent., saw the erection of the rectangular **nave** and the hemispherical **apse** (in total: 33 m. × 15 m.). At the end of the century, or early in the following one, significant decorative changes were made, including the insertion of some **pilasters** in the apse and the creation of semicircular corners within the rectangular nave. These alterations also included the insertion of pilasters that supported a new cupola-shaped roof over the nave. A small oblong **narthex** was added to the west end (20 m. × 4 m.). In the same phase 13 burials were made within the apse. These might be related to the legend of the martyrdom of the 13 members of the family of St Marcellus of LEÓN, though there is no

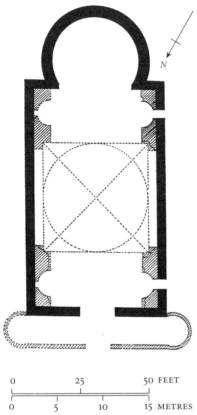

evidence relating to this cult earlier than the 13th cent. The structural changes might imply that the former nave, with its striking new roof, had become the liturgical focus of the building, and the apse had been relegated to the role of a funerary chapel. In the Visigothic period, probably in the later 6th or early 7th cent., further internal alterations took place, which included the construction of a stone **chancel screen**. Possibly at this time, if not earlier, a **baptismal font** was constructed in an extension off the south-west corner of the building. The presence of medieval burials in areas that would have been impossible if the church was still being used indicates that the building was later abandoned and probably robbed of its masonry, and the area reused for a cemetery. Unfortunately, it is not possible to date this precisely, though it may have been as early as the 8th cent.

| 0 | | 25 | | 50 FEET |
| 0 | 5 | | 10 | 15 METRES |

▲ Marialba: Roman and Visigothic church

Meca Iberian village

For El Castellar de Meca, within the parish bounds of Ayora (province of Valencia) head in the direction of Ayora, on the N 330; 12 km. north of Almansa take a small road on the left which leads towards Alpera; 8 km. on from this intersection, a track to the left goes to 'las Casas de Meca', at the northern foot of the hill; a site guardian may be found here.

On the summit of the hill, called 'El Mugrón', there is a 15-ha. site, 314 m. long, with cliffs on the northern and western sides, which has been identified as containing an Iberian village. There were originally three entries to the settlement, and traces of a defensive wall built of large stones can be seen at various points. A tower was uncovered in the eastern section of the wall during the 1983 excavations, and has now been restored. The most striking feature is probably the *Camino hondo* or sunken road, cut out of the rock at some points up to a depth of 2 m., which runs across the site. It is particularly impressive on the southern side, where steps have been carved out of the rock and it is possible to see the lower levels of houses adjacent to the road. There are a number of caves in the rocks, which show signs of artificial creation or enhancement, and which may have served as cisterns or granaries. The largest of these is the 'Cueva del Rey Moro' (Cave of the Moorish King) on the north-west side of the site. There is also a large cistern to be seen lower down the hillside to the west, outside the village. A Roman necropolis has been located, and there is clear evidence from the finds that the site was occupied in the later Middle Ages. At least some of the work on the sunken road may date to that period, as it is possible to see that pre-existing buildings were cleared to make way for this road. There is thus evidence for occupation in the Iberian (from 3rd cent. BC?) and Roman periods and for the existence of a medieval settlement here. The excavator has assumed there was continuity of occupation across the Visigothic and early medieval centuries too, but this does not seem to have been established archaeologically.

Medellín Roman town

On the N V/E 90, 24 km. east of MÉRIDA, continue east on the N 430 for 9 km. to its intersection with the C 520. The latter then leads 7.5 km. south to Medellín.

The Roman settlement of Caecilia Metellinum was built originally as a fort on the military road linking the Tagus and the Guadiana, and was named in honour of Caecilius Metellus, one of the commanders in the Sertorian War (82–72 BC). Little is known of its history, and continuous occupation of the site has limited its archaeological possibilities. In 1229 it was taken by Alfonso IX of León, who gave it to the Order of Santiago. Their **castle** on a hill outside the town is principally of 14th-cent. date; with dimensions of *c.*150 × 70 m., it is one of the largest fortresses in Extremadura. The town, which was the birthplace of Hernán Cortés (1485–1547), who destroyed the Aztec empire, was badly damaged by a French army in 1809. Part of a large **Roman theatre**, with a diameter of *c.*55 m., may still be seen on the side of the hill on the south side of the Guadiana, and there are sections of the town walls that contain Roman stonework. Some of the foundations of a **Roman bridge** over the Guadiana may also be seen in the river near to the present bridge immediately below the castle.

In an orchard on a farm called 'El Turuñelo', located about 5 km. due west of Medellín, on the banks of the Guadiana, is a remarkable Visigothic tomb.

The tomb, found in 1961, may have formed part of a much larger but now almost entirely lost necropolis, located about 1 km. from the Roman road linking Mérida to Medellín. In the form of a plain marble sarcophagus (2 × 0.5 m.), it contained a number of gold objects, notably a large circular brooch (5 cm. diameter) depicting the Adoration of the Magi, with a four-line inscription in Greek, indicating a Byzantine origin for the piece.

It has been dated to *c*.600. This brooch, a gold ring and earrings, a gilded belt buckle, a tangle of gold threads, some small cut-out sheets of pressed gold sheet, and other items found in the tomb may be seen in the Museo Arqueológico Nacional in MADRID. Two empty granite sarcophagi were also found close by.

Medina Azahara   Umayyad palace city
(Visit together with CÓRDOBA)

Take the C 431 west from CÓRDOBA for 8 km., when a small road to the right leads for a further 4 km. to the site (signposted).

This is a unique monument, being the palace city of the last Umayyad rulers. It was founded by the first caliph, ʿAbd al-Raḥmān III (912–61), around 936, and was named after his then favourite wife Zahra. Dated inscriptions indicate that its components were constructed at various times over at least the next twenty years. It was completely destroyed by the Berber army of Sulaymān al-Musta ʿīn (1009–10, 1013–16) in 1010, in the course of the civil wars that led to the extinction of the dynasty and of the caliphate. Although the *Hajīb* Al-Manṣūr (d. 1002), who dominated the Umayyad government in the last two decades of the 10th cent., is said to have built a similar complex called Medina Azahira, this has not been recovered. Material evidence of the violent end of this city includes the splashes of molten metal, caused by burning of the buildings, still to be seen on the floors of the *Salon Rico* (see below) and related areas. While there are no strictly contemporary literary records of it, accounts of the palace and its city are to be found in various later sources, notably the works of Al-Idrīsī (d. 1162) and Al-Maqqarī (d. 1632). Some of this information is highly fanciful, such as the claim that 12,000 loaves were required daily just to feed the fish in the palace ponds. Other information, such as the names of various gates and buildings, may be more reliable but this palace city also served as the literary image of a material wonder of a lost age.

While much of the northern and central sections of the site have been uncovered and reconstructed in excavations that began in 1910, something in the order of 30 ha. remain still to be explored. The city was said to have been structured hierarchically around three descending terraces, the ruler's palace being located at the highest, northern end of the complex, the administrative offices of the government and the dwellings of the courtiers coming in the middle section, and the lowest level being given over to the barracks of the caliph's guard and the houses of the numerous palace servants. The later sources give the numbers of the latter two groups as 12,000 and 4,000 respectively. There would also have had to be shops, store-rooms, and facilities for travellers and merchants. While a useful simplification, the reality of the site is more complex, as is its topography, with the three sections displaying considerable variation in their

▲ Medina Azahara: the reconstructed throne hall of the Caliphal palace

heights. The overall area of the city was roughly 1,500 × 750 m., defined by walls reinforced by a regular succession of towers. Only a limited section in the centre of the north wall may now be seen.

Entry is from the northern edge of the site, via a small museum containing some ceramics and a few fine capitals. (For other finds from the city see the Museo Arqueológico in CÓRDOBA and the Museo Arqueológico Nacional in MADRID.) So far only the middle part of the northernmost section has been investigated and restored in any detail, following the locating of the principal parts of the palace in 1944. Only a relatively small amount of this area is accessible to visitors. From the entry the approach is via the eastern side of this zone, taking in one of the streets of the palace area. From here you get a view over the **main mosque**, whose construction is dated by inscription and literary record to 941. Its foundations are now fully exposed. It is oriented to the south-east, at variance with all the other buildings in the site, other than for a dwelling immediately in front of the entry to the *sahn* or courtyard of the mosque. As in the Mezquita in CÓRDOBA, the entry to the court was flanked by the minaret. The prayer hall at the southern end was divided into five aisles, with the central one that leads to the *mihrab* exceeding the others in its width. A passage behind the *quibla* allowed the caliph private access to the mosque. Within the palace area proper, the central section is dominated by a large courtyard, now laid out as a garden, with the so-called **Salón Rico** ('Luxurious Hall') on its northern side. This has been reconstructed, with elements of its stucco decoration being replaced on modern concrete

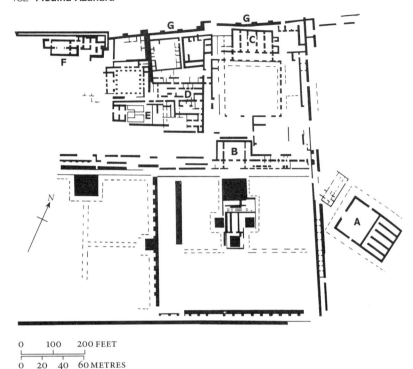

0   100   200 FEET

0   20   40   60 METRES

▲ Medina Azahara (after López-Cuervo)
  A. Mosque, B. The 'Salón Rico', C. The *Dar al-jund*, D. 'House of the Vizier
  Ja 'far', E. 'House of the Prince', F. Area of the Caliph's residence, G. Walls

reproductions of the original walls. The present interior of the hall can
hardly do justice to its probable opulence in its original state. Inscriptions
indicate that the construction of this area took place between 954 and 957.
Approaching the *Salón Rico* along the terrace from the east, you will
notice a number of small roofless chambers, in one of which is a fine if
shattered marble basin for a fountain.

Above and behind the *Salón Rico* is an area not normally accessible,
but which can be viewed from above, from the path by the entry. This
consists of two sections. The eastern one is centred on a large courtyard,
with a five-aisled hall, known as the **Dar al-jund** ('Hall of the Army') on
its northern side. The western section is more complicated, consisting of
a series of smaller courts, and an intricately divided-up building in its
south-east corner. This has been labelled 'The House of the Vizier Ja'far',
but this is more picturesque than sensible. Another building to the west of
this has been called 'The Prince's House'.

It is thought that the caliph's residential quarters were located to the
west of this group of courtyards and buildings, though little of this has so

far been exposed. Aerial photographs have helped to give a sense of other potential areas of excavation in the site, including a courtyard with at least two halls to the east of the area so far uncovered, and a series of zones of interest in the lower part of the city. In view of the importance of the site, and of the amount of time in which it has been subject to investigation, it might have been hoped that rather more effort would have been put into excavation and rather less into restoration. Large expanses of modern grey concrete and very limited access make this a far less appealing site than its intrinsic interest suggests or deserves. At least photography is now permitted, once a forbidden practice!

Medinacelli Roman and Arab town

Overlooking the N II/E 90 Madrid to Zaragoza motorway about 97 km. north-east of Guadalajara, Medinacelli is also approachable by train—-with a steep climb from the station in the valley up to the town!

Located on a large, roughly triangular, flat-topped hill, dominating the surrounding countryside, and above all the route leading from Toledo via the valley of the Río Jalón to the Ebro, Medinacelli is naturally placed to serve both as a fortress and the economic centre of its district. Excavations in the Plaza Mayor, made urgent by the recent renewal of building work in a previously rather neglected and decaying—if beautiful—small town, have uncovered traces of a Bronze Age settlement and of subsequent Celtiberian occupation of the site. This latter has been identified with the town of Ocilis, captured by Marcus Claudius Marcellus while Roman governor of Hispania Citerior in 152 BC. Of the Roman presence, the most tangible trace is the impressive **triumphal triple arch**, located on the brow of the hillside on the southern edge of the town. No inscription survives to help date this or indicate what it commemorated, but stylistically it can be assigned to the Severan period (*c.*193–235). There seems to be no evidence for continuity of occupation of the site through the later Roman and Visigothic periods up to the time of the Arab conquest.

Medinacelli takes its modern name from that given to it in the period of Arab occupation, when it was called *Madinat-Salim*. It was refortified in the reign of ʿAbd al-Raḥmān III (912–61), and became the military and administrative centre of the Middle March in the later 10th cent. Here the *Hajīb* Al-Manṣūr, who had made himself dictator of the Umayyad state by 980, died on campaign in 1002 and was buried. In 1123 the town was captured by Alfonso I (1104–34) the Battler, king of Aragón. Of the **medieval fortress**, approached around the edge of a field at the western end of the town, relatively little remains, and what does has been rather over-restored. This castle belonged to the Dukes of Medinacelli, descendants of one of the sons of Alfonso X (1152–84). Their family tombs are preserved in the 16th-cent. collegiate church in the Plaza Colegiata in the

▲ Medinacelli: the Roman triumphal arch

town (which also houses a small museum of liturgical objects in its *Sala Capitular*). A better impression of the medieval defences can be gained from the gate on the north-western edge of the present town, which gives access to the path to the castle, and from a section of wall to be seen beside that path, under the northern edge of the fortress. The church of the *Beaterio* (Spanish equivalent of a Beguinage, i.e. a sisterhood living as nuns but without vows) of San Román is believed to have been a synagogue, prior to the expulsion of the Jews in 1492.

*A right turn 20 km. further north on the N II/E 90 leads 3 km. south to **Montuenga de Soria**.*

Here there is a small but imposing castle of at least 12th-cent. origin. Built on a low but steep-sided oval hill, it consists of the remains of two square towers linked by walls.

*A right-hand road 6 km. further up the N II from the turn to Montuenga leads 1 km. to the Cistercian monastery of **Santa María de la Huerta**. On the N II/E 90, 26 km. beyond the turn-off to Santa María, a road to the right leads 2 km. to **Alhama de Aragón**.*

This is the site of the Roman settlement of Aquae Bilbilitanorum, which took its name from mineral springs that made it a health spa, in both Roman and Arab times. There is an impressive late medieval castle. See also BILBILIS.

Mérida   Roman city   ★★

In consequence of long centuries of neglect and relative obscurity in one of the less well-known parts of Spain, the small town of Mérida has preserved many traces of one of the most important cities of the peninsula in the Roman, Visigothic, and early Islamic periods. Augusta Emerita was founded in 25 BC by the legate Publius Carisius, as a *colonia* for retired Italian soldiers from the *Legio V Alaudae* and the *Legio X Gemina*, who had served in the recently concluded Cantabrian War, on a site previously occupied by a settlement of the Vettones. It was also intended to serve as capital of the recently (27 BC) created province of Lusitania. Amongst its governors was to be the future emperor Otho (AD 69). The location was a significant one, controlling a crossing of the Río Guadiana and the confluence of a network of roads linking Olisipo (Lisbon), Asturica (ASTORGA), Toletum (TOLEDO) and thence Caesaraugusta (ZARAGOZA), Corduba (CÓRDOBA), and Hispalis (SEVILLE). It benefited from the patronage of Augustus's intended heir Marcus Agrippa (d. 12 BC), and seems to have flourished economically and culturally throughout the imperial centuries. Under the administrative reorganization of the early 4th cent., Mérida became the residence of the *Vicarius Hispaniarum*, the deputy of the western Praetorian Prefect (who resided in Gaul), who was responsible for overseeing the civil administration of the whole peninsula. Amongst the holders of this office was the Spaniard Flavius Sallustius, friend of the Emperor Julian (361–3) and author of *On the Gods and the Universe*.

The city also had one of the earliest Christian communities in Spain, and its metropolitan bishops exercised authority over the province of Lusitania and, until the rise of Braga in the later 6th cent., over most of Galicia as well. In the middle of the 5th cent. it became the main royal centre of the Suevic kingdom (from 442), until taken over by the Visigoths in 456. A literary text, the *Lives of the Fathers of Mérida*, written around 630, records the substantial ecclesiastical and charitable constructions erected by a series of wealthy 6th-cent. metropolitan bishops, including Masona (*c.*570–*c.*600), one of the earliest Visigothic converts from Arianism. The coinage issued in the city in the Visigothic period rivals that of Toledo in terms of the number of examples found and in its geographical distribution.

Following the Arab conquest, the bishopric seems to have survived at least into the 9th cent., but the establishment of a Berber garrison caused much friction, and the city, again like Toledo, was the site of frequent revolts against the Umayyads. In some cases independent local rulers held the city for long periods. In 835 ʿAbd al-Raḥmān II (822–52) destroyed the city walls and built the still extant fortress known as the *Alcazaba* for an Umayyad garrison and as a place of refuge for partisans of the legitimate government. The rise of BÁDAJOZ, further down the Río Guadiana,

1 Roman bridge
2 Supposed 'river port'
3 Alcazaba
4 Area of Mithreum
5 Roman houses
6 Theatre
7 Amphitheatre
8 Temple 'of Diana'
9 Church of Santa María
10 National Roman Museum

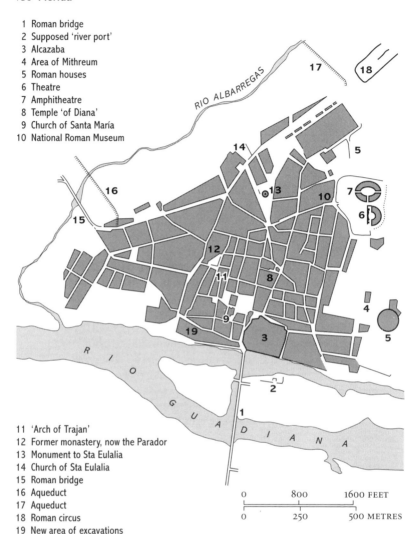

11 'Arch of Trajan'
12 Former monastery, now the Parador
13 Monument to Sta Eulalia
14 Church of Sta Eulalia
15 Roman bridge
16 Aqueduct
17 Aqueduct
18 Roman circus
19 New area of excavations

▲ Mérida (after Melida)

in this period led to an economic eclipse of Mérida and initiated a long process of urban decline. On 15 January 1230 it fell to Alfonso IX of León (1188–1230), who presented it to the archbishop of Santiago de Compostela, who in turn entrusted it to the Order of Santiago, which established a Commandery in the *Alcazaba*. In 1120 the long-vacant archbishopric of Mérida was formally transferred by Pope Calixtus II to the dynamic new metropolitan see of Santiago de Compostela, pending the Christian recovery of Mérida. However, by the time this was achieved in

1230 the power of Santiago was too deeply entrenched for the process to be reversed.

The Bridge

The now pedestrianized **bridge** over the Guadiana is one of the finest (and most picturesque) examples of Roman engineering in Spain. It now consists of sixty arches, the final four on the south bank being virtually invisible. Although it is sometimes said that the bridge was built under Trajan (98–117), there is no consensus on this, and a date in the time of Augustus (27 BC–AD 14) is more likely. An inscription (preserved in the 9th–10th-cent. MS Madrid BN 10029) records a repair that was carried out in 483 by Count Salla and Bishop Zeno, under the Visigothic king Euric (466–84). Other damage and repair is recorded in 865 and 1272. A major restoration was required by 1480 and work on this continued intermittently into the 1530s. A serious flood in 1603 caused renewed damage, and the completion of the ensuing repairs in 1610 is recorded in two inscriptions. Two of the sixty-four arches were deliberately wrecked in 1811 to impede a French attempt to relieve the siege of BÁDAJOZ, and were not repaired until 1832.

On the eastern side of the bridge, nearly half-way across the river, an opening leads down onto the small island on which this main section is anchored, and here some traces of Roman construction can be seen around its edge. This used to be taken as the site of a small dock forming the river port of the city. However, recent research has shown that the Guadiana is not navigable down to its mouth on the Atlantic, and it is highly unlikely that any significant trade connected with the city was river-borne. The stonework probably formed part of an embankment around the island to prevent its erosion by the river.

The Theatre

This is the best example of its kind to be found in western Europe. Although extensively restored, the unusual survival around the site of much of the fine marble columns, capitals and facing of the *scaenae frons* has enabled this to be reconstructed to a large degree. Normally such high-quality stonework was looted, from the Late Imperial period onwards, for reuse elsewhere (cf. the present state of the Roman theatres at SEGÓBRIGA and ITÁLICA). An inscription to be seen beside the stage indicates that the original patron of the theatre was Agrippa, but the style of much of the carving on the *scaenae frons* indicates that a major restoration and refurbishing took place in the 2nd cent., probably under the Antonines. Another major refurbishment is recorded for 333–5, in the reign of Constantine I. The seating of the theatre and the network of *vomitoria* or passages providing access around the perimeter and to the rows of seats have also been well preserved. Copies of statues found on the site,

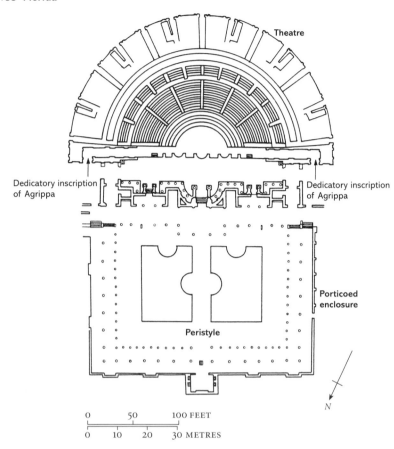

▲ Mérida: the theatre and portico (after Boschung)

but whose originals are now in the museum (see below) have also been erected in and around the *scaenae frons*. As these include figures of Ceres and Serapis, it is more likely that they came originally from a Serapeum in the vicinity of the theatre. On the other side of the *scaenae frons* was a colonnaded walk, around a central ornamental fountain that has now been recreated. Just west of the *scaenae frons* in a small area of excavated housing is part of a small villa of late imperial date: in the apsidal end of

Ceres

In Roman mythology she was the goddess who protects growing corn. From as early as the 5th cent. BC she was being equated with the Greek goddess Demeter.

one of the rooms may be seen frescos of the lower parts of the bodies of some standing figures, thought to be servants.

The Amphitheatre and Hippodrome

The **Amphitheatre** is located unusually close to the theatre. These, and the **Hippodrome** (see below), formed what was virtually a public-entertainments district of the city. This is another well-preserved example

▼ Mérida: the Roman theatre from the reign of Augustus

of its type. It was built in 8 BC, as evidenced by a series of inscriptions referring to Augustus in his 11th Consulship and 16th year of Tribunician Power. The box of the president of the games can be seen on the eastern side, and has one of the three extant examples of these inscriptions carved on it. The passages around and below the seating are very well preserved. Of the three sections of the *cavea* or seating area only the uppermost (the *summa cavea*) has been largely lost. In the centre of the floor of the arena a rectangular space (up to 5 m. deep) formed the concealed section in which animals and human performers in the spectacles were kept before their appearance.

The House of the Amphitheatre

This villa takes its modern name from its location, but there is no other relationship between the two monuments. It is the largest villa to have been uncovered in the city, and is notable for its collection of mosaics. The heart of the house is a porticoed atrium with fine geometric mosaic pavement, and construction of this area has been dated to the later 1st cent. AD. The central space was entered through a four-columned arcade on the western side; the three others were occupied by an ornamental pool. In the centre of the eastern side of this, a semicircular extension seems to have served as a Nymphaeum or shrine to the Nymphs. A number of chambers are arranged around this atrium. The one in the north-west corner has been identified as the kitchen by the presence of an oven in one corner. The *triclinium* or dining-room may well have been the room on the east side opening directly onto the Nymphaeum. A room of almost identical dimensions next to it on the north has retained its **mosaic decoration**. Within a large border of overlapping coloured rectangles are two panels thought overall to be depicting autumn. The one nearer the doorway shows three men trampling on grapes, whose juice runs into three vessels below, all within a pattern of vines inhabited by birds, bell-shaped vases, and a ladder. The other panel has a vegetal pattern, in the centre of which are two figures identified as Venus and Hero. Two birds on the right lack the symmetry of equivalents to the left, probably eliminated in a repair to be dated to the later 2nd or early 3rd cent. Traces of the original wall paint-

---

Venus

An Italian goddess who was identified, from at least the 3rd cent. BC, with the Greek divinity Aphrodite. She was goddess of married love (though her remit grew throughout the centuries). Her first temple in Rome, dedicated in 295 BC, was built on the proceeds of fines from women convicted of adultery.

Mérida: House of the Amphitheatre (after García Sandoval) ▶

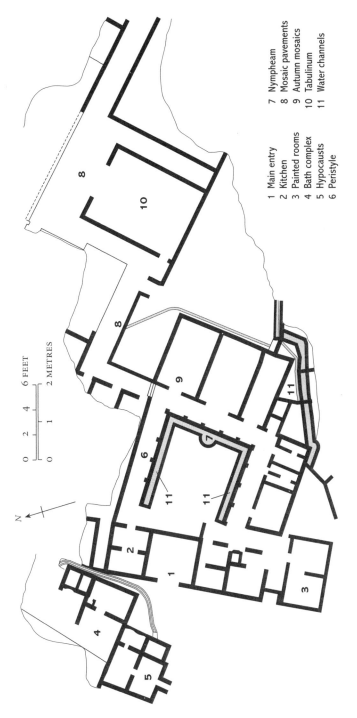

1 Main entry
2 Kitchen
3 Painted rooms
4 Bath complex
5 Hypocausts
6 Peristyle
7 Nympheam
8 Mosaic pavements
9 Autumn mosaics
10 Tabulinum
11 Water channels

Hero

In legend she was a priestess of Aphrodite (Venus) on the island of Sestos near the European shore of the Hellespont, who fell in love with a young man called Leander who lived on the Asiatic shore. He swam the Hellespont each night to visit her, guided by a light in her tower. When he was drowned one stormy night, she threw herself from the tower where she had been waiting for him.

ing may also be seen around the edges of the room. In the north-east corner of the atrium an L-shaped passage, retaining its mosaic decoration of coloured squares, led to another section of the house, whose construction is placed in the early 2nd cent. AD, in which the main feature is a large room surrounded on three sides by a passage with mosaic pavement. This has been identified as a possible *tablinum* or private art gallery or study. It has another fine mosaic floor, in the form of a series of fish each in separate and differently designed roundels, all within a large geometric-patterned border. Even more impressive is the mosaic in the expanded section of passage fronting the entry to the *tablinum*. This contains three great concentric circles of colour within a key-patterned border. The transition from the central circles to the rectangular border is effected via a series of bell-shaped-jar figures within spiralling lines placed in the corners of the space surrounding each circular whorl. In the central one, however, the jars are replaced by small towers with pointed roofs, out of which grow branches of pine trees. A further passage leads off this one to the east, into an unexcavated sector of the villa. At the west end of the house, placed at an angle to the corner of the kitchen, was another complex of rooms serving as a **bath house**. Some hypocausts at the southern end indicate the presence of a *caldarium* or steam room, and there are two plunge baths; one located next to the *caldarium* would have been used by those emerging from the steam room. Throughout the villa traces of its complex water-supply system can be seen, as for example between the kitchen and the bath house and next to the south-east corner of the central section.

The villa may have gone out of use in the later 3rd cent. AD, possibly as the result of destruction. Its site lay outside the line of the city walls then constructed, and the area was subsequently used as a **cemetery**. On the southernmost end of the west wing of the central sector are two chambers known as the 'Rooms of the Pictures', which retain good sections of fresco decoration around their walls, including some illusionist effects, in which paint is used to give the impression of stone. Within one of these rooms was found a burial under a roof-shaped arrangement of tiles. Another such tile burial was found in what had been the garden of the villa. Other burials within cists of large stones were also located; two more of these being within the 'Rooms of the Pictures'. Each contained a skeleton and a small pottery jar. In some of the cist burials the lid was formed with plates of marble from the villa. The tile burials have been assigned to the Late Roman period, and those in cists to the time of the Visigothic kingdom.

By the entry to the site may be seen part of another **villa**, of which only two rooms and a section of a peristyled court survive. Adjacent to it is a water conduit that was ultimately linked to the San Lazaro aqueduct (see below). Close to the perimeter fence, near the entry, is a recently excavated 3rd-cent. **mausoleum** of rectangular shape, with tombs in the interior.

The House of the Mithraeum

This villa, adjacent to the modern bullring, takes its name from the discovery in its vicinity of some statues (now to be seen in the Museum, see below) that must have come from a Mithraeum. The Mithraeum itself has not been located. Campaigns of excavation in this general area have located a zone of housing and part of the route of the principal road leaving the city eastwards towards MEDELLÍN. Much of the lines of the two major roads, the *Cardo* (north–south) and the *Decumanus* (east–west), and of several of the rectilinear subsidiary Roman streets are still detectable in the street pattern of modern Mérida. The villa is built around three colonnaded courts, the principal one being a rectangular atrium with central pool. Traces of fresco on the lower levels of the walls of some of the rooms indicate a 1st-cent. AD origin for the house. Although smaller than the House of the Amphitheatre, this villa outstrips it in terms of the quality of its **mosaic decoration**, in the form of the superb cosmographic mosaic that once covered the floor of the *triclinium*; this room is kept sheltered to preserve it. Although it has suffered considerable damage, this is still one of the finest Roman mosaics to be seen in western Europe. It depicts a range of celestial, terrestrial, and aquatic divinities in their respective elements, each clearly labelled. Above all, the quality of the workmanship and the richness of the colours (which can be enhanced if a benevolent custodian throws a bucket of water over it) mark this out as an exceptional piece.

> The smaller the *tesserae*, the individual cubes from which a mosaic is formed, and the wider the range of materials from which they are made, the greater the opportunity for the mosaic artist to provide a range of tone and detail of depiction that lifts the quality of his work.

This, in its use of relatively expensive blues and golds, is clearly the work of craftsmen of more than provincial skill (i.e. they must have been hired specially, possibly from North Africa or Italy) and of patrons with considerable financial resources, as can be seen by comparing it with any of the other mosaics to be seen in the city. Argument has raged over its dating. A 3rd-cent. date is now, rightly, regarded as more probable than the 2nd-cent. one favoured by the original excavator.

The *Alcazaba*

The fortress owes its existence to the Amir ʿAbd al-Raḥmān II (822–52), who ordered its construction in 835. An Arabic inscription over the west gate records its foundation and purpose. Recent removal of buildings from around its eastern side now enables the whole fortress to be seen. It is basically rectangular, with a fortified gateway on its west side that also dominated access to the north end of the bridge over the Guadiana. The southern side runs along the bank of the river, and the top of the wall here is normally accessible by stair. On the most vulnerable northern wall there is a series of free-standing towers only attached to the top of the wall by stone bridges. Although once thought to be of 9th-cent. date, these probably belong to a refortification of the city in the Almohad period. A similar tower belonging to the rebuilding of the town wall at that time is visible in the C/Arzobispo Masona, near to the Parador (a converted 18th-cent. monastery).

Almost in the centre of the southern half of the enceinte is the *aljibe* or **cistern**, linked to the waters of the Guadiana. It consists of a vaulted passage parallel to the south wall, from the middle of which two other passages descend side by side to the well chamber. This is a very good and massively constructed example of an Arab cistern, but even more striking are the numerous finely **carved pilasters** that are used to decorate the entries to the outer passage and to the two that lead down to the water. All of these are of Visigothic date, and are amongst the best representatives of a style of carving particularly associated with Mérida in that period. They will once have formed part of the internal structure and decoration of a (probably late 6th-cent.) church, whose nearest extant parallels are to be seen in North Africa.

The clearing of the interior of the *Alcazaba* provided the opportunity for a major excavation of the site, and the northern half of the interior in particular has been revealed. A road of early imperial date runs parallel to the river, with a house with central atrium and bath complex, located on its northern side. In the late imperial period a new street was constructed that cut through the eastern edge of this villa. The original Roman southern wall of the city did not run as close to the present bank of the Guadiana as does that of the *Alcazaba*. Thus it is possible to see the lowest levels of the line of that Roman wall running eastwards from the Arab gate. That itself was erected close to the site of a Roman city gate controlling access from the bridge, the foundations of which can be made out just outside the Arab gateway and at right angles to it. Between the Roman and Arab walls may be seen traces of houses built outside the fortifications of Roman date.

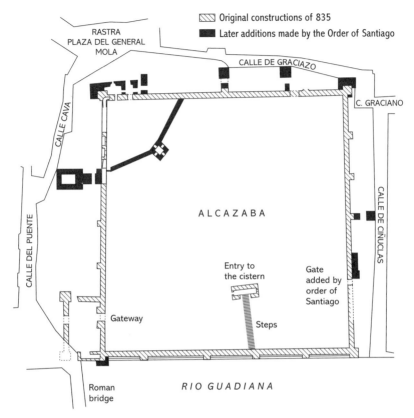

Key:
- ▨ Original constructions of 835
- ■ Later additions made by the Order of Santiago

RASTRA
PLAZA DEL GENERAL MOLA

CALLE DE GRACIAZO

C. GRACIANO

CALLE CAVA

ALCAZABA

CALLE DE CIÑUCLAS

CALLE DEL PUENTE

Entry to the cistern

Gate added by order of Santiago

Gateway

Steps

Roman bridge

RIO GUADIANA

▲ Mérida: the Alcazaba (after Melida)

Aqueducts

They formed part of a complex system of water distribution throughout the city. Some of the underground channels can be seen adjacent to the House of the Amphitheatre (see above), and part of a *castellum aquae* has survived in the Calle Calvario. Leading to this across the open countryside due north of the city are the remains of the aqueduct called 'Los Milagros' (The Miracles). It has been dated to the reign of Augustus. Only a small section of the aqueduct, consisting of ten arches, stands but it is very striking in the use of a double arcade and the interspersing of layers of red brick in the rows of ashlar. It has even been suggested, not very convincingly, that these two features were deliberately copied by the builders of the Great Mosque (**Mezquita**) in CÓRDOBA. Water was also led to the city via another aqueduct of similar construction, now called the Acueducto de San Lazaro. Only a small stretch of this has been preserved, and it has lost its upper arcades. Adjacent to it is a lower but much more complete aqueduct built in the 16th cent.

Temple of Diana

This is a good example of a temple that was preserved by having many of its columns enclosed in the walls of a 16th-cent. noble house. It had, however, survived in free-standing state until then, and is a reminder of the possibility of Roman structures enduring for centuries after their construction. Most of the 16th-cent. house has recently been demolished to free the remains of the temple. The dedication to Diana has no historical justification, and is just borrowed from the title of the Roman temple at Evora which, until this one was fully revealed, was the best example of such a building to be seen in the Iberian peninsula. More probably the temple was originally dedicated to the imperial cult. It has also been suggested, following excavations in the temple and the Calle de Segasta, that it fronted onto one of two fora. Amongst other buildings located in this zone are a bath complex and what may have been a basilica. There was also a portico, decorated with *clipei* (circular medallions) depicting Jupiter Ammon and Medusa, now to be seen in the museum, which fronted onto the forum.

Medusa

She was one of the Gorgons: three sisters who lived in the utmost West and had hair in the form of serpents. They could kill with a glance, and in early tradition were half-horse and half-human. Medusa was the only one of the three who was mortal, and she was killed by Perseus on the orders of Athena, the goddess of wisdom. Amongst her offspring was the horse Pegasus.

Museum of Roman Art

The **Museo Nacional de Arte Romano** (Calle José Ramón Melida) was inaugurated in 1986, and built over a section of Roman road and a house built around a porticoed court. This preserves some fine wall paintings. These remains and some tombs of 1st- to 3rd-cent. date may be visited in the basement of the museum. It contains an exceedingly fine collection of materials found all over Mérida and surrounding areas. Of particular note is a series of male and female portrait busts, principally of the 1st cent. AD, representing members of the leading families of the city in that period. There is also a particularly good bust of Augustus wearing the head covering indicative of the office of *Pontifex Maximus*. One or two other busts and some statues from Mérida may be seen in the Museo Arqueológico Nacional in MADRID. Mérida has also produced a very fine collection of mosaics from a variety of sites. Those not preserved *in situ* are now to be seen here (after several years of rather informal display in the *Alcazaba*). One of the most interesting is a mosaic depiction of the story of Bacchus and Ariadne in a rather non-spatial relationship and crude execution.

Argument continues as to whether this should be attributed to the 5th or to the 6th cent. The inscription *ex officina Anniponi* ('From the workshop of Anniponus') is of note, as it proves the continued existence of a mosaic factory in the city at this late point. This was found in a villa located near the railway station. A very fine mosaic of a man killing a wild boar, surrounded by a broad vegetal border containing busts representing the four seasons, dates from the 4th cent. and comes from a large rural villa, known as 'Las Tiendas', to the west of the city. Fragments of black and white 2nd-cent. mosaics with borders of comic pygmies are similar to some to be seen in ITÁLICA. Two other mosaics of the 4th cent., found in the Calle Masona, depict victorious charioteers driving four-horse chariots; inscriptions record their names as Marianus and Paulus. The Visigothic collections, including some fine pilasters from 6th-cent. churches, are now housed in the former archaeological museum in the Plaza de Santa Clara, behind the 16th-cent. Mendoza palace (now a hotel).

The Hippodrome

Due east of the theatre and amphitheatre, but with far less stonework extant, are the scanty remains of the **Hippodrome**. Excavations beginning in 1920 and culminating in 1982 have uncovered much of the stone supports of the seats on the long north and curved eastern sides. They also showed that at the eastern end at least an external wall ran round the back of the seats, creating a façade for the structure, which was decorated with a series of regularly placed pilasters on bases. It is easy to see the layout of the race track and its *spina*. The internal dimensions of the race track were 403 × 96.5 m. It is thought to have been capable of holding up to 30,000 spectators. This is one of only three hippodromes known from Roman Spain (the others being in TOLEDO and TARRAGONA). Although no inscriptions refer to the holding of circus games in Mérida before AD 135, this one probably originated in the Julio-Claudian period. It was extensively refurbished in the reign of Constantine II (337–40). Twenty-one fragments of the badly broken inscription (1.53 × 0.75 m.) that records this have survived. The name of Constantine was, however, erased from it, following his death in battle with his brother Constans (337–50), whose own name was then chiselled off when he was overthrown by Magnentius (350–3). The inscription makes it clear that the restoration involved the creation of a new façade for the exterior of the building, reconstruction of all or part of the *carceres* (starting places for the races), and the building of a new *euripus* (a trench that ran round the outside of the track) to replace an earlier barrier between the spectators and the races.

A New Development

The most recent excavations in Mérida promise to be amongst the most exciting in Spain. A substantial area along the river bank of the Guadiana,

adjacent to the Alcazaba and the Roman bridge is currently being excavated and conserved, with the intention of making it fully visitable in the
near future. New regional government offices have been built on stilts over
the site, leaving it accessible. Traces of Bronze Age occupation have been
found here, but the most significant feature of this extensive site is the
evidence it provides for the history of the town between the early Roman
empire and the 13th cent. The line of the Roman wall along the river has
been recovered, as has a road of early imperial date that parallels it. In
between the two is an extensive area of housing, initially of the same
period, but showing signs of having been restructured in the 4th cent.
The breaking up of the enlarged Late Roman houses into numerous small
units in the Visigothic period has been shown by the discovery of as many
as eight cooking hearths in what had previously been a single Roman villa.
The deliberate destruction of most of these houses has been associated
with the early Islamic period, and this was followed after an interval of
abandonment by the building of new residences in the ninth century. At
the same time, it is clear, as the Arab historians record, that the Roman wall
of the city was deliberately slighted, with sections of it being pulled down,
almost certainly at the time that the Alcazaba was constructed in 835. This
wall was hastily rebuilt at a later period, probably when the threat of
Castillian conquest grew during the time of the Almohads. The earlier
Islamic housing can be seen clearly in this site, especially where it disre-
gards the former Roman town plan and houses were built across what had
previously been streets. Later phases of Arab occupation can be detected
by the numerous wells and pits that cover the site, and which were dug
into the lower levels from the now vanished late Islamic dwellings. While
the site is not yet open for visiting, all of these features can be seen from
the numerous viewing points in the surrounding streets and from the
open stairways to the offices. Together with the recent excavations in the
church of Santa Eulalia, the new Museum and the wealth of its Roman
remains, this development will make Mérida the best of all Spanish locations for the study and visiting of archaeological sites of Roman to
Medieval date.

Minor Sites

A Roman **necropolis** was located across the Guadiana, taking the form of
a series of large tomb-houses lining the road leading south from the
bridge towards Seville. Only the foundations of seven of these were
uncovered, together with some skeletons and a few grave goods, on the left
side of the road, in the course of excavations in 1961–2. However, two
virtually complete examples of such tombs in the form of small houses, in
which families could forgather to take a ceremonial meal on the anniversaries of the deaths of those buried therein, can be seen in the monuments
called '**Los Colombarios**', north-east of the House of the Mithraeum.
These preserve sections of their original fresco decoration, and date to the

1st cent. AD. The roofs are modern. Inscriptions over the entries record that one was built by Caius Voconius Proculus for his parents and sister, and the other by Caius Iulius Modestus for members of his family. The '**Arch of Trajan**' is all that remains of a Roman arch, stripped of all its marble facings, which seems to have served as part of the linking of two forum areas, one in the vicinity of the so-called Temple of Diana (see above), and the other to the west, around the Plaza de la Constitución. Inscriptions found in the area suggest the presence of a temple dedicated to the imperial cult on the site of the present *parador* (a former monastery of 18th-cent. date) on the west side of the Plaza. There may also have been a basilica here. The podium of a temple has been located in this area, part of which may be seen in the C/Holguin. The patron saint of the city from the Late Imperial period onwards was **St Eulalia**, who was said to have been executed during the persecution in the reign of Trajan Decius (249–51), and whose virtues were extolled by the Christian poet Prudentius (*c.*400). The place of her burial in an extramural cemetery became a cult site in the 4th cent. A basilica, substantially rebuilt around 560, gave way to the present largely 13th-cent. church, which certainly retains some Visigothic capitals that may have come from its predecessor. The whole area beneath the church has now been excavated and may be visited. The original 4th-cent. tomb-shrine is visible, as are some of the later ones that were built around it. All of these were subsumed into the basilica built in the Visigothic period, the outline of whose walls and internal structuring may be seen. There is a useful small museum of the site at the point of entry on the north side of the church. In the Calle de Santa Eulalia a rather chaotic-looking monument to the saint, called the **Hornito de Santa Eulalia**, includes Roman capitals, columns, and cornices, some of which may have come from a temple of Mars. This is indicated by the inscription MARTI SACRUM VETTILLA PACULI, 'Dedicated to Mars by Vettilla (wife of) Paculus. This is probably of 2nd-cent. date.

Head north-west on the C 537 out of Mérida, and take a small road due north that leads off to the right just before the C 357 intersects with the N V/E 90. This crosses over the N V/E 90 and then leads exclusively to a lake, some 4 km. north.

This artificial lake, called the 'Lago de Proserpina', was the source of the water conveyed to the city via the Los Milagros aqueduct. You can see the Roman granite dam and water tower built to contain and regulate it.

Near the lake was fought the battle of La Albuera, on 24 February 1479, in which the Extremaduran partisans of the claims to the Castilian throne of Juana 'la Beltraneja', the daughter of Enrique IV (1454–74), were defeated by the latter's sister Isabel (1474–1504) and her husband Fernando of Aragón (1479–1516).

Montánchez Castle

*On the N 630 heading from **Mérida** to **Cáceres**, turn right on to the CC 801 (31 km. from Mérida). After 12 km. a road leads right up to the large if ruinous castle, which provides fine views over the surrounding area.*

Within the fortress fragments of Visigothic carving have been recovered in sufficient quantities and of such quality as to make the previous existence on the site of a church of that period more than probable. The earliest Arab fortress on the site was briefly taken by Ordoño II of León (913–24). A substantial refortification is probably to be dated to the Almohad period. The castle changed hands a number of times in the late 12th cent., but was definitively conquered by the Order of Santiago around 1230. Although parts of the present castle date to a 13th-cent. refortification by the Order, there is considerable evidence of the earlier Arab occupation of the site, including a well-preserved twin-chambered cistern. Reused Roman stones may be seen throughout the fortress.

*Returning to the CC 801 (which soon becomes the CC 800) it is possible to continue to **Trujillo** (38 km.); 21 km. along the way to Trujillo a minor road to the right leads an additional 9 km. to the village of **Ibahernando**.*

This is the site of a small Visigothic basilica and Roman necropolis, excavated in 1973. The church, according to an inscription, was dedicated by Bishop Orontius of Mérida in 635. This damaged inscription and other finds from the site may be seen in the Museo Arqueológico Provincial in Cáceres.

Monte Mollet and Monte Marinet Berber settlements

Monte Mollet is located about 2 km. south-west of Vilafamés (c.20 km. north-west of Castellón de la Plana via the C 238), but has to be approached from the south-west on the CS 814. Monte Marret is about 3 km. north-east of Monte Penyagolosa (1814 m.) and is best approached from Vistabella del Maestrazgo (c.40 km. on from Vilafamés via the small and winding CS 812 to La Pelejaneta, CS 820 to Adzaneta, and CS 821 to Vistabella); ask for detailed guidance in Vilafamés and Vistabella respectively.

Although very difficult of access, these two sites are of great importance, in that they date from an early phase of the Arab conquest, and their distinctive features relate them to North African parallels. They may therefore be rare early evidence of the Berber military settlement in Al-Andalus (cf. FONTANAREJO).

Monte Mollet

The **Monte Mollet** site, partially excavated in 1976–7, seems to be that of a substantial and well-preserved village. On the top of Monte Mollet (at 704 m.) there is a roughly rectangular fortress (approx. 90 × 40 m.), with two towers on its short southern wall. Some sections of the longer east and west walls are missing, and there are traces of domestic buildings in the northern half, culminating in a tower, with large stones in its corners and

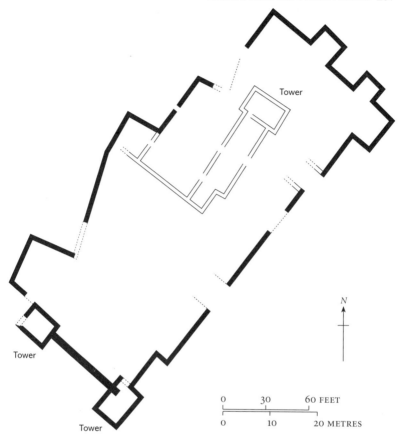

Tower

Tower

N

Tower

| 0 | 30 | 60 FEET |
| 0 | 10 | 20 METRES |

▲ Monte Mollet: the fortress (after Bazzana)

generally built in a style whose nearest equivalents are to be seen in North Africa. The outer wall (2 m. thick) is constructed from two faces of unmortared or clay-bonded stones of medium size, the space between being filled with earth and pebbles. The northernmost point of the village is some 200 m. south of the fortress. While most of the rest of the village consists of rectangular detached houses of differing sizes, mainly built around central courtyards, at this northern end there is a much larger triangular construction, made up on the eastern side of a series of linked long rooms (*c.*14 × 5.5 m.), and reinforced in each of the three corners by roughly square structures with thicker walls, which may have been towers.

Monte Marinet

The **Monte Marinet** site, excavated in 1983–4, stands on top of the mountain at a height of 1,467 m., on the boundaries between the villages of Chodos and Vistabella, and covers an area of about 8,000 sq. m. The

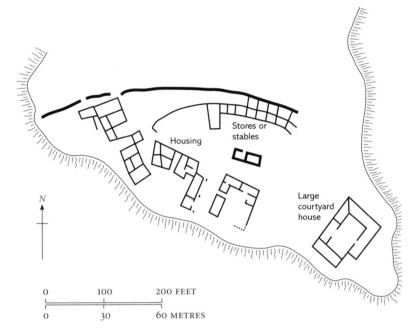

▲ Monte Marinet (after Bazzana)

main part of the site, of triangular shape, is on the flat top of the hill and is defined by a defensive wall of dry stone, very similar in construction to those found on Monte Mollet. A change of level divides this area into two zones. In the upper, western sector a secondary, less well-constructed, dry stone wall parallels the outer defensive wall, before curving away towards the corner of the most easterly house in this area, thus cutting this zone off from the one below it. A series of square chambers between the two walls and along the inner face of the interior wall lack doorways and have been interpreted as serving as granaries or stores. In the centre of this upper part of the site a two-room building was constructed with particularly thick walls (up to 1.2 m.). Two periods of occupation have been detected. Amongst the houses are examples of those built around three sides of a courtyard, as seen in Monte Mollet. There is no equivalent here to the fortress seen in the latter, but a large building with central courtyard in the southernmost corner of the settlement enjoyed a wide view over the surrounding countryside. Here also two phases of occupation have been detected, with the material finds being of better quality than those found in the other, smaller houses. In particular fragments of glazed pottery found here contrast with the grey coarse wares of the rest of the site. Scientific analysis of the former has given it a possible chronological range from the 7th to the early 9th cent. The lack of Visigothic and earlier and also of later types of Arab ceramics have led the excavators to favour the later 8th or 9th cent. for the period of occupation of both these sites, which they also deduce were inhabited for perhaps no more than about fifty years. Despite the poor quality of most of the ceramics and of the constructional techniques, the size and layout of most of the houses have led them to suggest these were for a population of relatively high status, 'a military upper class'.

Monte Naranco Asturian palace and churches

Located half-way up the hillside on Monte Naranco, immediately to the north of Oviedo and overlooking the city; accessible by local bus.

The late 9th-cent. Asturian chronicles record the erection by King Ramiro I (842–50) of 'a church and palaces with remarkable vaulting in the place called *Lignum*' (*Chronicle of Albelda* XV. 10), and locate this on Monte Naranco, two (Roman) miles from his capital of OVIEDO. The probably later 'Ad Sebastianum' version of the *Chronicle of Alfonso III* also mentions the construction on the site of a bath house, of which no trace has been found. But the church and palace(s) are substantially represented in the two buildings called **Santa María de Naranco** and **San Miguel de Lillo**.

Santa María de Naranco consists of a rectangular hall (12 × 6 m.) located over a barrel-vaulted lower storey (which is not normally accessible). It is entered via a flight of steps on the northern side, leading into the centre of the hall. At either end of the hall there is an arcaded loggia (4 × 6 m. each). In the eastern one may be seen a stone altar with an inscription around its edge, recording how King Ramiro I had restored the church of Santa María in the year 848. The layout of this building, even as briefly described, suggests that it was not constructed initially to serve as a church, and it has long been assumed that it once formed part of the palace complex, serving either as some form of throne room or just as a *mirador* or viewing pavilion offering exceptional views over the hillside below. An alternative explanation is thus needed for the presence of the clearly dated altar. This can be derived from the current state of the second building, the church of San Miguel de Lillo, located about 300 m. to the

Chronicle of Alfonso III

This Asturian chronicle takes its name from the king who it is thought wrote the original text. It survives in two distinct versions. One of these, known as the *Rotense* from the 11th cent. manuscript in which it may be found, dates from the time of Alfonso's son Ordoño II (913/14–24), while the other, known from an introductory letter to a bishop as the *Ad Sebastianum*, may be 11th cent. in origin. The work provides the main narrative history of the Asturian kingdom.

west. It is immediately clear that this is incomplete. A large and relatively complex west end dwarfs a small and unornamented chancel. Excavation around the eastern end of the church easily confirmed what the present state of the building suggests. The original crossing and chancel of the church collapsed at some relatively early point, and were eventually replaced by the present small chancel in the later Middle Ages. As this would indicate a period of abandonment, it has been possible to suggest that the altar now in Santa María de Naranco was originally situated in San Miguel de Lillo, and was transferred to the other building following the latter's collapse. Indeed, it seems probable that the dedication was transferred with it. Thus the building now called Santa María de Naranco was in origin a secular building associated with King Ramiro's palace, and the church of San Miguel was then called Santa María. It was given a new dedication, to the Archangel Michael, when it was restored in the late Middle Ages. The implication of the altar inscription is also that the church (the present San Miguel) pre-dated the reign of Ramiro I, only being revived by him. However, it has not been possible to gauge its original period of construction, and the extant western section suggests that Ramiro's work on the building was fairly substantial Excavations by German archaeologists in 1990/1 have confirmed this reconstruction of the history of the buildings, not least by demonstrating that the present church of San Miguel in the form it enjoyed in the reign of Ramiro had a barrel-vaulted construction similar to that to be seen in the main hall (and in the under-chamber) of Santa María de Naranco.

Both buildings have notable traces of their original sculptured decoration, and in the case of San Miguel a small section of fresco painting can be seen on the ceiling of the south-west bay. The carved capitals of the loggias of Santa María are particularly interesting, being filled with a series of small figures. There is also a series of roundels on the walls, in the centre of which are figures of stags that are strangely reminiscent of the animal-figure art of the Russian steppes.

Nothing is known of the use of the palace on Monte Naranco after Ramiro I's death in 850 and the transfer of the seat of the monarchy from Oviedo to LEÓN after 910. Only the collapse of the east end of the present San Miguel, necessitating the transformation of the hall into a church in its place, may have preserved this section of an otherwise redundant complex.

Monteagudo   Arab villa (and fortress)

*On the left 4 m. from the centre of MURCIA, heading north-east up the C 3223 towards **Yecla**.*

At Yecla there is a Museo Arqueológico Municipal in the Casa de Cultura (Calle España, 37), housing Iberian finds, especially from the Cerro de los Santos site.

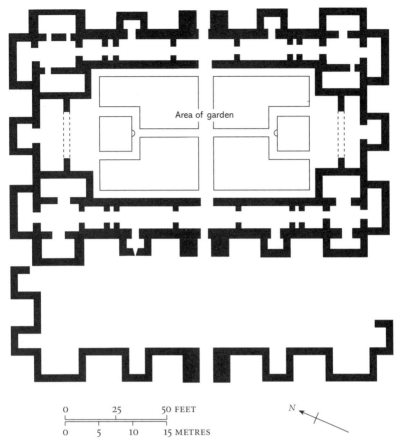

Area of garden

0   25   50 FEET

0   5   10   15 METRES

N

▲ Monteagudo: the Castillejo (after Gómez-Moreno)

The **Castillar** constitutes the remains of a small hilltop fortress of Arab construction, built on a Roman site with reused materials, and now much restored.

Cf. other such fortresses of Arab origin at **Aledo** (*13 km. west of the 617 km. marker on the N 340-E 15*), held by the Order of Calatrava from 1085 to 1160); **Mula** (*45 km. west of Murcia on the C 415*), rebuilt by the Velez family in the 15th–16th cents.—see also museum in former palace of the Marqués de Menahermosa (Calle Marqués), to house finds from the Iberian necropolis of **El Cigarralejo**; and **Orihuela** (*24 km. east of Murcia on the N 340*)—see also cathedral of 1305–55, with 16th-cent. additions.

Once thought to be of Almoravid construction, the **Castillejo** of Monteagudo (400 m. north-east) has been reattributed to the reign of a local potentate called Muḥammad ibn Mardanish (1147–72), who made himself ruler of Murcia and Valencia. He also gained control for a time over Granada, Jaén, and Almería. The poorly preserved *tabiya* or rammed-earth complex is now thought to be a *munya* or country villa of a wealthy inhabitant of Murcia. It has a fortress-like aspect, with multi-angular corner towers and defended entrances, but within these stood a rectangular garden, quartered by raised paths, with pavilions at either end. Traces of painted decoration and stucco have been found in the ruins of the chambers within the outer walls. On the western side another wall paralleled the main structure, defining a space whose use is not known.

Montgó (Denia) Iberian fortress

The fortifications are located on the western end of the dominating massif of Montgó or Mongo (c. 750 m. high), 4 km. south of Denia (province of Alicante). Although no road leads over the mountain itself, it may be skirted on its southern side on a small road leading from Jávea/Xàbia to the village of La Xara. The latter can be approached via the C 3311 running west from Denia. It stands immediately below the Alto de Benimaquía, on the summit of which is located one of the forts.

The narrow western end of the massif, known as the Pico de Aguila, is fortified by three parallel walls. Due west and divided from it by a narrow valley is the lower hill called the Alto de Benimaquía (225 m. high), which is crowned by a fortress. Here a platform has been artificially flattened and fortified. Using the precipitous slope for its southern defences, two walls, one of *c*.100 m. and the other of *c*.25 m., set at right angles to each other and strengthened by the remains of six rectangular towers, protect the approaches from the north and the west. The southern end of the shorter wall has been obscured by the erection of relatively modern walls for penning stock. These structures, none of which now rise much more than 2 m. above ground level, have been dated to the 5th–4th cents. BC.

The siting and careful angling of the three walls on the adjacent Pico de Aguila is held to indicate the knowledge of more sophisticated defensive techniques, making use of salients that could enable the defenders to launch flanking attacks on besiegers. These in consequence have been assigned to a second phase of occupation, dating to the 3rd–2nd cents. BC. Many shards of Iberian pottery were discovered in excavations conducted in 1961, but the lack of any finds of Greek pottery in either site seems to indicate that there was no commercial centre on the coast in the vicinity of Denia in these periods.

Muñigua Roman town

Muñigua is situated in the southern fringes of the Sierra Morena, about 2 km. west of the Arenillas halt on the railway line that, in leisurely fashion, links SEVILLE and MÉRIDA. The site, now called Castillo de Mulva, is not directly accessible by road. It can be approached by a track that may not be suitable for all vehicles The track begins at Villanueva del Río y Minas, 2.5 km. north of the C 431 about 50 km. east of Seville.

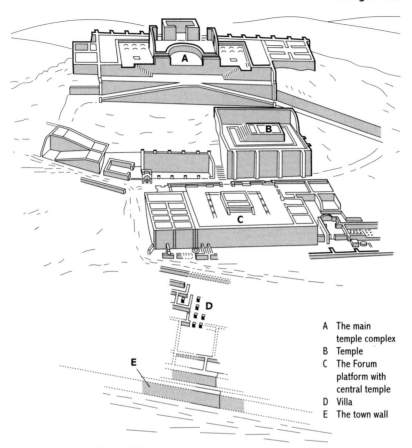

A   The main
    temple complex
B   Temple
C   The Forum
    platform with
    central temple
D   Villa
E   The town wall

▲ Muñigua (after Hauschild)

This Roman *municipium*, granted the *Ius Latii* by the Emperor Vespasian in 73/4, is known, from finds of kilns and metal waste, to have been a centre of the mining and iron-working industries in the Early Imperial period. Little is known of its history, but a significant number of public and private inscriptions have come from the site. Virtually all its major structures that are now known seem to date from the second half of the 1st cent. AD. The chief urban feature of Muñigua, and its most attractive feature, is the substantial site of a temple complex (A) on an artificial plat-form, dramatically situated on the hillside, facing eastwards across the site of the forum. Situated in the dominant position in the town, this has been recognized as an attempt by the citizens of Muñigua to create, on a smaller scale, a copy the famous temple of Fortuna at Praeneste (Italy). There is a smaller temple of more orthodox form on a levelled space below it (B). Below this is the terrace of the forum (C), in the centre of which stood another temple. Across the road that runs at the foot of the east wall of the forum platform, sections of a villa (D), also dating from the second half of the 1st cent. AD, have been excavated. Centring on a peristyled atrium, nine rooms of this villa have been located. On the east side of the villa there is a small section of the town's outer wall. A necropolis has also been found just outside the town wall at this point. The town is notable for the survival of an inscription bearing a rescript, or reply to a petition, of the Emperor Titus (79–81). Interestingly, this was far from favourable to the town, being the rejection of the local magistrates' appeal to the emperor to be released from the obligation of paying a debt the municipality owed to a certain Servilius Pollio, a tax collector. The emperor waived the fine (of 50,000 sesterces: the largest denomination of Roman bronze coin) due for a wrongful appeal, in the light of the town's claim of civic poverty.

*On the C 431, to the east of the turn to Villanueva del Río, and about 5 km. beyond Alcolea del Río, is the site of **Arva**, situated on the hillside (Peña de la Sal) north of the road.*

This is another Roman *municipium* of the age of Vespasian, and of Turdetanian origin. A ruined arch, a pottery factory, oil presses, the site of a public bath house and a Roman necropolis have been found, together with several inscriptions. There is also evidence of the existence of a cult of Attis, in the form of a funerary statue.

Murcia   Arab town defences

This settlement goes back to the 8th cent. AD, when the Arab town of Mursiya was founded, but evidence of reuse of Roman masonry and numerous Visigothic finds (in the Museo de Murcia: see below) suggest the presence of earlier occupation sites in the vicinity, if not in the same location. The most distinguished period in the history of the town began in 1224 when it became the centre of the independent kingdom of Ibn Hud (d. 1238), who made himself master of much of eastern Al-Andalus, including CÓRDOBA, as the power of the Almohads disintegrated. However, acute political instability following his death and military threats from both Castile and Aragón led to Abū Bakr ibn Hud submitting his kingdom to Fernando III of Castile in 1243. In 1264 there was a successful local rebellion, in alliance with the Nazirids, but the town was forced in 1266 to surrender to Jaume I (1213–76) of Aragón, who returned it to the rule of his Castilian son-in-law, Alfonso X. The latter expelled most of the Muslim population and it was repopulated, largely by Catalans. It remained a frontier fortress until the fall of Granada in 1492; the massacre of the Christian population of Cieza (40 km. north-west of Murcia) in a Nazirid raid in 1449 indicates the continuing need for strong defences.

The principal legacies of the Islamic presence in Murcia are the foundations of a small but very significant part of the 12th-cent. system of

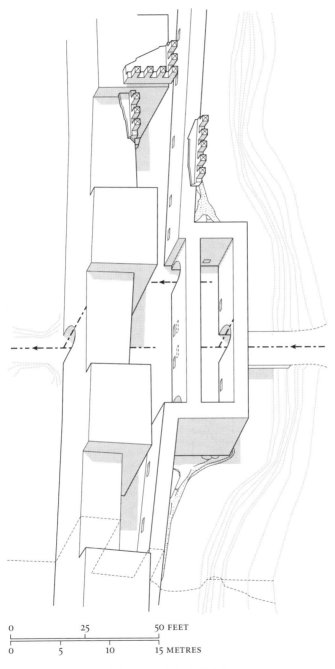

▲ Murcia: reconstruction of the Gate of Santa Eulalia as it would have been in 12th cent.

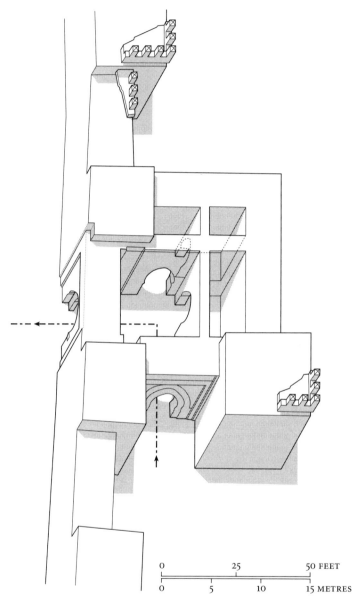

▲ Murcia: Reconstruction of the Gate of Santa Eulalia as it would have been in 15th cent.

defences. That a powerful set of walls around the city existed by the end of the 12th cent. is established by references in both Muslim and Christian sources, and administrative documents relate to various repairs and restorations in the 14th and 15th cents. Excavations, from 1963 to 1965, uncovered part of this 12th-cent. city wall, a tower, and a section of a second, outer wall of the same date in the Plaza de Santa Eulalia. Also discovered were parts of a tower and wall belonging to a 15th-cent. refortification, standing about 4 m. in front of the earlier gateway. The Almohad barbican (12th cent.) took the form of a rectangular projection from the outer wall, entered via two arches in the latter, but with only a single centrally placed gateway to the exterior. In the 15th cent. this was massively reinforced by the construction of two great linked towers in front of the exit from the outer wall, and the creation of two gateways in between, facing each other and parallel to the line of the wall. The other significant discovery of the excavations was the presence in the same location of an **Islamic cemetery** of 10th–11th-cent. date. As this was built over by the Almohad walls, and must have been originally established outside the then perimeter of the city, it is clear that an earlier but almost certainly shorter line of walls existed within the circuit of the later ones.

A Museo de la Muralla Arabe, once located on the site in the Plaza de Santa Eulalia, seems to have expired, and the ceramic and other finds from the excavations are to be seen in the archaeological section of the Museo de Murcia (Calle Alfonso X el Sabio, 5). There is a late Gothic cathedral (1394–1465) hidden within 16th- and 18th-cent. exterior features, situated on the site of the former main mosque of the city. The Museo Diocesano, in the 14th-cent. chapter house, contains a Late Roman sarcophagus, reused in the Middle Ages.

Niebla Roman, Visigothic and Arab town

26 km. east of Huelva on the N431 to Seville.

This was Roman Ilipla, and site of the Visigothic see of Elepla, of which five late 6th- and 7th-cent. bishops are known. It was called Lebla by the Arabs. For part of the Almoravid period it, together with Mertola and Silves, was in the hands of the disciples of a rebel messianic leader called Abū al-Qasim ibn Qasī. Although (as usual) over-restored, substantial sections of the Arab walls with forty-six towers and four of the gates of the town may be seen. The lower courses of the towers suggest Umayyad origins, but most of what may be seen dates to the Taifa and Almohad periods, as does the ruined Alcázar. The Puerta del Agua (water gate) is a good example of a defensive bent-entry, forcing attackers to turn once inside it (see also GRANADA and BÁDAJOZ). The church of Santa María de la Granada has a complex building history. It is thought to contain traces of an earlier, 10th-cent. Mozarabic church, converted into a mosque under the Almohads. The minaret now serves as the bell tower. Something of

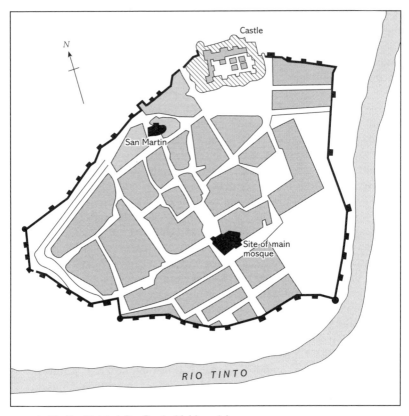

▲ Muslim Niebla (after Pavón Maldonado)

another Almohad mosque may be seen in the form of a brick arcade now forming part of the ruined church of San Martín. The bridge is of Roman creation, retaining much original stonework. The town fell to Alfonso X in 1262 after a ten-month siege.

Numantia   Iberian and Roman town

On the N III 7 km. north of Soria; the site is signposted from the village of Garay.

Historically highly significant, as the centre of indigenous opposition to Roman conquest, this Iberian town of the Arevacos was subject to a siege by Caius Hostilius Mancinus in 137 BC. This proved a fiasco, with the Roman commander and his army eventually surrendering to the Arevacos. A more determined effort, however, led to the town being besieged and taken by Scipio Aemilianus in 134–133 BC. The second siege, like that of Masada (in Israel), involved the construction in the surrounding hills of seven camps with walls between them around the beleaguered town. The total length of this perimeter was about 9 km. The wall, about 3 m. high and 2.5 m. wide, was stone-built. Watch towers were inserted

▼ Numantia and the Roman siege camps

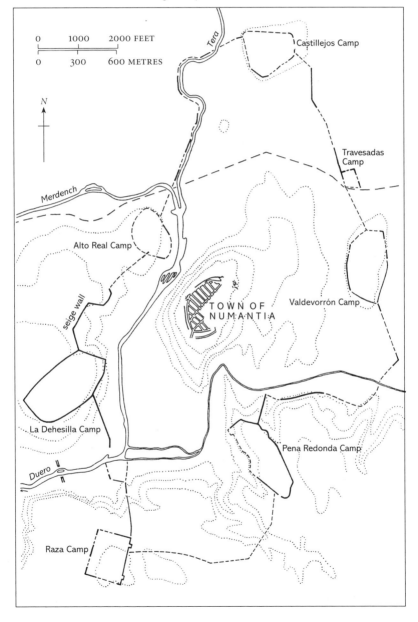

into the wall every 33 m., and a palisaded ditch was thrown up in front of the wall. The locations of these siege camps have been recovered, and their positions are marked, but few traces may be seen of them on the ground. Stones thrown by siege weapons have been recovered from the site. The inhabitants were eventually starved into surrender, and the survivors were sold into slavery. The town was completely destroyed. Excavations have revealed traces of the final phase of violent conflict, in the form of arrow-heads, sling shots, spearheads and Roman ballista bolts. After destruction of the town a minor Ibero-Roman settlement, called Numantia, developed on the site, of which several features can now be seen. These include a number of houses and streets, and traces of the town wall.

The settlement and the military sites around it were the subject of much excavation in the earlier part of this century by Spanish and German archaeologists. Finds from the site, as well as reconstructions, can be seen in the Museo Numantino in Soria (Paseo Espolón, 8), which is only 7 km. away. It may be better to visit the museum prior to going to the site.

Olérdola Medieval fortress and church

From Vilafranca del Penedès (which has an interesting museum devoted to the local wine industry)—on the N 340 from BARCELONA *to* TARRAGONA—*head south on the B 211 for about 5 km. A signposted turn to the right indicates the way up to the site, which is a cul-de-sac. (NB Being walled, this site is inaccessible outside its opening hours.)*

On a naturally defensible hilltop site (358 m. high), Olérdola has shown signs of occupation from the Neolithic and the Bronze Age onwards. The earliest recorded excavations of the site took place in 1921, and concentrated on what came to be recognized as an indigenous settlement (within an area under Roman rule) dating from between the 3rd and the 1st cents. BC. To this period, possibly during Marcus Porcius Cato's suppression of indigenous revolts in 197 BC, is attributed the earliest stages of the wall that runs across the whole breadth of the hilltop and the ruins of a watch tower at the southern end of it. As there have been no finds of *terra sigillata*, the site may have been abandoned by the late Republican period.

It may not have been reoccupied until the late 9th or 10th cent. By that time the County of Barcelona, established after the Frankish conquest of that city in 801, was expanding its frontiers gradually westwards along the Mediterranean coast. Settlements in this vicinity can be documented at Ribes in 942 and La Granada in 950. Olérdola itself is first mentioned as a settlement in a charter of 911. Another one dated to 929 records Count Sunyer I (912–54) of Barcelona erecting a castle in the ruins and founding a church dedicated to the Archangel Michael. A reference to the reconstruction of the church in 991 may suggest that the earlier building had suffered in Al-Manṣūr's destructive raid on Catalonia in 985. The Ibero-

Roman cistern that can be seen on the western side of the site is mentioned in another document of 987. The settlement seems to have become the centre of a wider district in the course of the repopulation of the Penedès region around 1000. A member of the comital family, Mir Geribert, who had substantial estates in Penedès, took the title of 'Prince of Olérdola' in 941/2, but was forced to recognize the authority of Count Ramón Berenguer I (1035–76) of Barcelona in 1058. In 1060 he and his son Bernardo were captured during a failed expedition against the Taifa fortress of Mora de Ebro and were executed at Tortosa.

Olérdola was probably sacked in 1108 by the Almoravids, as the church had once more to be restored late that year. A new charter of liberties was also conceded to the population by Count Ramón Berenguer III (1096–1131), but the settlement seems to have gone into further decline, paralleling the growth of the more conveniently located settlement of Vilafranca del Penedès. A small castle built around the former Roman watch tower remained in the hands of the Lords of Sant Martí Sarroca (a small town 11 km. north-west of Vilafranca), descendants of Mir Geribert, and a village-size population continued to live on the site for several centuries.

The **walls** give indications of at least two different phases of construction. The earlier phase, associated with the Celtiberian/Roman settlement, can be distinguished by the use of large blocks. This included the construction of the large square tower on the right side of the gate, and the rectangular tower on the western section of wall. The smaller and cruder stonework of the upper levels of the walls and towers just mentioned, and all the left-hand gate tower can be attributed to the various stages of fortification and restoration under the counts of Barcelona, between 929 and 1109. The unique semicircular tower, which you can visit internally through the museum, belongs to the last stage of this period, though it may replace an earlier construction destroyed in 1108. The **church** is thought to show evidence of four phases. The earliest part may now be the chamber on the north side of the chancel and the horseshoe-arched doorway (perhaps once a chancel arch) leading into it from the west. This has been interpreted as being all that survives of the east end of a small rectangular church in Mozarabic style, built perhaps in the 9th cent. Of the church built by Count Sunyer in 929–35, the present chancel is all that may be seen. The nave belongs to the rebuilding of 991, but it was re-vaulted and roofed in Romanesque style, probably after the sack of 1108. To this last phase also belongs the damaged tower over the cupola of the crossing. The hideous bellcote is a more recent aberration. The church continued in use for the much reduced population of the settlement until the 19th cent., when it was downgraded to the level of *Ermita*. It was vandalized during the Civil War, and finally restored to its present state in 1963.

There is a small site museum inside the walls, adjacent to the main gate.

Olmos Arab fortress

Located within the municipal boundaries of El Viso de San Juan (province of Toledo; about 6 km. due west of Illescas) on two adjacent hills overlooking the Río Guadarrama. The northern hill is currently thought to mark the location of the 12th- to 14th-cent. village, and its companion to the south that of the Arab and later fortress.

The Umayyad fortress of Walmus was certainly in existence by July 933, when ʿAbd al-Raḥmān III (912–61) stayed there on campaign (Ibn Hayyan, *Muqtabis* V). Like MADRID and CALATALIFA, it may have been built by Muḥammad I (852–86) to defend the routes leading from the passes of Berrueco and Tablada in the Sierra de Guadarrama towards Toledo. In the Taifa period the small fortress seems to have become a *ribat*, as grave markers of two Muslims who came there to devote themselves to *jihad* or 'holy war', have been found. In 1083 it was ceded by Yahyā b. Ismāʿīl (1075–80, 1081–5), the last Muslim ruler of Toledo, to Alfonso VI (1072–1109) of Castile-León, but it was besieged and destroyed by the Almoravids in 1109–10. In 1140 it was given by Alfonso VII (1126–57) to the Hospitallers, but soon passed to the diocese of Toledo and in 1166 was granted by Alfonso VIII to the town council of Segovia. It had become deserted and was known only as a hideout of felons by the reign of Juan II (1406–54). Little may now be seen, but excavations in 1983–4 recovered many fragments of medieval pottery; the earliest of these have been dated

▼ Arab towns and fortresses in the vicinity of Toledo

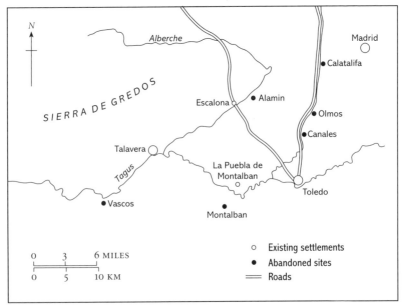

to the 9th cent., strengthening belief in the foundation of the fortress by Muḥammad I.

Orce Palaeolithic site

On the picturesque N 432 from Granada to Baza and Puerto Lumbreras, at Cúllar de Baza, 22 km. east of Baza, take the C 2239 northwards for 28 km. to Galera. Here a small road leads east for 8 km. to Orce (where the owner of the site lives: enquire at Ayuntamiento *to find him for permission and for details of the location on the Cerro de la Virgen).*

Although little is visible apart from some signs of excavation, this area is of the greatest importance, in that it has revealed traces of possibly the **earliest hominids** known in Europe. In particular, worked flints have been found here that have been accepted as being well over a million years old, and the product of activity probably attributable to *Homo erectus*. Although many of the flints found are not worked, their nearest geological place of origin is 5 km. away, indicating that they were transported to this location. The sites excavated here were once on the shore of a long-vanished lake, and two layers of possible early human occupation have been detected palaeomagnetically. The older of these has been dated to a period around 1.8 million years ago, and the other to a time between 1.6 and 1.4 million years ago. Actual human remains found on the site come from the higher and thus later of the two levels. These consist of three bone fragments, one from a skull and the other two from an upper arm. There are also animal bones showing signs of having been broken artificially and being worked on with stone tools. While the recent nature of the discoveries leaves the conclusions still provisional, their acceptance would make this the oldest site of hominid occupation in Europe, and would also undermine the previous belief that human occupation of the continent did not begin until about 500,000 years ago. Other discoveries at GRAN DOLINA, dating to about 780,000 years ago, help to substantiate this revision of the chronology of man's first presence in Europe.

On the road between Galera and Orce a track on the right leads 1 km. to a chapel, visible from the road, beside which may be seen traces of round houses dating from the Late Neolithic.

Oviedo Asturian royal sites   ★

Oviedo succeeded **Pravía** as capital of the Asturian kingdom early in the reign of Alfonso II the Chaste (791–842). A number of buildings to be seen in the city date to his reign. To that of his successor Ramiro I (842–50) are ascribed those on the adjacent MONTE NARANCO. After the death of Ramiro's grandson Alfonso III the Great in 910 the centre of the kingdom moved south to LEÓN and Oviedo declined in importance. The

The church of San Juan, founded by King Silo in 780, but rebuilt in the 9th cent. and substantially reconstructed in the 17th and 18th cents., may be seen at Santianes de Pravía.

present cathedral, replacing a church first built by Fruela I the Cruel (757–68) and restored by Alfonso II, was begun in 1388. The tower flanking the west door on its southern side was only built in 1556, and its companion on the north side was never completed.

San Tirso (immediately south-west of the cathedral; entered via the Plaza de Alfonso II) retains only the complete east end of the church built by Alfonso II (to be seen from the street), including a now blind triple-arcaded window, and some evidence of earlier work in its present north wall. Most of the rest is 14th-cent., affected by a restoration following a major fire in 1521.

The **Cámara Sancta** (so named from the treasure chamber which contains the *arca sancta*: see below) is attached to the south transept of the cathedral, whence entry is gained to the upper storey and its treasury. The outside of the building and its lower storey are approached via the cloister. Excavated and extensively restored following damage during the October Revolution in the Asturias in 1934, this is best known as repository of the cathedral treasures. These (stolen in 1977 but recovered and repaired) include a gold equal-armed (Greek) cross set with classical gems, made for Alfonso II, and the great gold and jewelled Cross of Victory of Alfonso III. The latter contains a wooden cross, supposed to have belonged to King Pelayo (718–37), the founder of the dynasty, and used in his victory at the battle of Covadonga in 718. There is also an ivory diptych of the consul Flavius Strategius Apion (AD 539), a gold and agate casket given by Fruela II (924–5), a wooden relic box, the *arca sancta*, which was covered with decorated silver plates by Alfonso VI (1072–1109), the portable altar known as the Diptych of Gundisalvo (1162–74), and a large collection of relics in a variety of medieval and later reliquaries. The antechamber to the treasury was reworked in the reign of Alfonso VI, when the six columns containing very fine paired figures of the twelve apostles were added, together with new vaulting. Although normally attributed to Alfonso II, the building of the Cámara Sancta is not one of the works attributed to him in the 9th–10th-cent. Asturian chronicles, and is not recorded before the 12th cent. The excavations of 1934 established the existence of two phases, represented by the present structure and by part of an adjacent tower (visible in the west wall of the lower storey), that must have preceded it and onto which the Cámara Sancta was built. It is possible that it was only that tower that belonged to the time of Alfonso II, and the main part of the building dates to a later period, such as that of Alfonso III. Adjacent to the Cámara Sancta to the west were found traces of what was identified as the royal palace of Alfonso II, and a reconstruction of its plan has been attempted. You can see features of this site outside the south wall of the cathedral, west of the south transept.

San Julián de los Prados (*to the left of the A 66 to Gijón about 500 m. north-east of the cathedral*) is recorded as a construction of Alfonso II, and is one of the best-preserved of the Asturian churches. It is reported to have stood close to a palace, but of this no trace has been found. The most striking feature of the building is its fresco decoration, of which substantial traces can be seen in the nave, the crossing and the triple-apsed chancel. Not only is there much use of illusionism, with paint, imitating marble and coloured stone and also employed to give three-dimensional effects, but the decoration is strikingly classical. In the nave and the transepts in particular this takes the form of stylized villas and draperies, distantly reminiscent of features to be seen in the mosaics of Ravenna (especially Sant'Apollinare Nuovo) and even in the mosaics of the Umayyad mosque in Damascus. No human or animal figures are to be seen, nor any element of specifically Christian art, beyond centrally placed crosses. These latter are very close in form to the Cross of Victory of Alfonso III (see above), and it is possible that these frescos—and even possibly the present building itself—should be dated to his reign rather than that of Alfonso II. In general the ideological underpinning of the decoration of this church seems to be opposed to religious imagery (cf. the Iconoclast movement in Byzantium) but there is no documentary record of such ideas circulating in Christian Spain.

The **Museo Arqueológico** (Calle San Vicente, 5) is located in the medieval monastery of San Vicente, which came into being around 781, and was the major male monastic house (San Pelayo on an adjacent site was the female equivalent) in the city. It contains an important collection of Asturian decorative carvings, mainly from the sites on MONTE NARANCO. There are also a number of Roman and Visigothic pieces. Some columns with very stylized Corinthian capitals are thought to have come from the palace of Alfonso III. On the inner edge of the pavement towards the eastern end of the Calle de Arguëlles, around the corner from the museum, may be seen slight traces of the 9th-cent. and later wall of the city.

About 36 km. south of Oviedo, on the east side of the N 630 is the small Asturian church of **Santa Cristina de Lena**. *Approach by leaving the N 630 at Pola de Lena 6 km. to the north; the key is kept in the house at the bottom of the hill on which the church stands.*

Quite undocumented, this is stylistically and in its decorative details very reminiscent of the buildings on MONTE NARANCO. It was restored after partial destruction in 1934. There is a well-preserved west gallery and an elevated chancel with its arcaded screen, which includes a central section of Visigothic date.

Palencia Visigothic crypt

The site of a settlement of the Vaccaei and then the Roman town of Pallantia, the modern city offers few traces of its antiquity. However, beneath the late medieval cathedral (begun in 1321) is the crypt of San Antolín (St Antoninus), which can be dated to the Visigothic period by the style of the two capitals in a triple arcade at the east end. The crypt was modified in 1034 (while the diocese of Palencia was being first established), when new supporting arches were added throughout. These divide the crypt into three small sections. The original Visigothic section at the eastern end may have been used at this time to house relics of St Antoninus, a Gallic martyr thought to have been killed in the persecution under Trajan Decius (249–51); they may have been displayed in a precious metal reliquary in the rectangular space between the two small columns. It is likely that the main altar of the cathedral that preceded the present one stood at ground level immediately overhead. However, there is no evidence at all for the existence of the cult of St Antoninus in Spain in the Visigothic period, and the function of this chapel at that time may have been quite different. The presence of a spring (cf. SANTA COMBA DE BANDE and SANTA EULALIA DE BÓVEDA) might suggest this is another case of a Christian reuse of a site of previous pagan worship.

There was a university at Palencia, the first in Spain, between 1208 and 1239, when it was transferred to Salamanca. One possible consequence of this was that by the 1280s 20 per cent of the canons of the cathedral were found to be illiterate. In 1217 Enrique I of Castile (1214–17) was killed by a falling brick when riding through the city.

Pla de Nadal Visigothic building

Located close to Manises, which is on the east side of the E 15 bypass around Valencia, about 6 km. due west of the city. Enquire at the Oficina de Turismo *in Valencia or the* Ayuntamiento *in Manises.*

This is a unique survival from the Visigothic period, subject to excavation from 1981 onwards. Only the southern sector survives of what appears to be a very grand villa, possibly rectangular in shape, centred on a large peristyled court. In the excavated sector there is a striking buttressed façade, with central entry, opening into a vestibule (17 m. × 5 m.). This opens at either end, via rectangular lobbies, onto small porticoes flanked by towers. What may be other towers extend forwards, at right angles to the façade, to flank the main entry. As the walls only survive to a height of little over a metre, it is not possible to be sure how many storeys the building may have had or how high the rectangular tower-like sections may have once risen.

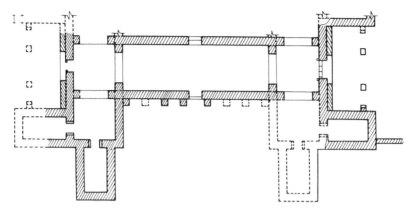

▲ Pla de Nadal: the excavated section of the Visigothic villa (after E. Juan and I. Pastor)

The Visigothic origin of the building is attested by surviving fragments of its decoration, in the form of some vegetal friezes, and a column with attached cuboid capital. Some crosses within circles of laurels are reminiscent of those found in the sites of the basilicas of Casa Herrera and RECCOPLIS. A stone disc contains a (damaged) monogram within a stylized interleaved vegetal border.

Parallels have been drawn between this building and some of the greater Late Roman villas of the Moselle valley (in particular that of Pfalzel), leading to the suggestion that this was the residence of a noble family of the Visigothic period. Further excavation may modify or strengthen this conclusion.

For finds from sites in this region see the Museo de Prehistoria (Calle Corona, 36) and the Museo Histórico de la Ciudad (Plaza Arzobispo, 3) in **Valencia**, and the Museo de Paterna (Calle San Agustín, 7) in the dormitory town of Paterna. There is also a Museo Maritimo in the late 14th-cent. gateway, the *Torres de Serranos* (Plaza de los Fueros) in Valencia.

Puig Castellet (Lloret de Mar) Iberian village

*In the town of Lloret, on the coast 39 km. north-east of **Mataró** (see TORRE LLAUDER), in the suburban housing estate of Roca Grossa, at the east end of the town and about 1 km. inland, approached via the Avenida Puig de Castellet.*

A section of a fortified 3rd-cent. BC Iberian village on the slope of a small hill may be seen. An entry, defended by a tower (cf. ULLASTRET) gives access to a rectangular enclosure divided up into a series of adjacent small houses, all enclosed within an outer wall.

*Continue on for 11km. to **Tossa de Mar.***

Puig de les Muralles/Puig Rom (Roses, Gerona)

Visigothic fortress

On the coast road 2 km. south-east of Roses/Rosas (which is 17 km. east of Figueres/Figueras on the C 260).

On a hilltop overlooking the bay of Roses, this location was first excavated by Professor Pere de Palol in 1946, but he revised his original analysis in 1988 (though this remains unpublished). He has described it as a complete walled site, with rooms of 'definitely military' purpose being built into the inner face of the walls, and has identified it as part of a system of defences controlling access across the eastern end of the Pyrenees. An area some 70 m. wide was uncovered in the south-west corner, incorporating an angled section of the defensive wall overlooking the bay. At the point of the angle is the only gateway into the fort, which is flanked by two solid rectangular towers. One other shallow rectangular tower protrudes from the western section of wall, which stands to a height of 2–3 m. This tower and the western tower of the gate are not bonded into the wall, and may represent a secondary phase of fortification. The techniques of construction used have been thought to indicate haste. In the interior, the foundations of a series of rooms can be seen abutting the walls. Visigothic period belt buckles were found on the site, together with a coin weight and some agricultural and carpentry tools. A gold *triens* of the mint of Gerona of the reign of Achila (710–13) suggests the site was still occupied at the time of the Arab conquest.

*Within the Ciudadela (citadel) (1543) of **Roses**, to the right of the main road to Figueres, lies the monastery of Santa María (foundation charter of 1022).*

You can see part of the church of **Santa María de Roses**, in particular the apse and parts of the side walls. The church was restored in 1966–9. This is the earliest example of the 'Lombard' style of architecture known in

▼ Puig Rom (after Palol)

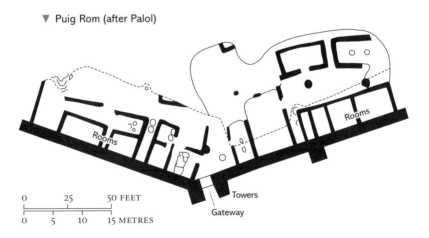

0   25   50 FEET

0   5   10   15 METRES

Towers

Gateway

Rooms

Rooms

Spain. There are parts of the monastic ranges visible to the south of the church.

Follow a hillside track starting half a km. beyond the military base at Peni.

You can see the ruins of another church of the same period, of basilican shape, **Sant Tomàs de Peni.**

Reccopolis and Zorita de los Canes Visigothic and
medieval towns   ★

Reccopolis

The site (*c*.30 ha. in area), which was discovered in 1893, is located on the flat-topped hill of La Oliva, overlooking the River Tagus, 1.5 km. north-east of the present village of Zorita de los Canes, which itself began to develop in the 9th cent. The *Chronicle of John of Biclar*, written about 602, records that the Visigothic king Leovigild (569–86) built a town, which he named after his second son and eventual successor Reccared (586–601). Little more is recorded of this foundation, which did not become the seat of a bishop, though coins minted in it in the names of Kings Leovigild, Reccared, and Wittiza (sole reign 702–10) are known (Miles, pp. 96–9). These include some from a hoard of 90 gold *trientes* discovered on this site. The site's identification with the Visigothic town derives primarily from the text of the 10th-cent. Arab historian and geographer Al-Razi, who states that the castle of Zorita (see below) was built with stone taken from 'Racupel'.

Excavations were conducted by Juan Cabré in 1944–5; they concentrated on a Visigothic church and what came to be seen as a palace, but his premature death left these unpublished, other than for an account of the coin hoard. This has also meant that little new work can usefully be done on the section of the site then excavated. Other excavations in the 1970s found domestic housing in the centre of the site. Renewed work from 1993 onwards under Lauro Olmo has added to knowledge of the site's chronology and extent. In particular, it has been shown that the town was occupied, with varying levels of intensity, between the late 6th and early 9th cents., before being completely abandoned, probably in favour of the adjacent fortified village and castle. A small Romanesque church was built on the site after the Castilian conquest of this region in the late 11th cent. This is the only building standing above the levels of its foundations, and should not be confused with the earlier Visigothic church, whose plan has been recovered by excavation.

The earlier excavations established the presence of a **long thin building** (133 m. by between 9 and 13.5 m.) along the edge of the hill directly overlooking the Tagus, and this forms the principal item to be seen on the site at the moment. A line of bases in the middle of the two principal parts into which this divides indicates that arcading once ran along the spine of

▲ Reccopolis (Zorita de los Canes): ruins of the 12th-cent. church and the Visigothic palace

the building supporting the floor above. On the southern side of the western part six semicircular buttresses can be seen against the outside of the wall. At the east end another shorter line of buildings leads southwards to the site of the church. The church was cruciform, with a three-aisled nave, a western narthex, and a peculiar northwards inclination of its plan at the eastern end.

This complex of buildings was identified as and continues to be considered to be a palace, though it should be stressed that this has not been proved archaeologically. The recent excavations have uncovered parts of two more rooms in the buildings in the east wing that linked the rest of the complex with the church, which indicate that this section continued even further towards the east than previously recognized. At the same time, another building began to be detected to the south, seeming to mark the limits of the complex in that direction. This structure was on two levels, with the upper having a floor of *opus signinum*. The lower consisted of two bays (roughly 3 m. wide), divided by a wall 1.2 m. thick.

The town was surrounded by a wall (*c.*2 m. wide), interspersed with irregularly placed square towers. One gate, in the west, has so far been located and excavated. It was defended by two rectangular towers, which unlike the others protrude further into the area behind the wall than into that in front. An aqueduct bringing water into the town from the east has also been discovered, opening up possibilities that the area around the town was artificially irrigated. Within the town and adjacent to the palace complex on its southern side have been located a group of houses. These consisted of a series of rectangular rooms opening onto central spaces, probably patios, in which a well was normally to be found.

Recent studies have also uncovered something of the economy of the area in the Visigothic period, showing the coexistence here of agriculture and stock-rearing—mainly goats and cattle, together with some hunting of deer and rabbits. There is evidence of woodland, now hard to envisage in the bare landscape, which included sizeable amounts of oak. Oak was used in the construction of buildings in the town, as finds of it there have indicated.

The finds of Visigothic pottery have been particularly significant, as the site has provided the most varied range of types so far encountered, including both fine and coarse wares. These have also included at least two types of imported North African oil amphorae, some of which have been found in 8th-cent. levels. This is a surprisingly late date for such items.

The recent excavations have shown that, while the houses continued in use, the palace changed its functions after the Arab conquest. The upper floor of the newly discovered southern building seems to have been abandoned in the 8th cent. and stripped of its tiles. Probably by the end of the century it had been destroyed by fire. Around this point the adjacent housing also seems to have been abandoned, and by the early 9th cent. the whole area was being used for agriculture, with the palace being systematically robbed of stone, perhaps for reuse in the new settlement in Zorita and in the fortress.

Zorita: The Medieval Town and Castle

This area was the centre of the territory of a Berber messianic leader called Shaqya (768–77), and generally proved difficult for the Umayyads to control. The capture of a fortress at Zorita is recorded for the year 926 (Ibn Hayyan). The town, which had developed as Reccopolis, declined, and the castle became part of the kingdom of Castile around 1086, but was retaken briefly by the Almoravids in 1113. It was repopulated from Aragón in 1148, and was given to the Order of Calatrava in 1174 by Alfonso VIII. The king granted a set of *fueros* to the town in 1180, which includes reference to a Jewish community amongst the population. The Jewish quarter was probably located in the northernmost part of the town within the walls. Zorita went into decline in the later Middle Ages, and in the 16th cent. the Order transferred its base to the nearby town of **Almonacid** (Arabic *al-munayster*, i.e. 'the monastery', suggesting this was once the site of a *ribat*; two 14th-cent. fortified gateways of the late medieval wall are visible). In the reign of Felipe III (1598–1621) the Order sold the town to Ruy Gómez de Silva.

The walls of the castle and of the small town that nestles below it on the northern and western sides are principally of Arab construction, dating to the 9th and 10th cents. The Order of Calatrava enhanced the defences of the castle at various points in the 13th and 14th cents. by adding three major towers, one of which also serves as the apse of the castle chapel. To the north of it, the next tower but one is rounded, and may be a rare example of the use of such a shape in Islamic fortifications (cf. the towers of Albaicín in GRANADA and in the Aljafería in ZARAGOZA. The tower with a gateway in the middle of the west wall of the castle is a fine example of late Umayyad work. The northern wall of the castle, especially around the gate and its two flanking towers, shows much evidence of repair, suggestive of damage inflicted during the taking of the fortress, but whether in the Almoravid siege of 1113 or the subsequent Castilian reconquest cannot be determined. The Calatravan southern tower of the castle (now heavily restored) is a fine example of late medieval military architecture, defending the most vulnerable point in the outer walls. There is a subterranean Arab cistern located in the centre of the castle bailey, just north of the chapel.

Ronda la Vieja Roman town
Ronda Arab town

*From **Ronda** take the C 339 north-west; turn off to the right after about 7 km. onto the MA 449, which leads directly to the site (approx. 14 km.).*

On an extraordinarily sloping site (beware the unprotected upper edge!) the main surviving elements of Roman Acinipo to be seen consist of part of the theatre, including the lower levels of the seating and much of the *scaenae frons* (the back wall) but not the colonnades that would have decorated the stage; lower down the hillside there are sections of a bath house. There was an Iberian settlement on the site, which came under Roman rule following the end of the Second Punic War, of which the best traces are the foundations of some round houses very close to the present entry. You can see the remains of an aqueduct that brought water to the town on either side of the C 344 (to Coín and MÁLAGA) at a point 1.7 km. east of Ronda. In the Late Republican period the town issued its own coinage, to pay its annual tribute to Rome, depicting one of its major economic assets, grapes. Near Ronda itself, in the Serranía de Ronda, a hoard of 29,860 Roman coins was discovered—one of the largest such finds ever made. They were virtually all 3rd-cent. debased silver *antoniniani*, the latest dating to 268.

Despite the name, there is no particular relationship between this site and that of **Ronda** itself. The latter, in its naturally defensible site defined by the Río Guadalevín, was the location of both an indigenous and then a Roman settlement (Arunda). Continuous occupation has, however, left few traces of these. Following the Arab conquest this became an area of settlement for some clans of Nafza Berbers. In the late Umayyad period Ronda (Arab Runda) was the capital of the *qura* (administrative district) of Takurunna, and it was one of the main towns of the Nazirid kingdom, before being conquered by Castile in 1485. A Muslim revolt was crushed in the mountains around Ronda in 1501.

In the Calle del Marqués de Salvatierra see the small minaret of a Nazirid sectional mosque. The church, dedicated to San Sebastián, that had reused the minaret as its bell tower, was destroyed in the Civil War. The principal mosque stood on the site of the 16th-cent. church of Santa María la Mayor, which incorporates some of its stonework, not least in the brick bell tower on the west front. This retains most of a 13th-cent. minaret, though ornamental elements were later added to the top. Other features of the mosque may be seen over the doorway adjacent to the belfry and in the interior of the church, especially in the inner western wall. The *mihrab* of the mosque has also been found inside the church. Below the old city, on its eastern side, you can see the substantial remains of an Arab bath house. The *Alcazaba* was largely destroyed by the French in 1809, but much of the wall, including some *torres albarranas*, surrounding the old city survives, and dates from the Nazirid period. It is particularly easy to see from the path below it on the west side, continuing from the Puente San Miguel past the Arab baths to the site of the *Alcazaba*. Two original gates, the Puerta Almocábar and the Arco de Cristo, survive. Three houses in the old city, the Case del Rey Moro, the Casa de Mondragón, and the Casa del Gigante, although much restored and rebuilt, are of Nazirid origin.

Sádaba Roman villa and mausoleum

The small town of Sádaba (province of Zaragoza) is located 43 km. south of Sangüesa on the A 127, which then continues another 62 km. southwards to join the N 232 30 km. south-east of Tudela. The ruins are located 1 km. south-east of the town just west of the Canal de las Bárdenas, and approached by a footpath from Sádaba (get directions locally). The mausoleum is situated about 80 m. due east of the villa.

The mausoleum is a relatively well-preserved structure that was long thought, in local tradition, to be the ruin of a medieval Jewish synagogue. A campaign of excavation in 1962 revealed instead that it was a Roman mausoleum of the 4th cent. AD. This led to the suspicion that, if this had served as a family tomb, then there should be traces of a residence to be found in the vicinity. This was discovered in a second campaign later the same year. Of the **villa**, situated on a rocky hillock, little more than some of the foundations were found, though these proved to be of part of the domestic quarters, and their dimensions and plan indicate something of the size and sophistication of the dwelling.

The **mausoleum** (externally 16 × 14 m.) consists internally of a central chamber with four almost equal arms (like the Mausoleum of Galla Placidia in Ravenna of *c*.AD 425), the northern and southern ones having squared ends and the eastern and western ones being apsidal in shape. Some of the walls of the building still stand to a height of 4 m., though all the vaulting has been lost. There is a small vestibule on the south side, originally entered through a twin-columned arcade. Niches were located in the northern wall of this vestibule and in the north and west arms of the central chamber. Human remains and part of a large stone sarcophagus were uncovered in the vestibule. The lack of decoration made it impossible to date the sarcophagus. The central chamber had been dug over by treasure hunters in earlier times and revealed little.

Turn right off the A 127 about 1 km. north of Sádaba, heading in the direction of Sangüesa, onto a track that appears immediately after the road crosses the Canal de las Bárdenas.

Here is another, unrelated, Roman tomb, dating from the 2nd cent. AD. This is known from an inscription to have belonged to the family of the Atilii. It is known locally as the *Altar de los Moros*.

See also the well-preserved 13th-cent. castle of Sádaba, and **Uncastillo** (16 km. north-east on the A1202), which is dominated by the ruins of a castle of the 12th to 14th cents., built on Roman foundations and on the site of a 9th–10th-cent. fortress.

▼ Sádaba: Roman villa and mausoleum (after García y Bellido)

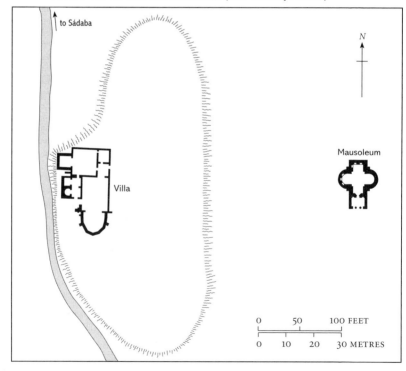

*At the end of a track 1.5 km. east of Layana (on the A1202 about 3 km. north of Sádaba) are the remains of a Roman town now called **Los Bañales** (original name unknown) and part of the aqueduct that served it.*

The aqueduct is visible from the A 1202. On the site of the town some partly reconstructed baths and water channels may be seen, together with traces of a small temple.

Sagunto   Roman and Medieval town

*Sagunt/Sagunto is located near to the mouth of the **Río Palància**, 23 km. north of VALENCIA on the N 340.*

There appears to have been a settlement of the Iberian people called the Editani on the flat-topped hill, now called the **Cerro del Castell**, from early in the Iron Age. That it came under Greek cultural influence is shown not least in a lead copy of a document, found at AMPURIAS, which refers to commercial arrangements made by a local entrepreneur with Sagunto. There are also indications of Greek influence in some of the building techniques used by the Iberians in their town, and possibly also in their political organization, in which a powerful local oligarchy seems to have played a predominant role. The threat of Cathaginian expansion led the inhabitants to make an alliance with Rome, and so, when Hannibal besieged and sacked the town in 219 BC, this was the immediate cause of the outbreak of the Second Punic War the following year. The Romans took Sagunto from the Carthaginians in 214 BC, and after the war the town was given federate status. Clear indications of Roman ideas of town planning have been detected in the Iberian settlement of the Late Republican period, and between 40 and 30 BC Sagunto was refounded as a *municipium*. As with so many such towns in Spain, a major programme of public building took place in the reigns of Augustus (27 BC–AD 14) and Tiberius (AD 14–37). It served as a major port for the export of wine in the early imperial period and for imports, not least of olive oil from North Africa, by the time of the later Empire. Its economic significance seems to have declined in the latter period, and it did not become the site of a bishopric. Little is known of its history under Islamic rule, when it was eclipsed by VALENCIA. The town was taken by king Jaume I of Aragón in 1238.

Traces of an Iberian defensive **wall** can still be seen on the east side of the Cerro del Castell, under a medieval mill resting on Roman foundations, in the **Plaza de Armas** (which is entered via an Islamic horseshoe arch). Little else is visible from the early period, but some Iberian **inscriptions** and a stylized figure of a bull, possibly suggesting the existence here of the kind of cult known from other Iberian settlements, have been discovered in the town. Around 175 to 100 BC a temple or *capitolium* was built, with a cistern close by it, that was later incorporated into the early imperial Forum. The **foundations** of part of this, and also of some other Iberian buildings (just to the west of the Roman basilica), can be seen in the Forum area.

The Roman settlement is primarily represented by the relatively well-preserved remains of the seating of the **theatre** and by traces of the main early imperial **Forum** buildings, excavated in 1985. The theatre is built out of the rock on the north side of the Cero dell Castell, and the Forum site is located on the top of the hillside, about 50 m. above the theatre and to the south-east of it. The original Forum of Late Republican date seems largely to have been demolished, in order to be replaced by a new one, built at the expense of a local aristocrat called Gnaeus Baebius Geminus in the reign of Augustus. Its construction involved flattening of the ground and the building of **buttressed walls** to support the artificial terrace thus created. Some of these supporting walls and buttresses can be seen below the terrace, especially on the northern side. Around a central plaza (60 × 36.5 m.) are ranged a **basilica** (40 × 20 m.) on the west and a range of *tabernae* or shops on the east. On the southern edge of the plaza is a relatively well preserved double-aisled **cistern**. Facing this on the northern edge of the plaza are the remains of the **temple** or *capitolium* of the 2nd cent. BC (14 × 12 m.) and a more complex building in the north-east corner, which has variously been interpreted as a *curia* and as an *aedes Augusti*. With its two large, parallel northern chambers, it may have served for both. Only parts of the foundations of these buildings are visible.

The theatre probably dates to the time of Tiberius. Thirty-three rows of seats may be seen, though the top levels were destroyed during a French siege of the town in 1812. The width of the theatre is 90 m. across, and it has been calculated that it could have held an audience of about 8,000. Only the foundations of the orchestra, the stage, and the *scenae frons* can now be seen. Stone robbed from here may well have been incorporated in the Islamic and later medieval fortress above.

There are slight traces of a Roman **hippodrome** in a public garden on the north side of the town, and columns from Roman buildings may be seen reused in the Plaza Mayor. From inscriptions found in the town it is known that there were associations of worshippers (*collegia*) of both Apollo and Diana here. Another inscription commemorates Scipio's capture of the town from the Carthaginians, which seems to have continued to be commemorated, and there is the base of a statute of Germanicus, Tiberius's intended heir. For finds of Roman and earlier date visit the Museo de las Muralla de Sagunto, adjacent to the theatre in the Calle Castillo. Apart from parts of the fortress, there are few traces of the Islamic period to be seen. The **church** of Santa María, built in 1334, replaced the principal mosque of the town.

Saltés (Huelva) Islamic town

Located on the Isla de Saltés in the estuary of the Río Odiel, immediately south-west of the town of Huelva, this site may be approached via a road from the north that leads onto the island via the neighbouring island of Bacuta. The settlement site is located in the north-west edge of the island, which is generally very marshy.

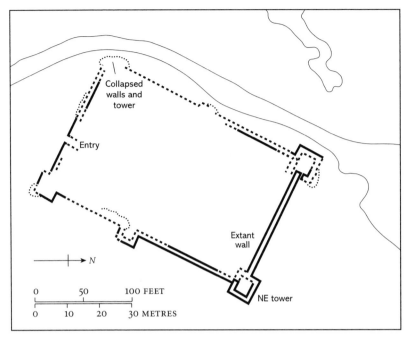

▲ Saltés (after Bazzana/Cressier)

Although this was once thought to be a possible contender for the site of Tartessos, recent excavations have found no traces of pre-Roman settlement on this site. The small town that then came into existence seems, like many along this southern Spanish coast, to have been primarily devoted to fish-salting and the production of *liquamen*, the Romans' much appreciated fish sauce. There is no evidence to prove continuity of occupation of the site between the 4th cent. AD and the emergence of the Arab town of Shaltish, which is known from literary sources to have existed here by the time of the Viking raids of the mid-10th cent. It is probable from what has been found that this settlement came into existence in the later 9th cent. It survived until the Castilian conquest of Seville in 1248 but would seem to have been abandoned very soon after, and there are no indications of later occupation of the site. Thus, like LOS VASCOS and CIEZA, this is a rare and important example of an Arab town that developed in the late Umayyad period, with no immediate non-Islamic antecedents.

The most obvious feature of Arab Shaltish now to be seen is the rectangular **fortress** in the north-west of the town site; the lines of some of its walls are still visible. Sections of the north and east walls, and of the corner towers of the eastern and southern corners, are particularly easy to see. The defences appear to have been built of *tabiya*, of which small sections remain intact. Surprisingly, in view of its vulnerability to attacks from the sea (Vikings in the 10th, and Portuguese maritime raids in the 12th cents.) no traces have been found of walls around the town itself, either on the single landward side or along the shore. Some outlines of buildings have been made out and there are some large blocks from what must have been a major structure in the north-east. A ditch is thought to have divided the small town (with an area of *c*.6 ha.; cf. LOS VASCOS) from the uninhabited part of the island. No traces have been found of suburbs. Archaeological study of the site, especially between 1980 and 1985, has revealed that fishing and metal-working were the main economic activities of the Arab town. As for its Roman predecessor, immediately south of the short southern wall of the fortress fish-salting vats have been found. Significant finds of Islamic ceramics have also been made (mostly of 12th–13th-cent. date), but only one item of glass and hardly any coins have been discovered.

San Juan de Baños Visigothic church   ★

In the village of Baños de Cerrato, 2 km. east of the railway junction at Venta de Baños (10 km. south of PALENCIA) on the N 620/E 80 between Burgos and Valladolid. If closed, the key is to be found at the priest's house, at the other end of the village.

This is unique amongst Visigothic churches in having its foundation precisely dated, thanks to the survival *in situ* over the chancel arch of the inscription recording how King Reccessuinth (649–72) dedicated the church to St John the Baptist in the (Spanish) era 699, which is AD 661 (Vives no. 314).

Spanish Era

This system of dating takes what was regarded as the formal completion of the Roman conquest of Spain in 38 BC as its starting point. Its use is attested from at least the 5th cent. AD, and it was the exclusive system of dating for documents in Christian Spain until the 11th. From then on it gave way gradually to the system of dating by Years of the Incarnation (i.e. AD dating).

About 100 m. due south of the church you can see the entry to a spring fronted by two horseshoe-shaped arches of clearly Visigothic date. It seems most likely that Reccesuinth's dedication of the church was connected with the presence of this medicinal spring (cf. SANTA COMBA DE BANDE), and also that Roman masonry reused in the construction of the church came from a previous building, possibly a pagan shrine or an earlier church, located in this vicinity. The latter, however, was certainly not in the same position as the present church, as the only evidence of

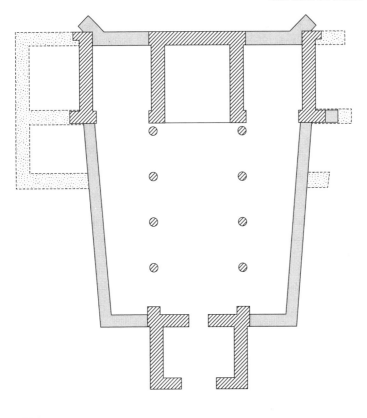

☑ Sections of original Visigothic stonework

☐ Later walls (medieval and 19th century)

▨ Foundations uncovered by excavation or deduced (c. 1900)

▲ San Juan de Baños (after Palol)

prior occupation of the site is some Late Bronze Age/Early Iron Age pottery, found under the chancel.

The construction history of this building is more complex and less secure than its present appearance (see plan) might indicate. Engravings indicate that it was in a ruinous state by the 18th cent., and remained so until given a major, if unscientific, restoration in 1865. This involved the re-creation of the outer walls of the nave, with their bizarre semicircular niches, and the addition of the top two rows of stone in the otherwise original arcading of the central aisle of the nave; the addition is clearly detectable by comparison with the earlier work below it. The bellcote over the outer doorway to the church is also a work of whimsy by the restorer, and should be disregarded. The first serious study of the building was carried out between 1898 and 1903 by Professor Aníbal Alvarez, who claimed to find evidence of a distinctive arrangement of the eastern end of the building. This took the form of a central rectangular chancel matched by two parallel chambers attached to the outer wall of the eastern end of the nave, producing a trident shape. This did not survive intact, as the existing masonry at the eastern end indicates that the two spaces thus created had been filled in, probably in the 14th cent., and at some point the two outer chambers have clearly been demolished, and are now only represented by two sections of wall. That this occurred after 1601 is proved by a reference to the existence of five chapels in the east of the church at that time.

Excavations conducted in 1956, 1961, 1963, and 1983 by Professor Pere de Palol found only limited traces of these lost extremities, but confirmed their previous existence, if not necessarily the full details of the reconstruction of their arrangement suggested at the beginning of the century. In 1963 a small part of a Visigothic cemetery on the northern edge of the parking area west of the church enclosure was also excavated, producing a few 7th-cent. lyre-shaped belt buckles. In 1983 a 10th–11th-cent. cemetery was studied; it contained a number of sarcophagi with internal head-shaped recesses, located along the northern side of the church itself, and in part built over by the 1865 reconstruction of the outer wall of the nave. The modern excavations have raised the question of how different the original plan of the church may have been both to its present appearance and to the reconstruction worked out in 1898 and 1903. Professor Palol has suggested that Reccesuinth's church may have taken the form of a simple three-aisle basilica with rectangular chancel and protruding western porch, and that the development of the eastern end into its trident shape, by the addition of the external chambers on the north and the south, may have taken place around the 10th cent. (However, the triple-apsed church of SANTA LUCÍA DEL TRAMPAL, with which parallels were drawn, has been declared to be Visigothic by its excavator.)

The decoration of this church is restrained compared to that of SAN PEDRO DE LA NAVE or the architectural fragments preserved from Visigothic churches in MÉRIDA, in that the capitals are non-figurative, and the frieze outlining the arch over the outside of the west door, and the string courses around the chancel and above the windows in the nave are composed of simple vegetal motifs. The former are mainly rather stiff Visigothic adaptations of Late Roman Corinthian capitals, but there is one reused Roman original (the one nearest the chancel on the north side, of the 4th or early 5th cent.). Some Roman column bases may also be seen in use. Fragments of a shattered Visigothic chancel screen were found during excavations in 1963; this too was decorated with very stylized vegetal and geometric shapes. Other carvings of leaf and floral shapes, now wrongly located (in 1865) in the outer wall above the arch surrounding the west door, may once have formed a decoration around a window in the east end of the chancel. Two sections of finely carved if repetitive string course have survived on the outside of the building between the eastern buttresses (put in in 1865) on both north and south sides of the building. These would originally have been the inner walls of the two otherwise destroyed flanking chambers. The pattern used in this string course differs from the stylized vegetal design employed in the arch around the west door and in the interior of the building, and has been seen as belonging stylistically to the Asturian period. This deduction forms part of the argument for the addition of these external chambers in the 10th cent.

San Miguel de Escalada   Mozarabic church

Take the N 601 south-east from **León** *for 14 km. before turning east onto a small road leading for 16.5 km. via the villages of Villafalé and Villiguer to the site of the church, beyond the village of the same name.*

Founded as the church of a monastery in 913 and consecrated by Bishop Genadius of Astorga in 914, this building is often taken to represent the purest example of the 'Mozarabic' style in architecture.

By this is meant the buildings erected in the kingdom of León in the 10th and early 11th cents. that were the work of refugees from Islamic Spain, who brought with them distinctive artistic traditions that had developed in the south since the end of the Visigothic period. Such movements of refugees from Al-Andalus can be documented, though not all Arab or Arab-seeming names in documents are now taken as proof of such origins. The style of the Mozarabic churches, with the use of fully developed and very thin horseshoe arches (see the arcading of the nave and of the south portico) of the kind to be seen in Umayyad CORDOBA and MEDINA AZAHARA is clearly different in both plan and decoration to that of the churches of the Asturian kingdom (see OVIEDO and MONTE NARANCO).

This church, which in its foundation inscription was described as being built 'amongst ruins', was the subject of a major excavation of its interior in 1983–4.

From this it emerged that a Late Roman building, of 4th–5th-cent. date, had once occupied the site. This was probably a villa. The outlines of some rectangular rooms with *opus signinum* flooring and the bases of their walls have been found. This seems to have been reconstructed at some point between the 6th and 9th cents. to form what in the 10th cent. was thought to have been a monastery dedicated to St Michael. This earlier monastery was clearly abandoned before the foundation of the Mozarabic monastery on the same site in 913. At least four burials of the

Visigothic period have been found in the bedrock under the present church, including one of a child under the south apse of the chancel. Although most of the church dates from the first half of the 10th cent., sections of 11th- and 12th-cent. stonework have been found in various parts, including the south apse and the portico. The tower is 11th cent., and served as a place of refuge. There are also a few burials from these later periods, including that of Prior Esteban Raunulfo, dated by an inscription in the portico to 1223. The greater success of other monastic houses in this area, including Eslonza (see below), led to the subsequent eclipse and decline of San Miguel. Various works of restoration were carried out on the building in the late 19th cent., and more extensively in 1946.

*Continuing along the same road, to return in a near circle to the N 601, you pass the ruins (signposted) of the once important Benedictine abbey of **Eslonza** (first recorded in a charter of 912 and much patronized by the monarchy in the 12th cent.) near the village of Santa Olaja de Eslonza.*

San Pedro de Alcántara Roman remains and early Christian basilica

The pleasant coastal resort of San Pedro has retained some interesting traces of its past. The N 340 runs parallel to the shore between the town centre and the Mediterranean. All the sites are approached via roads heading south from the N 340 towards the beach. Full access to the villa and the basilica involves obtaining a key from the Oficina de Turismo (Avenida Marqués del Duero) in the centre of the town; both may be viewed from outside their enclosures.

The 'Torre de las Bovedas' and Roman Baths

Take Avenida 9 which starts by the 170 km. marker on the N 340.

This impressive but enigmatic structure on the beach consisted of a central octagonal tower, with a four-apsed lower chamber and octagonal pool, within a series of seven mostly interconnecting vaulted chambers, of which much can still be seen. On the upper level, an internal gallery gave access to a series of small rooms. The flat roof above these may have served as a terrace. An open cupola above the central pool provided light for the lower level. This building is thought to have been primarily a water tower, part of a luxurious bath complex of probably Late Imperial date, of

Antonine Itinerary

This is a rare survival of a Roman road map, indicating the major settlements on each highway and the distances between them. It is thought to have been prepared for the Emperor Marcus Aurelius Antoninus (211–17), hence its title.

which there are other traces to the west. The ornate central chamber, however, would indicate that it served other functions of a less strictly practical kind. Precisely what these were is not clear. The bath complex belonged to the Roman town of Cilniana, whose existence in this vicinity is proved by the Antonine Itinerary. Much destruction may have been caused to the town by an earthquake and ensuing tidal wave on 21 July 365.

The Basilica of Vega del Mar

Just under half a km east from the previous site a road leads from the N 340 to the 'Linda Vista' playa; the ruins are in the middle of a small copse of eucalyptus trees, close to but not on the beach.

The wider site in which the church is located, east of the Arroyo del Chopo, is likely to have been an extramural cemetery of the Roman town. The lower levels of the walls of the entire building have survived, thanks to their being covered in the sand. The final plan was rectangular, with an eastern apse protruding, but this conceals a more complex building history. As is easily seen, the central part of the church is double apsed, the western apse being encased within later rectangular external walls. In the chamber between this apse and the outer walls to the north-west can be seen a very well preserved baptismal font, for full immersion. Other rooms of less obvious purpose surround the central, quadruple-arcaded nave on both north and south. Numerous burials can be seen inside and around the church, especially around the west end and on the north side. A number of these were of children.

The initial date of construction of a double-apsed basilica on this site has been placed in the last quarter of the 4th cent., and there is evidence of extensive reuse of earlier materials, perhaps resulting from the destruction wrought in 365. The greater part of the present building was probably erected around 500, reusing the earlier double-apsed church, and it may have had to be repaired after an earthquake in 526, as suggested by the asymmetry between the piers on the northern and southern sides of the nave. In the mid-6th cent. the baptismal pool and the rooms to the south of the nave were added. At the same time, possibly as the result of Byzantine liturgical practices, access to the eastern apse was restricted by the construction of walls leaving only a narrow central entry. When the basilica went out of use cannot be determined, but a find of coins of Liuva II (601–3) indicates its continued functioning into the 7th cent.

Finds from the tombs were taken to the Museo Arqueológico Nacional in MADRID. Other items from the site may be seen in the Museo de Málaga in MÁLAGA (Calle San Agustín, 8).

Roman Villa

Heading east, after passing the 175 km. marker the N 340 crosses the Río Verde. Once across take the first road on the right, and then the first right again. The villa has been left uncovered in the middle of a suburban street.

A section of a small rural villa around a central courtyard may be seen. There is a particularly nice black and white 2nd-cent. mosaic in the corridor around two sides of the atrium and leading to the *triclinium* or dining-room, depicting cooking utensils and food.

San Pedro de la Mata   Visigothic church

From TOLEDO take the N 401 26 km. south-east to Sonseca, whence a minor road leads south to the villages of Casalgordo and Arisgotas. The church is approached by farm tracks from both villages: it is best to ask for guidance in either of them, as the way is not signposted.

Although in a ruinous (but restored) state, the visible plan of this church would by itself argue in favour of its Visigothic dating. There are no documentary records of it, but it shows strong similarities in its design to both SANTA MARÍA DE MELQUE and SANTA COMBA DE BANDE. Only one aisle of the nave survives, but the walls of the crossing, chancel, and two flanking chambers still stand to a height of several metres, and there is one restored arcade over the crossing, as well as several internal doorways. As with some other Visigothic churches, the area of the chancel is subdivided, with the altar located within an inner sanctuary. Hardly any of the decorative elements survive *in situ* (just two carvings with stylized vegetal motifs, reused as imposts under the springing of the arch between the south aisle of the nave and the crossing) but small sections of carving of clearly Visigothic date can be seen reused in the south wall of the church of the nearby village of Arisgotas. That these came from San Pedro is a very reasonable assumption.

The history of the site is more complex than cursory inspection might suggest. Analysis of the ruins has led to the identification of different phases of construc-

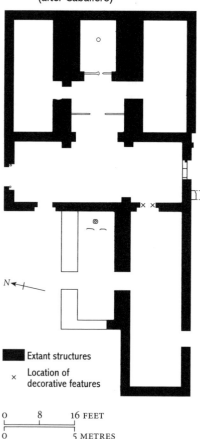

▼ Church of San Pedro de la Mata (after Caballero)

N

■ Extant structures
× Location of decorative features

```
0        8       16 FEET
0                5 METRES
```

tion, though without being able to offer a precise chronology. The original church appears to have been cruciform (21.5 × 13 m.). To this were added three additional chambers, including those flanking the chancel, before the church suffered a major destruction. It was subsequently restored on at least two occasions, and after the first continued in use as a place of worship. The second major reconstruction, however, transformed it into some kind of workshop. This may be associated with the blocking off of the surviving south aisle of the otherwise vanished nave. Initial construction and amplification can reasonably be dated to the Visigothic period, and destruction to some point after the Arab conquest. The first rebuilding is not likely to have occurred before the Castilian conquest of this area in 1085; it is even more likely after the battle of las Navas de Tolosa in 1212. The final secularization and reuse of the structure cannot be dated, but may relate to the abandonment of a settlement here.

Continue 8.5 km. south-east of Sonseca on the N 401) to **Orgaz**.

Orgaz has traces of walls of Arab origin, a castle (12th-cent., with several later additions), and a bridge (on the N 401) on Roman foundations, that formed part of the Roman road between TOLEDO and CÓRDOBA.

San Pedro de la Nave   Visigothic church   ★

On the N 122 (Zamora to Bragança) 11 km. from Zamora a turning to the right leads to El Campillo, 12 km. up a no through road.

▼ San Pedro de la Nave

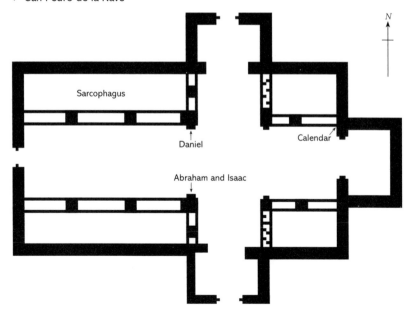

▲ San Pedro de la Nave: a capital depicting Daniel in the lions' den

A substantial church, dating from the 7th cent., situated on the western edge of the village of El Campillo, this has long been regarded as one of the most important architectural survivals of the Visigothic period. Indeed, it has sometimes been taken as the paradigmatic example of a Visigothic monastic church. No documentary evidence survives relating to it, and it cannot be dated more precisely. Nor is there any clear proof that it was of monastic origin. Indeed, the whole building raises more problems than it gives answers to, in that it does not stand in its original location, which was some 1.5 km. further west. The church was moved to its present site in 1930 to make way for a reservoir, and in the process was substantially reconstructed. In particular, the present crossing tower and the two enormous external doorways into the transepts may owe more to the restorers' preconceptions than to the realities of Visigothic architecture.

Despite this reservation, much of the ground-plan of the building may be trusted, as may its internal decoration, which represents its most significant and also most appealing feature. While the nave of two bays is essentially plain, the crossing and the chancel, with its additional small sanctuary, are all highly ornamented with carvings. Especially notable are the **capitals** of the western side of the crossing, which are triangular in shape and are decorated on three faces. The sacrifice of Isaac by Abraham and Daniel in the Lions' Den are depicted on the principal faces of the capital on the south and north sides respectively. The sides of these capitals contain small carvings of some of the Apostles, identified by carved inscriptions (the Daniel scene is flanked by Saints Philip and Thomas; the sacrifice of Isaac by Saints Peter and Paul). The depiction of St Philip (on the east side of the north capital) is particularly notable, as the iconography of the saint holding a crown over his head derives from the apocryphal Greek Acts of Philip. The figure of St Thomas (on the other side of this capital) holds a stylized book, with the inscription EMANUEL. On the southern capital Paul holds a scroll and Peter a book, inscribed LIBER ('book'!). The two capitals on the eastern side of the crossing are decorated with stylized representations of human heads and very formal vine-scroll interlace inhabited by peacocks. Why they are less ornate than those of the western side, and why there are no depictions of the other Apostles, is not known. It is possible that the four figures on the sides of the two eastern capitals of the crossing should have represented particular individuals, but they lack any inscriptions. The side windows of the sanctuary are surrounded by very fine low-relief carvings of crosses, vines, and highly stylized human figures. Apart from the principal capitals with their explanatory inscriptions, no clear iconographic scheme can be detected in the decoration, which is technically, however, of the highest quality and overall the finest example of relief carving to survive from the Visigothic period. Also of note are the remains of a liturgical calendar (only January and February survive) carved high up to the left of the sanctuary arch in the chancel, and an undecorated sarcophagus in the north aisle of the nave. On the outside of the east wall of the south transept some small carved crosses, probably of medieval date, can be seen.

Santa Comba de Bande   Visigothic and Asturian church

*From **Orense/Ourense** take the N 540 southwards for about 50 km. The church is situated at the west end of the small village to the right of the road.*

This church is of Visigothic origin, but was restored 'from its foundations', by the Asturian king Alfonso III in 872, according to a contemporary document preserved in the cartulary of the cathedral of Zamora. It has suffered subsequent modifications, most notably in the form of the large west porch erected in the 16th cent., which served as village meeting place. Some early features subsequently destroyed can be made out in the

On the N 540 26 km. south of Orense/Ourense is **Celanova**, site of one of the most important monasteries in Galicia, founded in 936 by St Rudesind, bishop of Dumio (Guimarães in northern Portugal). Although most of the existing buildings date from the 16th to 18th cents., in the garden may be seen the mid-10th-cent. chapel of San Miguel, a small but perfect example of Mozarabic architecture. At Orense there is an excellent cathedral, mainly of 1218–48, with fine if damaged north portal.

ground, particularly on the north side. The problem has been to sort out original Visigothic elements from the later Asturian restoration, and it cannot be said that there is complete agreement on this. As can be seen from the plan, published in 1919, the church is essentially cruciform, the arms being filled by four additional chambers (three of which have been destroyed). There are also indications of a narthex across the western end. It has been argued that the Visigothic church was purely cruciform, with a horseshoe arch-shaped apse, similar to that of SANTA MARÍA DE MELQUE, and that the side chambers were all 9th-cent. additions. There is no argument that the vaulting must all belong to the Asturian rebuilding. It is also certain that the two phases can be distinguished in terms of internal decorative features. The rather crude rope-work string courses, to be seen for example in the lower stages of the crossing tower, can be paralleled with similar features in the Asturian buildings of MONTE NARANCO. The much finer vegetal string course to be seen in the apse probably belongs to the Visigothic period. Similarly, the cruder capitals on the two easternmost of the four columns flanking the entry into the apse are more likely to be Asturian than Visigothic. The other two, in much purer Corinthian style, are of Late Roman origin. However, all the probable Visigothic elements, including reused Roman columns probably brought here from a Roman site a little to the north at Bande, may have been re-employed, and if the charter of 872 can be taken literally the whole structure could be essentially of that date.

The building of a church here in the Visigothic period may relate to the presence of a spring, about 25 m. south of the south-west corner of the church. It is encased in a stone arch, bearing a small cross on the left side. The close proximity of Visigothic churches to springs, possibly previously sites of pagan veneration, can also be seen in the cases of SAN JUAN DE BAÑOS, SANTA EULALIA DE BÓVEDA, and the crypt of San Antolín at PALENCIA.

Santa Eulalia de Bóveda Temple and early medieval church

The church of Santa Eulalia is in the village of Bóveda. Leave LUGO heading south-west down the N 540, and about 4 km. after leaving the city turn right onto the LU 232, which goes directly to the village (c.8 km.). Enquire at the post office (Correos) if the site is not open.

Discovered in 1926, this represents an unusual combination of Late Roman shrine, of the 4th or even 5th cent., reused as a church, probably in the Visigothic period and again from the late 8th or 9th to 11th cents. The structure has two storeys, of which the lower is better preserved. This is entered via a portal with carved decoration, including strangely distorted human figures dancing, and a small narthex, and then through a Visigothic horseshoe arch. In the inner wall of the narthex (*c.2 × 6.5 m.*) there are two rectangular windows divided by a lintel from triangular

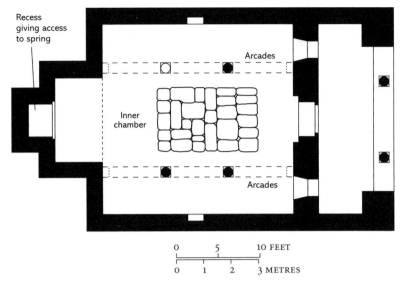

▲ Santa Eulalia de Bóveda (after Gómez Moreno)

upper lights. The inner chamber (*c.*7 × 6.5 m.) is barrel-vaulted with two small arcades (the arches are missing but the springing can be seen in the outer walls) of two thin marble columns each (one is missing). In the centre of the floor between the columns a rectangular space made up of closely fitting stones of various sizes has been left exposed. At the far end another horseshoe arch leads into a recess (*c.*2 × 2.5 m.), whence a rectangular opening gives access to the spring, which may have been the original focus of devotion. It is likely that the original purpose of the building was for it to serve as a *nymphaeum*. The vaulting is extensively decorated with faded frescos depicting birds and other animals, together with a variety of geometric patterns. The style of the decoration is clearly Late Roman. The association of church buildings with springs is a marked feature of several of the surviving Visigothic sites (see SANTA COMBA DE BANDE, SAN JUAN DE BAÑOS, and above all the crypt of San Antolín under PALENCIA cathedral).

A Castro site, with much Roman material, has been located about 1 km. away.

Santa Lucía del Trampal Visigothic church

Located on the side of the Pico del Centinela (also called the Siera del Monasterio), the church can be reached via a track leading from the village of Alcuéscar. On the N 630/E 803 between MÉRIDA and CÁCERES, turn east onto the CC 801 31 km. north of the former (38 km. south of the latter). The turn south to Alcuéscar is 4 km. along the CC 801.

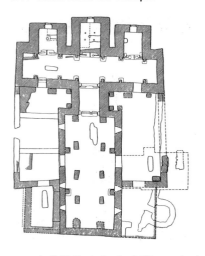 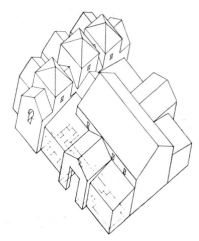

▲ *(left)* Santa Lucía del Trampal: plan based on 1988 excavations
(right) Santa Lucía del Trampal: reconstruction based on modified plan established by 1989 excavations

This relatively well-preserved Visigothic church was first discovered only in 1974, and it was not until 1981–2 that its existence began to be made known more widely. Since then it has been cleaned and restored, excavations being carried out from 1983/4 to 1989. In the process about a dozen inscriptions dedicated to the goddess Atacaina (a deity primarily associated under the Romanized form of Proserpina with MÉRIDA) were found reused in the walls or as supports for (now lost) chancel screens in the church, which also contained other Roman masonry. Traces of earlier foundations have also been located in the east end of the church, suggesting the prior existence of a sanctuary of Atacaina in the vicinity, ultimately replaced by the Visigothic building. This latter has been seen as being more than just a church. Excavations conducted in 1988 and 1989 have indicated the presence of a series of chambers on both the southern and northern side of the nave. These have been interpreted as being monastic cells, and thus it has been suggested that the building was a self-contained monastery. The only certain Visigothic monastic complex is that of SANTA

Proserpina

She was the daughter of the corn goddess Ceres (Greek: Demeter). Known to the Greeks as Persephone, she was goddess of the Underworld, with *Dis Pater* (Hades to the Greeks) as the god. Their cult was first introduced into Rome in 249 BC, during the First Punic War. In Spain the Iberian goddess Atacaina was equated with Proserpina.

MARÍA DE MELQUE, although similar claims have been made for SAN PEDRO DE LA NAVE. If this is the case such a monastic community should probably be seen not as leading the kind of complex communal life envisaged in such texts as the *Rule of Benedict* or the Spanish rules of Fructuosus of Braga, but more as a group of hermits. The 'autobiographical' works of the Visigothic recluse Valerius of Bierzo (690s–700s) give an impression of such a lifestyle.

What may be seen now of the original church is the crossing and the eastern end, which consists of three small parallel apses, and the narrow passage dividing the eastern end from the nave. It seems that the crossing was covered by three small tower-like structures covered by (now vanished) wooden roofs. The towers were supported on a series of undecorated horseshoe arches extending from west to east across the crossing, which are still to be seen *in situ*. The nave seems to have been entered via large porches on the northern and southern sides, but the original arcading of the nave, perhaps of reused Roman work, has been lost. It may have been removed for use elsewhere during the period of Islamic occupation of the area. In the 14th or 15th cent. the nave was restored in Gothic style, with new pointed arches resting on pillars built onto the outer walls. At this time, if not before, must have occurred the demolition of the chambers and porch flanking the south side of the nave. Of the original decoration only a few carved fragments have been found. Five burials have been located within or adjacent to the church.

Santa María de Melque   Visigothic church   ★

From TOLEDO head south-west on the C 401 for 41 km. before turning right onto the C 403 towards La Puebla de Montalbán. The turn-off to the site is on the right 10 km. down this road (very vaguely signposted).

Of all Visigothic ecclesiastical sites this is perhaps the most extensively excavated and published; a process that indeed led to its being re-dated to that period. It had hitherto been regarded as 10th-cent., and more typical of the style of Mozarabic architecture. It is also now the best-established example of a Visigothic monastery (cf. SAN PEDRO DE LA NAVE), as the excavators were able to locate the presence of dependent buildings and a perimeter wall. Traces of these are still visible in the area to the east of the church, which is the most substantial feature of the site. Although the internal decorative features are almost entirely lost and there has been some structural damage (notably in the south side of the nave and the tower), most of the building still stands. It includes an unusual small cloister-like area between the north transept and the nave. Substantial finds of pottery from the site establish its continued occupation well beyond the Visigothic period. Islamic wares from as late as the 11th cent. indicate occupation (though not Christian use) up to the time of the Castilian conquest of Toledo in 1085. It has an unusual horseshoe-shaped apse, which its excavator believes may once also have been used in the much rebuilt churches of SANTA COMBA DE BANDE and SAN PEDRO DE LA MATA.

*Immediately opposite the turn off the C 403 to the site of the church a track leads for about 1 km. in the opposite direction to the castle of **Montalbán**.*

The castle is 13th cent. and later. This is impressively sited on the edge of a ravine, with a variety of powerful defences including two large *torres albarranas* on the more vulnerable eastern side.

Santa María de Quintanilla de las Viñas

Visigothic church

*Head south from **Burgos** on the N 1; after 6.5 km. turn onto the N 234 to Soria; 26.5 km. further south a small road to the left leads 3.5 km. to the village of Quintanilla de las Viñas. Continue through the village for less than 1 km. to find the **church of Santa María** to the left. A custodian should be on the site in normal hours.*

Only the chancel and transepts of the church of Santa María are still standing, though the outline plan of the nave is marked out on the ground. Although of simple rectangular shape, the exterior of the chancel and the two short arms of the crossing are immediately striking by virtue of the quality of their stonework and, even more, for the two bands of carved decoration that run all the way around what remains of the outside of the building. Probably these bands continued around the whole outer wall of the nave. The decoration consists of a rather stiff and geometric vine scroll, inhabited by stars, leaves, palms or 'trees of life', bunches of grapes, and at least three different types of bird. On the east wall of the chancel this repertoire is increased by the addition of a short third band of decoration at a higher level, in which are depicted some stylized animals, including bulls and griffins. Even more significantly, in the central band to the north of the window can be seen three monograms, made up of the letters FNLA, DNLA, and FNCR respectively. These have been interpreted as the names, possibly Flanola or Flainus and Danila or Dilanus, of the presumed founders of the church, together with the verb 'FeCeRuNt', meaning 'made (this)'. Blank roundels in the same band to the south of the window suggest the intention of adding further monograms or repeating the existing ones.

The interior of the building contains a chancel arch and some displaced carvings of considerable interest. The arch is topped by a panel of vine scroll inhabited by bunches of grapes and by birds, clearly related to the external decoration. The columns supporting the arch have rectangular figured capitals containing central roundels with representations of the Sun (south side) and the Moon (north side), supported by flying angels in a distinctly Late Antique style. Above the solar relief is an inscription: +OC EXIGUUM EXIGUA OFF DO FLAMMOLA VOTUM, meaning

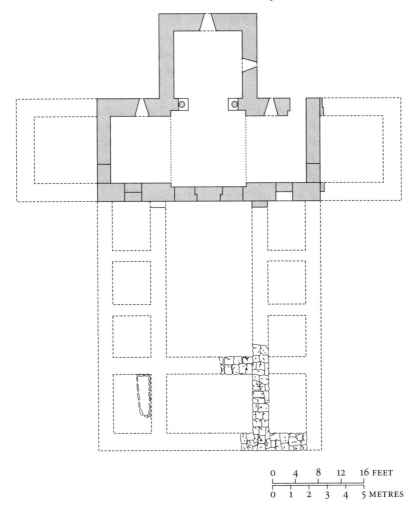

▲ Santa María de Quintanilla de las Viñas (after Iñiguez)

'Flammola, the least of the least, makes this promised offering to God'. It is also notable, but inexplicable, that the figure of the Moon, clearly inscribed as LUNA, should be bearded. The displaced reliefs consist of three single busts, two of whom carry books and may be Evangelists. The third is similar to the representation of Christ found on Visigothic coins of the reign of Ervig (680–7). Two slightly larger reliefs depict the busts of a female figure and of a male figure holding a small cross on a short staff; both figures are supported by angels of the type that accompany the Sun and Moon. Stylistic differences between the reliefs and the bands of decoration found in the walls have led to arguments over dating. Some see the reliefs as Visigothic and the building as being probably 10th-cent. Others suggest the reverse. An easy answer cannot be given, but the Flammola inscription and the Late Antique elements in the reliefs support a Visigothic dating. The Sun and Moon reliefs were probably not originally intended as capitals, and their reuse here implies at least a later date for the building.

The base of an altar of Visigothic type that came from the church, carved with depictions of a cross with pendant a and w, and a stylized vine, can be seen in the Museo Arqueológico Provincial in Burgos. Some fragments of Roman inscriptions and ceramics found on the site are also held, if not displayed, in the museum.

*Continue on the same road 1.5 km. further to the very ruinous 10th–11th-cent. **Castillo de Lara**, on the summit of the hill to the left of the road. A climb up will be rewarded with a fine view, and a site associated with the 'Infantes de Lara', the villainous sons-in-law of the Cid in the* Poema de mío Cid. *It may date from the time of Count Fernán González of Castile (d. 970), who used Lara as one of his residences. On the nearby Peña de Lara are the slight remains of an Iberian castro, accessible on foot (long walk) from the village of Lara de los Infantes.*

Santa Olalla de Cáceres Visigothic church

Located in the site of the deserted village of La Aldehuela, 5 km. south of CÁCERES.

The church was remodelled in the 18th cent., losing its original nave, but it retains its Visigothic chancel. Documents from the time of the rebuilding prove that the church had previously been of basilican form.

Santa Pola (la Picola) Iberian village

The town itself stands on the coast, 1.5 km. east of the N 332, 20 km. south of Alicante. The site is located in the western suburbs, about 750 m. north-west of the castle.

Santa Pola was Roman Portus Ilicitanus, the port for the nearby town of Ilici, itself once an important Iberian settlement. Excavations in 1987 revealed part of a Roman fish-curing factory, in the form of five fish-salting tanks, dating from the reign of Augustus (27 BC–AD 14), located next to the Iberian site. It appears that the Iberian site was extensively robbed of its still standing stonework to construct the factory.

First excavations on the La Picola site took place in the 1970s, leading to the discovery of some very fine Greek pottery (see in particular a beautiful red-figure crater in the Museo Arqueológico Provincial in Alicante: Avenida de la Estación). Further programmes of excavation took place in 1989 and 1991–4. As well as the damage inflicted in Roman times, the site has suffered from agricultural terracing in recent centuries and the urban spreading of Santa Pola. However, enough has survived to give clear indications of the size and structure of the settlement.

Like the earlier village of EL ORAL, it had a short lifespan. It came into existence around 430 BC and survived for no more than a century. Only one phase of construction has been detected. This took the unusual form of an almost square layout for the village, within a powerful **system of fortifications**. These consisted of an inner wall (*c*.1.5 to 2 m. thick) of mud bricks, detectable as a thin layer of red clay, with a berm or flat platform about 5 to 5.5 m. wide all around the outside of it. The berm ended in a narrower outer wall, which fronted directly onto a shallow but water-filled ditch. In the north-east angle (and perhaps in the south-west one as well) there was a solid rectangular tower (4.75 × 3.2 m.) attached to the wall. Surprisingly this overlooked only one of the walls adjacent to it. Although this system is unusual in an Iberian context, and has evoked parallels with the excavated Hellenistic defences of both AMPURIAS and even Athens, the crude nature of the building techniques employed and the peculiar nature of the tower argue against actual Greek construction.

Within **the village**, which had an internal area of 3,400 sq. m., something of the organization of space has been discovered. A row of five houses has been located running along the inside of the north wall, faced across a street (4 m. wide) by a less well preserved parallel row of dwellings. The houses themselves were of more or less uniform size (*c*.7 × 3.5 m.) and consisted of two rooms. The buildings were constructed of mud bricks of a standard size (and also half-bricks) on stone footings. The implication of the apparent structuring of the settlement is that at least two other such rows of houses could have been accommodated in the southern part of the village. The regularity of the size of the buildings and the orthogonal grid of the overall plan of houses and streets are unusual features in an Iberian context. It is clear from the pottery finds that considerable Greek commercial and cultural influence was being exercised in this area when this settlement was flourishing. Further discoveries may help to set the peculiarities of the site more clearly in their context.

See the archaeological material in the Museo Municipal Arqueológico-Pesquero y Acuario in Santa Pola (Plaza Castillo).

The French archaeologist Pierre Rouillard has suggested that **Santa Pola** may be the site of Alonis, a Greek colony founded from Massilia (Marseilles; see AMPURIAS), whose existence is known only from literary sources. However, this has been doubted and his recent excavations have not been able to settle the issue.

Santiago de Compostela Early churches

The principal archaeological site in the city is the cathedral, which is constructed on the same location as its two predecessors, churches built respectively by Alfonso II (791–842) and Alfonso III (866–910). The second of these was destroyed in Al-Manṣūr's raid into Galicia in 997. Work on the present cathedral commenced *c*.1075. Access to the excavations, carried out between 1946 and 1959 below the nave, which include some of the foundations of the earlier buildings and a Late Roman and Early Medieval cemetery, is via a stairway concealed beneath a flagstone in the south-west portion of the nave. The site is not normally open for visiting, but a request in writing or in person *may* succeed. It has to be said that these excavations were conducted on the basis of a strong a priori assumption that the site was that of the burial place of the Apostle James. This in part derived from earlier, highly unscientific, excavations in the chancel in 1878–9, which were claimed to have uncovered the Apostle's shrine.

The 1878–9 excavations are said to have found a rectangular two-storeyed mausoleum, dated to the 1st cent. AD, located within a slightly larger surrounding structure. The relationship of this to a wider area, under the nave and the south transept, and to buildings of later periods was the product of the excavations of the 1940s and 1950s. The findings of the latter extend up to the 11th cent. Below the first two columns of the north arcading of the nave lie the foundations of a square tower, part of the outer defences of the town in the Asturian period, and dated to the 9th cent. East of this up the centre of the nave were found a large number of burials, either in stone sarcophagi or more crudely in cists. Just below the penultimate columns of both nave arcades ran the west wall and doorway of Alfonso III's church. Traces of the equivalent western entry to Alfonso II's church have been located about 2 m. due east of this. Of the eastern end of the Alfonsine churches less is known archaeologically, but the 19th-cent. reports suggest the presence of a square-ended chancel that terminated about where the curve of the apse of the present chancel begins. This was taken to be three sides of a building of early Roman date built around the mausoleum, and subsequently incorporated into the Asturian church. The exterior walls of Alfonso III's building ran between 1 and 2 m. in from and parallel to the line of the present north and south walls of the nave and chancel. Further burials and the foundations of walls of some rooms probably of Roman date have been located under the south transept. An altar dedicated to Jupiter was also found reused in the foundations of the central column of the east side of this transept. A few of the sarcophagi found under the cathedral have inscriptions, dating them to the late 9th, 10th, and 11th cents. Amongst these were two found in rectangular chambers under the north-east corner of the south transept; one of these was of Bishop Theodemir (d. 847) of Iria Flavia, who is recorded as having found the relics of St James in this site.

While elements of these excavations must now seem unreliable, it appears that a complex of Roman buildings, probably a villa, existed on the southern edge of the present cathedral, which in the Late Imperial and/or Visigothic periods became a burial site. For reasons that are and will remain unclear this became associated with the legend of the burial of St James in Spain. Isidore of Seville (d. 636) testified to this in *On the Deaths of the Fathers*. From this resulted the erection of the two successive Asturian churches, and the development of a fortified settlement on this site. From these foundations developed both the medieval city and the powerful archbishopric.

Sasamón   Roman town

Head west from BURGOS *on the N 120; after 30 km. a road to the right leads 2 km. to Sasamón.*

The Roman settlement of Segisamo is recorded in the Antonine Itinerary and by Pliny, and the identification was established by an inscription found in the church of Santa María la Real (13th–15th cent.). It formed part of the *conventus* of CLUNIA. There was a bishopric here in the second half of the 11th cent., which was merged with that of Burgos by 1128, when Alfonso VII (1126–57) of León-Castile gave the church of Santa María to the cathedral of Burgos.

Pliny the Elder and Pliny the Younger

Gaius Plinius Secundus (c. AD 23–79) is known for his *Natural History* of AD 77, an encyclopaedic treatment of the natural world as the Romans then knew it. He was killed in the eruption of Vesuvius that destroyed Pompeii. His nephew, Pliny the Younger (61–112), left an important collection of letters in ten books.

Of Roman Segisamo you can see a section of wall with a square tower, reused in the Middle Ages, and, outside the modern village, two bridges over the Río Brullés. Both may be crossed on foot. The smaller, with two arches, stands 2 km. north-west of the town on the BU 120. The larger, with a four-arch span, may be seen on the parallel road that makes a detour to Villasidro before joining the BU 120. On the far side of this bridge you can see over 100 m. of paved Roman road, now leading into fields.

*At the intersection on the N 120 30 km. west of Burgos the left turn leads directly to **Olmillos de Sasamón**, which has a ruined 15th-cent. castle. The village of **Villadiego**, 3 km. further south, is the birthplace of Enrique Flórez (1702–73), the many volumes of whose España Sagrada contain items of documentary, epigraphic, and antiquarian lore still of the greatest value.*

*A road to the right 5 km. beyond this village leads for 13 km. to **Castrojériz**.*

This is the site of a Roman camp (in a field on the edge of the town, opposite the Collegiate Church or 'Colegiata'). In 974 Castrojeriz received the first genuine set of Castilian *fueros*, from Count García Fernández (970–92), though they are only preserved in a confirmation and extension issued by Alfonso VII. About 4 km. before entering Castrojeriz, to the south of the road lie the ruins of the 14th-cent. monastery of San Antón.

Segóbriga (Cabeza del Griego) Roman town and
Visigothic church   ★

Heading south on the N III/E 901 from MADRID *to Albacete, turn off to the right (south) at Exit 104, on the CU 304 towards Casas de Luján. The entry to the site is marked less than 3 km. down this road.*

▼ Segóbriga

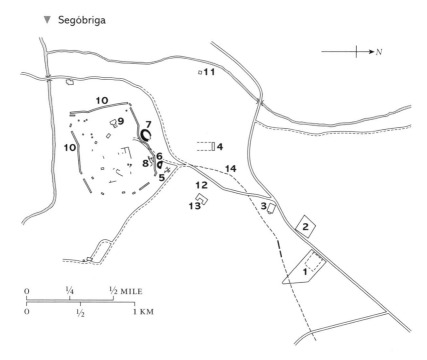

1 Roman necropolis 1st cent. AD
2 Remains of large building, not yet excavated
3 Traces of Visigothic basilica, excavated 18th cent.
4 Unexcavated buildings
5 Baths outside walls
6 Theatre
7 Amphitheatre
8 Baths within walls, located between theatre and amphitheatre
9 Area of Roman buildings, with chapel of San Bartolomé built on top
10 Remains of Roman Wall
11 Ruins of large Roman tomb
12 Site museum
13 Visigothic necropolis
14 Line of aqueduct, almost entirely destroyed, that brought water to town from 'La Fuente de la Mar' spring, near village of Saelices

▲ Segóbriga: the amphitheatre

The **Visigothic basilica** is located to the left of the road after turning into the entry to the site but well before reaching the museum and car park. Unfortunately, this was excavated in the 18th cent. Although only the outline of the building can now be seen, the church was built to a plan unique in Visigothic architecture, whose nearest equivalents can be seen in North Africa. There is a model of the building with a reconstruction of its probable interior, together with some decorative fragments, in the Museo Arqueológico Nacional in MADRID, which is best seen prior to visiting the site.

The **Segóbriga museum**, about 500 m. further on to the left, contains a small exhibition of finds. These include a number of damaged statues, fine capitals, and busts of Augustus (27 BC–AD 14) and of his wife Livia (d. AD 29), all found in the theatre. The statues had been reused as part of the stonework of a Late Roman wall. At the back of the museum is a Visigothic cemetery, in which 8th-cent. muslim burials took place. These muslim burials sometimes reused the east–west orientated Christian sarcophagi. Some bronze grave goods were found in the tombs. The walk to the town, on a small hill to the south-west of the museum, is another half km.

The **principal Roman structures**, the theatre and amphitheatre, are situated on the side of the hill nearest the entry, and between them can be seen the remains of a public bath house. Both of these major public buildings were probably erected in the reigns of Vespasian (69–79) and Titus (79–81). A much damaged inscription records that the theatre was paid

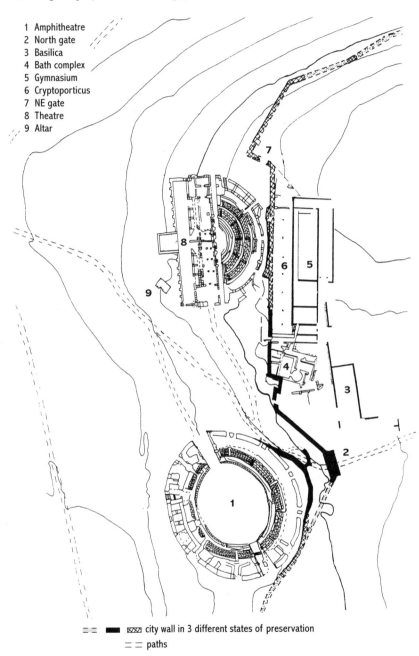

1 Amphitheatre
2 North gate
3 Basilica
4 Bath complex
5 Gymnasium
6 Cryptoporticus
7 NE gate
8 Theatre
9 Altar

▨▨ ▬▬ ▨▨ city wall in 3 different states of preservation
= = paths

▲ Segóbriga

for by a Senator, whose name is lost but who had held the office of Governor of Aquitaine in AD 76–9. The style of some ornamental fragments from the *scaenae frons* of the theatre (now in the Museo de Cuenca) indicates that a major restoration took place in the late 2nd cent. Little trace remains of the finer decorative features of the amphitheatre. Of the theatre, the two lower tiers of seats, which were carved out of the hill, have been preserved, together with the ground plan of the stage. The lowest part of the amphitheatre is substantially intact. Although not now visible, excavation revealed that both theatre and amphitheatre had been filled by low-quality housing, probably dating to the late 4th or 5th cent. Starting behind the seating of the theatre and then running between the amphitheatre and the hill is the line of a pre-Roman wall, which once provided the defences for the preceding Celtiberian settlement. It was roughly rectangular in shape, turning to the south about 200 m. beyond the amphitheatre and then following around the line of the hill. Very little of it can be made out on the ground now, especially on the eastern and southern flanks of the hill.

A path leads over the hill from the back of the amphitheatre but, although various indentations in the soil can be easily seen, especially in the area of the Ermita de San Bartolomé, no further structures have been fully uncovered. About 700 m. west of the amphitheatre, near the Arroyo del Cañar, stands the remains of a large Roman tomb (easily seen from the hilltop).

Over 300 inscriptions have been found on the site. Many of these, however, are no longer extant, and are only recorded in publications by antiquarians from the 16th cent. onwards. As well as many funerary records, these include inscriptions indicating phases of construction of public buildings in the reigns of Tiberius (AD 14–37) and Claudius (AD 41–54).

The existence of an earlier, Iberian, settlement on this site has been established by finds of metalwork and pottery, including an imported Etruscan vase dating to the 5th cent. BC. Other finds and stonework from the site may be seen in the Museo de Cuenca (Calle Obispo Valero, 6, Cuenca).

Returning northwards on the N III/E 901, at Exit 91 turn off north to **Uclés** *(6 km.).*

Near here was fought the battle of Uclés in 1108, in which Sancho, the only male heir of Alfonso VI of León-Castile, was killed by the Almoravids. Uclés itself retains an impressive set of medieval walls, and a castle, both dating in part from the Taifa and Almoravid periods. Following conquest by Alfonso VIII of Castile, Uclés was given in 1174 to the Order of Santiago, one of whose major centres it became. The large monastery that dominates the town was built by the Order in the early 16th cent. to replace their earlier constructions on the site.

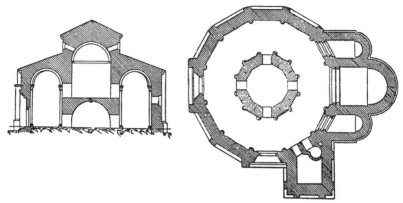

▲ Segovia: church of la Vera Cruz

Segovia Roman and medieval town

The Iberian settlement on this naturally defensible site was taken by the
Romans in 80 BC. Little is known for sure of the history of the town in the
Visigothic and early Islamic periods. It may have been deserted following
raids across the Meseta by the Asturian kings Alfonso I (739–57) and
Fruela I (757–68), but this is not certain. If so it was probably reoccupied
in the 10th cent. as an Umayyad frontier fortress. The tower of the church
of San Millán (south-east of the walled town) has been dated to the 10th
cent., implying the presence of a Christian community. After the end of
the Umayyad state, Segovia became part of the Taifa kingdom of Toledo.
After the Castilian conquest of 1085, a bishopric was established here, and
the 12th and 13th cents. saw the building of a number of impressive
churches in the Romanesque tradition. Several of these survive (e.g. San
Martín, San Estebán, and San Juan de los Caballeros), and their arcaded
porches with elaborately carved capitals represent a distinctive local
architectural and decorative style.

The **Aqueduct** is the finest Roman example in Spain. It was probably
first erected in the reign of Augustus (27 BC–AD 14) and was substantially
restored under Trajan (98–117). Thirty-five of the arches were destroyed
by the garrison in 1071, to prevent the aqueduct from being used by
besiegers, but the town was captured by Alfonso VI of León-Castile in
1085. The damaged arches were restored in 1483. The total length of the
structure is 813 m., with a greatest height of 128 m. from the ground. The
central section is constructed in two layers, and the total number of
arches is 165.

At the **Church of the Santissima Trinidad** (Calle de San Agustín)
recent excavation has revealed the foundations of a small church of late
11th-cent. date, as well as finds of the Roman period, under the present
building.

The **Church of La Vera Cruz** (located on a ledge of rock below and to the north of the Alcázar) is unique in Spain as an example of a building modelled on the Holy Sepulchre in Jerusalem (cf. the Temple Church in London, and Tovar in Portugal). Its dedication, recorded in an extant inscription, took place on 13 April 1208 (the inscription uses the Spanish era, not abolished in Castile until 1383). It was built by the Order of the Temple, and after the suppression of that Order in 1312, it was given to the Knights of the Hospital, under whom it became the church of the parish of Zamarramala. It seems to have been virtually abandoned by the late 17th cent., and entirely so when the monastic orders were abolished in Spain in 1835. It was restored and reconsecrated in 1951. The church was constructed to house a relic of the True Cross, which was kept in the upper chapel in the central section of the twelve-sided nave. This two-storeyed central section is parallel to the outer walls of the nave. Access to the upper floor, the chapel of the *Lignum Crucis* ('Wood of the Cross'), is via a stone staircase that curves around the exterior. Four large windows and door openings give a cross shape to the structure of the upper storey. The lower section has large open arcades, to provide communication between the west door of the nave and the triple-apsed chancel. A south doorway is located next to the bell tower, the upper sections of which are entirely restored. Sections of 16th-cent. wall paintings can be seen in one of the subsidiary apses, and there are damaged 15th-cent. frescos (and a fine carved altar stone) in the chapel of the *Lignum Crucis*. A fragment of 13th-cent. painting, of the lower part of a man holding a round shield bearing the red cross of the Templars, is located near the south door.

There is an impressive 16th-cent. cathedral in Gothic style in the heart of the old town. The medieval Alcázar, at the western edge of the old town, was almost entirely rebuilt in the 14th and 15th cents. but was badly damaged by fire in 1862. It was rebuilt, somewhat under the influence of Viollet le Duc's Romantic ideas of medieval fortress architecture in 1882, but is still worth a visit for the reconstructed royal apartments. The church of Corpus Christi, whose apse forms part of the defences of the south wall of the town (see it from the Paseo de Salón) was once a synagogue, and retains its original internal arcading, despite fire damage in 1899. Photographs dating from before the fire show that its decorative features were very reminiscent of those of the synagogue of Santa María la Blanca in TOLEDO, and thus it should probably be dated to the late 13th cent. After a legal dispute, it was confiscated by the Crown in 1402 and given to the Friars of the Order of Merced (Mercy), who used it as a hospital. At the foot of the aqueduct the long-established Castilian 'Mesón de Cándido', in a building dating from the 15th cent., has almost as grand a reputation for its *cochinillo asado*: roast sucking-pig.

Seville Islamic and Roman remains
(Visit together with ITÁLICA)

The Roman city of Hispalis was established on the site of an Iberian settlement, and was given the enhanced status of *colonia*, under the title of Colonia Julia Romula, by Caesar in 45 BC. It became the capital of the province of Baetica in the Late Roman Empire, and was the seat of a metropolitan bishopric. In the Visigothic period it was briefly the capital of the independent kingdom of Hermenegild (579–83), and was the intellectual centre of Spain under its bishops Leovigild (d. 599/600) and his brother Isidore (d. 636). After the Arab conquest, when its name became Ishbiliya, it was the residence of the first governors, but was quickly replaced by Córdoba. After the collapse of the Umayyad caliphate it became the capital of the most powerful of the Taifa kingdoms (1023–91/2). The Almoravids and the Almohads made it the seat of their administration in Al-Andalus, and some of the monarchs of these North African dynasties resided there. It was conquered by (St) Fernando III (1217–52) of Castile in 1248. He and his son Alfonso X the Wise (1252–84) were buried in the Gothic cathedral, as was Pedro I the Cruel (1350–69).

The Northern Sector of the City

The **Church of San Salvador** (southern end of the Calle de Cuna) was built on the site of an Umayyad mosque, probably serving as the 'Friday' or principal mosque of the city. This was founded by the Amir ʿAbd al-Raḥmān II in 829/30, as recorded in an inscription on a column, now to be seen in the Museo Arqueológico (see below). The minaret was replaced after an earthquake in 1079; part of this forms the lower section of the present bell tower. Also preserved is the upper half of an arcade that may have formed part of the courtyard of the enlarged and rebuilt mosque, and which is now to be seen in the façade of the present church, which dates from 1671–1712. Reused Roman Corinthian capitals were employed in the construction of the arcade. Its present truncated appearance testifies to the height of the modern city above its medieval predecessor. Literary accounts testify that the mosque had a breadth of 50 m. and consisted of a larger central nave in the middle of ten aisles, all placed perpendicularly to the *quibla*. This plan conforms to that of the earliest stage of the great mosque in CÓRDOBA.

Three Roman mosaics and some sculptural fragments, all brought from ITÁLICA, may be seen in the 16th-cent. Palacio de la Condesa de Lebrija, also in the Calle de Cuna.

Amongst other churches in the northern sector of the city that retain traces of Islamic architecture or stand on the site of former sectional mosques or oratories are **San Juan de la Palma** (Calle Gerona), which retains part of a minaret erected in 1085 (the foundation inscription

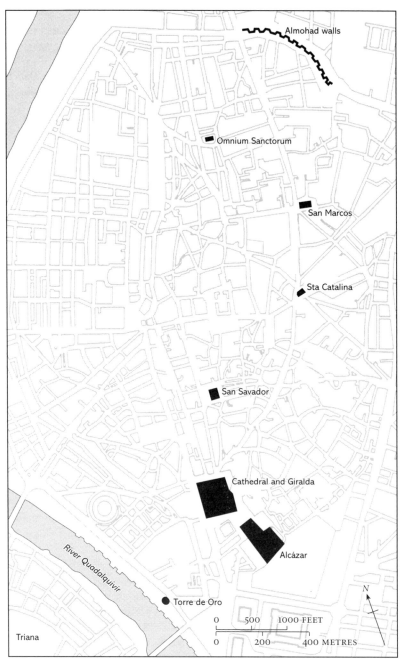

▲ Seville

recording that this was undertaken on the orders of the favourite wife of the Taifa king Al-Mu'tamid can be seen in the Museo Arqueológico); **San Marcos** (east end of the Calle Castellar), whose tower of 1350 rises from the base of a minaret; and **Omnium Sanctorum** (Calle Relator), with some of a minaret preserved in its tower. **Santa Catalina** (Plaza Ponce de León) has a Mudéjar tower of c.1350, and was built on the site of a mosque.

An Arab bath house has been excavated in a site (now an apartment block) located between the Calles de Baños, Juan de la Vera Cruz, and Miguel del Cid, and called by 16th-cent. antiquaries '**The Baths of the Moorish Queen**'. The buildings were given to the cathedral of Seville by Alfonso X in 1278, and were recorded in 1396 as 'The Baths of Don Fadrique', before becoming a noble residence and later a convent. A central patio was surrounded by an arcade formed of Almohad columns of the 12th cent. The original roofing of the patio is long gone, but in some of the rooms to the east were found the star-shaped apertures in the vaulted ceilings typical of steam rooms of Arab baths. An Arab cistern was also located just to the south-west of the patio. Ceramic finds from the rescue excavation of 1983 dated from the 11th to 13th cent.

In the Calle de Muñoz, between the Puerta Macarena and the Puerta de Córdoba, is preserved a stretch of the **Almoravid defensive wall**, erected around 1100, and much restored in the Almohad period. The rest of the medieval walls of Seville, other than those surrounding the Alcázar, were demolished in the 1860s.

The Central Sector of the City

The **Alcázar** may be on the site of the judicial and administrative centre of the Roman *conventus* of Hispalis. Little is known of its use in the Umayyad and Taifa periods, but it was the location of the main palace and administrative centre of the Almohad regime in Al-Andalus, up to the fall of the city to Fernando III of Castile in 1248. A Gothic palace was erected on the site in 1258 for his successor Alfonso X the Wise (1252–84). However, most of the present structure dates from a substantial rebuilding in Mudéjar style in 1366 undertaken for Pedro I the Cruel of Castile (1350–69), further alterations and additions being carried out by the Emperor Charles V and c.1624 by Felipe IV. The outer wall may date originally from the reign of 'Abd al-Raḥmān II (822–52), but it was much restored in 1176. In the first courtyard, the Patio de la Montería, which is entered by passing through the Puerta del León, was the site of the *Mexuar* or council chamber of the Almohad palace. Of the latter the only traces may now be found in the Patio de Yeso of 1171–6. A rectangular formal garden, known as the *Crucero*, dating from the 12th cent., has been shown to lie on top of a similar garden of Taifa date. The park that lies between the palace complex and the south wall of the Alcázar, which contains a pavilion built for Charles V, may have been first created for the Almohads. It has also been suggested, but not generally accepted, that the present *Salón de los Embajadores* incorporates much of the 'Hall of the Pleiades' of the Taifa poet-king Al-Muʿtamid (1068/9–1091/2).

A new 'Friday mosque' of substantial proportions was erected for the Almohad ruler Abū Yaʿqūb Yūsuf (1163–84) in 1171/2. A church may once have occupied the site, as indicated by a reused fragment of a Visigothic doorway, now in the Museo Arqueológico. The Almohad mosque was converted for use as a church following the Christian conquest of 1248, but was then demolished in 1401 to allow construction of the present **Gothic cathedral**. Only the minaret of the mosque, now known as the **Giralda**, was retained to serve as a bell tower. Work on this began in 1184 under an architect called Aḥmad ibn Bāso, and it was completed in 1198. It is 16 sq. m., and now stands to a height of 94 m., but the bell chamber at the top was added in 1568. The balconies and panels of decorative brick-work that may be seen on all sides of the tower are original. This is the finest example of the religious architecture of the Almohad period still to be seen in Spain. Much of the original forecourt of the mosque has also been preserved in the *Patio de los Naranjos*, on the north side of the cathedral. You can still see a large Visigothic basin, once reused for Muslim ritual ablutions before prayer, in the middle of the patio.

The *Torre de Oro* ('Tower of Gold'), on the bank of the Guadalquivir due west of the Alcázar, dates to 1220 and formed part of an extension of the Almohad defences from the Alcázar to the river. A chain stretched between it and a comparable tower on the opposite bank served to stop traffic on the river at night or to prevent hostile shipping from approaching the city. It was much rebuilt in 1760, when the present upper storeys and the enlarged lower windows were added. Only the bottom two floors of the building represent its original state. It received its name from the coloured tiles with which it had originally been roofed.

You can see a small section of an early imperial Roman **aqueduct** in the Calle Luís Montoro.

West of the Guadalquivir

Excavations have been conducted across the river in the market of the suburb called Triana, which stands on the site of a 12th-cent. **Almohad fortress**. This became the seat of the Tribunal of the Inquisition, from 1481 until 1785. It was demolished and the site reused for the market in the early 19th cent. Traces of a barbican tower have been found, but so far there is no evidence of earlier Umayyad or even Visigothic fortifications that some believe to have stood on the same site. Back on the eastern side of the river, traces of the Almohad Puerta de Triana, one of the principal gates of the city, were also uncovered in 1983, at the point where the Calles Gravina and Zaragoza intersect the Calle de San Pablo.

Provincial Archaeological Museum

The Museo Arqueológico is housed in part of a Neo-Mudéjar complex in the Parque de María Luisa, built for the Spanish-American Exhibition of 1929. The museum has twenty-seven rooms, and contains fine collections of Roman mosaics, sculptures, and inscriptions (mostly from ITÁLICA), as well as Visigothic and Islamic ceramics, bronzes, and inscriptions. A few pieces from MEDINA AZAHARA can be seen here, as well as items found in Seville. There is also a range of prehistoric items, primarily in the basement. These include 8th-cent. BC funerary stelae from CARMONA, Phoenician ceramics from **Río Tinto**, a 2nd-cent. BC bust and finds from MUNIGUA.

On the SE 620 12 km. west of Seville lies **Bollullos de la Mitación**.

Close to it may be seen an Almohad mosque, converted into a church called the Ermita de Cuatrohabitan. The present entry is in the location of the former *mihrab*, but the rest of the double-arcaded prayer hall has been preserved, if in restored form, as has the brick minaret.

The south coast   Phoenician settlements

From around the middle of the 8th cent. BC a series of Phoenician colonies was established along the southern coast of Spain. These trading settlements were the entrepôts through which eastern Mediterranean pottery and other items entered the Iberian peninsula, and the primary channel for eastern cultural influence on the Iberian tribes. The rise to power in the western Mediterranean of the former Phoenician colony of Carthage led to these settlements being absorbed into its empire. They then became the centres of Punic (Carthaginian) cultural and political influence in the south. The most westerly was **Gadir** (modern Cádiz). Other such settlements with modern equivalents include **Baria** (Vera), **Abdera** (Adra), **Sexi** (ALMUÑECAR) and **Malaka** (MÁLAGA). Other sites have been found at **Cerro del Prado**, the mouth of the River **Guadalhorce**, and **Morro de Mezquitilla**.

The site of the Phoenician settlement of **Abdera** has been located on the Cerro de Montecristo, east of modern Adra. Excavations in 1970 and 1971 located Roman and Punic buildings, but nothing, other than Greek and Phoenician pottery fragments, dated from before the 4th cent. BC. A rescue dig in 1986 produced definite evidence of Phoenician and Phoenico-Punic occupation of the site from the mid-8th cent. BC.

Gadir was located on the easily defensible peninsula that is still the heart of the modern city. Traces of Phoenician or Punic masonry are said to be detectable in the lowest levels of a square tower (dating from 1613) in the Castillo de San Sebastián on the western point. Finds, including those from the necropolis at Punta de la Vaca, may be seen in the archaeological section of the Museo Provincial (Plaza de Mina).

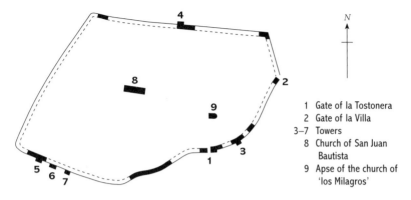

1 Gate of la Tostonera
2 Gate of la Villa
3–7 Towers
8 Church of San Juan
    Bautista
9 Apse of the church of
    'los Milagros'

▲ Talamanca del Jarama (after Rubio Visiers and Paloma López del Álamo)

Talamanca del Jarama Arab fortress town

On the N I heading north from MADRID, after 16 km. turn east onto the M 100 at Fuente del Fresno. After 7 km. this intersects the M 103. Take this road northwards for 17 km. to the turn-off to Talamanca, which is situated just to the west of the road.

Like **Buitrago de Lozoya** Talamanca was an Umayyad fortress town, guarding the route from Toledo to the Pass of Somosierra. However, in origin it probably dates back to the Roman period, and small items of Roman and Visigothic stone carving can be seen incorporated into later work, notably in the walls. The fortification of the town was undertaken by Muḥammad I (852–66), probably around the time when the walls of MADRID were constructed. Ibn Ḥayyan records a governor of the town in 929 called García b. Aḥmad. Castilian raids are reported in 1047 and 1059, before the definitive capture of the town by Alfonso VI in 1085. Of the **Arab defensive walls** little now remains beyond the basic outline and the lowest levels of construction in some of the four remaining towers. Substantial refortification seems to have taken place in the 12th cent. Excavations carried out in 1981 and 1982 in and around the 13th-cent. Romanesque/Mudéjar apse (all that now survives) of the church of los Milagros have produced stratified indications of the phases of Roman, Visigothic, and Islamic occupation of this site. The **church of San Juan**, in the centre of the town, has a fine 12th-cent. Romanesque apse, but the rest of the church was rebuilt in the 16th cent.

About half a km. north-west of Talamanca may be seen a Roman bridge (sign-posted), restored in the Middle Ages and in the 16th cent.

Continue northwards from Talamanca on the M 103 in the direction of **Torrelaguna** (taken by Alfonso VI in 1085; birthplace of Cardinal Cisneros in 1436). Torrelaguna retains parts of a 12th-cent. defensive wall and numerous 15th/16th-cent. houses.

*Beyond Torrelaguna, on the M 131 in the direction of Sieteiglesias, a road heads north from the village of **El Berrueco** towards Manjirón. About 2 km. up it, on the left, may be seen the Umayyad atalaya of Arrebatacapas, of which the bottom storey and part of the one above it survive. Another ruinous atalaya of the same period may be seen (south of the road) between El Vellón and El Espartal, villages on the minor road linking the N 1 and the M 103, whose eastern end is about 4 km. north of Talamanca. A third of this group of interconnected Arab watch towers is situated near Venturada, just to the west of the N 1, about 4.5 km. north of El Vellón.*

Tarifa Arab fortress

The most southerly town in the Iberian peninsula, Tarifa is 21 km. south-east of Algeceiras, and is little over 16 km. from the North African coast.

Tarifa is thought to be the site of the Carthaginian settlement of Josa, and was renamed Julia Traducta by the Romans. It was captured by Sancho IV of Castile in 1292, and held against a Nazirid counter-attack in 1294 by Alfonso Pérez de Guzmán who is said, in a document of 1297, when the attackers threatened to kill his hostage son, to have thrown down his own knife from the walls 'with which they should kill his son, so that they might be sure he would not give up the town'. They did, but Guzmán was rewarded by the king with the sobriquet of 'El Bueno' (the Good).

It is possible that the crucial battle fought by the Arab invaders against the Visigothic king Roderic 'in the transductine promontory' (*Chronicle of 754*, ch. 52) was fought in this area, though Arab sources locate it further north-west in the valley of the Guadalete, near JEREZ DE LA FRONTERA.

Some of Tarifa's Almohad defensive walls survive, though much repaired and restored, as do some horseshoe-arched gateways. An inscription records that the ruined Alcázar was built in 950–60, making it one of a small number of surviving Caliphal fortresses. (See BAÑOS DE LA ENCINA, EL VACAR, GORMAZ, and TURÉGANO). An irregular quadrilateral, with two entries, the fortress has been subjected to much modification internally, but the basic external structure, with its shallow rectangular towers of equal height with the wall, probably remains faithful to its Umayyad original.

The church of San Mateo (partly 15th-cent.) was built on the site of a mosque. It contains a Visigothic funerary inscription of a penitent called Flavianus, who died on 30 March 636.

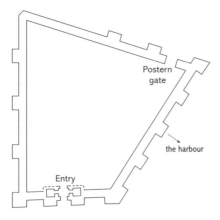

▼ Tarifa (after Bednorz)

Postern gate

the harbour

Entry

Chronicle of 754

This anonymous chronicle was probably written in Toledo around the year 754, and provides the nearest we have to a contemporary account of the Arab conquest and of the succeeding decades. The earliest extant Arab sources date from no earlier than the 10th cent.

Tarragona Roman and Iberian town ★★

An Iberian settlement, located in the lower part of the present city, southeast of the bullring, has been identified as the Kissa or Kese of early sources. It seems to have come into existence in the 5th cent. BC, and to have survived up to the Roman conquest. It was under Roman rule, during the Second Punic War, that the famous '**Cyclopean Wall**' in the east of the city was built to defend the military headquarters or *praesidium*, situated on the site of the medieval cathedral. The Roman development of Tarraco was twin-centred: the higher part of the town around the *praesidium* remained military in character, essentially a fortress, while in the mid-2nd cent. BC a residential and commercial district developed in the area of the former Iberian settlement, close to the mouth of the Río Francolí. This was

▼ Tarragona: possible line of the Roman walls and principal areas

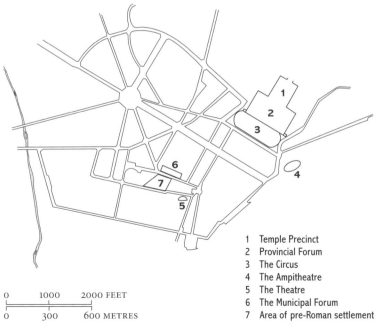

| 0 | 1000 | 2000 FEET |
| 0 | 300 | 600 METRES |

1 Temple Precinct
2 Provincial Forum
3 The Circus
4 The Ampitheatre
5 The Theatre
6 The Municipal Forum
7 Area of pre-Roman settlement

the site of the forum, which was certainly in being by the time an inscription was set up in it in 71 BC to honour Pompey, though it was extensively remodelled under Augustus (27 BC–AD 14), who had visited the town during his participation in the Cantabrian War in 26 BC.

Between 45 and 27 BC the status of *colonia* was conceded to the city, under a new name of Colonia Iulia Urbs Triumphalis Tarraco, and it was made capital of the newly constituted province of Hispania Citerior. The size of the forum was increased, and some reliefs depicting captives have been found that seem to have come from a triumphal arch, probably erected to mark the successful conclusion of the Cantabrian War. A theatre was also built next to the forum; the theatre went out of use in the 3rd cent. A temple dedicated to Augustus, testified to on local coinage, was also probably built in this area soon after his death. Amongst the governors of Hispania Citerior was the future emperor Galba (68–9), whose revolt led to the overthrow of Nero (54–68).

Excavations undertaken in the 1980s have revealed that in the Flavian period (AD 69–96) a major programme of public works was undertaken in the upper town, to create a monumental complex suitable for housing the *Concilium Provinciae Hispaniae Citerioris*, the administrative assembly of this large province. This period also marks a considerable increase in the use of expensive imported marble as opposed to local limestone for the decoration of public works.

The enormous province of Hispania Citerior was subdivided in the administrative reorganization of the time of Diocletian (284–305) and Constantine I (306–37), but Tarraco remained capital of the new, if smaller, province of Tarraconensis.

A sizeable Christian community, with its own bishops, had come into existence by the middle of the 3rd cent. In the 5th cent. the lower part of the city appears to have been almost entirely abandoned, with the population concentrating instead in the more defensible upper part. Traces of building activity at this time may represent the creation of an episcopal complex—church(es), baptistery, bishop's palace—of the kind known from other sites, especially in southern France. Rubbish pits in the circus indicate that it was no longer used for its original purposes. Finds from these and other pits indicate a wide range of commercial contacts continuing between the city and other parts of the former Roman Empire.

An inscription honouring the emperors Leo I (457–73) and Anthemius (467–72) indicates the continued political adherence of the city to the empire around 470, but immediately after the overthrow of Anthemius in Rome the armies of the Visigothic king Euric (466–84) overran Catalonia and the Ebro valley, incorporating the Roman province of Tarraconensis into the Visigothic kingdom. The city remained the capital of the province and its bishops the metropolitans of the church in Tarraconensis until the end of the Visigothic period. Held by the Visigothic king Achila (710–13), who minted coins there, Tarragona fell to

▲ Tarragona: the Roman amphitheatre, containing a 12th-cent. church, on top of a 7th-cent. Visigothic church

the Arabs between 714 and 720, and was given a Berber garrison. Conflicts led to the latter massacring the civilian population in 794, and the city was abandoned for about a decade. Archaeologically little is known of Arab Taraquna. A small but fine 10th-cent. *mihrab* is normally to be seen in the cloister of the cathedral, but nothing is known of where it came from. The growth of the power of the counts of Barcelona and the Christian resettlement of northern Catalonia seems to have led to a definitive abandonment of Tarragona in the 11th cent. It was occupied and resettled around 1089. The cathedral, possibly replacing a mosque, began to be built in 1171 and was finally consecrated in 1331.

The **wall** used to be taken as predating the Roman occupation of the site, at least in its lowest levels where the largest stones repose, but has now been proved to belong to the Early Roman period. In particular, masons' marks visible on the stones of the wall have been shown to be identical to those found on other military constructions in Italy of Republican date. The exact date of construction is not clear, but may be associated with the Second Punic War. A substantial extension of the wall, together with a heightening and broadening of the existing sections, took place around 150–125 BC, at the time when Rome was expanding its control over the interior of Spain. It is probably to this period that the development of a real Roman town of Tarraco, as opposed to a military cantonment, belongs. You can best observe the wall in the 'Passeig Arqueológico' that runs between it and the Vaubanesque outer defences erected by British engineers during the War of Spanish Succession (1700–12). The entry is by the Puerta del Rosario, and the walk extends along most of the northern and eastern stretches of the wall. Various statues are displayed *en route*. (The bronze statue of Augustus was a present from the Fascist government of Italy in 1936 and not a local discovery!)

The **amphitheatre** is located in a small park (Parc del Milagro) adjacent to a beach in the angle between the upper and lower sections of the city. The amphitheatre was built in an area previously used as a cemetery in the early 2nd cent. It was a personal benefaction for the city by a local notable, as is known from the recent discovery of part of the dedicatory inscription. A substantial reformation of the building was undertaken in 220 under the patronage of the Emperor Marcus Aurelius Antoninus, known as Elagabalus (218–22), and is recorded in the largest Roman inscription known from Spain, set up all around the podium of the amphitheatre. Not much of the eastern end of this structure has survived, but there is enough to get a sense of its dimensions (111.5 × 86.5 m. for its external walls; 61.5 × 38.5 m. for the area of the arena). Stone from the amphitheatre was clearly reused for the construction of the 12th-cent. church whose ruins occupy the south-east corner of the floor of the arena (a location dictated by the subterranean passageways and storage areas that take up the centre of this space). This replaced an earlier, smaller church of Visigothic date, whose foundations may be seen clearly in the area of the nave of the later building. This was of a simple cruciform shape with a semicircular chancel. As in the case of the Coliseum in Rome, the presence of Christian structures in the middle of a former amphitheatre indicate the existence of a cult of martyrs thought to have perished there in the course of the persecutions. Here the cult was that of Bishop Fructuosus of Tarragona and his deacons Augurius and Eulogius, who were burnt to death in this amphitheatre in 259 in the short period of persecution at the end of the reign of Valerian (253–60). An early *Passion* records their fate, and their cult extended well beyond the city in the Late Roman period; they were referred to by the African bishop Augustine of Hippo (d. 430). They were originally buried in an extramural cemetery (see below), but their relics were translated in the 6th cent., possibly to this church if not to the cathedral.

The **redevelopment of the upper city**, begun by Vespasian (69–79) and completed by Domitian (81–96), resulted in the creation of three great related structures, each separately terraced, and rising in ascending order from south to north. The most northerly component, at the highest point, was a rectangular enclosure, probably containing a large temple dedicated to the imperial cult. This was probably located under the medieval cathedral, whose construction started in 1171, but no trace of it exists. It fronted onto another but larger rectangular enclosure, set at right angles to it, which would have been the new forum, housing the buildings of the *Concilium* of the province of Hispania Citerior (only traces of the outer walls of this enclosure have been discovered). The third element, the last to be built, was a great **hippodrome or circus** that ran across the southern front of the enclosure of the *Concilium*, which would have had to be entered around either end of the circus. Some of this has been preserved in the form of subterranean vaults around the east end and in the eastern half of the north side. You should be able to visit some of this area if further excavation is not taking place, and something of the site can be glimpsed from the south-eastern corner. The outer wall that runs along the south side of the site is of 14th-cent. date. A 13th–14th-cent. tower, part of the former Castell del Rei and located next to what would have been the south-east corner of the Provincial Forum, houses the Museo de Historia de Tarragona ('Pretorio Romano', Escaleras San Hermenegildo), which contains an important collection of finds from the city, including a fine bust of Marcus Aurelius (161–80). One side of a fine 4th-cent. Christian sarcophagus may be seen high up on the west wall of the cathedral, to the right of the main door. There is also a medieval inscription in Hebrew in the wall of house no. 6 in the Calle de Escribanias, which once formed part of the *Judería* or Jewish quarter.

In the southern sector of the modern town (between the Calle de Lérida and the Calle Fortuny) has been preserved a substantial section of a basilica, and an adjoining street, that are thought to have formed part of the municipal **forum** of the Roman city. When reconstructing the site in 1969, the excavator, Serra Vilaró, believed that the rectangular colonnaded area in the middle was the *curia* of the forum and the arcaded chambers along the outer wall and opening into the central space were shops (*tabernae*). It is now thought, not least because of the small scale of the constructions implied by the earlier view, that they all formed part of a single basilican building. The arcaded chambers would thus have served as offices, and the rectangular extension in the middle of the north wall may have been dedicated to the imperial cult (an *aedes Augusti*). Fronting the main entry to the basilica on the east was a rectangular square, once adorned with statues, probably erected by the Council (*Curia*) that governed the city. This in turn is approached via a street flanked by unidentified buildings and possible shops. In the area of the city immediately south of the site (across the Calle del Gasómetro) have been found indications of other Roman buildings, consisting of at least two temples and a theatre. A Julio-Claudian date seems likely for these and, by comparison with CLUNIA, for the construction of the basilica of the forum.

The urban development of Tarragona in the last two centuries has obliterated many of the traces of the street plan and residential quarters of the Roman city, but rescue digs have provided some information on both aspects. However, an important **early Christian cemetery**, around the ruins of a basilica of the 4th cent., was discovered by chance in the Paseo Independencia in 1923, when a tobacco factory was about to be constructed on the site. The earliest burials probably date to the 3rd cent., and a fragment of an inscription from an altar suggests that the bodies of Saints Fructuosus, Augurius, and Eulogius were buried and venerated here (Vives, no. 321). Burials continued until the mid-6th cent., and a variety of styles of inhumation may be seen, as well as a range of sarcophagi ranging in date from the 4th to the 6th cent.

The **Arch of Berà**, a triumphal arch (12.5 × 5 m.) stood on the Via Augusta, which ran from Tarraco towards the Pyrenees and ultimately to Rome. It was built in the reign of Augustus by Lucius Licinius Sura, who came to live in Tarraco at this time. A descendant of his of the same name was a friend of the younger Pliny. (*The N 340 runs around it about 20 km. east of the city.*)

A funerary monument of the 2nd cent. AD (*c.*9 m. high) is misleadingly called the **Torre de los Escipiones** (*located on the north side of the N 340 about 6 km. east of the city*). The carving of two male figures (very worn) on one side of the structure led to the belief that it commemorated the brothers Scipio, who were both killed in battle with the Carthaginians in 212 BC.

An impressive section of one of the aqueducts that would have brought water to Tarraco survives in a woodland park just north of the city. Known as the **Acueducto de les Ferreres**, it may date from the reign of Trajan (98–117). (*It is approached by a track off the N 240, just north of where it is crossed over by the A 7/E 15; signposted and normally visible from the main road.*)

See also CENTCELLES *(about 5 km. north of Tarragona), and* OLERDOLA *(about 55 km. east)*

Teba   Arab castle

*On a hill overlooking the MA 465, which leads southwards from the N 342 (*GRANADA *to* JEREZ DE LA FRONTERA*) 7 km. west of Campillos before joining the C 341 (Campillos to* RONDA*).*

The lack of any ceramic finds datable to the time of the Umayyad dynasty would seem to place the origin of this fortress in a later period. Its defensive system also argues for a relatively late date, probably in the Almoravid or Almohad periods. At this time it seems to have served as a ḥiṣn for the defensive needs of a local Muslim population. Under the Nazirids it was enlarged by the building of the outer circuit of walls, and its functions altered. In the centre of the fortress a high-status residential complex was

Here Sir James Douglas, taking the heart of the Scots king Robert I (1306–29) the Bruce to Jerusalem, fell in battle with the Nazirids. He is said to have thrown the casket containing the king's heart ahead of him as he charged. It was later recovered and returned to Scotland for burial in Melrose Abbey.

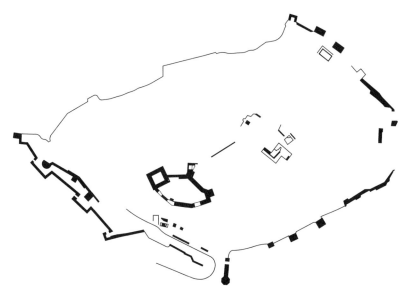

▲ Teba: castle (after Vallejo Triano)

constructed, in the form of the so-called *Torre de Homenaje*, which would seem to have been the dwelling of a noble family. The outer parts of the castle continued to serve as a fortified settlement for a local population until the late 15th cent., when a move to the site of the present village seems to have occurred. The noble residence was occupied by the family of the Condes de Teba, until 1603. By the mid-17th cent. the sector of the castle within the inner curtain wall had begun to be used as a village cemetery and the whole site had been abandoned for settlement purposes.

South-west from the town of Teba, on the northern slopes of the Sierra de Peñarrubia, is an important Visigothic necropolis.

'El Tesorillo' of 7th-cent. date, was excavated in 1980. The necropolis was established in the ruins of a small Roman villa, of the late 1st cent. AD. Twenty burials were found scattered in apparently random fashion around the site, but with a common west–east orientation. Seven of them were in open cists of stones; others were contained within tiles or by small walls of stone. One lacked any form of delimitation. Some jars and a few fine bronze buckles, including one of cruciform shape, were recovered. In 1983 another 7th-cent. Visigothic necropolis was found in the deserted village of Peñarrubia., 1 km. from this site.

Tiermes Roman town (Termantia)

On the N 110, between SEGOVIA and El Burgo de Osma, turn right 4 km. north of Ayllón onto a small road to the south, marked to Torraño. Continue on this rather winding road through the villages of Torraño, Cuevas, Liceras, Montejo de Tiermes and Torresuso. A road to the right 4 km. after Torresuso leads directly to the site (2 km.).

This Roman town on a site previously occupied by a Celtiberian settlement has been excavated in stages over several years. It is located on a promontory of land defined by the 1,200 m. contour on the western edge of the valley of the Río Manzanares. There is a museum displaying finds at the point of entry, together with a car park. These are adjacent to a probably late 11th-cent. Romanesque chapel (see below). Little remains above ground, but you can reach a number of excavated buildings by clearly defined paths.

Part of the **wall of the Roman town** is visible in the north-eastern corner of the site. On the northern side, visible from the approach road to the site, are traces of two semicircular towers. Following excavation of a section of the wall in 1979 it has been dated to the second half of the 3rd cent. There are clear parallels to walls of the same period to be seen at LUGO, LEÓN, ASTORGA, and BARCELONA.

Immediately to the west of the Romanesque chapel a substantial area has been excavated, leading to the identification of the main square of the

▼ Tiermes: the forum area (after Argente Oliver)

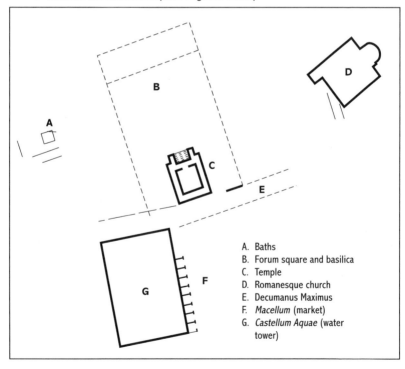

A. Baths
B. Forum square and basilica
C. Temple
D. Romanesque church
E. Decumanus Maximus
F. *Macellum* (market)
G. *Castellum Aquae* (water tower)

Roman forum, with a temple (visible foundations) located on its southern edge. Across the *Decumanus Maximus*, one of the two main thoroughfares of the city, which ran immediately to the south of the temple, has been discovered a large *castellum aquae* or water tower. To the west of the forum have been found traces of a public bath house.

The excavation of a square section located due north of the apse of the chapel has uncovered parts of buildings belonging to three phases of occupation. The first, dated by traces of wall painting and ceramics, belongs to the late 1st and 2nd cents. AD. The second, related to the building of the chapel and an 11th-cent. phase of the necropolis (see below), has been dated by coins to the time of Alfonso VI of Castile (1072–1109). The third has been dated, also by coin finds, to the reigns of Enrique III (1390–1406) and Juan II (1406–54). Documentary records indicate that a settlement still existed in Tiermes in 1499, but also that it was classified as unpopulated in the 16th cent.

The 'House of the Aqueduct' was excavated between 1979 and 1986, and is the first complete **Roman villa** to be uncovered on the site. It is situated on a slope of the hill, and its plan, based around two peristyled courtyards, takes account of this. Running parallel to it immediately to the north was an aqueduct bringing water into the town. Traces of this also continue to the west. The villa was probably built in the middle of the 1st cent. AD, and pottery finds suggest that it continued in occupation until at least the 5th cent. Traces of painted plaster decoration have been uncovered at floor level in seven of the rooms and in the eastern peristyle and around the basin in its courtyard. These indicate several stages of redecoration, to accommodate changing tastes in the 1st and 2nd cents. The principal entry was from the east. To the right of the main entry, on the lower level, are what are thought to be the kitchen, wine cellar, and storerooms, with a small stairway carved out of the rock to provide access to the dining area above. To the left of the main entry the rooms are believed to be the quarters of the domestic slaves. On the higher level and in the north-east corner of the building were latrines. Passing through the main entry, guests would have proceeded straight along a corridor rising into the eastern atrium, and thence to the reception and dining-rooms that open to the north of it. The large centrally located room with a semicircular northern end is thought to be the summer dining-room (*triclinium*). Because of the open nature of both courtyard and rooms, it is probable that this area was used primarily at that time of year. To the west of this atrium a single room provides access to the area of the smaller western courtyard, around which are assumed to be the private quarters of the family owning the villa. Three adjacent rooms in the north-west corner that do not open into this complex are taken to be storerooms. Finally, along the southern façade, to the east of the western atrium and south of the eastern one, are a group of interconnected rooms that would only have been entered via a doorway to the left of the corridor leading up from the main entry. These may have been the winter reception rooms, with the largest, the westernmost of them, serving as the dining-room.

The **Romanesque chapel** of Nuestra Señora de Tiermes stands on the eastern edge of the site, close to the museum. Finds from the necropolis north of it (see above) have dated it to the reign of Alfonso VI (1072–1109). It was given to the Cistercian monastery of **Santa María de Huerta** in 1191. Excavations to the east of this site have revealed traces of Roman houses and a paved Roman road, as well as a medieval cemetery, which also extended around to the west of the chapel. This cemetery appears to have come into existence in the 11th cent., and continued in use into the 15th. A number of medieval coins and of discoidal tombstones have been discovered. Material finds from this area have also established the continued existence of a settlement at Tiermes in the Visigothic period, though its centre has yet to be located. The reuse of Visigothic stonework in the northern outside wall of the chapel and in one of the medieval tombs, as well as other carved fragments from this period found in the nearby small chapel (23 × 7 m.) of Nuestra Señora del Val (in the village of Pedro), prove the existence of buildings of Visigothic date in the vicinity. No evidence has emerged to prove Arab occupation of the site.

Toledo   Roman and Islamic remains   ★★

Built upon a naturally defensible elevated site within an incised meander of the River Tagus, Toledo has been continuously occupied from at least Roman times. This has limited both the potential for and the quantity of archaeological investigation of the site. Little is known of Roman Toletum before it became the capital of the Visigothic kingdom in the mid-6th cent. From 589 onwards an important series of church councils were held here, and the metropolitan bishops of Toledo secured primacy over the rest of the Church in Spain in the course of the 7th cent. Following the Arab conquest, when it became known as Ṭulayṭula, the political and ecclesiastical importance of the city gradually declined. In the 8th and 9th cents. it was frequently in revolt against the Umayyads. Following the collapse of their caliphate it became the capital of a Taifa kingdom, before falling to Alfonso VI of Castile in 1085. A distinctive Mozarabic community survived in the city, using Visigothic liturgical rites and the Arabic language (until the 13th–14th cents.). Descendants of this group still live in the city, and the Visigothic or Mozarabic liturgy, as revised by Cardinal Cisneros (1436–1517), is still said daily in one chapel of the Gothic cathedral. This was built in stages from 1227 to 1493, and is the burial place of King Sancho IV the Valiant (1284–95) of Castile, and of the first three kings of the Trastámara dynasty: Enrique II (1369–79), Juan I (1379–90), and Enrique III (1390–1406).

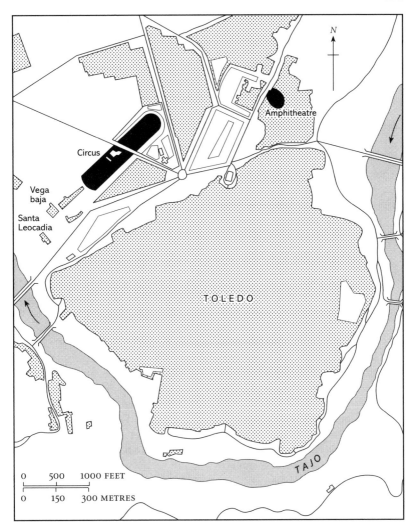

▲ Roman sites in Toledo

The Roman Circus

Located in a park just north of and parallel to the western half of the city walls and the Paseo de Recaredo, the circus is the most substantial surviving trace of Roman Toletum, largely thanks to its position outside the city. In the same way, traces of the Roman amphitheatre have been preserved immediately to the east of the Hospital de Tavera (1541–99) on the other side of the Paseo de Merchán. You can see the foundations of the seating of the circus and parts of the vaulted chambers that lay under it around the northern end, especially on the west side. The outline of most of the structure can be made out. Although not substantial, this is one of the best preserved of all Roman circuses. Excavation has shown that the site was previously used for some form of market, and the building of the circus itself appears to be datable to the mid-1st cent. AD. The circus, probably by then denuded of most of its visible stonework, was reused as an Islamic cemetery; tombs found there date from the 9th to the 11th cent. In a second phase the area was a burial place for Toledan Muslims, now under Christian rule, in the 13th and 14th cents. Some tombs, in the form of low-lying vaulted sarcophagi made of thin bricks, may also be seen in the area of the circus. These are believed to be later medieval Jewish burials.

The Church of Santa Leocadia

One of the three most important Visigothic churches and scene of several of the 7th-cent. Councils of Toledo, attended by bishops from all over the Visigothic kingdom, its site is thought to lie in the vicinity of the present, much restored, Ermita de Cristo de la Vega, at the end of the Paseo de los Canónigos, and immediately south-west of the Roman circus. Largely unpublished excavation of this site took place in 1972–5. Burials, probably of pre-11th-cent. date from the medieval Islamic cemetery, were found around the site of the former Roman circus. Some of the tombstones were reused for Mozarabic Christian burials around the Ermita later in the Middle Ages. A fragment of a Visigothic funerary inscription also emerged, as did deep-lying traces of a massive construction built of large granite blocks, oriented along an east–west axis. There is evidence that it was buttressed. This building appears to have been almost totally obliterated, but it has been suggested from its scale and quality that it formed part of some palace-like structure of Late Roman or Visigothic date. (Professor Palol prefers the latter, but support for the earlier dating might now come from some features of a Tetrarchic palace found at CÓRDOBA.)

Santo Cristo de la Luz/Bab al-Mardum

The Arabic name is taken from the nearby Gate of Al-Mardum. It is a small mosque, possibly built on the site of a former Visigothic church. As can be seen from the inscription on the outer wall, it was erected in 999/1000 by Aḥmad ibn Hadidi, a member of a local noble house, using an architect called Mūsā ibn ʿAlī. The view that such small nine-domed mosques as this, and the Mosque of **Tornerías** (see below) were funerary buildings is now discredited. Following the Castilian conquest it was put into the hands of the Knights Hospitaller and turned into a church, which was then extended in the 1190s by the addition of the present apse, built in Mudéjar style. The dimensions of the prayer hall are 7.5 × 8.5 m. It is 8 m. high, rising to 10.5 m. in the central cupola, where the strap-work vaulting is reminiscent of that to be seen in the late 10th-cent. sector of the Mezquita at Córdoba. It has been suggested that the *maqsura*, or royal enclosure, of the latter was the direct inspiration for this building. The original *mihrab*, facing south-east, was destroyed, and is now a doorway. Originally the building would have been open on all the other three sides. Very stylized Visigothic capitals were reused on the four central columns, which divide the interior space into nine roughly equal sections. No trace remains of the original plaster or other decorative features of the interior of the mosque, but small sections of fresco are preserved in the later apse.

The Mosque of Tornerías

This is located in the upper parts of Calle Tornerías 21 and 23, (but entered from the Plaza de Solarejo) in what was the commercial heart of the city throughout the Middle Ages. It served as the mosque for the Muslim community in Toledo until closed down by the Catholic Kings between 1498 and 1505, when it was turned into a house and given to the Hospital de la Misericordia. Its true origins were rediscovered in the 19th cent. Lacking inscriptions, the date of construction of the mosque is not certain, but may be as late as 1159, when the mosque on the site of the church of **San Salvador** (see below) was closed down. Its location on the first floor of a dwelling and the unorthodox orientation of the *quibla* towards the south-west suggest it may have been built after the Christian conquest of the city, yet its small dimensions and its plan make it an unlikely choice for a congregational mosque, even after 1085. Furthermore, its clear similarities in design to the **Bab al-Mardum** mosque (see above) have led some scholars to suggest an early 11th-cent. date for it. In size, with dimensions for the prayer hall of *c.*8.5 × 7 m., it is very close to the **Bab al-Mardum**. The issues of its date and purpose remain open. Recent excavation also revealed that it was built on top of a Roman *castellum aquae* or water tower. Restoration work seeks to bring out both features, and to house a museum devoted to Islamic Toledo.

The Church of San Salvador

This church stands on the site of a mosque, as indicated in an inscription found in the church and dating to 1041. It is not clear if this records the first building or the restoration of the mosque. Its present orientation towards the south-east is that normally used to give the direction of Mecca. Although it initially survived as a Muslim place of worship after the Castilian conquest of 1085, the decision to turn it into a church was taken in 1159. Some decorative fragments of Visigothic date are to be seen in the outer walls, but the most important feature is a unique Visigothic pilaster that now serves as part of the arcading of the nave (the pillar nearest to the chancel and to its right). It is carved on three sides with vine scroll and formal vegetal motifs, and with three miniature columns in relief; the fourth side is unparalleled in depicting four New Testament scenes in rows, one above the other. These are (top to bottom): the Raising of Lazarus, Jesus and the Woman at the Well of Samaria, the Healing of the Blind Man, and the Healing of the Woman with an Issue of Blood. The nearest parallels to the iconography and the structuring of these scenes may be found in some Late Antique ivories.

Walls and Bridges

Toledo boasts a substantial section of **defensive walls** across its northern frontage, now somewhat over-restored in some areas. As with most medieval town walls, these have been rebuilt and repaired at various dates, and precise chronology is rarely possible. It has been claimed that some sections may be of Visigothic date, while others, especially between the Puerta del Cambron (built in 1576 on the site of the Arab Bab al-Maqabia) and the Puerta de Alfonso VI, have some obvious Islamic features, especially in the towers. The **Puerta de Alfonso VI** or **Puerta vieja de Bisagra**, in front of the justly famed Hostal del Cardenal, has long been thought to date to the 9th cent. However, recent analysis has revealed that it was constructed in the 12th or 13th cent. It may thus belong to the same phase of refortification of the city as the Mudéjar **Puerta del Sol**. Southwest of the church of San Juan de los Reyes (1476–92) and on the riverbank adjacent to the **Puente de San Martín** (first built in 1203) may be seen a roofless rectangular structure, known popularly as the *Baños de la Cava* and traditionally said to be the bathing place of the daughter of 'Count Julian', whose rape by King Roderic led to her father betraying the Visigothic kingdom to the Arabs. In reality this is the defensive structure placed on the city end of a now lost 9th-cent. bridge. Another Arab bridge, built in 871, occupied the site of the present **Puente de Alcántara** (Arabic *al-Qantara* = bridge), which was erected in 1259 and restored in 1484. To the latter date belongs the tower at the city end. The portal on the other end was erected in 1721.

Santa María la Blanca

This church, in the Calle de los Reyes Católicos, used to be identified with the 'New Synagogue' built in 1203 by Joseph ben Shushan, *Almojarife* or Tax Collector of King Alfonso VIII of Castile. However, recent rescue excavations, necessitated by damage from damp, make this unlikely. A date in the second half of the 13th cent. seems more likely, as the construction of the synagogue involved demolition of a building lying under the west wall, which contained painted decoration attributable to the 12th cent. Walls of earlier buildings of Roman and Visigothic date have been discovered under and supporting the western arcades of the synagogue. The building was seized by the Christians of Toledo in 1411 and turned into a church, following an inflammatory sermon by (St) Vincent Ferrer delivered in the church of **Santiago del Arrabal** (*c.*1265, with tower of *c.*1179; note the 14th-cent. Mudéjar pulpit), but may have returned briefly to use as synagogue after 1477. In the 16th cent. it became a convent.

Traces of buildings associated with this phase have been uncovered in the garden, as have tombs and the foundations of walls for side chapels within the church. After a period of abandonment in the 18th cent. it was turned into a barracks in the 1790s. The decorative non-functional capitals in the arcades were restored in 1798. Substantial finds of Roman, Islamic, and late medieval ceramics were made during the excavations, which also disproved the theory that the foundations of a women's gallery for the synagogue were located in the garden.

The Visigothic Museum

The **Museo de los Concilios y de la Cultura Visigoda** is located in the **Church of San Román**. The church is rather more interesting than the museum; it was consecrated in 1221, and has a Mudéjar tower of the mid-12th cent. and some fine 13th-cent. mural frescos, including some Arabic as well as Latin painted inscriptions. Apart from some folios from four liturgical manuscripts in Visigothic script, the museum contains only some sculptural fragments and a selection of finds from the Visigothic cemetery of **El Carpio del Tajo** (see LOS VASCOS). There is a notable paucity, in terms of both the quantity of items and their quality, of contents of the individual tombs. These are the burials of a 6th-cent. rural population, whose ethnic origin was not necessarily Germanic. The limited and damaged nature of the items of Visigothic stonework found in Toledo has led to the suggestion that the city was deliberately ill-treated after 711 by the Arab conquerors, who sought to undermine its former special status in the kingdom. However, this may be no more than further evidence of the problems imposed by continuous occupation of a geographically limited site. As well as three 6th-cent. funerary inscriptions, also you can see two fragments of a finely carved credal statement, which may have come from the **Basilica of St Leocadia**.

The Archaeological Museum

This is currently housed in the claustral buildings attached to the Hospital of Santa Cruz, now itself a fine museum of painting and decorative arts. At present the **Museo Arqueológico** is but a fragment of its former self, being confined to a series of pre-Roman displays in the basement of the south range of the cloister. Of the once extensive Visigothic and Islamic displays no trace is to be seen.

The Jewish Museum

The **Museo Sefardi** is housed in the Synagogue of *El Tránsito* (= the Death of the Virgin), which was built around 1357 for Samuel ha-Levi, the Treasurer of King Pedro I of Castile, who subsequently had him executed. It is said that a passage originally connected this synagogue with ha-Levi's residence. Following the expulsion of the Jews from Spain in 1492, Isabel of Castile gave the building to the Order of Calatrava. Not only is the synagogue interesting, having retained much of its Mudéjar decoration and fine Hebrew inscriptions, but the site should also be visited for the museum, which contains collections relating to the whole history of the Jewish presence in Spain and the subsequent Sephardi diaspora. Of particular interest are the medieval funerary inscriptions of a number of rabbis, a Corinthian capital with Hebrew and Arabic inscriptions (of the text of Deuteronomy 28: 6), possibly coming from a lost Toledan synagogue, and a trilingual (Hebrew, Latin, and Greek) marble basin, decorated with carvings of a menorah, a tree, and two peacocks, that has been dated to the 6th cent.

Torre Llauder (Mataró) Roman villa

On the coast, 20 km. north of BARCELONA Mataró is now primarily an industrial town, but stands on the site of the Roman settlement of Iluro (see also ILDURO). Of the latter, the well-preserved villa of Torre Llauder is the best representative. The site is located in a walled enclosure on the Avinguda President Lluís Companys, which is one of the roads radiating from the junction where the A 19 ends.

According to the elder Pliny (d. AD 79) Iluro was a small town of Roman citizens in his day. It has been established that the town walls of Iluro were built in the reign of Augustus (27 BC–AD 14).

▼ Roman villa of Torre Llander (after Prevosti and Clariana)
  Phase 1: traces of Late Republican construction

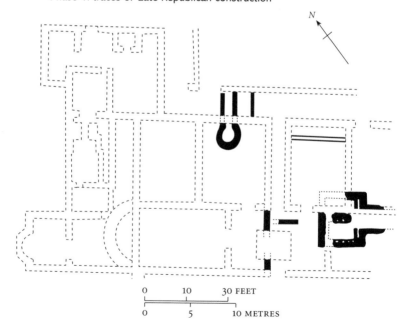

0	10	30 FEET
0	5	10 METRES

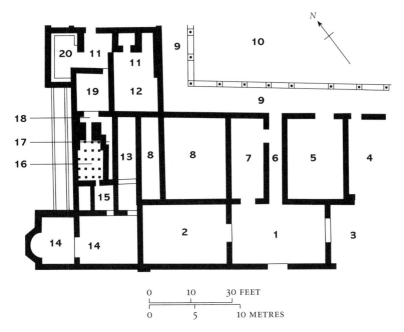

▲ Roman villa of Torre Llander (after Prevosti and Clariana)
Phase 2: the villa in the time of Augustus

Of that settlement, the section of the villa on the Torre Llauder site is the best-preserved remnant. Finds of Roman objects on the site are recorded as early as 1601, and the presence of some form of Roman building on this location was recognized in the late 18th cent. Excavations were undertaken throughout the 1960s. Unfortunately the demolition of the Torre Llauder, the former residence of the Llauder family, built around a 16th-cent. tower and atrociously modernized in 1927, as well as various programmes of public works, resulted in the destruction of much archaeological evidence. Thus only part of the villa, principally some sections of rooms around the southern and western patios of the central garden courtyard (*viridarium*), has been fully excavated and made visitable. Some agricultural outbuildings have also been detected slightly to the south-west, but only the main site has been left exposed.

Here various phases of construction and restoration have been identified. In the Late Republican period (1st cent. BC) an amphora factory seems to have functioned on the site. Some traces of its walls and a large ceramic oven, capable of firing up to 110 amphorae at a time, were discovered in 1927. In the last fifteen years of the 1st cent. BC this factory was replaced by a large and luxurious villa, which was given a substantial restoration in the Severan period (193–225). From then on it experienced a gradual decline in the care devoted to it and the uses to which it was put, and it had clearly become more of a rural farmhouse than an urban villa by the 4th and 5th cents. The addition of an apsidal end to one of the larger rooms in this period has been interpreted as evidence that some of the building may have been used as a Christian church at this time, but this is not certain. Evidence has emerged of the villa's continued use in the post-Roman period, when storage areas were created that damaged some of the now hidden Early Imperial mosaics. The final stage of occupation of the villa is thought to have ended violently, if the condition of some apparently unburied skeletons found in the rooms has been interpreted correctly. Unfortunately, it is not possible to get precise dating for these events, which theoretically may be associated with the Arab conquest of the region around 720.

The three plans given here indicate the structural changes of the main phases of the villa's use. In the first, datable to the middle of the reign of Augustus (c.15–1 BC), the surviving rooms of the southern wing (nos. 1–8) were probably part of the domestic quarters of the owners of the house, serving either as bedrooms or reception areas. Adjacent to them on the west (rooms 11–20) was the bath house. Entry to this bath complex would have been via a vestibule (11) and changing-room (12). Off the vestibule lay a communal latrine, with eight open stalls; some of these have been restored to show the original appearance. Otherwise, a corridor

▼ Roman villa of Torre Llander (after Prevosti and Clariana)
Phase 3: the Severan period (AD 193–235)

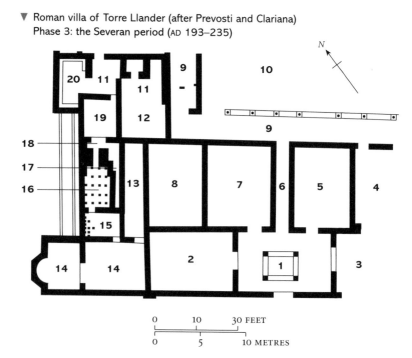

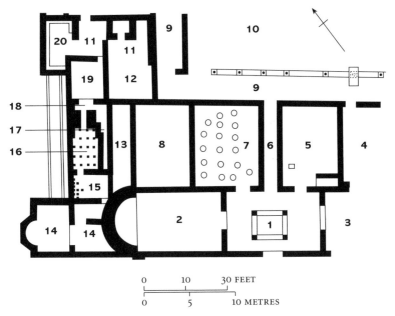

▲ Roman villa of Torre Llander (after Prevosti and Clariana)
Phase 4: the Later Roman period

(13) led from the vestibule and changing-room to the various baths. In room 16 may be seen the hypocausts supporting the floor of the steam bath (*caldarium*), and also the underfloor flue connecting it to the furnace room (19). A cold-plunge bath was located in the polygonal room in the south-west corner of the building (14), with a small antechamber preceding it. Between this and the *caldarium* lay the warm-water bath (*tepidarium*), the base of whose tank is visible (15).

In the Severan period (late 2nd–early 3rd cent. AD) some major work was done on the domestic rooms. Room 1, which served as the point of entry for many of the surrounding chambers, was turned into a small atrium with a central pool (*impluvium*). Room 2 probably functioned as either a dining-room (*triclinium*) or some kind of reception hall. The internal walls of rooms 7 and 8 were entirely replaced, to produce two rooms of more or less equal size, of similar dimensions to room 5. As a consequence of these changes new mosaics had to be laid, of which those of room 7 and of the new atrium (room 1) have in part survived, as has some of the central section of a new polychrome mosaic laid out in room 2. New marble facings and half-columns on the door jambs were added to the room at this time, to further enhance it. No significant structural changes seem to have been made to the bath complex.

In the 4th cent. a major alteration was made to room 2, the most important of those leading off from the small atrium. It was given a new apsidal western end, at the expense of the antechamber of the *frigidarium* in the bath house adjacent to it. Some archaeologists have speculated that this new basilican shape given to the room was the result of its being converted for use as a church. It has to be said that there is no other evidence to support such an interpretation, and no trace of an altar has been found. It is likely that this was merely a stylistic change, that can be paralleled in some other sites of this period, and the room continued in use as a *triclinium*. In the same period room 5 and the southern peristyle of the main atrium beside it (9) were converted to agricultural use, by the creation of small rectangular pits. In the case of room 5 this was at the cost of an earlier mosaic floor, of which a small fragment survives by the door. At a later date still, almost certainly after the end of Roman imperial rule, the process of turning this sector of the building into a farmhouse was taken further by the establishment of a series of small circular pits, probably intended to support round-bottomed pottery storage jars, all over the floor of room 7; one example is preserved in the north-east corner. This process, which also seems to have involved rooms 1, 2, and 5, as well as the southern patio (9), severely damaged the surviving mosaics below, which must have been hidden by this time.

Some early imperial portrait busts were found near the villa, probably having formed part of a now lost funerary monument; they were presented to the Museu Comarcal del Maresme (Calle Carrero, 17–19), where they may now be seen. They provide a very rare opportunity for the visitor to see lifelike portraits of people once directly associated with a site. One of the female busts has a hair-style identical to that of Agrippina Senior, mother of the Emperor Caligula (37–41), and this gives a stylistic dating for the portrait of around AD 20–30. In the ruins of the bath house the base of a lost statue (dating from the late 1st or early 2nd cent. AD) was found, bearing an inscription in honour of a certain Gaius Marius Aemilianus. He was a member of the class of *Equites* (the social order immediately below that of the Senators) and obviously a man of some importance in the region, as the base of another lost statue of him has been found in the forum of Barcinona (BARCELONA). That he too once resided in this villa or was related to the family that did is a reasonable assumption. Ceramic (including several items of fine *terra sigillata*), metal, glass, and coin finds from the site are also to be seen in the Museu Comarcal del Maresme (see above).

Tossa de Mar   Roman villa

On the coast 11 km. north of LLORET DE MAR *by the GE 682. The site is located opposite the Casa de Cultura in the town.*

The villa site of 'Els Ametllers' or the *Villa Vitalis* comprises the remains of a large Roman residence, including some of its bath house, occupied from the 1st to 5th cent. A floor mosaic, probably to be dated to the early 5th cent., has an inscription SALVO VITALIS | FELIX TURISSA | EX OFFICINA FELICES, which gives the name of one of the last owners of the villa, Vitalis, and of the maker of the mosaic, Felix.

Objects from the site may be seen in the Museo Municipal ('Vila Vella', Plaza Roig y Soler, a house which belonged to the Falguera family, who formerly held the hereditary office of Batlle de Sac, the local representative of the abbey of Ripoll, to which the town had once belonged). There are also remains of the medieval walls of the town and of a castle.

Trayamar   Phoenician tombs and settlement site

The N 340/E 15 coastal road crosses the Río Algarrobo 37 km. east of MÁLAGA at Algarrobo Costa. The tombs are on the western side of the river and the settlement site on the opposite bank. For the tombs, take the MA 103 that heads north from the N 340, just before Algarrobo Costa, to the village of Algarrobo which now runs across the site; indeed, its construction in 1965 was the cause of the destruction of two of the tombs! Less than 1 km. along the road, a right turn leads to the Residencia Trayamar, where a key for the one intact tomb may be obtained.

The settlement site (of which there is little to see) is located on the Morro de Mezquitilla, 250 m. north of the village of Mezquitilla on the coast. Access is via a private farm track.

The Phoenician funerary monuments on the Trayamar site are of a type known elsewhere in southern Spain and in North Africa, but are amongst the finest examples. They consisted of rectangular chambers, built of large finely cut stone blocks buried in the hillside, and had full-size doorways to provide access to the burial chamber. Funerary offerings were found in each, which have provided evidence for their chronology. Of the five tombs known from this site, only one survives intact and is visitable. Two were demolished (!) in 1965 to make way for a road, and the other two are less well preserved. Although perhaps intended for single burials, a variety of periods and types of burial are here represented. Thus, tomb no. 1 can be dated to *c.*650 BC, but also contains a secondary burial of about half a century later. Practices of burial both by inhumation and by incineration have been found in the tombs. In the latter cases the remains were deposited in fine alabaster funerary jars. Goods found in tombs 4 and 2 (excavated prior to its destruction) indicate a date of around 600 BC for their construction, and this seems to mark the latest period of the building of such monuments. Their reuse for burials, either intrusively or by descendants of the original builders, may have continued thereafter; at least until the disappearance of the settlement on the opposite bank. Finds from the site may be seen in the Museo de MÁLAGA (Calle San Agustín, 8).

On the Morro de Mezquitilla, across the river, traces of a **Phoenician factory** were discovered in 1964, and the site excavated in 1967. Following on from a Late Neolithic and Bronze Age occupation of this hill, a Phoenician settlement dating to around the mid-7th cent. BC was established. This seems to have continued in being into the late 6th- or early 5th cent. BC. There were also traces of use of the site in the Roman period, but the exact chronology of this is not clear.

Turégano   Arab and Christian fortress

Head north-west from SEGOVIA on the CL 601 in the direction of Valladolid; after 9.5 km. turn right onto the C 603, which leads 24.5 km. to Turégano.

An interesting but poorly recorded and little studied site, this consists of a small **Late Medieval castle**, probably built by Bishop Juan Arias Dávila of Segovia (1461–97) around the 13th-cent. church of San Miguel. Bishop Dávila's castle consists of a rectangular set of low battlemented walls, with circular corner towers and a ditch. He also constructed a massive tripartite tower over the triple-apsed east end of the church. In 1498–1501 the bishop's successor, Juan Arias de Villar (1498–1512), continued the work by fortifying the nave of the church with ornate battlements, three narrow but high circular towers on the west end, another tower in the middle of the north wall, and an elaborate fortified gateway on the south side, with a balcony between its two towers. A circular tower was inserted into the centre of the church by Bishop Diego Rivera (1512–43), to the top of which was added a baroque bellcote.

Much less well preserved are an **outer line of walls**, constructed of *tabiya* (rammed earth), probably of Islamic date. Little of the wall stands above a few metres, but three towers on the north-west side give good indications of the methods of construction and style of this earliest part of the fortress. A date in the 10th cent. is most probable, though little is known of the history of this castle, which must have fallen into Castilian hands no later than 1085, when Alfonso VI captured SEGOVIA. There seems to have been a royal palace in Turégano in the Late Middle Ages, probably located in this fortress, as the presence of various kings of the Trastámara dynasty is recorded here on a number of occasions from 1390 to 1474. Excavation should reveal more of this unusual site.

Continue on the C 603, the SG 231, and the C 112 for about 28 km. in a direct line to **Sepúlveda** *(Roman Septempublica), where a small castle is located immediately behind the Ayuntamiento in the Plaza Mayor.*

Some of the medieval walls survive and the gorge of the Río Duratón makes a dramatic curve around the northern edge of the town. Asturian chronicles record the depopulation of the town in the time of Alfonso I (739–57), and according to 11th- and 12th-cent. annals it was re-occupied in 940 by Count Fernán González of Castile. There are several Romanesque churches, notably El Salvador of 1093.

Ullastret   Iberian town

From Gerona/Girona take the N II north for 4 km. and turn east onto the C 255 and continue on this for about 25 km., until about 1.5 km. beyond La Bisbal d'Empordà the GE 644 leads northwards (left) to Ullastret. The site, which is signposted, is just north-east of the town.

This 11-ha. site is the best example of an Iberian town so far uncovered in Spain. Finds from the Late Neolithic/Chalcolithic and Early Bronze Ages have proved the existence of earlier occupation of this site and the surrounding area. The site of the Iberian settlement of Indika, the settlement of the Indiketes, is located on a small hill, the Puig de Sant Andreu. It is only 14 km. from AMPURIAS and may have developed thanks to the presence of the Greek commercial centre. Its origins may date to the late 7th cent. BC, as imported Greek wares of that period have been found on the site, but its cultural and economic apogee seems to have been in the later 6th and 5th cents. It was abandoned by the end of the 3rd cent., around the time of the Second Punic War. The establishment of the Roman fortress at Ampurias in 218 BC and rapid Roman domination of the area may have contributed to its abandonment. The fortifications, internal organization of the settlement, and plans of the houses, together with the porticoed market-place, indicate strong Greek influence. Many of the finds from the site also testify to the impact of the Greek presence at Ampurias. Significant remains of the outer walls, built around 500 BC, which extend for 880 m. and still stand up to 4 m. high, may be seen. Seven gates have been found, and the walls were defended by still visible solid round towers. The acropolis, on which the main religious and political buildings once stood, became the site of the medieval castle, but some traces of the Iberian sanctuaries have been found around it. The central square has yet to be excavated, but traces of domestic buildings and streets may be seen in various areas within the walls. It is as the find-site of large quantities of **imported Greek, mainly Attic, ceramics** that Ullastret is famous. These include mid-5th-cent. BC late black-figure cups, and the low twin-handled cups known as 'Castulo cups', which appear in 4th-cent. contexts. It has been suggested that these latter, which normally are assigned to the late 5th cent., may have been imported via southern Italy and Sicily.

There is small site museum in the upper part of the former town, established in a 14th-cent. chapel.

Uxama Roman town

*As you approach El Burgo de Osma from the west on the N 122 (**Valladolid** to **Soria**), the site is on top of the hill to the north immediately before the town is reached. A path on the left of the road leads to the hilltop.*

A Celtiberian settlement of the Arevaci, Uxama supported Sertorius in his rebellion in the 70s BC, and following his death was conquered by Pompey. Excavations have continued on the site since 1976. Centuries of erosion and of agricultural use of this site have limited the amount of information that it can now provide. The site of the forum, built in the reign of Tiberius

Adoptionism

This was the theological argument that spoke of Christ's humanity as being adoptive, developed by Bishop Elipandus of Toledo during a conflict with a heretical group in Al-Andalus in the 780s. In the Frankish empire its most influential exponent was Bishop Felix of Urgell (d. 818). It was criticized by the Asturian abbot Beatus, and condemned by the Papacy and by the Frankish bishops at the Council of Frankfurt in 794.

(AD 14–37), has been located, though little is now known of the public buildings that surrounded it. Some of the terrace on which the forum was located has been exposed, as have elements of a double *cryptoporticus* that formed part of it. The presence of a temple and shops has been deduced. Two major cisterns are located close to the forum, which have yielded up finds of early 1st-cent. AD date. An excavation was conducted in 1913 of what was then thought to be a temple; this has now been reinterpreted as a basilica, and it seems as if the creation of a second forum, or of a replacement of the original forum by a new one, took place in the Flavian period (AD 69–96). A number of houses, including one to the south-east of Late Imperial date, have been located and studied. It appears that the town developed principally in the Julio-Claudian period, but it may have expanded, or perhaps its centre moved, in the 4th cent. A bishopric existed here throughout the Visigothic period, but whether the ecclesiastical sites were located in or close to the Roman town or down in the valley below is unknown. A Bishop Etherius of Osma joined the Asturian abbot Beatus in opposing the Adoptionist theology of Elipandus of Toledo in the 780s. His existence may hint at that of a surviving Christian community here in the same period.

On the south side of the N 122 between the site of Uxama and the town of El Burgo is situated the castle of Osma.

One of the towers, known as the *Torre de Agua* ('Water Tower'), of the outer or third curtain wall is situated beside the road, but the rest of the fortress is on top of the hill. This upper part consists of a double enceinte, of which sections of the walls and one tower still stand. The size of the site, which has yet to be excavated, suggests this was the location of an **Islamic frontier fortress** and settlement, replacing Roman Uxama. This Arab fortress of Osma was captured by King García of León in 912, but changed hands again on various occasions in the 10th cent. It was surrendered to Count Sancho García of Castile in 1011, but a Christian repopulation of the settlement was first undertaken by Alfonso VI in 1088, following his conquest of Toledo in 1085. In the early 12th cent. a new settlement was begun on the site of the present town, and a **cathedral** was founded in

Beatus of Liébana

Abbot of the Asturian monastery of Liébana, Beatus took the lead in Spain, along with Bishop Eterius of Osma, in criticizing the Adoptionist theology of Elipandus of Toledo. He is also, most probably, the author of a large *Commentary on the Apocalypse*, derived from a wide range of sources, which was written around 776. Some of the 9th–12th-cent. manuscripts of this work are notable for a distinctive series of illustrations.

1110. The present cathedral was begun in 1232: as well as the building and the tomb of San Pedro de Osma (1258) see a fine if late manuscript of the *Commentary on the Apocalypse* of Beatus of Liébana, dated 1086. The castle, however, continued in occupation throughout the Middle Ages and displays work from a wide range of periods, and is in need of study. The castle overlooks a medieval bridge over the Río Ucero on the N 122.

Valeria (Cuenca) Roman town

*On the N 320 to Albacete, 8 km. south of **Cuenca**, a right turning onto the CU 712 leads 27 km. to the village of Valera de Arriba. The site is just over 1 km. beyond the village, to the left of the road.*

A Roman town on an earlier site, this settlement continued to be occupied throughout the Visigothic period, when it was the seat of a bishopric (recorded as late as 693). Like its not too distant neighbour RECCOPOLIS (90 km. north-east), it may have continued in occupation well into the 8th cent., but is likely to have been abandoned by the end of it. Remains of a castle and of the ruined Romanesque church of Santa María testify to the reuse of some of the site following Alfonso VIII's conquest of Cuenca in 1182.

Excavations on this site have been undertaken since 1974, concentrating primarily on the area of the forum. Compared with such sites as BAELO, all too little has survived, but this is still one of the most studied and earliest of the Roman *fora* of central Spain. Under the artificial platform of the forum (86 × 80 m.), the earliest feature of the site, constructed in an otherwise steeply angled location between two hills, have been found four cisterns (21.5 × 3 m. each), dating probably from the reign of Claudius (AD 41–54). Two of these were known prior to the modern excavations, as was the ruin of a probably Late Republican Nymphaeum, located along the eastern edge of the forum, and possibly representing the only part of the site never completely buried. The Nymphaeum (55 m. long) is a vaulted gallery housing the canal used to feed a long monumental fountain via a series of openings that take the form of alternating rectangular and semicircular niches. At a lower level in front of the

Nymphaeum, but not extending as far as it does, are a group of thirteen rooms (11.5 × 4 m. each) that have been interpreted as once forming shops, datable to the time of Augustus (27 BC–AD 14). These appear to have been reused in the Late Imperial period. Above them on a platform at the level of the Nymphaeum may once have stood an ornamental patio, giving a commanding view eastwards, and in which the waters of the Nymphaeum would have flowed out of the alternating niches.

Along the northern side of the forum, immediately at the foot of the hill of La Horca, lies a basilica (44 × 19 m.), excavated from 1976 onwards, of which the bases of the internal arcades may be seen. Although the dating is not entirely certain, it looks at least as if it received its definitive form around the reign of Claudius. This building seems to have lost its original function by the end of the 3rd cent. AD.

On the west side of the forum have been discovered a group of rooms located over a hemispherical foundation, probably forming part of an earlier building. The rooms appear from their techniques of construction to be originally of Augustan date, but were subjected to much rebuilding and reuse as late as the 4th cent. The nature of what lay beneath them is not clear, but there may have been a portico in front of them facing across the forum. To the south of the forum, although some traces of a structure have been found, little has so far materialized.

Finds from the site may be seen in the archaeological section of the Museo de Cuenca (Calle Obispo Valero, 6, Cuenca). Part of a small column carved with stylized geometric and floral decoration, dating from the Visigothic period, is displayed in the Museo Arqueológico Nacional in MADRID. This probably came from a so far unlocated church of that time.

Zaragoza   Roman and Islamic cities   ★

The oldest evidence of settlement in the centre of the present city belongs to the Early Iron Age, in the form of some 7th-cent. BC finds made in the Calle Gavín-Sepulcro. Despite some earlier doubts, it now seems certain that this was also the location of the subsequent Celtiberian town of Salduia (3rd–2nd cents. BC). Finds from this period were made in the Calle Echegaray y Caballero, the Calle de D. Jaime I, and the Calle del Sepulcro, amongst others. In the last of these the line of a wall of Celtiberian construction was discovered, near to the episcopal palace. All of the sites of this period are located in the north-west corner of the old city centre close to the river bank, and this must be where the town was situated. Amongst the most interesting finds of this period is a granite statue of Egyptian origin, found in the river bank in front of the church of San Juan de los Panetes. Although unique as an item of its kind in the Iberian penninsula, this is further testimony to eastern Mediterranean contacts, mediated through the Phoenicians. The town, previously known to the Romans as Salduba, was made into a *colonia* for veterans of the

Cantabrian War by Augustus (27 BC–AD 14), under the title of
Caesaraugusta. It was still in imperial hands when visited by the Emperor
Majorian in 460, but was incorporated into the Visigothic kingdom of
Euric (466–84) in 477. It was the seat of a bishopric, whose most notable
holder was Braulio (631–51), friend of Isidore of Seville (d. 636). In 714
the city was sacked by the Arabs. Its local Arab rulers appealed to the
Frankish ruler Charlemagne for help in 777 when faced by the rising
power of ʿAbd al-Raḥmān I (756–88), but he was refused admission when
he led an army into the Ebro valley in 778, and the city soon fell into
Umayyad control, under which it became one of the principal centres of
the *Ṭagr al-ʿalā* or Upper March. Following the collapse of the Umayyad
caliphate in 1031 the Tujibid dynasty, formerly governors of the *Ṭagr*,
made Zaragoza (Sarakusta) their capital. The city was taken by Alfonso I
of Aragón in 1118. It thereafter became a major centre of the Aragonese
monarchy, but was eclipsed politically and economically by the Catalan
coastal cities of BARCELONA and Valencia.

The Roman City

The roughly rectangular outline of the Roman city of Caesaraugusta can
still be made out from a map of the modern street plan of Zaragoza. The
city, then as now, fronted to the north onto the River Ebro. Its southern
extent is defined by the Calle del Coso. Quite a lot of the pattern of Roman
streets can be made out from their modern replacements. The *Cardo
Maximus*, the main north–south thoroughfare, is now paralleled by the
Calle de D. Jaime I, while the *Decumanus* is even more closely paralleled
by the line of the Calle Espoz y Mina/Calle Mayor. The forum was probably situated immediately south-west of the junction of these two Roman
roads; a view substantiated by the discovery of a civic basilica datable to
the reign of Augustus under the Palacio de los Pardo (but see below).
Rectilinear arrangements of streets, especially in the south-west corner of
the area of the former Roman city, look like further survivals of early
arrangements. Only in the centre has the Roman grid pattern disintegrated, a process that probably started with the establishment of the earliest Christian sites inside the city in the 4th cent.

Extensive campaigns of excavation were carried out from the later
1980s onwards in the Plaza de la Seo, west of the medieval cathedral and
south of the Basilica del Pilar, which have uncovered part of what appears
to be a **forum**. This is a location further to the north and to the east of that
previously presumed to be its site. Indications from the layout of the
Roman roads and drains in this area indicate a major development in this
part of the city. Probably, as in TARRAGONA and MÉRIDA, there were two
fora in this important settlement, an urban one and a provincial one, serving the economic and administrative needs of the city and of its wider
territory. So far, this site has revealed two wings of twin-arcaded porticoes
with at least thirteen shops on the outer side of the eastern one. What is

more, this is located over a slightly simpler and earlier structure of similar character. There thus appear to be two phases of construction. The date of the first construction of a forum on this site has been placed around 10 BC, with a major rebuilding taking place about AD 10–20. The explanation for the reconstruction seems to lie in difficulties with the drainage of the area, which were rectified in the second phase through the construction of the substantial *cloaca* (drains) still to be seen on the site.

Traces of occupation at a later period have also been found. The two main drains were linked in the 2nd or 3rd cent., but they apparently ceased to be cleaned and probably went out of use by the end of the 4th cent. (It was also at this time that mosaic floors found under the Calles de Torrenueva (nos. 4–6) and D. Jaime I (no. 26) ceased to be used.) Unfortunately, no traces of major structures of later date have been found here, but there have been significant finds of Late Roman and Visigothic pottery. From a 6th-cent. level has come a possible circular grain store that was filled in by the end of the Visigothic period. A stone-faced well of Arab construction has also been found, containing substantial quantities of 10th- and 11th-century pottery, and also a gold coin of the Byzantine emperor Justin II (565–78).

The location of the **Roman theatre** of Caesaraugusta has been shown to be between the Calle de la Verónica and the Calle Pedro Joaquín Soler (a little may be seen). Study of this site has led to the dating of the construction of the theatre to late in the reign of Tiberius (AD 14–37); it was abandoned at some point after the mid-3rd cent., and definitely before the middle of the 4th. You can see traces of a Roman bath house in the Calle de San Juan. This has been dated to the reign of Augustus (27 BC–AD 14).

Islamic and Medieval Sites

In the north-west corner of the old town, adjacent to the church of San Juan de los Panetes (13th-cent. brick tower), a short stretch of Roman wall, of later 3rd-cent. date, has been preserved. This was also once incorporated into the Arab town walls (now destroyed), which once followed the line of the Calle de Coso. Adjacent to the church on the east is the Torre de la Zuda, which once formed part of a fortress of the Taifa kings and that was later the residence of the first Aragonese kings. Roman mosaics have been found here. Jewish baths, dating from the mid-13th cent., have been discovered under houses nos. 126–32 of the Calle de Coso (towards its eastern end).

On the western fringe of the city stands the **Aljafería**, the much reconstructed fortress palace of the second dynasty of Taifa-period rulers of Zaragoza, the Banu Hud (1039–1110). Construction began under Aḥmad ibn Sulaymān al-Muqtadir (1049/50–1082/3), but it was not completed until the reign of his grandson Aḥmad al-Mustaʿīn (1083/4–1110). It was taken over, together with the city, by the Almoravids in 1110, and fell to

Alfonso I the Battler of Aragón in 1118. An occasional palace of the Aragonese rulers, its subsequent employment included periods serving as headquarters of the Inquisition in Aragón from 1485 onwards, and as a barracks in the late 18th cent. It was badly damaged in the French siege of Zaragoza in 1809, and was hospital, prison, and barracks again in the 19th cent. The building is surrounded by the outline of fortifications of the time of Felipe II (1556–98), the eastern part of which have been reduced to their foundations and used ornamentally. The Aljafería itself is roughly 95 m. square, and is surrounded by a dry moat, walled in brick. In its original state as far as this can be gauged (see plan) it had circular towers on each corner, and an unequal number of hemispherical towers on each wall. The northern wall also includes a massive rectangular keep that rises above the level of all of the other defences. The principal entry, via a horse-shoe arch, lies on the east side, and is flanked by two towers higher than those in the corners. There is a modern *mirador* or viewing gallery on top of the whole of the eastern wall, and all the battlements are reconstructions.

The palace within has suffered numerous modifications from the Late Middle Ages onwards and also stringent modern restoration. Relatively little original work survives, but a reasonable impression can be formed of what the central part of the Banu Hud residence may have been like. A series of interconnected porticoed halls and salons in the northern sector are moderately convincing. The most southerly of the porticoes is built around a rectangular pool, which is linked by a channel across the central court of the palace, the Patio de Santa Isabel, to other pools at the southern end. The elaborate interlocking multi-lobed arcading on doubled columns in the northern area is reminiscent of that to be seen in the *maqsura* of Al-Ḥakam II (961–76) in the Mezquita in CÓRDOBA. Although of modern workmanship, these are copied from surviving originals, which may be seen in the Museo Arqueológico Nacional in MADRID. In the centre of the eastern edge of this group of rooms and halls is a small polygonal chamber rising to a height of two storeys, with a scallop-shaped *mihrab* entered via a horseshoe arch in its south-east corner. This was the ruler's private mosque, for his performance, while in the palace, of the required five daily acts of prayer. The public mosque was probably on the site in the main courtyard now occupied by a church. Substantial changes were made to the interior in the reign of Fernando II of Aragón (1479–1516) and Isabel of Castile (1474–1504). To this period dates the monumental stairway (1492) and the throne room, whose elaborate wooden-coffered ceiling incorporates their heraldic badges.

Glossary

aedes Augusti: 'house of Augustus', a term used to refer to the shrine of the imperial cult, where offerings would be made both to the memory of the divinized founding emperor (Augustus) and also for the health and safety of his current successor. This was normally located on or by the forum.

Al-Andalus: a name, of disputed origin, used by the Arabs to refer to that part of the Iberian peninsula (primarily the south and the centre) under their rule.

alcázar: Hispanic word for an Arab fortress (from the Arabic al-qasr).

aljibe: an Arab fresh-water cistern. Good early examples exist at **Mérida** and **Cáceres**.

Almohads: a Berber ruling dynasty and its following that replaced the Amoravids in both North Africa and Spain; see the Introduction.

Almoravids: a Berber ruling dynasty and its followers; see the Introduction.

Amir: 'king', i.e. an Islamic ruler with secular authority over his subjects.

amphitheatre: a place of large-scale public entertainment, oval in shape with raked seating, that was normally used for gladiatorial and beast fights. They were usually built entirely of stone, but some early examples were wooden on stone foundations. The Colosseum in Rome is the largest and best-known example of such a building. Several of them, e.g. the one at Nîmes in France, are known to have been transformed into fortresses in the Early Middle Ages. Good examples in Spain may be seen at **Mérida** and **Itálica**.

amphora (pl.: amphorae): a large Roman coarse-ware-pottery container with a round or pointed bottom, usually used for the storage and transportation of liquids such as olive oil and wine, and of *garum*. Finds of Spanish-made amphorae, e.g. in the vicinity of Rome and in the Rhineland, give important indications of the patterns of trade that existed within the Empire.

apodyterium: the changing-room in a Roman public bath house.

ashlar: carefully cut and squared-off blocks of stone, used in the best buildings. In some cases (e.g. at **Los Vascos**) walls were constructed of two parallel facings of ashlar with the space between being filled with rubble.

atalaya: Arab watch tower. These nearly always formed part of a complex network, in which each tower was in sight of its neighbour.

atrium: a courtyard, open to the sky, surrounded by a peristyle, and usually having a central pool or fountain, that provided a major feature in Roman villas, and around which the main public rooms, such as the *triclinium*, were arranged. In larger and more sumptuous villas there might be more than one atrium, with the family's private quarters being concentrated around a secondary, more secluded one.

baldachino: a canopy over an altar, supported on four columns (or suspended from the ceiling).

ballista: a large Roman catapult on a stand that fired large iron bolts.

Berbers: indigenous North African tribal peoples of distinct ethnic and linguistic origin, involved in the Arab conquest of Spain in 711. More

Berbers were recruited as mercenaries by Al-Manṣūr in the late 10th cent., and some of them formed Taifa kingdoms in the 11th.

burj: a tower, of relatively simple design, used as a local place of refuge in the Umayyad period.

Caesar: the title given to a junior Roman emperor from the 2nd cent. onwards.

caldarium: hot-water bath room in a private or public bath house.

Caliph: 'Successor' (to the Prophet Muḥammad). This title conferred spiritual as well as political leadership of the Muslim community. It was first used in Al-Andalus by ʿAbd al-Raḥmān III in 929, and retained by his successors until 1031.

cardo: the general name for a minor street in a Roman town running at right angles to the *Decumanus Maximus*. The *Cardo Maximus* was one of the two main roads, and bisected the settlement. running north–south.

castellum aquae: Roman water tower.

cavea: the area of seating of a Roman theatre or amphitheatre.

cist/cists: funerary chambers formed out of slabs of stone placed on their ends to form a rectangular chest. In some cases these would be covered by other horizontal stones.

collegium: a corporate body, e.g. a guild of merchants or a youth organization, and the building used by it.

colonia: Initially this would have been a settlement, usually of veterans from the army, to whose inhabitants the emperor gave the status of Roman citizens. Although initially associated with settlements founded after the Punic and Cantabrian Wars, in the 1st cent. AD it became increasingly common for this status to be granted to successful *municipia*. The distinctions in classes of citizenship ceased when Caracalla (211–17) granted Roman citizenship to all free-born inhabitants of the empire.

columbarium: ('dovecot') a funerary building, in whose interior there would be a series of niches for placing urns containing cremations: thus (slightly) resembling the nesting-boxes of the traditional dovecot.

conventus: In the early Roman Empire this was a grouping of towns whose inhabitants enjoyed full Roman citizenship. The capital of the *conventus* served as the judicial centre for the region.

cryptoporticus: an enclosed gallery.

curia: the name of both the muncipal council that ran a Roman town, and of the building in which it met. The latter would be located in close proximity to the forum.

Decumanus Maximus: one of the two main roads in a Roman town, the other being the *Cardo Maximus*. It ran from east to west, and would normally bisect the *Cardo Maximus* or *Via Principalis* near the forum.

exedra: an apse, i.e. a semicircular end or side of a building.

forum: the principal public area of a Roman town, where the main temples, the law courts, markets, shops, and administrative offices would be located. In particular the term is used of the open central court, usually artificially flattened, around which these buildings were placed.

fresco: a form of painting in which water-based pigments are applied directly onto freshly laid plaster. This was used extensively in the Roman period for the decoration of the interior walls of the principal rooms of a villa.

frigidarium: the sector of a bath house (public or private) in which the cold plunge baths were located.

fueros: a set of local laws and privileges conceded by the monarch or a major landowner to the inhabitants of a new settlement. They were often given as an inducement to form such a settlement.

garum: Roman sauce that was highly regarded as a culinary and digestive aid, made from decomposed and salted fish blood and guts. Spain was a major producer, and a number of salting tanks have been found at sites along the south coast, indicating the presence of *garum* factories.

Hajīb: the chief minister of the Umayyad state, in charge of the administration. Al-Manṣūr (d. 1002) used this post to achieve dictatorial power under a child Caliph, Hishām II.

hamman: Arab bath house. It was very similar in principle to that of the Romans, in that it combined steam baths and hot and cold pools. (Its modern equivalent is the Turkish bath.)

hippodrome: Roman race course, for both chariot and horse racing. Substantial remains of these may be seen in Spain, at **Mérida** and **Toledo**.

ḥiṣn (pl.: *ḥuṣūn*): garrisoned fortresses. These were regularly distributed over at least some areas of Al-Andalus in the Umayyad period.

hypocausts: small piles of cemented tiles, or arches of brick, used to support floors under which steam was circulating. They were mainly to be found under the *caldarium* of a bath house, but in some sumptuous villas the circulation of steam was employed more extensively to provide a form of under-floor central heating. This could also be extended up the walls through flues in the brickwork.

hypogeum: a cellar or underground room (cf. Vitruvius VI. xi).

impluvium: a pool. This was notably a feature to be found in the middle of an *atrium*.

imposts: supports protruding from a wall on which the ends of an arch rested.

insula (pl.: *insulae*): a block of buildings surrounded by streets in a Roman town.

'Latin citizenship': the right to the *Ius Latii* or 'Law of Latium', the second level of citizenship, originally conceded to the towns of Latium. The highest level, with the fullest legal privileges, was that of Roman citizenship. The distinction was abolished by Caracalla (211–17).

liquamen: another word for *garum*, the Roman fish sauce.

macellum: a covered-market building, divided up into stalls and alleys.

maqsura: the section of mosque, close to the *mihrab*, reserved for a ruler and his family.

martyrium: a chapel or shrine erected in the Late Roman period over the burial place of a Christian martyr, where his or her relics would be venerated, and which might become a centre of pilgrimage. From the 5th cent. onwards such relics were frequently translated from the cemeteries outside the towns to intramural churches.

mihrab: niche in the wall of the *quibla* indicating the direction of Mecca towards which worshippers should face in order to pray. In the grander mosques it could be elaborately shaped and decorated (e.g. in the Mezquita in Córdoba).

mirador: Spanish term for a viewpoint or platform built for the sake of the view it affords.

mithraeum: a shrine of the god Mithras, a saviour divinity of Iranian origin, whose worship was popular in the Roman army in the 3rd cents. Worship was secret, and rites included the *taurobolium*, in which the devotee was showered with the blood of a dying bull. No actual *mithraeum* has been found in Spain, but the existence of several, including one in Mérida, has been deduced from inscriptions.

Moriscos, the: the population of the former Nazirid kingdom of Granada, who in 1502 were forced to choose between conversion to Christianity or expulsion to North Africa. Those who converted and stayed were responsible for a series of revolts in the 16th cent., and the majority of them were finally expelled from Spain in 1609–10.

Mozarabs/Mozarabic: although in Arab sources the term is used of indigenous converts to Islam who became culturally arabized, in modern parlance it tends to refer to Christians in Al-Andalus who absorbed much of the linguistic and material culture of the Arabs. Several Mozarab monastic and lay communities migrated north to the Christian kingdoms in the late 9th and 10th cents. Most of the remainder were expelled to North Africa by the Almoravids in 1126.

Mudéjar: an artistic and architectural style deriving from Islamic traditions that was widespread in the territories conquered by the Christian monarchs in the centre and south of Spain in the 12th–14th cents. Even in the north (e.g. the monastery of Las Hulegas, Burgos) it is possible to see examples of Mudéjar workmanship, including the decorative use of cufic script.

municipium: a settlement of the indigenous population, enjoying a status, given by imperial grant, which conferred the privileges of Roman citizenship on its magistrates and those of the lesser Latin citizenship on the rest of the inhabitants.

nymphaeum: a shrine to the nymphs. The latter are minor female divinities, of which there are various kinds, including the *Naiads* who preside over water, lakes, and springs, and the *Napaiae* who are the nymphs of mountain valleys.

octastyle temple: a classical temple with an eight-columned façade.

opus sectile: paving made from small stones set to form patterns.

opus signinum: decorative plasterwork for walls, made from lime and fragments of pots. It takes its name from the Latin town of Signia (modern Segni).

orthogonal: right-angled or rectangular.

parador: a member of a chain of Spanish state-run hotels, many of which are built in former medieval castles and monasteries.

peristyle: A passageway, opened on one side by the use of arcading, that would be found around the edge of an *atrium* or, on larger scale, surrounding part of a forum. It thus provided both a sheltered route around or immediate access into the open central space.

piscina: a swimming pool.

praesidium: garrison headquarters.

praetorium: the official residence of a provincial governor.

quibla: the southern wall of a mosque where the principal features—the *mihrab*, the *maqsura* and the imam's *mimbar* (pulpit)—would be located.

qura: an administrative region of the Umayyad state.

ribat: an early Islamic institution comprising a fortress to which men could come on a voluntary basis, and stay for as long as they wished, to live an ascetic life and fight in the defence of Islam. Such institutions were prevalent in North Africa and Islamic Spain. There is a very fine early example at Sousse in Tunisia.

scaenae frons: the ornamented wall immediately behind the stage of a Roman theatre, which provided both a decorative backdrop and also a location from which celestial characters could appear. It also served as the outer wall of the theatre, and in some Spanish cases (e.g. **Mérida**) overlooked a large porticoed plaza.

Serapeum: the temple to Serapis in Alexandria.

spina: the central spine of a hippodrome, around which horses and chariots were raced.

sudatoria* or *laconicum: the steam baths in a Roman public or private bath house. The floor would have been heated from the furnace room via the hypocausts, and when water was thrown on it steam would be produced. The bather's skin would be oiled and then the sweat (and dirt) which had been brought to the surface by the steam would be scraped off with the aid of a curved bronze instrument called a *strigil*, prior to his proceeding into the *frigidarium*.

***tabiya* or 'rammed earth'**: (cf. Spanish tapial: 'cement') an Arab style of construction, involving the making of walls of compacted earth, built around a containing wooden scaffolding. In consequence of this method of building, such walls always display a uniform pattern of parallel rows of small holes, where the scaffolding once stood. This was a technique widely used in North Africa, and can appear both in buildings of the Umayyad period and again in Almohad constructions. The survival of fortresses such as **El Vacar**, built entirely in this fashion, indicates the strength of this technique.

tablinum: a large reception room in a Roman villa that served as a study or in some cases as a private gallery for the display of sculptures.

tepidarium: the warm water (as opposed to hot—see *caldarium*) bath section of a bath house. The pools were heated from the main furnace through flues that first served the *caldarium*, which required the most intense degree of heat.

terra sigillata: a high quality red pottery with a particularly hard and shiny surface, usually decorated with moulded figures.

tetrapylon: a gateway with four towers, thus having entries facing in four directions.

Tetrarchic: relating to the period of the Tetrarchy (286–313), when the Roman Empire was divided between four emperors, with two normally holding the higher title of Augustus and two the junior title of Caesar.

tetrastyle temple: a classical temple with a four-columned arcade across its front.

torres albarranas: towers on the outside of and detached from the walls of a castle or town, but linked to them by a bridge at the upper level. These produced fighting platforms set well ahead of the walls, from which it was easier to defend them. Their dating is controversial. Some scholars see them as being introduced as early as the 9th cent.; others would see them only as a 12th/13th-cent. development.

triclinium: the dining-room in a Roman villa. This was normally to be found to one side of the *atrium* and opening directly onto the passage that surrounded it. In some villas in Spain, due to the variation in climate between the seasons, there would be a second, fully enclosed winter *triclinium*.

tympanum: the space between the lintel of a doorway and the arch above it.

Vaubanesque: in the style of Sebastian Le Prestre de Vauban (1633–1707). He was the military architect of the reign of Louis XIV, famous for his complex geometrically shaped fortifications.

villa: a Roman house, either urban or rural. A wide variety of styles and degrees of comfort and luxury are encompassed within the single category. By the Early Middle Ages the term is to be found in legal documents as applying to a whole estate rather than just to a building.

Visigothic period: AD 409–711; see the Introduction.

vomitoria: the passages and tunnels in an amphitheatre or theatre whereby the audience reached the seating (*cavea*).

Chronology to AD 1248

BC

c.1.8–1.6 million	possible first appearance of hominids in Spain
c.300,000	beginning of the Lower or Early Palaeolithic (or Stone Age)
c.100,000–c.40,000	the Middle Palaeolithic
c.40,000–c.10,000	the Upper or Late Palaeolithic
c.10,000–c.5000	the Mesolithic (Middle Stone Age)
c.5000–c.2500	the Neolithic (New Stone Age)
c.2500–c.1700	the Chalcolithic or 'Copper Age'*
c.1700–c.1200	the Early Bronze Age*
c.1200–c.700	the Middle and Later Bronze Ages*
c.800/700–c.200	the pre-Roman Iron Age*

*These dates apply to Spain; other parts of Europe and the Mediterranean saw these periods begin at slightly different points, according to the diffusion of the knowledge of these technologies

814	traditional date of the foundation of Carthage (more likely c.750)
c.780	beginning of Phoenician trading settlements on the south coast
c.600	legendary foundation of Rhode (modern Rosas) by the Rhodians (more likely to be 4th cent.)
c.600	Phocaean Greeks found Massilia (Marseille)
c.600/580	the Phocaeans found the *palaiopolis* (old town) at Ampurias
c.570	foundation of the *neapolis* (new town) of Ampurias
mid-6th cent.	decline of the Phoenician settlements
247–241	First Punic War
by 237	Carthaginian conquest of most of Spain south of the Ebro
218	Carthaginian attack on Sagunto, resulting in:
218–201	Second Punic War; ejection of Carthaginians from Spain
206, 205	revolts against Rome by the Ilergetes suppressed
205	foundation of Itálica
197–178	revolts by and Roman campaigns against the indigenous peoples in north-east and central Spain
197	Roman Spain divided into the two provinces of Citerior ('Nearer') and Ulterior ('Further')
195–94	M. Porcius Cato's Spanish campaign: Rhode sacked
180–78	governorship of Tiberius Gracchus in the province of Hispania Citerior
179	victory over the Lusitani by Lucius Postumius Albinus
178	treaty between Gracchus and the Celtiberians
155–133	the Celtiberian and Lusitanian Wars
151	Lusitanian victory over Servius Sulpicius Galba, governor of Hispania Ulterior
147	Lusitanian victory under Viriathus at Tribola: c.10,000 Romans killed
146	destruction of Carthage by Scipio Aemilianus

141	Viriathus' victory over Quintus Fabius Maximus at Erisana
139	murder of the Lusitanian leader Viriathus
138–136	Roman expedition into Galicia
137	Roman army surrenders to the Numantines
134–133	siege and sack of Numantia by Scipio Aemilianus
82–72	Sertorian War
72–61	Lusitanian raids
49–45	civil war between Caesar and Pompey; partly fought in Spain
46	Gnaeus Pompeius lands in Spain; campaigns in the south
45	victory of Caesar at battle of Munda; execution of Gnaeus Pompeius
27–AD 14	reign of Augustus, first Roman emperor
29–27	planning of Cantabrian War
27–22	Cantabrian War
25	foundation of Augusta Emerita (Mérida)
19	last Cantabrian revolt suppressed

AD

14–37	reign of Tiberius, under whom several Spanish cities are endowed with new public buildings
41–54	reign of Claudius; further imperial patronage of Spanish towns
68	Galba, governor of Hispania Citerior, becomes emperor
69	reign of Vitellius; grant of municipal status to some Spanish towns
69–96	Flavian dynasty in Rome; much patronage of Spanish towns and grants of municipal status
98–117	reign of Trajan, born in Itálica
117–38	reign of Hadrian, also from Itálica
193–235	rule of the Severan dynasty in Rome
249–51	reign of Trajan Decius; persecution of Christians
253–60	reign of Valerian; persecution of Christians (257–9)
259/60	Franks and Alamans raid Gaul and north-east Spain, possibly sacking Tarragona
260–9	reign of Postumus over an independent Gallic Empire, including Spain and Britain
269–71	reign of Victorinus in the Gallic Empire; Spain recovered by the legitimate emperor Claudius II Gothicus (270–2)
c.277	Frankish raids on Gaul, possibly extending to Spain
285–305	reign of Diocletian; 'Great Persecution' begun in 303
306–37	reign of Constantine the Great
312	Constantine's conversion to Christianity
350	overthrow of Constans (possibly buried at Centcelles nr. Tarragona)
376	Visigoths enter the Roman Empire
379–95	reign of Theodosius I, from Spain, over Eastern Roman Empire
406	Vandals, Alans, and Sueves cross the Rhine
407–10	usurper Constantine III rules part of Spain
409	Vandals, Alans, and Sueves enter Spain
410	sack of Rome by the Visigoths, who move into Gaul in 411
417–18	Visigoths campaign in Spain for the Empire
418–30	Hasding Vandals dominant in Iberian peninsula
429	Vandals and Alans invade North Africa

430–56	Sueves dominant in Iberian peninsula, except for the north-east
455	murder of Valentinian III; end of the dynasty of Theodosius
456	Theoderic II (453–66) and the Visigoths invade Spain and defeat Suevic king Rechiarius (448–56)
466–84	reign of Euric, who completes the Visigothic conquest of the peninsula
507	battle of Vouillé; Alaric II (484–507) defeated by the Frankish king Clovis; loss of most of Visigothic kingdom in Gaul
511–26	Visigothic kingdom ruled by viceroys of the Ostrogothic king Theoderic the Great (493–526)
551	revolt of Athanagild leads to Byzantine seizure of south-east coast
561	First Council of Braga, marking conversion of the Suevic kingdom in Galicia to Catholicism
569–86	reign of Visigothic king Leovigild, who reunites most of the peninsula
589	Third Council of Toledo: conversion of the Visigoths from Arianism to Catholicism
c.600–36	episcopate of Isidore of Seville
624	last Byzantine fortresses in south-east fall to Suinthila (621–31)
632	death of the Prophet Muhammad
643	beginning of Arab attacks on the Byzantine and Persian empires
641	Arab conquest of Egypt
647	first Arab raid on North Africa
654	issue of Visigothic law code known as the *Forum Iudicum*
680–90	episcopate of Julian of Toledo
694	Seventeenth Council of Toledo; Egica (687–702) decrees enslavement of most of the Jewish population
698	Arabs take Carthage (completion of their conquest of North Africa)
710	death of Wittiza (692/4–710), followed by civil war
711	Arab invasion and defeat of King Roderic (710–11)
710–13	reign of Agila in north-east
714	Arab conquest of Ebro valley and Catalonia
718(?)	revolt in the Asturias against the Arabs
721	failure of Arab attack on Toulouse
732 or 733	Frankish defeat of an Arab raid in battle of Poitiers
740s	wars between Arabs and Berbers in Spain and North Africa
747–56	rule of Yūsuf b. ʿAbd al-Raḥmān in Spain
750	Abbasid revolt leads to fall of Umayyad Caliphate in Syria
756	Umayyad seizure of power in Al-Andalus under ʿAbd al-Raḥmān I (756–88)
778	Charlemagne's expedition to the Ebro, and defeat at Roncesvalles
781	beginning of the construction of the Mezquita in Córdoba
791–842	reign of Asturian king Alfonso II the Chaste
801	Frankish capture of Barcelona
806	Franks capture Pamplona
808/10	Franks fail to take and hold Tortosa and Tarragona
824	revolt in Pamplona and defeat of Frankish army in second battle of Roncesvalles leads to the creation of an independent kingdom (later known as Navarre)
839	Council of Córdoba
844	first Viking raid on Spain; Seville looted

851–9	time of the Martyr Movement in Córdoba
878	Wifred I the Hairy becomes Count of Barcelona, establishing a dynasty
880–918	revolt of ʿUmar ibn Hafṣūn in Al-Andalus
886–912	reigns of Amirs Al-Mūndhir and ʿAbd Allah: endemic civil wars in the south; Umayyad power in decline
910	deposition of Alfonso III the Great of Asturias by his sons
912–61	reign of ʿAbd al-Raḥmān III, who restores Umayyad control over all of Al-Andalus
914	León replaces Oviedo as the capital of the Asturian kingdom
927	elimination of the sons of ʿUmar ibn Hafṣūn
929	ʿAbd al-Raḥmān III takes the title of Caliph
939	battle of Simancas: ʿAbd al-Raḥmān defeated by Ramiro II (931–51) of León
mid-10th cent.	Umayyad state at its height
959	Sancho I the Fat of León restored to his throne by Umayyad forces; flight of Ordoño IV the Bad (958–9)
961–76	reign of Caliph al-Ḥakam II
966 and 971	Viking raids in the south
980–1002	ascendancy of the Hajīb Al-Manṣūr in Al-Andalus
985	Al-Manṣūr sacks Barcelona
988	Al-Manṣūr sacks León
997	Al-Manṣūr sacks Santiago de Compostela
1002–6	ascendancy of Al-Manṣūr's son ʿAbd al-Malik; poisoned by his brother
1004–35	reign of Sancho III the Great of Navarre
1008	murder of Al-Manṣūr's son 'Sanchuelo'
1009	deposition of Hisham II; outbreak of civil wars in Al-Andalus
1010	sack of Medina Azahara
1016–23	usurpations of the Caliphate by the Hammudids
1031	end of the Umayyad Caliphate
1035	kingdom of Sancho III divided between his sons
1037	Vermudo III of León killed by Fernando I of Castile
1054	battle of Atapuerca: García Sánchez IV of Navarre killed by his brother Fernando I of León-Castile (1037–65)
1064	French knights take part in Aragonese capture of Barbastro
1085	Castilian capture of Toledo
1086	Almoravid intervention in Spain; their defeat of Alfonso VI of León (1072–1109) at the battle of Zallaqa
1090–4	Almoravid conquest of most of the Taifa kingdoms
1094	Valencia captured by El Cid (d. 1099)
1118	Alfonso I the Battler (1104–34) takes Zaragoza
1128–37	Portuguese revolt against Alfonso VII of León (1126–57)
1137–62	kingdom of Aragón ruled by Petronilla and Ramón Berenguer IV of Barcelona; their son becomes King Alfonso II (1162–96)
1137	independent kingdom of Portugal recognized by León-Castile; ruled by Afonso Henriques (1128–85).
1147	overthrow of the Almoravids in North Africa by the Almohads
1158	founding of the Order of Calatrava

1195	Alfonso VIII of Castille (1158–1214) defeated at Alarcos by the Almohads
1212	Castilian and Aragonese victory over the Almohads at the battle of Las Navas de Tolosa
1213	Pere II of Aragón (1196–1213) killed at battle of Muret; collapse of Aragonese–Catalan power in south-west France
1229	Mallorca conquered by Jaume I (1213–76) of Aragón–Catalonia
1230–1	collapse of Almohad rule in Al-Andalus
1230–1492	rule of the Nazirid (Nasrid) dynasty in Granada
1236	Córdoba falls to Fernando III of Castile-León
1248	Fernando III takes Seville

Select Bibliography

Prehistoric

Actas del Congreso, 'Homenaje a Luís Siret (1934–1984)' (Seville, 1986).
Bahn, Paul, *Pyrenean Prehistory* (Warminster, 1984).
El Calcolítico a debate (Seville, 1995).
Chapman, Robert, *Emerging Complexity: The Later Prehistory of South-East Spain, Iberia and the Western Mediterranean* (Cambridge, 1990).
Euskal Herriaren Historiari Buruzko Biltzarra/Congreso de Historia de Euskal Herria, i. *De los orígenes a la cristianización* (San Sebastián, 1988).
Evolución humana en Europa y los yacimientos de la Sierra de Atapuerca, 2 vols. (Valladolid, 1995).
Fernández Castro, María Cruz, *Iberia in Prehistory* (Oxford, 1995).
Martín, C., Fernández-Miranda, M., Fernández-Posse, M. D., and Gilman, A., 'The Bronze Age of La Mancha', *Antiquity,* 67 (1993), 23–45.
Moure Romanillo, A., and González Sainz, C. (eds.), *El Final del Paleolítico Cantábrico* (Santander, 1995).
Schubart, H. *Die Kultur der Bronzezeit im Südwesten der Iberischen Halbinsel,* 2 vols. (Berlin, 1975).
Waldren, W. H., and Kennard, R. C. (eds.), *Bell Beakers of the Western Mediterranean: Definition, Interpretation, Theory and New Site Data,* BAR int. series, vol. 331 (Oxford, 1987).

Iberian and Punic; Roman Republic (c.700–27 BC)

Almagro-Gorbea, M., and Martín, A. M. (eds.), *Castros y oppida en Extremadura* (Madrid, 1995).
Asensio Esteban, José Angel, *La ciudad en el mundo prerromano en Aragón* (Zaragoza, 1995).
Aubet, M. E., *The Phoenicians and the West: Politics, Colonies and Trade* (Cambridge, 1993).
Barceló, Pedro A., *Karthago und die Iberische Halbinsel vor den Barkiden* (Bonn, 1988).
Blázquez Martínez, José María, *Religiones primitivas de Hispania* (Rome, 1962).
Boardman, John, *The Greeks Overseas: Their Early Colonies and Trade* (2nd edn.; London, 1980).
Galsterer, H., *Untersuchungen zum römischen Städtewesen auf der iberischen Halbinsel* (Berlin, 1971).
García Merino, C., *Uxama I: Campañas de 1976 y 1978* (*EAE* 170; Madrid, 1995).
Harrison, R. J., *Spain at the Dawn of History: Iberians, Phoenicians and Greeks* (London, 1988).

Keay, S. J., 'The "Romanisation" of Turdetania', *Oxford Journal of Archaeology*, 11 (1992), 275–315.

Niemeyer, H. G. (ed.), *Phönizier im Westen* (Cologne, 1979).

Perex Agorreta, María Jesús, *Los Vascones* (Burlada, 1986).

Richardson, J. S., *Hispaniae: Spain and the Development of Roman Imperialism, 218–82 BC* (Cambridge, 1986).

Rouillard, P., *Les Grecs et la Péninsule Ibérique* (Paris, 1991).

Santos Velasco, J. A., *Cambios sociales y culturales en época ibérica: el caso del sureste* (Madrid, 1994).

Seibert, Jacob, *Hannibal* (Darmstadt, 1993).

Shefton, B. B., 'Massalia and Colonization in the North-Western Mediterranean', in G. R. Tsetskhladze and F. de Angelis (eds.), *The Archaeology of Greek Colonization* (Oxford, 1994).

Sopeña Genzor, G., *Etica y ritual: aproximación al estudio de la religiosidad de los pueblos celtibéricos* (Zaragoza, 1995).

Warmington, B. H. *Carthage* (Harmondsworth, 1964).

Texts

Livy:

A. De Sélincourt (trans.), *The War with Hannibal* (Harmondsworth, 1965): bks. XXI–XXX (222–201 BC).

H. Bettenson (trans.), *Rome and the Mediterranean* (Harmondsworth, 1976): bks. XXXI–XLV (201–167 BC).

Polybius:

I. Scott-Kilvert (trans.), *The Rise of the Roman Empire* (Harmondsworth, 1979) (selections).

Roman Empire (27 BC–AD 409)

El Anfiteatro en la Hispania romana (colloquio) (Mérida, 1995).

Aranegui Gascó, C. (ed.), *Los Foros romanos de las provincias occidentales* (Madrid, 1987).

Arce, Javier, *El último siglo de la España romana: 284–409* (Madrid, 1982).

Cortijo Cerezo, M. L., *La administración territorial de la Bética romana* (Córdoba, 1993).

Cunliffe, Barry, and Keay, Simon (eds.), *Social Complexity and the Development of Towns in Iberia, from the Copper Age to the Second Century AD* (Oxford, 1995).

Curchin, Leonard A., *Roman Spain: Conquest and Assimilation* (London, 1991).

Fear, A. T., *Rome and Baetica: Urbanization in Southern Spain c.50 BC–AD 150* (Oxford, 1996).

García y Bellido, A. *Les Religions orientales dans l'Espagne romaine* (Leiden, 1967).

Humphrey, John H., *Roman Circuses* (London, 1986), 337–87.

Keay, S. J., *Roman Spain* (London, 1988).

Montenegro Duque, Angel, et al., *Historia de España*, iii. *España Romana* (Madrid, 1986).

Palol, P. de, *Arqueología cristiana de la España romana* (Madrid and Valladolid, 1967).
——**(ed.),** *Il Reunió d'arqueologia paleocristiana hispànica* (Barcelona, 1982).
Percival, John, *The Roman Villa* (London, 1976).
Potter, T. W., *Towns in Late Antiquity: Iol Caesarea and its Context* (London, 1995). (For comparison with N. Africa.)
Richardson, J. S., *Roman Spain* (Oxford, 1996).
Sillières, P., *Baelo Claudia: une cité romaine de Bétique* (Madrid, 1995).

Visigothic Kingdom (409–711)

Claude, Dietrich, *Adel, Kirche und Königtum im Westgotenreich* (Sigmaringen, 1971).
Collins, Roger, *Early Medieval Spain, 400–1000* (2nd edn.; London, 1995).
Díaz y Díaz, M. C., *Del Isidoro al siglo XI* (Barcelona, 1976).
Ferreiro, Alberto, *The Visigoths in Gaul and Spain A.D. 418–711: A Bibliography* (Leiden, 1988).
García Moreno, Luís, *Historia de España Visigoda* (Madrid, 1989).
Godoy Fernández, C., *Arqueología y liturgia: iglesias hispánicas (siglos IV al VIII)* (Barcelona, 1995).
Hillgarth, J. N., *Visigothic Spain, Byzantium and the Irish* (London, 1985).
***Historia de España Menéndez Pidal* iii,** J. M. Jover Zamora (ed.), *España Visigoda*, 2 vols. (Madrid, 1991).
James, E. (ed.), *Visigothic Spain: New Approaches* (Oxford, 1980).
López Requena, M., and Barroso Cabrera, R., *La Necrópolis de la Dehesa de la Casa: una aproximación al estudio de la época visigoda en la provincia de Cuenca* (Cuenca, 1995).
Orlandis, José, *La vida en España en tiempo de los Godos* (Madrid, 1991).
Ripoll, G., and Velázquez, I., *La Hispania visigoda: del Rey Ataúlfo a Don Rodrigo* (Madrid, 1995).
Thompson, E. A., *The Goths in Spain* (Oxford, 1969).

Islamic (711–1492)

Arié, Rachel, *España musulmana (siglos VIII–XV)* (Barcelona, 1982).
Ashtor, Eliyahu, *The Jews of Moslem Spain,* 2 vols. (Philadelphia, 1973; reprinted 1992).
Chalmeta, Pedro, *Invasión e islamización* (Madrid, 1994).
Collins, Roger, *The Arab Conquest of Spain, 710–797* (rev. edn.; Oxford, 1995).
Dodds, Jerrilynn (ed.), *Al-Andalus: The Art of Islamic Spain* (New York, 1992).
Epalza, Mikel de (ed.), *La Ciudad islámica* (Zaragoza, 1991).
Fletcher, Richard, *Moorish Spain* (London, 1992).
Glick, T. F., *From Muslim Fortress to Christian Castle* (Manchester, 1995).
Guichard, Pierre, *Al-Andalus: estructura antropolológica de una sociedad islámica en occidente* (Barcelona, 1976).
——*La España musulmana: al-Andalus omeya (siglos VIII–XI)* (Madrid, 1995).

Harvey, L. P., *Islamic Spain 1250 to 1500* (Chicago and London, 1990).

Hernández, Miguel Cruz, *El Islam de al-Andalus* (Madrid, 1992).

Historia de España Menéndez Pidal **viii,** J. M. Jover Zamora (ed.), *Los Reinos de Taifa* (Madrid, 1994).

Huici Miranda, Ambrosio, *Las grandes batallas de la Reconquista durante las invasiones africanas* (Madrid, 1956).

Kennedy, Hugh, 'The Muslims in Europe', in Rosamond McKitterick (ed.), *New Cambridge Medieval History,* ii. *c.700–c.900* (Cambridge, 1995), 249–71.

Ladero Quesada, Miguel Angel, *Granada: historia de un país islámico (1232–1571)* (2nd edn.; Madrid, 1979).

Lagardère, Vincent, *Les Almoravides* (Paris, 1989).

Lévi-Provençal, E., *Histoire de l'Espagne musulmane,* 3 vols. (Paris and Leiden, 1950/1).

Lirola Delgado, Jorge, *El poder naval de al-Andalus en época del Califato Omeya* (Granada, 1993).

Manzano Moreno, Eduardo, *La frontera de al-andalus en época de los Omeyas* (Madrid, 1991).

Torres Balbás, L. *Ciudades hispano-musulmanas* (2nd edn.; Madrid, 1985).

Vallvé Bermejo, J., *Nuevas ideas sobre la conquista árabe de España* (Madrid, 1989).

Wasserstein, David, *The Rise and Fall of the Party-Kings* (Princeton, 1985).

Wolf, Kenneth Baxter, *Christian Martyrs in Muslim Spain* (Cambridge, 1988).

Medieval Christian States (711–1492)

Bisson, Thomas N., *The Medieval Crown of Aragon* (Oxford, 1986).

Cavadini, John C., *The Last Christology of the West: Adoptionism in Spain and Gaul, 785–820* (Philadelphia, 1993).

Collins, Roger, *The Basques* (Oxford, 1986). (Covers from Prehistory to the sixteenth century.)

——— 'Spain: The Northern Kingdoms and the Basques', in Rosamond McKitterick (ed.), *New Cambridge Medieval History,* ii. *c.700–c.900* (Cambridge, 1995), 272–89.

Fletcher, Richard, *St. James's Catapult: The Life and Times of Diego Gelmírez of Santiago de Compostela* (Oxford, 1984).

García de Castro Valdés, C., *Arqueología cristiana de la Alta Edad Media en Asturias* (Oviedo, 1995).

Hillgarth, J. N., *The Spanish Kingdoms, 1250–1516,* 2 vols. (Oxford, 1976/8).

Jiménez Esteban, Jorge, *El Castillo medieval español y su evolución* (Madrid, 1995).

Kendrick, T. D., *St. James in Spain* (London, 1960).

Linehan, P., *History and the Historians of Medieval Spain* (Oxford, 1993).

McKay, Angus, *Spain in the Middle Ages: From Frontier to Empire, 1000–1500* (London, 1977).

O'Neill, John P. (ed.), *The Art of Medieval Spain A.D. 500–1200* (New York, 1993).

Proctor, Evelyn S., *Curia and Cortes in León and Castile 1072–1295* (Cambridge, 1980).

Reilly, Bernard F., *The Kingdom of León-Castilla under King Alfonso VI 1065–1109* (Princeton, 1988).

—— *The Conflict of Christian and Muslim Spain 1031–1157* (Oxford, 1992).

Salrach, Josep M., *El procés de formació nacional de Catalunya (segles VIII–IX),* 2 vols. (Barcelona, 1978).

Santos Yanguas, N., *Asturias hasta la época medieval* (Madrid, 1996).

Vones, Ludwig, *Geschichte der Iberischen Halbinsel im Mittelalter 711–1480* (Sigmaringen, 1993).

Linguistic

Wright, Roger, *Late Latin and Early Romance in Spain and Carolingian France* (Liverpool, 1982).

—— **(ed.),** *Latin and the Romance Languages in the Early Middle Ages* (London and New York, 1991).

—— *Early Ibero-Romance* (Newark, Del., 1994).

Abbreviations

BAM	*Boletín de Arqueología Medieval*
BAR int. ser.	*British Archaeological Reports,* international series (Oxford)
Barrucand and Bednorz	Marianne Barrucand and Achim Bednorz, *Moorish Architecture in Andalusia* (Cologne, 1992)
Blagg, Jones, and Keay	T. F. C. Blagg, R. F. J. Jones, and S. J. Keay (eds.), *Papers in Iberian Archaeology,* 2 vols. (Oxford, 1984)
Cunliffe and Keay	Barry Cunliffe and Simon Keay (eds.), *Social Complexity and the Development of Towns in Iberia* (Oxford, 1995)
CIL	*Corpus Inscriptionum Latinorum* ii. *Spain*
EAE	*Excavaciones Arqueológicas en España*
Los Foros	C. Aranegui Gascó (ed.), *Los Foros romanos de las provincias occidentales* (Madrid, 1987)
Keay	S. J. Keay, *Roman Spain* (London, 1988)
Miles	G. C. Miles, *The Coinage of the Visigoths of Spain, Leovigild to Achila II* (New York, 1952)
MM	*Madrider Mitteilungen*
MCV	*Mélanges de la Casa de Velazquez*
Schlunk and Hauschild	Helmut Schlunk and Theodor Hauschild, *Hispania Antiqua. Die Denkmäler der Frühchristlichen und westgotischen Zeit* (Mainz, 1978)
Vives	J. Vives (ed.), *Inscripciones cristianas de la España romana y visigoda* (2nd edn.; Barcelona, 1969)

Sources

AISTRA Achim Arbeiter, 'Die vor- und frühromanische Kirche San Julián y Santa Basilisa de Aistra bei Zalduondo', *MM* 35 (1994), 418–39. ALANGE J. Alvárez, 'Las termas romanas de Alange', *Habis*, 3 (1972), 267–90. ALAVA José Ignacio Vegas, *Dolmenes en Alava: guia para su visita* (Vitoria/Gasteiz, 1983). ALCALÁ DE GUADAIRA Jorge Jiménez Esteban, *El castillo medieval español y su evolución* (Madrid, 1995), 94–6. ALCALA DE HENARES Dimas Fernández Galiano, *Complutum i and ii* (*EAE* 137 and 138; Madrid, 1984) (vol. ii is devoted to the mosaics); Basilio Pavón Maldonado, *Alcalá de Henares medieval: arte islámico y mudéjar* (Madrid and Alcalá, 1982). ALCALÁ LA REAL Pedro Can Avila, *Alcalá la Real en los autores musulmanes* (Jaén, 1990); Angela Mendoza *et al.*, 'Cerro de los Infantes', *MM* 22 (1981), 171–210. ALCÁNTARA F. Gutton, *L'Ordre d'Alcantara* (Paris, 1975); J. Jiménez Esteban, *El Castillo medieval español y su evolución* (Madrid, 1995), 92–3. ALMERÍA Lorenzo Cara Barrionuevo, *La Almería islámica y su alcazaba* (Almeria, 1990); P. Cressier *et al.*, *Estudios de arqueología medieval en Almería* (Almería, 1992)—mainly on rural sites in the vicinity; M. C. Fernández Castro, *Iberia in Prehistory* (Oxford, 1995), 3–32. ALMONASTER LA REAL A. Jiménez Martín, *La Mezquita de Almonaster* (Huelva, 1975). AMPURIAS E. Sanmartí and J. M. Nolla, *Empuries: Guide and Itinerary* (Barcelona, 1988); E. Sanmartí-Grego, 'El foro romano de Ampurias', *Los Foros*, 55–60; B. B. Shefton, 'Massalia and Colonization in the North-Western Mediterranean', in G. R. Tsetskhladze and F. de Angelis (eds.), *The Archaeology of Greek Colonization* (Oxford, 1994), 61–86; E. Sanmartí-Grego, 'Recent Discoveries at the Harbour of the Greek City of Emporion', in Cunliffe and Keay, 157–74. ASTORGA V. García Marcos and J. M. Vidal Encinas, 'Recent Archaeological Research at Asturica Augusta', in Cunliffe and Keay, 371–94; *Actas del I Congreso internacional sobre Astorga Romana* (Astorga, 1986). BÁDAJOZ Fernando Valdés Fernández, *La Alcazaba de Bádajoz I* (*EAE* 144; Madrid, 1985); Fernando Valdés Fernández, 'Excavaciones en la Alcazaba de Bádajoz', *Revista de Estudios Extremeños*, 34, 35, 36 (1978–80)—especially for non-Islamic periods; María Cruz Villalon, 'Los antecedentes visigodos de la Alcazaba de Bádajoz', *Norba*, 2 (1981), 23–9. BAELO C. Domergue *et al.*, *Excavaciones de la Casa de Velázquez en Belo (Bolonia—Cádiz)* (*EAE* 79; Madrid, 1974), relating to campaigns of 1966–71; annual reports will be found in the volumes of the *MCV*, starting in 1967, as well as further monographs published by the Casa de Velázquez; J. N. Bonneville *et al.*, *Belo V: L'Épigraphie* (Madrid, 1988); A. Pelletier, S. Dardaine, and P. Sillières, 'Le Forum de Belo: Découvertes recentes', *Los Foros*, 165–72. BALAGUER Christian Ewert, *Hallazgos islámicos en Balaguer y la Aljafería de Zaragoza* (*EAE* 97; Madrid, 1979); J. Giralt i Balagueró, 'Fortificacions andalusines a la marca superior d'al-andalus', in Philippe Senac (ed.), *La marche supérieure d'al-Andalus et l'occident chrétien* (Madrid, 1991), 67–76. BAÑOS DE LA ENCINA Ramón Revilla Vielva, *Patio Arabe del Museo Arqueológico Nacional* (Madrid, 1932), 92–3; Derek Lomax, *The Reconquest of Spain* (London,

1978), 124–34 for the battle of Las Navas de Tolosa and its aftermath. BAÑOS DE VALDEARADOS J. L. Argente, *La villa tardorromana de Baños de Valdearados (Burgos)* (*EAE* 100; Madrid, 1979). BARCELONA P. Banks, 'The Roman Inheritance and Topographical Transitions in Early Medieval Barcelona', in Blagg, Jones, and Keay, 600–34; Jordi Vigué, *El monastir romànic de Sant Pau del Camp* (Barcelona, 1974); E. Ripoll i Perelló *et al.*, *Guia del Museu Arqueològic de Barcelona* (Barcelona, 1981). BILBILIS—CERRO DE LA BAMBOLA Manuel Martín-Bueno, 'La inscripción a Tiberio y el centro religioso de Bilbilis', *MM* 22 (1981), 244–53; M. Martín Bueno, 'El Foro de Bilbilis', *Los Foros*, 99–112. BOBASTRO J. Vallvé, 'De nuevo sobre Bobastro', *Al-Andalus*, 30 (1965), 139–74. BONETE Santiago Broncano Rodríguez and Juan Blánquez Pérez, *El Amarejo (Bonete, Albacete)* (*EAE* 139; Madrid, 1985). BOTORRITA J. S. Richardson, 'The *tabula contrebiensis*: Roman law in Spain in the Early First century BC', *Journal of Roman Studies*, 73 (1982), 33–41. BUITRAGO DE LOZOYA María Paloma López del Alamo and María Jesús Rubio Visiers, 'Las murallas de Buitrago de Lozoya', *Mayrit*, 1 (1992), 33–43. BUJARRABAL Basilio Pavón Maldonado, *Guadalajara medieval: arte y arqueología arabe y mudejar* (Madrid, 1984), 151–2. CABEZO DE ALCALÁ José Angel Asensio Esteban, *La ciudad en el mundo prerromano en Aragón* (Zaragoza, 1995), 146–67; M. Beltrán, *El poblado ibérico del Castillejo de la Romana* (*EAE* 103; Madrid, 1979). CÁCERES G. Ulbert, *Cáceres el Viejo: ein spätrepublikan-isches Legionslager in Spanisch-Extremadura* (Mainz, 1984). CALATALIFA Daniel Pérez Vicente, 'Excavaciones arqueológicas en Calatalifa', *Madrid del siglo IX al XI* (Madrid, 1990), 141–4; M. Retuerce, 'La cerámica islámica de Calatalifa',

Boletín del Museo Arqueológico Nacional, 2 (1984), 117–36. CALATRAVA LA NUEVA F. Gutton, *L'Ordre de Calatrava* (Paris, 1955); anon., *Guia del Sacro Convento y Castillo de Calatrava la Nueva* (Ciudad Real, 1993). CALATRAVA LA VIEJA M. Retuerce and I. Lozano, 'Calatrava la Vieja: primeros resultados arqueológicos', *I Congreso*, iii. 57–75. CANCHO ROANO Martín Almagro-Gorbea *et al.*, 'Cancho Roano: un palacio orientalizante en la Península Ibérica', *MM* 31 (1990), 251–308. CAPARRA J. M. Blázquez, *Caparra* (3 vols., *EAE* 34, 54, and 67; Madrid, 1965/66/70). CARMONA M. Bendala, *La necroplois romana de Carmona*, 2 vols. (Seville, 1976). CARRANQUE J. Arce, 'El mosaico de "Las Metamorfosis" de Carranque (Toledo)', *MM* 27 (1988), 365–74; J. F. Matthews, 'A Pious Supporter of Theodosius I: Maternus Cynegius and his Family', *Journal of Theological Studies*, 18 (1967), 438–46; Dimas Fernández Galiano, 'The Villa of Maternus at Carranque', in Peter Johnson, Roger Ling, and David Smith (eds.), *5th International Colloquium on Ancient Mosaics* (Ann Arbor, 1994) = *Journal of Roman Archaeology*, suppl. ser. 9/1: 199–211. CARTEIA Francisco J. Presedo Velo *et al.*, *Carteia I* (*EAE* 120; Madrid, 1982). CASTILLO DE ALBA José Avelino Gutiérrez González, 'Sistemas defensivos y de repoblación en el Reino de León', *III Congreso*, i. 169–91. CASTILLO DE DOÑA BLANCA D. Ruiz Mata, 'Castillo de Doña Blanca', *MM* 27 (1986), 87–116. CASTRO DE LA CORONILLA María Luisa Cerdeño and Rosario García Huerta, *El Castro de la Coronilla* (*EAE* 163; Madrid, 1992). CASTULO José María Blázquez Martínez (ed.), *Castulo i–v* (*EAE* 105, 117, 131, and 140; Madrid, 1975–), A.A.H. viii (vol. v relates to La Muela); J. M. Blázquez, 'Castulo, Capital of the Mining District of Oretania', in Blagg, Jones, and Keay, 396–429. CENTCELLES

T. Hauschild and H. Schlunk, *La villa romana i el mausoleu constantinià de Centcelles* (Tarragona, 1986); Cesar Martinell, *El Monestir de Santes Creus* (Barcelona, 1929). CIEZA J. Navarro Palazón, 'La conquista castellana y sus consequencias: la despoblación de Siyasa', *Castrum*, 3 (1988), 208–14; id., 'La casa andalusí en Siyasa', in *La casa hispano-musulmana* (Granada, 1990), 177–98. CLUNIA P. de Palol, *Clunia: Historia de la ciudad y guia de las excavaciones* (Burgos, 1994); P. de Palol and J. Vilella, 'Un sanctuario priápico en Clunia?', *Koine*, 2 (1986), 15–25; P. de Palol, 'El Foro romano de Clunia', *Los Foros*, 153–64; J. M. Gurt Esparraguera, *Clunia III: hallazgos monetarios* (*EAE* 145; Madrid, 1985). CÓRDOBA Rafael Hidalgo Prieto and Pedro Marfil Ruiz, 'El yacimiento arqueológico de Cercadilla: avance de resultados', *Anales de Arqueología Cordobesa*, 3 (1992), 277–308; Rafael Hidalgo Prieto and Angel Ventura Villanueva, 'Sobre la cronología del palacio de Cercadilla en Corduba', *Chiron*, 24 (1994), 221–40; Rafael Hidalgo Prieto, *Espacio publico y espacio privado en el conjunto palatino de Cercadilla* (Córdoba, 1996); F. Cantera Burgos, *Sinagogas de Toledo, Segovia y Córdoba* (Madrid, 1973), 151–86; B. Pavón Maldonado, *Tratado de arquitectura hispano-musulmana I: agua* (Madrid, 1990); P. Cressier, 'Les Chapiteaux de la grande mosquée de Cordoue', *MM* 25 (1984), 216–81 and 26 (1985), 257–313. DUEÑAS R. Revilla Vielva, P. de Palol Salellas, and A. Cuadros Salas, *Excavaciones en la Villa Romana del 'Cercado de San Isidro'* (*EAE* 33; Madrid, 1964). EL BOVALAR Pere de Palol i Salellas, *El Bovalar (Seròs; Segrià)* (Lérida, 1989). EL ORAL Lorenzo Abad Casal and Feliciana Sala Sellés, 'El Oral: un poblado ibérico antiguo en el Sureste de la Península Ibérica', *MM* 35 (1994), 183–209; P. Rouillard, *Les Grecs et la péninsule ibérique du VIIIe au IVe siècle avant Jésus Christ* (Paris, 1991), 556 (for the finds at El Molar). FONTANAREJO Amador Ruibal Rodríguez, 'Un primitivo enclave islámico: Fontanarejo', *I Congreso*, iii. 237–48. FRAGA F. J. Montón Broto, 'Un asentamiento musulmán cerca de Fraga', *I Congreso*, iii. 113–27; J. Serra Rafols, 'La villa Fortunatus de Fraga', *Ampurias*, 5 (1943), 5–35; Walter Oakshott, *Sigena Paintings* (London, 1972). FUENGIROLA Carmen Román Riechmann, 'Aproximación historico-arqueológico al castillo de Fuengirola', *I Congreso*, iii. 405–26. GAUCÍN Carmen Peral Bejarano, 'Actuación arqueo-lógica en el castillo de Gaucín', *I Congreso*, iii. 325–46. GORMAZ P. J. Banks and J. Zozaya, 'Excavations in the Caliphal Fortress of Gormaz (Soria): A Summary', in Blagg, Jones, and Keay, 674–703 (incl. photographs). GRAN DOLINA CAVE N. Hammond, *The Times*, Tuesday 26 September 1995, p. 18; *Evolution humana en Europa y los yacimientos de la Sierra de Atapuerca*, 2 vols. (Valladolid, 1995). GRANADA J. Bermúdez López, 'Contribución al estudio de las construcciones domésticas de la Alhambra', in *La Casa Hispano-Musulmana* (Granada, 1990), 341–54; C. Gómez González and C. Vilchez Vilchez, 'Baños árabes de la época almohade de la Judería de Granada', *I Congreso*, iii. 545–67; J. A. García Granados and V. Salvatierra Cuenca, 'Excavaciones en el Maristan de Granada', *I Congreso*, 617–39; M. Roca Roumens, M. A. Moreno Onorato, and R. Lizcano Prestel, *El Albaicín y los orígines de la ciudad de Granada* (Granada, 1988). GUARDAMAR R. Azuar Ruiz, 'Una rábita hispanomusulmana del Siglo X', *Archéologie Islamique*, 1 (1990), 109–45. HUELVA J. P. Garrido Roiz, *Excavaciones en la necrópolis de 'La Joya', Huelva (1 y 2 campañas)* (*EAE* 71; Madrid, 1970); J. P. Garrido and E. M. Orta, *Excavaciones en la* necrópolis de 'La Joya', Huelva (3, 4 y 5 campañas) (*EAE* 96; Madrid, 1978); J. P. Garrido and E. M. Orta, *El Habitat antiguo de Huelva* (*EAE* 171; Madrid, 1994); J. Fernández, Jurado, 'Die Phönizier in Huelva', *MM* 26 (1985), 49–60. HUESCA Carlos Esco Samperiz and Philippe Senac, 'La muralla islámica de Huesca', in *II Congreso de Arqueología Medieval Española* (Madrid, 1987), ii. 589–601. IRUN *Diario Vasco*, 19 and 24 January 1993. ITÁLICA J. Luzón, *Arte hispalense: la Itálica de Adriano* (Seville, 1975); Alicia María Canto, 'El acueducto romano de Itálica', *MM* 20 (1979), 282–338; anon. (ed.), *Itálica* (*EAE* 121; Madrid, 1982); A. García y Bellido, *Andalucía Monumental: Itálica* (Seville, 1985); J. M. Rodríguez Hidalgo and S. Keay, 'Recent Work at Italica', in Cunliffe and Keay, 395–420. JEREZ DE LA FRONTERA Barrucand and Bednorz, *Moorish Architecture*, 158–61. LA HOYA Armando Llanos Ortiz de Landaluce, *La Hoya—un poblado del primer milenio antés de Cristo* (Vitoria/Gasteiz, 1983). LA PEDROSA DE LA VEGA P. de Palol, *La villa romana de la Olmeda de Pedrosa de la Vega (Palencia)* (Palencia, 1986). LACIPO Rafael Puertas Tricas, *Excavaciones arqueológicas en Lacipo (Casares, Málaga). Campañas de 1975 y 1976* (*EAE* 125; Madrid, 1982). LAS MÉDULAS D. G. Bird, 'Pliny and the Gold Mines of North-West Iberia', Blagg, Jones, and Keay, 341–63. LAS VEGAS DE PUEBLA NUEVA T. Hauschild, 'Das Mausoleum bei Las Vegas de Puebla Nueva', *MM* 10 (1969), 296–316; id. 'Das Mausoleum von Las Vegas de Pueblanueva … Grabungen in den Jahren 1971/1974', *MM* 19 (1978), 307–39; L. Klappauf, 'Zur Keramik aus dem Mausoleum von Las Vegas de Pueblanueva (Prov. Toledo)', *MM* 19 (1978), 340–78. LEÓN M. Gómez-Moreno, *Iglesias Mozarabes* (Madrid, 1919), i. 253–9; *Legio VII Gemina* (León, 1970;

= conference proceedings); J. Rodríguez-Fernández, 'La monarquía leonesa de García I a Vermudo III (910–1037)' and J. L. Martín, 'La monarquía leonesa. Fernando I y Alfonso VI', in J. M. Fernández Catón (ed.), *El Reino de León en la Alta Edad Media III* (León, 1995), 131–705; A. Viñayo González, *Panteón Real de San Isidoro* (León, 1971). LÉRIDA/LLEIDA P. Scales, 'La red militar en el Tagr-al-'ala', *I Congreso*, 221–36; Federico Lara Peinado, *Lérida: Museo Arqueológico* (Lérida, 1974); Manuel Guallar Pérez, *Lérida visigoda* (Lérida, 1974); Rodrigo Pita Merce, *Lérida arabe* (Lérida, 1974). LOS VASCOS Ricardo Izquierdo Benito, 'Excavaciones de Vascos: resultados y planificación', in *Actas del Primer Congreso de Arqueología de la Provincia de Toledo* (Talavera, 1990), 433–58; Ricardo Izquierdo Benito, *Excavaciones en la Ciudad Hispanomusulmana de Vascos (Navalmoralejo, Toledo). Campañas de 1983–1988* (Madrid, 1994); Gisela Ripoll, *La Necrópolis visigoda de El Carpio de Tajo* (*AEA* 142; Madrid, 1985). LUGO Manuel Vázquez Seijas, *Lugo bajo el imperio romano* (Lugo, 1939); Manuel Vázquez Seijas, *Fortalezas de Lugo y su provincia*, i (repr. Lugo, 1983). LUMBIER Julio Altadill, 'Vías y vestigios romanos en Navarra', in *Homenaje a D. Carmelo de Echegaray* (San Sebastián, 1928), 465–556; M. de Mézquiriz and B. Taracena, in *Excavaciones en Navarra II* (Pamplona, 1956), 189–215 and 45–106. MADRID Various authors, *Madrid del siglo IX al XI* (Madrid, 1990); Fernando Valdés (ed.), *Mayrit: Estudios de arqueología madrileña*, i (1992). MÁLAGA Luís Baena del Alcazar, *Catálogo de las esculturas romanas del Museo de Málaga* (Málaga, 1984); C. Ewert, 'Spanisch-islamische Systeme sich kreuzender Bögen II', *MM* 7 (1966), 232–53. MARI-ALBA T. Hauschild, 'La iglesia martirial de Marialba (Léon)', *Boletín de la Real*

Academia a de la Historia, 163 (1968), 243–9. MECA Santiago Broncano Rodríguez, *El Castellar de Meca, Ayora (Valencia)* (*EAE* 147; Madrid, 1986). MEDELLÍN María Jesus Pérez Martin, *Una tumba hispano-visigoda excepcional hallada en El Turuñelo. Medellín (Bádajoz)* (Madrid, 1961). MEDINA AZAHARA Basilio Pavón Maldonado, *Memoria de la excavación de la mezquita de Medinat al-Zahra* (*EAE* 50; Madrid, 1966); Felix Hernández Giménez, *Medinat al-Zahra, arquitectura y decoración* (Granada, 1985). MÉRIDA J. M. Alvares, J. L. de la Barrera, and A. Velasquez, *Mérida* (Léon, 1995); *Augusta Emerita. Actas del Bimilenario de Mérida* (Madrid, 1976); José María Alvarez Martínez, *El puente romano de Mérida* (Bádajoz, 1983); Eugenio García Sandoval, *Informe sobre las casas romanas de Mérida y excavaciones en la 'Casa del Anfiteatro'* (*EAE* 49; Madrid, 1966); E. Alföldi-Rosenbaum, 'Mérida Revisited: The Cosmological Mosaic in the Light of Discussions since 1979', *MM* 34 (1993), 254–74; Alicia M. Cantó, 'Sobre la cronología augustea del acueducto de Los Milagros de Mérida', *Homenaje a Sáenz de Buruaga* (Madrid, 1982), 157–76; John H. Humphrey, *Roman Circuses* (London, 1986), 362–76; José Bueno Rocha, 'Restos de época visigoda en la iglesia de Santa Eulalia de Mérida, *II Congreso*, ii. 321–30; Antonio García y Bellido, *Mérida: La gran necrópolis romana de la salida del puente* (*EAE* 11; Madrid, 1962). MONTÁNCHEZ Antonio González Cordero, 'Templo visigodo en el castillo de Montánchez', *Revista de Estudios Extremeños*, 40 (1984), 513–26; Enrique Cerrillo Martín de Cáceres, *La Básilica de época visigoda de Ibahernando* (Cáceres, 1983). MONTE MOLLET AND MONTE MARINET André Bazzana, 'Asentamientos medievales en las sierras del Bajo Maestrazgo: Monte Marinet y Monte Mollet', *I Congreso*, iii. 147–61. MONTE NARANCO Sabine Noack-Haley and Achim Arbeiter, *Asturische Königsbauten des 9. Jahrhunderts* (Mainz, 1994); V. J. González García, *La iglesia de San Miguel de Lillo* (Oviedo, 1974). MONTEAGUDO Barrucand and Bednorz, *Moorish Architecture*, 146–8. MONTGÓ H. Schubart, D. Fletcher Valls, and J. Oliver y de Cárdenas, *Excavaciones en las fortificaciones del Montgó cerca de Denia (Alicante)* (*EAE* 13; Madrid, 1962). MUÑIGUA Theodor Hauschild, 'MUNIGUA. Untersuchungen im Stadtgebiet östlich vom Forum', *MM* 10 (1969), 185–98. MURCIA Manuel Jorge Aragonés, *Museo de la muralla árabe de Murcia* (Madrid, 1966). NIEBLA A. Marín Fidalgo, *Arquitectura gótica del sur de la Provincia de Huelva* (Huelva, 1982), 60–5. NUMANTIA José Ramón Melida, *Excavaciones de Numancia*, various volumes (Madrid, 1916, 1918, 1920, 1921, 1923, 1924); A. Schulten, *Numantia. Die Ergebnisse der Ausgrabungen*, 4 vols. (Munich, 1914, 1927, 1929, 1931). OLÉRDOLA E. Ripoll Perelló, *Olérdola* (Barcelona, 1977). OLMOS S. Martínez Lillo, 'El poblado fortificado de Olmos', in *Madrid del siglo IX al XI* (Madrid, 1990), 131–40. ORCE *British Archaeology*, 7 (September 1995), 4; N. Hammond, *The Times*, Tuesday 26 September 1995, p. 18. OVIEDO J. Manzanares Rodríguez, *Las joyas de la Cámara Sancta* (Oviedo, 1972); Roger Collins, 'Doubts and Certainties on the Churches of Early Medieval Spain', in id., *Law, Culture and Regionalism in Early Medieval Spain* (Aldershot, 1992); M. Escortell Ponsoda, *Catálogo de las salas de arte prerrománico del Museo Arqueológico de Oviedo* (Oviedo, 1978); María Soledad Alvarez Martínez, *Santa Cristina de Lena* (Oviedo, 1988). PLA DE NADAL Empar Juan and Ignacio Pastor, 'Los visigodos en Valencia. Pla de Nadal: ¿una villa aulica?', *BAM* 3 (1989),

137–79; P. de Palol, in *HE* iii. 363–4. PUIG DE LOS MURALLES/ PUIG ROM Pere de Palol, in R. Menéndez Pidal (ed.), *Historia de España* (new edition), iii, pt. 2 (Madrid 1991), 358–60; Miguel Oliva Prat, *Arquitectura Románica Ampurdanesa: Santa María de Roses (Gerona)* (Gerona, n.d.). RECCOPOLIS AND ZORITA DE LOS CANES Lauro Olmo Enciso, 'Proyecto Recopolis: ciudad y territorio en época visigoda', *Arqueología en Guadalajara* (Toledo, 1995), 209–23; K. Raddatz, 'Anmerkungen zu Reccopolis', *MM* 36 (1995), 310–19; Basilio Pavón Maldonado, *Guadalajara medieval* (Madrid, 1984), 185–201. SÁDABA A. García y Bellido, *La Villa y el Mausoleo Romanos de Sádaba* (*EAE* 19; Madrid, 1963). SAGUNTO C. Aranegui, 'Evolucíon del área cívica saguntina', *Journal of Roman Archaeology*, 5 (1992), 56–68; C. Aranegui *et al.*, 'El Foro de Saguntum: La Planta arquitectónica', *Los Foros*, 73–97. SALTÉS A. Bazzana and P. Cressier, *Shaltish/ Saltés (Huelva): une ville médiévale d'al-Andalus* (Madrid, 1989). SAN JUAN DE BAÑOS Pere de Palol, *La Basílica de San Juan de Baños* (Palencia, 1988); J. M. de Navascués, *La dedicación de San Juan de Baños* (Palencia, 1961). SAN MIGUEL DE ESCALADA Hortensia Larren Iz-quierdo, 'Excavaciones arqueológicas en San Miguel de Escalada (León)', *I Congreso*, 103–23. SAN PEDRO DE ALCÁNTARA Carlos Posac Mon and Rafael Puertas Tricas, *La Basilica paleocristiana de Vega del Mar* (Málaga, 1989). SAN PEDRO DE LA MATA L. Caballero Zoreda, *La iglesia y el monasterio visigodo de Santa María de Melque* (Madrid, 1980), 501–43. SAN PEDRO DE LA NAVE M. A. Rodríguez, *San Pedro de la Nave* (Zamora, 1980). SANTA COMBA DE BANDE L. Caballero Zoreda, *La iglesia y el monasterio visigodo de Santa María de Melque* (*EAE* 109; Madrid, 1980), 545–87. SANTA EULALIA DE BÓVEDA Manuel Nuñez, *Historia da arquitectura galega: arquitectura prerromanica* (Santiago, 1978), 131–9. SANTA LUCÍA DEL TRAMPAL L. Caballero Zoreda, 'Santa Lucía del Trampal, Alcuéscar (Cáceres)', *Información cultural*, 75 (December 1989), 12–19. SANTA MARÍA DE MELQUE L. Caballero Zoreda, *La iglesia y el monasterio visigodo de Santa María de Melque* (*EAE* 109; Madrid, 1980). SANTA MARÍA DE QUINTANILLA DE LAS VIÑAS Salvador Andrés Ordax and José Antonio Abásolo Alvarez, *La ermita de Santa María, Quintanilla de las Viñas, Burgos* (Burgos, 1982); Achim Arbeiter, 'Die westgotenzeitliche Kirche von Quintanilla de las Viñas', *MM* 31 (1990), 393–427. SANTA OLALLA DE CÁCERES José Bueno Rocha, 'La iglesia visigoda de Santa Olalla de Cáceres', *BAM* 3 (1989), 181–93. SANTA POLA Pierre Moret *et al.*, 'The Fortified Settlement of La Picola (Santa Pola, Alicante) and the Greek Influence in South-East Spain', in Cunliffe and Keay, 109–25. SANTIAGO DE COMPOSTELA José Guerra Campos, *Exploraciones arqueológicas en torno al sepulchro del Apostol Santiago* (Santiago, 1982); Richard Fletcher, *St James's Catapult* (Oxford, 1984), chs. 1–4. SASAMÓN Enrique Flórez, *España Sagrada*, xxvi (1771), 21–8. SEGÓBRIGA Martín Almagro Basch, *Segóbriga I* (*EAE* 123; Madrid, 1983); id., *La Necrópolis hispano-visigoda de Segóbriga, Saélices (Cuenca)* (*EAE* 84; Madrid, 1975). SEGOVIA J. M. Santamaría, *La Vera Cruz* (Segovia, 1979). SEVILLE María Jesús Carrasco, 'Avance del estudio de la cerámica hispano-musulmana procedente de los "Baños de la Reina Mora" (Sevilla)', *II Congreso*, ii. 529–38; José Guerrero-Lovillo, *Al-Qasr al-Mubarak, el Alcázar de la benedición* (Seville, 1974); Fernando Fernández Gómez and Juan Campos Carrasco, 'Panorama de la arqueología medieval en el casco antiguo de Sevilla', *I*

Congreso, iii. 37–55; *Catalogo del Museo Arqueológico de Sevilla*, i and ii (Seville, 1980). SOUTH COAST Angela Suárez *et al.*, 'Abdera: una colonia fenicia en el Sureste de la Península Ibérica', *MM* 30 (1989), 135–48; *Los Fenicios en la Península Ibérica*, i (Sabadell, 1986); H. G. Niemeyer (ed.), *Phönizier im Westen* (Cologne, 1979). TALAMANCA DEL JARAMA María Jesús Rubio Visiers and María Paloma López del Alamo, 'Talamanca del Jarama: fortificación y defensa', *Mayrit*, 1 (1992), 45–55. TARIFA Vives, *Inscripciones*, no. 142, p. 45. TARRAGONA Taller Escola d'Arqueologia, *L'Amfiteatre romà de Tarragona, la basílica visigòtica i l'església romànica* (2 vols.; Tarragona, 1990); Xavier Dupré i Raventós *et al.*, *El Circ romà de Tarragona I: Les voltes de Sant Ermenegild* (Tarragona, 1988); R. Cortés, 'Los Foros de Tarraco', *Los Foros*, 9–24; Xavier Dupré i Raventós, 'New Evidence for the Study of the Urbanism of Tarraco', in Cunliffe and Keay, 355–69; J. Benages i Olive, *Les monedes de Tarragona* (Barcelona, 1994). J. M. Carreté, S. Keay, and M. Millett, *A Roman Provincial Capital and its Hinterland* (*Journal of Roman Archaeology* supplementary series vol. 15, 1995). TEBA Antonio Vallejo Triano, 'Actuación arqueológica en el castillo de Teba', *I Congreso*, iii. 281–305; Encarnación Serrano Ramos and Rafael Atencia Páez, 'La necropolis de época visigoda de 'El Tesorillo'', *I Congreso*, ii. 279–95; E. García Alfonso, V. Martínez Enamorado, and A. Moragado Rodríguez, *El bajo Guadalteba (Málaga): espacio y poblamiento. Una aproximación arqueológico a Teba y su entorno* (Málaga, 1995). TIERMES Jose Luis Argente Oliver *et al.*, *Tiermes*, 4 vols. to date (*EAE* 111, 128, 166, and 167; Madrid, 1983–94). TOLEDO Julio Porres Martín-Cleto, *Historia de Ṭulayṭula* (Toledo, 1985); F. Javier Sánchez-Palencia and María Jesus Sainz Pascual, *El Circo romano de Toledo: estratigrafia y arquitectura* (Toledo, 1988); Antonio de Juan García, *Los Enterramientos musulmanes del Circo romano de Toledo* (Toledo, 1987); P. de Palol, 'Resultados de las excavaciones junto al Cristo de la Vega', *XIV Centenario: Concilio III de Toledo, 589–1989* (Toledo, 1991), 787–832; Clara Delgado Valero, *Toledo Islámico* (Toledo, 1987), 283–317; Geoffrey R. D. King, 'The Nine Domed Mosque in Islam', *MM* 30 (1989), 332–90; John Beckwith, *The Andrews Diptych* (London, 1958); Schlunk and Hauschild, 195–6, pl. 95; Fernando Valdés Fernández, 'La puerta vieja de Bisagra. Notas para una cronología de la muralla de Toledo', *II Congreso*, ii. 281–94; Germán Prieto Vázquez, 'Santa María la Blanca y la Mezquita de Tornerías: dos excavaciones de urgencia en Toledo', *Actas del Primer congreso de Arqueología de la Provincia de Toledo* (Talavera, 1990), 459–81; Matilde Revuelta, *Museo de los Concilios de Toledo* (Madrid, 1973); Ana María López Alvarez, *Catálogo del Museo Sefardi, Toledo* (Toledo, 1986); Francisco Cantera y Burgos, *Sinagogas de Toledo, Segovia y Córdoba* (Madrid, 1973). TORRE LLAUDER M. Ribas Bertrán, *La villa romana de la Torre Llauder de Mataró* (*EAE* 47; Madrid, 1966); M. Prevosti i Monclús and J.-F. Clariana i Roig, *Torre Llauder, Mataró, Vil.la romana* (Barcelona, 1988). TRAYAMAR Hermanfrid Schubart and Hans Georg Niemeyer, *Trayamar; los hipogeos fenicios y el asentamiento en la desembocadura del río Algarrobo* (*EAE* 90; Madrid, 1976); H. Schubart, 'Morro de Mezquitilla. Vorbericht über die Grabungskampagne 1976 auf dem Siedlungshügel an der Algarrobo-Mündung', *MM* 18 (1977), 33–61; *MM* 23 (1982), 33–45 for 1981 excavations. ULLASTRET Marina Picazo, *Las cerámicas áticas de Ullastret* (Barcelona, 1977); B. B.

Shefton, 'Greek Imports at the Extremities of the Mediterranean, West and East', in Cunliffe and Keay, 127–55. UXAMA Carmen García Merino, 'Noticias preliminares sobre el Foro de Uxama Argaela', *Los Foros*, 147–51. C. García Merino, Uxama 1: campañus de 1976 y 1978 (*EAE* 170; Madrid, 1995). VALERIA M. Osuna *et al.*, *Valeria Romana I* (Cuenca, 1978); A. Fuentes Domínguez, 'Avance del Foro de Valeria (Cuenca)', *Los Foros*, 69–72. ZARAGOZA Andrés Alvarez Garcia *et al.*, *La Plaza de la Seo. Zaragoza. Investigaciones histórico-arqueológicas* (Zaragoza, 1989); Christian Ewert, *Hallazgos islámicos en Balaguer y la Aljafería de Zaragoza* (*EAE* 97; Madrid 1979); Salvador Barbera, 'A Poem on the Master Builder of the Aljafería', *MM* 31 (1990), 440–4.

Index